CANUCK ROCK:
A HISTORY OF CANADIAN POPULAR MUSIC

The Guess Who. Gordon Lightfoot. Joni Mitchell. Neil Young. Stompin'
Tom Connors. Robert Charlebois. Anne Murray. Crowbar. Chilliwack.
Carole Pope. Loverboy. Bryan Adams. The Barenaked Ladies. The Tragically Hip. Céline Dion. Arcade Fire. K-oS. Feist. These musicians are national heroes to generations of Canadians. But what does it mean to be
a Canadian musician? And why does nationality even matter? Canuck
Rock addresses these questions by delving into the myriad relationships
between the people who make music, the industries that produce and
sell it, the radio stations and government legislation that determine
availability, and the fans who consume it and make it their own. An invaluable resource and an absorbing read, Canuck Rock spans from the
emergence of rock and roll in the 1950s through to today's international
recording industry. Ryan Edwardson combines archival material, published accounts, and new interviews to explore how music in Canada
became Canadian music.

RYAN EDWARDSON is a Canadian music fan with a PhD in History from
Queen's University.

RYAN EDWARDSON

CANUCK ROCK

A History of Canadian Popular Music

UNIVERSITY OF TORONTO PRESS
Toronto Buffalo London

© University of Toronto Press Incorporated 2009
Toronto Buffalo London
www.utppublishing.com
Printed in Canada

ISBN 978-0-8020-9989-1 (cloth)
ISBN 978-0-8020-9715-6 (paper)

Printed on acid-free paper

Library and Archives Canada Cataloguing in Publication

Edwardson, Ryan, 1974-
  Canuck rock : a history of Canadian popular music / Ryan Edwardson.

  Includes bibliographical references and index.
  ISBN 978-0-8020-9989-1 (bound)   ISBN 978-0-8020-9715-6 (pbk.)

  1. Popular music – Canada – History and criticism – Textbooks. I. Title.

  ML3484.E265 2009   781.64'0971   C2009-903288-0

Cover illustrations: (front) Martin Tielli of the Rheostatics, Vogue
Theatre, Vancouver, 1997 © Suzanne Goodwin; (back) Poster image
courtesy of Bob Masse Studios.

University of Toronto Press acknowledges the financial assistance to its publishing program of the Canada Council for the Arts and the Ontario
Arts Council.

University of Toronto Press acknowledges the financial support for its publishing activities of the Government of Canada through the Book Publishing
Industry Development Program (BPIDP).

This book has been published with the help of a grant from the Canadian
Federation for the Humanities and Social Sciences, through the Aid to
Scholarly Publications Program, using funds provided by the Social Sciences
and Humanities Research Council of Canada.

Contents

vi   Contents

Illustrations follow page 120

Acknowledgments

First and foremost, I want to thank Mary Vipond and the History Department at Concordia University for their support during the Social Sciences and Humanities Research Council Postdoctoral Fellowship that funded this project. I also want to extend appreciation to Claire Campbell, the History Department at Dalhousie University, and the Killam Foundation for supporting my subsequent project, an exploration of east coast music and identity. Ian McKay at Queen's University has been my rock of academic support for many years. Tim Smith has proven to be a constant supporter and friend. Finally, the publishing of this book has been made possible in part by funding from the Aid to Scholarly Publication Program.

Many rock and rollers and industry folks in the trenches took time to share their experiences and stories, most notably Dave Bingham, Alan Cross, Peter De Remigis, Bill Henderson, Dov Ivry, Stan Klees, Jurgen Peter, Jeffrey Ridley, Norm Sherratt, and Ritchie Yorke. Other people offered photos from their personal collections. And I extend thanks to John Einarson, Nicholas Jennings, and all the authors, few as they are, that set a foundation for Canadian music history scholarship upon which this book is built.

University of Toronto Press, and my editor Len Husband, have once again proven to be tremendously supportive. One could not ask for a better editor. I wish to thank the anonymous readers who took the time to offer constructive feedback and suggestions. This book is better because of their efforts. Frances Mundy at UTP has helped bring this project to fruition. Jim Leahy deftly copy-edited the text, and I thank him on behalf of myself and the readers.

On a personal note, I wish to extend thanks to the people who have brought so much to my life. Long-standing friendships, laughter, and love have been provided by Keren Bromberg, William and Keely Speechley, Steve Noakes, Ross Cameron, Neel Jethwa, Adrian Elliot, Jeff and Heather Wilson, Scott Wilson, Christina Dabrowski, Mark Sampson, Andre Dupuis, Sarah Morrison, Michelle Fleming, Tonia Moore, and Maren Larson. East coast antics were aided by the likes of Vincent Perez, Kristen Healy, Allison Nolting, Dawn Kellett, Birgit Greiner, Geniva Liu, Marla Cranston, Saman Jafarian, Angus Ross, Ella Henderson, Sanja Pecelj, Natalie Jean Slater, and the various ragamuffins at Steve-O-Renos. Steven Edwardson and Laura Devlin have been wonderful caretakers of my belongings and have always been there for me. Finally, my mother, Jenny Strachan, has been unwavering in her support and encouragement. Thank you all.

CANUCK ROCK:
A HISTORY OF CANADIAN POPULAR MUSIC

Introduction: From Rock and Roll in Canada to 'Canadian' Rock and Roll

I don't think there is anything intrinsically Canadian in our music. I am just a member of a band which expresses the way it sees the world.
                                                                          – Burton Cummings, the Guess Who, 1971[1]

I often say that there is no such thing as a Canadian song style – this may sound a bit ungracious of me, but it conveys what I mean … There is the Quebec style, and there is the American style.
                                                                          – Gilles Vigneault, 1974[2]

My songs are Canadian because I am a Canadian, and my observations are made from living here. Occasionally I've wasted a little bit of time trying to define the national character, and realized that to a large extent the effort was futile.
                                                                          – Murray McLauchlan, 1974[3]

We have that Canadian rock band sound. It's there. I don't know what it is, but it's there.
                                                                          – Neil Osborne, 54-40, 1986[4]

'Musicians Play a Canada Rock': Courtney Tower made a rather bold assertion in choosing this title for a February 1970 *Maclean's* article. Rock and roll was still widely thought to be little more than an entertainment of questionable substance. The Canadian content regulation was still a few months away from being proposed by the Canadian Radio and Television Commission as an aid to industry, and with the exception of a few nationalistic voices in the media, the coverage of rock, folk, and psychedelia was usually seeped in bewilderment if not lack of interest. Yet, Tower informed the readers, 'Canadian pop songs, contrary to the notions of most adults, don't deal exclusively with sex, drugs and the

hassles of adolescent love ... increasingly, composer-performers such
as [Ian] Tyson, Gordon Lightfoot, Neil Young (of Crosby, Stills, Nash
and Young) and Robbie Robertson (of the Band) are producing songs
that celebrate a fresh awareness of Canada.'[5] Tower based this claim on
Lightfoot's 'Canadian Railroad Trilogy,' Ian Tyson's 'Four Rode By,' and,
though not mentioned by name, Young's 'Helpless' (given its mention of
Ontario) and Robertson's 'We Can Talk.'[6] This was evidence enough for
Tower to inform readers of a 'beginning in English-speaking Canada ...
of a vocal nationalism that French-Canadian chansonniers have celebrated for many years.'[7]

The reality was much less patriotic. Unlike chansonniers – traditional
folk singers – such as Félix Leclerc and Gilles Vigneault who had joined
in on fervent celebration of Québécois nationhood, Tyson and Lightfoot
were professedly apolitical while Young and Robertson both lived in the
United States outside the orbit of the 'new nationalism' that was thriving at the time. Even 'Canadian Railroad Trilogy,' the song most open
to being read as nationalistic, was in fact commissioned by the Canadian
Broadcasting Corporation (CBC) for a television program celebrating
the country's centennial in 1967. Further, other songs penned by these
four songwriters dealt just as directly, if not more so, with the United
States, notably Ian and Sylvia's big hit 'Some Day Soon' about a rodeo
rider born in southern Colorado, Lightfoot's 'Black Day in July' reflecting on the Detroit riots in 1967, Young's reaction to the Kent State shootings in 'Ohio,' and 'The Night They Drove Old Dixie Down' by the Band.

That is to say, it was not these songwriters but Tower, like many other
Canadians, who was beginning to use music to connect, individually and
collectively, to a national sense of self and in turn vest musicians, particularly the famous expatriates who could be reclaimed, with special status as national representatives.[8] Such a nationalistic assertion was novel
and rather tenuous, owing more to the socio-economic complex than to
the activities of musicians. Tellingly, 'Musicians Play a Canada Rock' was
slipped into a special five-page editorial, 'Canada Report,' that led off
by declaring 'either you're *for* Canada, or you just don't care. Editorially,
Maclean's cares intensely. We present this report, frankly, with an ulterior
motive. *Maclean's* wants to fan the flames of what we take to be "The
Heartening Surge of a New Canadian Nationalism."'[9] The special section included reports on grassroots publishers fighting American literary
imperialists, attempts to contain 'the flood of American TV,' steps forward in the struggle to 'buy back' Canada from American investors, and
warnings about how non-Canadian university and college faculty were

rejecting Canadian works with the result that 'students lose the insights into this country of a Hugh MacLennan or a Gabrielle Roy.'[10] Rock and roll was being mixed in with a sovereign economy and high culture as the mortar of nation-building.

'Musicians Play a Canada Rock' was a sign of the paradigm shift that is at the heart of this book. *Canuck Rock: A History of Canadian Popular Music* explores the evolution of rock and roll and related forms of 'pop' music from their continental and regional ebb and flow in the late 1950s through the entanglement with nationalization at the turn of the 1970s and the combination of national ideology and multinational industry that followed. Music went from being a means for baby boomers to mediate gender, class, and generational identities to embracing a national identity and membership in a nation as they became politically aware citizens. What transpired was a transition from 'music in Canada' to 'Canadian music.' The singers of lyrics and slingers of guitars came to be celebrated alongside the most revered of scientists and humanitarians and were bestowed the country's highest honours, yet, when rock and roll first came about in the mid-1950s, it was treated as a continental entertainment that was at best frivolous and at worst debauched, prompting parents, clergies, city councils, and moral authorities at large to call for the music to be banned. The degenerative qualities ensured that the mainstream found little of national value and character in rock and roll. Even Americans sought to distance themselves from the 'jungle' and 'hillbilly' music taking place within pockets of their country. To social critics and moral leaders the music may have started in the United States but it was certainly not reflective of the American nation they envisioned.[11] For youths, on the other hand, the songs of Bill Haley, Elvis Presley, Buddy Holly, and the like offered a means of negotiating identities and differences through the pleasurable emotions and energies outside of, and at odds with, the status quo.[12] A continental economic and demographic baby boom, cross-border radio signals and shared setlists, Canadian reliance on U.S. material sources, and the mingling and exchange of musicians through touring circuits and relocation (Paul Anka left, Ronnie Hawkins arrived) ensured that, although Canadians were not at the epicentre of rock and roll, they were nonetheless in its radius.

With the British Invasion of the early to mid-1960s, national identifiers became all the rage, although it was not so much about the music as representing British nationhood as it was about the need to respond to a new music that was geographically situated and defined. Aspiring Canadian acts, loving the new sounds but finding themselves shut out

by an industry that was cashing in on the latest fad, adapted by appropriating not only musical but national identifiers. They took monikers
derived from British cities, spoke in faked accents, plastered Union Jacks
on clothing and record album covers, and even invented stories about
having recently arrived from Liverpool. Bands like the Lords of London,
the Liverpool Set, Jack London and the Sparrows, and the British Modbeats almost bordered on caricature (an approach common around the
world). Bands outside of Britain latched onto the identifiers more than
did their British counterparts. Placing a group like the British Modbeats
beside the Rolling Stones reveals how identifiers are co-opted for the
sake of 'authenticity' and to attract fans and industry alike. Yet, although
many groups came across as over-eager cover bands, others, like the Ugly
Ducklings and the Haunted, shared with the British groups a love for
American rock and roll, R&B, and blues; many Canadians had learned
their styles from the same albums as their British counterparts. For them
the Rolling Stones, the Kinks, the Who, and others were not so much
groups to copy as they were examples of how a career could be built in
an era of whitewashed Frankie Avalons and Paul Ankas.

Whereas rock and roll threatened the social and moral order upon
which the nation rested, or at the very least seemed to have little positive
to offer, folk music shared with national narratives a nostalgic connection to the past, although the musical roots connected to socialism and
black field workers were relegated to the margins until their middle-class
sanitization during the folk 'revival' of the mid-century. Long considered
to be pejoratively folksy and quaint, the music gathered steam during the
1950s with the popularity the Weavers and the Travellers, had its breakthrough with the Kingston Trio's version of 'Tom Dooley' in 1958, and
by the early 1960s achieved new heights at bohemian cafes, music clubs,
and university campuses. Jazz, blues, and folk music melded together
among the cigarette smoke and coffee cups in often haphazardly assembled clubs frequented by beatniks, hipsters, folkies, and assorted artists
and wannabes. The baby boom generation and its like-minded compatriots were drawn to a music that offered an anti-modern escape from Cold
War tensions, and, as they matured into politically conscious adults, folk
songwriting became a means of expressing opinions on, and lodging
protests against, issues of the day. Vancouver's Kitsilano was a west coast
haven, Calgary had the Depression, in Edmonton the Yardbird Suite was
popular, and, perhaps more musically important than all the others (at
least for the career-minded), Toronto had the vibrant Yorkville Village.
A crossroads for domestic and foreign talent, Yorkville became a hub for

musicians from across the continent to share old tunes while crafting new ones, spurred on by the likes of Woody Guthrie, Pete Seeger, Joan Baez, Bob Dylan, and domestic talents such as Ian Tyson, Sylvia Fricker, and Gordon Lightfoot.

Few musicians, though, stayed in Yorkville for more than a year or two. Venues sought established acts, and, without a name to draw a crowd, performers often found themselves with only the occasional opening spot, accepting loose change from a basket passed among the audience. Toronto became a stepping stone to the United States, particularly New York City and California, where youths joined their American peers in casting off the values of their parents in favour of utopian projects. Situated on the margins of the mainstream alongside like-minded folks, songwriters expressed common resentment and anger at social inequality, the military-industrial complex, and the tragedies that were befalling the world. Neil Young decried the 1970 Kent State shootings in 'Ohio.' Joni Mitchell lamented America's militarism and social disenfranchisement in 'The Fiddle and the Drum' and then made a seminal mark with 'Woodstock,' calling upon the 'nation' of youth to 'get back to the garden.' Denny Doherty and his band mates in the Mamas and the Papas beckoned others to join them in 'California Dreamin,' the upbeat appeal of southern California made all the more attractive by Zal Yanovsky and the Lovin' Spoonful's 'Do You Believe in Magic?' For those who were more concerned about freedom than communities, 'Born to Be Wild,' by several ex-Yorkville musicians who had taken on a new life in Steppenwolf, became an anthem. And when those who had cast the mainstream aside, many of them now parents themselves, became disenfranchised by crumbling utopias, Robbie Robertson and the Band invited them to reclaim America and the continent as a whole through such nostalgically rooted heartland songs as 'The Night They Drove Old Dixie Down,' 'Up on Cripple Creek,' and 'King Harvest (Has Surely Come).'

This was not the music with its allusions to sexual promiscuity and the abandonment of social virtues that had horrified the public back in the 1950s. Although many rock songs, fashions, and lifestyles continued to ostracize the general public – sexualized, bubblegum, and psychedelic variations added little to the social and cultural capital of rock – there was a growing appreciation for hybrids of folk and rock that displayed literary and socially valuable qualities. In some cases, rock and rollers were even becoming spoken of as a cultural avant garde who challenged placid society. Peter Gzowski, the famed national commentator, admitted to the readers of *Maclean's* in early 1966 that his feelings towards rock and roll were transformed upon watching Bob Dylan and his band (later to be the Band) perform at Massey Hall in Toronto during the infamous electrified tour. In 'Dylan: An Explosion of Poetry,' Gzowski confessed that

> like most grown-ups of the 1960s, I had until recently spent as little time as possible listening to rock-and-roll music. To me, rock and roll had seemed what I suppose the popular music of all younger generations has seemed to all older generations: too loud, too boorish, too dull … To my astonishment, I have learned while many of the rest of us have had our backs turned and our radios off, 'rock and roll' has quietly – well, I do admit *that's* hardly the word, but unobtrusively – become the most fascinating form of music of the 1960s.[13]

This re-evaluation occurred within a broader cultural shift in which 'mass' entertainment, long shunned for its commercialism and for pandering to base instincts, was starting to be thought of as the basis of a 'popular culture.'

Popular music's rising capital made musicians and their songs valuable to a Canadian population caught up in the thriving 'new nationalism' that emerged in the mid-1960s. After decades of continentalism, many people feared that economic prosperity had come at the cost of national sovereignty, a concern made all the more pressing by the decline of the United States into internal riots and external military conflicts. Along with calls for the federal government to economically overhaul Canada through 'buying back' areas of industry owned by Americans, the arts and mass media sectors undertook activities that ranged from founding grassroots playhouses and book publishing companies to petitioning for citizenship requirements in universities and a minimum quota of domestic work in art galleries. Popular music became interwoven into this nationalist imperative, with laments over the loss of songwriters now achieving acclaim in the United States and attempts to latch onto popular musicians as national brethren speaking for the nation, as typified by Tower's 'Musicians Play a Canada Rock.' Just as the Group of Seven were revered for supposedly channelling the essence of Canadiana, so too, in the view of nationally charged Canadians, could the new generation of musical artists. That so many of them lived in the United States made the desire to lay claim to them even stronger.

This nationalization of popular music came about more so at the hand of non-musicians than of musicians themselves. Truth be told, songwriters were largely apprehensive and suspicious of nationalism, and the notable ones who would go on to make political statements had already exited Canada, leaving behind those who were more interested in using their talent to write commercial rather than national songs. A national, let alone nationalistic, music scene was absent not only in ideological but geographical terms as well. Acts in Canada shared more with groups in the United States than they did with other Canadian ones because of highly regionalized scenes shaped by geography and a lack of pan-Canadian exposure on the airwaves. At the turn of the 1960s this had meant that Little Caesar and the Consuls, Robbie Lane and the Disciples, and other southern Ontario groups were tied into a rock and roll, R&B, and rockabilly circuit that ran through the 'rust belt' and brought many of them under the tutelage of Ronnie Hawkins and the Hawks. When psychedelia emerged in the mid- to late 1960s, the Collectors and the United Empire Loyalists in Vancouver shared stages with such California acts as Grateful Dead and Jefferson Airplane, or likewise travelled up and down the coast for the sake of musical inspiration with no need to cross the mountains that blocked them off from the rest of the country. Likewise, Toronto's the Paupers and Kensington Market mingled with those same American acts (and others visiting Toronto) during tours in the United States while having minimal connection with bands in other regions. And although many musicians may have heard of the Guess Who thanks to exposure on the CBC and as jingle singers for Coca-Cola, that band lived in the Prairies and might as well have been living across an ocean. Canadian acts shared little with their distant counterparts other than citizenship, an interest in foreign recordings and bands, and an inability to sustain a career.

Although the nationalist imperative was becoming intertwined with popular music, the initial attention to developing a 'national' music scene occurred in the mid-1960s among entrepreneurs who found themselves and others largely shut out from the publicly owned airwaves by radio stations that relied upon popular foreign recordings. *RPM*, an industry trade paper founded in 1965 by Walt Grealis and supported by close friend and record producer Stan Klees, took the lead in directing the attention of radio programmers to up-and-coming acts and quality recordings and, as of 1968, pressuring the federal government to ensure domestic access to the airwaves. In this, *RPM* was doing more than were the musicians who routinely distanced themselves from the nationalist imperative. At least this was the case in English-speaking Canada. The situation was significantly different in French-speaking Canada, where the Quiet Revolution of the early 1960s brought artists and audiences together in a celebration of Québécois nationhood, with chansonniers using their songs to glorify the past while laying out the destiny of a Québécois nation. Eager Quebeckers came together in such clubs as le Patriote in Montreal to musically celebrate and reify their dream of nation. The Québécois, thus, were years ahead of English-speaking Canada in using music to mediate a national sense of self.

In English-speaking Canadian music scenes, the push for musical and recording opportunities eventually took hold in legislation that made radio stations accountable for their use of the publicly owned airwaves. Prime Minister Pierre Trudeau, coming to power in 1968, and Pierre Juneau, chairman of the Canadian Radio and Television Commission (CRTC),[14] fought against the opposition of the Canadian Association of Broadcasters and members of parliament, who believed that music was no more than an industry best left to the private sector. In the end, the CRTC held off its challengers in legislating a 30 per cent content quota for AM-band radio as of 1971 (AM being the dominant band at the time; the quota was extended to FM in 1975).

The Canadian content regulation has been characterized in many ways over the years, perhaps most controversially and inaccurately as a qualitative assessment of Canadianness, rather than as an industry-minded quantitative system designed to ensure opportunities for a variety of talent to access the airwaves. The legislation, tellingly, gave equal weight to singers, composers, lyricists, and recording studios on a four-point system that required a song to meet a minimum two of four points in order for it to be counted towards the airplay quota. In the words of Juneau soon after the legislation was passed, 'I think the thirty percent Canadian music requirement should be looked upon not as a regulation, but as an instrument to all who are interested in the greater development of these varied talents.'[15] Although radio stations commonly abused the Canadian content system by overplaying the singles of a few established artists, enshrining the likes of the Guess Who, Gordon Lightfoot, and Anne Murray, opportunities nonetheless trickled down for aspiring acts, leading to investment in recording studios and record labels.

Musicians were divided on the legislation, with up-and-comers tending to praise the opportunities and established acts decrying a change that they did not need (and a resulting overplay that threatened to 'burn' their singles). Suspicion and unease with nationalism continued to proliferate within musical communities, songwriters in particular concerned that their work was being usurped for the nation's sake. But among consumers, who had been raised with popular music and were maturing into members of a nation, it seemed only natural to mediate national identity through songs and bands just as they did for gender, class, peer group, and other identities. Musical experiences offered rallying points for inclusion and identity, a sense of self and collective, of expressing oneself and finding kinship within the lyrics, concerts, and famed musicians. Neil Young is Canadian and since you are Canadian and I am Canadian, and even if he lives in the United States and Americans see him as theirs, he is nonetheless ours, or so the emotive logic goes. As members not only of a political state but of a collective nation, there is an inherent claim upon the works produced by other members no matter how far removed. A familial kinship exists within the emotive national imperative. Thus it did not matter that Canada lacked a national music scene by any measure: the ability to state that one existed, stretching a national skin across the skeletal regional music scenes, made it an ideological reality.[16] The national imperative, Gillian Mitchell has noted in *The North American Folk Music Revival: Nation and Identity in the United States and Canada, 1945–1980*, meant 'that songwriters who came from "the regions" of Canada (i.e., places other than southern Ontario), such as Neil Young and Joni Mitchell, were now considered, by the press and by nationalists, Canadians first and foremost and regional musicians secondarily.'[17] That Neil Young and Joni Mitchell, among many others, now had identities that derived on a substantial level from communities in the United States did not of course come into consideration.

For the recording industry spawned in the wake of the CRTC regulations and the multinational labels who could cash in on the airplay, there was much to be gained by capitalizing on the growing connection between music and national identity. Doing so, however, meant using media to brand musicians and their work in national terms, because the music itself usually lacked such identification. As record producer Jack Richardson, a force behind the breakthrough of the Guess Who, opined to music journalist Ritchie Yorke in 1971, 'there isn't a Canadian flavor or sound in music. That kind of musical identity usually comes through a factor of isolation from the mainstream. Canada just doesn't have that.'[18] Or, in the words of newspaper columnist Bob Johnston, 'Who is going to know when Canadian music is being played, unless someone announces it? Canadian music is, after all, just North American music which happens to be performed or written by Canadians. It has no unique sound, because it is a mixture of other influences such as those gained from our British and American contemporaries.'[19]

That 'announcement,' as Johnston put it, had been taking place in the media for a few years. Tower's article 'Musicians Play a Canada Rock' is an obvious example. Television, though, offered an even greater means of identifying and selling musical commodities to a population immersed in music as a component of their national identity. To this end, the Canadian Academy of Recording Arts and Sciences, representing the interests of the recording industry, seized control of the Juno Awards in 1975 and turned the industry-only celebration of domestic talent and entrepreneurs into a televised promotional tool for selling domestic and expatriate 'border jumpers' alike on the labels of multinational record companies. The Juno Awards served, and continues to do so, as a framing device, a means for the recording industry to use the national imperative to identify, promote, and encourage the consumption of the most popular and profitable of recordings. The event is not simply celebration but 'sell-abration.'

Television has had a significant impact on the relationship between music and the nation, from house bands performing Top 40 radio hits on *Let's Go* and *After Four* in the 1960s to variety shows like *Stompin' Tom's Canada* and *Nashville North* in the 1970s to the national showcase of the Juno Awards, but perhaps nothing did more to link audiences and musicians together in a national discourse than did MuchMusic, the self-proclaimed 'nation's music station' launched in 1984. Lacking a supply of videos to fill its Canadian content quota, and carrying over the grassroots feel of CITY-TV and *The NewMusic*, MuchMusic filled a significant amount of its airtime with interviews and special events that emphasized music as a national experience.

By the late 1980s this discourse was thriving not only on television but among the likes of radio station CFNY-Toronto, small domestic record labels, and music periodicals *Canadian Musician* and *Chart*. A celebration of Canadian music took place that brought domestic talent to the forefront as musical acts and national brethren, from 54-40 and Spirit of the West on the west coast to Sloan and Thrush Hermit on the east coast. Multinational labels, long underwriting the domestic music industry, pumped massive amounts of money into a scene that was ideologically national but industrially multinational, only to see the boom collapse by the late 1990s, ruptured by label overspending, declining consignment opportunities among retailers, MuchMusic's growing reliance on non-music content, and the shifting of radio formats towards an older demographic that was disinterested in new music.

As MuchMusic, radio stations, and record retailers turned away from grassroots domestic acts, aspiring bands and keen audiences made increasing use of the Internet and MP3 devices as alternative delivery systems. Official and fan tribute band websites, music and video streaming, community sites such as MySpace, YouTube, and Facebook, and online sales and pay-per-track downloads became the new means for up-and-coming acts to break through. The grassroots nature of the Internet made it possible for acts like Arcade Fire, Broken Social Scene, Metric, the Trews, and Hedley to come to the forefront while maintaining the feel of independence so qualifying of rock and roll (particularly in Canada). That even these groups owed much to multinationals for distribution did not matter.

From Paul Anka and the Guess Who to Bryan Adams and Feist, musicians have become celebrated as not only musicians but as Canadians. Not surprisingly, much of the literature written on music in Canada is less inquisitive and analytical than it is celebratory; emotive national discourses have reigned supreme among a generation raised with music as a means of mediating their individual and collective connections to the nation. Nicholas Jennings's *Before the Gold Rush: Flashbacks to the Dawn of the Canadian Sound*, compiled from his years as a music journalist, is a wonderfully detailed look at music scenes in Toronto during the 1960s yet is typical in using such familial language as 'this is the story of how Canadian pop was born.'[20] Similarly, Michael Barclay, Ian A.D. Jack, and Jason Schneider's *Have Not Been the Same: The CanRock Renaissance, 1985–95* offers the disclaimer that 'our intention is not to make some flag-waving, faux-nationalist claim about the superiority of Canadian music' only to then assert that 'this book is meant to celebrate what happened here and to argue that it's as valid as any other nation's music.'[21]

For some authors, the task goes beyond celebrating and into supposedly identifying quintessential Canadianness by sifting through the 'American' and 'imitative' in order to find a thread, pattern, or some other vein of a 'truly' Canadian music.[22] This pursuit shows a tremendous predilection towards the songwriters who came to fame during a 'golden age' spanning the late 1960s to early 1970s, their careers not only coinciding with the rise of songwriters as artists but also existing in a time commonly romanticized as being less corporate and thus truer to the music and muse. In 'McRock: Pop as a Commodity,' Mary Harron well summarized how in the late 1960s 'the stress on private sufferings and the storms of creation, the reverent attention paid to a performer's technique and inspiration, all served to build up a romantic vision of the artist that would have made Shelley blush.'[23] This sense of an unadulterated musical creativity truer to the spirit of the music has been empowered by nationalistic narratives that praise singer-songwriters for their ability to sense or tap into the 'Canadian' experience. Douglas Fetherling, author of *Some Day Soon: Essays on Canadian Songwriters*, has been among the more brazen in selectively identifying within the songs of Neil Young, Joni Mitchell, Leonard Cohen, Robbie Robertson, and Gordon Lightfoot a 'conscious Canadianism' supposedly evident in the 'sense of polite, distracted anguish,' 'sense of isolation,' and 'loneliness of the landscape.'[24] He further, and very tellingly as to the subjectivity of his claim, argues that 'a truly sensitive listener, for instance, should be able to feel if not articulate the Canadianness of Judy Collins' rendition of "Some Day Soon," a tune rich in implication and intellectualized emptiness, even though it is not immediately recognizable as an Ian Tyson song and all the place names are American.'[25] Such a position is in line with Fetherling's long involvement with the more nationalistic of periodicals in Canada.[26]

Fetherling is not alone in making such assertions. One has only to look at another prominent book in the field, Marco Adria's *Music of Our Times: Eight Canadian Singer-Songwriters*. According to Adria, the Canadian musical archetype is 'frontierness,' a conclusion based upon a narrow selection of songwriters drawn almost exclusively from 'golden age' folk and folk rock (Gordon Lightfoot, Leonard Cohen, Neil Young, Joni Mitchell, Bruce Cockburn, Murray McLaughlan, Jane Siberry, and k.d. lang).[27] The assertion, for Fetherling and Adria alike, is made all the easier because it plays upon the pre-existing and deeply entrenched idea that the 'true' Canada is one of the outdoors and open spaces and that several of these acts, notably Young, Mitchell, and lang, were raised in the Prairies; the notion is easily extended to Lightfoot's relatively rural upbringing in Orillia and the 'back-to-the-country' narratives of Cockburn and McLaughlan.

Greg Potter, in his journalistic *Hand Me Down World: The Canadian Pop-Rock Paradox*, has similarly identified golden age songwriters as more Canadian than those who followed, a position buttressed by decrying that national authenticity has been surrendered as part of the often-discussed (and lamented) national inferiority complex:

The Canadian pop-rock paradox is simply stated: in a quest to win international celebrity, Canadian musical artists have gradually and unwittingly lost their Canadian identity. Twenty-five years ago it was obvious that Ian Tyson, Gordon Lightfoot, Anne Murray, the Guess Who and Bachman-Turner

Overdrive were Canadian acts. Today, that distinction is irrelevant unless you work for the [Canadian Radio-television and Telecommunications Commission]. The problem stems from a deep-rooted sense of playing second banana to the industrialized world, a part of our heritage that predisposes us to snatch at hand-me-downs like a wino rifling a Goodwill bin.[28]

This sort of humorous metaphor takes the place of analysis, allowing Potter to argue that, back in the day, 'songs like Ian and Sylvia's "Four Strong Winds" and Gordon Lightfoot's "Early Morning Rain" verily reeked of back bacon and beer for breakfast.'[29]

'Polite, distracted anguish'; 'isolation'; 'loneliness of the landscape'; 'frontierness'; 'a deep-rooted sense of playing second banana' – to this list has been added 'irony.' Rick Salutin, noted journalist, author, and playwright, argued in *Queen's Quarterly* that

> [Neil] Young and [Leonard] Cohen may have lived in the United States for decades, but they are, in my opinion, clearly Canadian in their sensibility. When Leonard Cohen, for instance, sings, 'Democracy is coming ... to the U.S.A.,' this has an ironic detachment which I don't believe Americans are generally capable of with regard to their own mythologies. Americans tend to be too identified with those mythologies; when they critique them, they tend to express themselves with deep anger, as in the case of Bruce Springsteen. A satirical or ironic mode is largely beyond them.[30]

Putting aside Salutin's questionable and unqualified use of 'clearly Canadian ... sensibility,' the reductive and representative treatment of Bruce Springsteen, and the 'us' versus 'them' dichotomy, it is important to note that Salutin was not the first to argue on the behalf of irony. Barry Grant had earlier argued that 'ironic distance' was the quintessentially Canadian trait not only in music but popular culture as a whole.[31] According to Grant, 'Canadian rock artists have sought to distinguish themselves from the dominant American sounds by taking an ironic distance toward these musical forms themselves.'[32] Yet, as Bart Testa and Jim Shedden have already pointed out about Grant's position, the argument is flawed not only in its selectivity but because irony exists within rock and roll as a genre. 'The trickle of Canadian rock irony does not offer much national-cultural distinction when we compare it with the steady flow of parody underwriting American rockers,' in careers that range from Bo Diddley to Frank Zappa. Rock and roll is 'inclined to ironic self-subversion without respect to national cultures.'[33]

Reductionism and juxtapositions have also been used to evaluate the nationalness of Canadian musicians; it is not simply a matter of *being* Canadian but of being *more* Canadian. Timothy Rice and Tammy Gutnik, in 'What's Canadian about Canadian Popular Music? The Case of Bruce Cockburn,' have claimed that Cockburn is more Canadian than 'Joni Mitchell and Neil Young … [who] emigrated to the United States to cash in on their popularity' and that they, like 'most Canadian musicians have not followed Cockburn's eclectic past, but have adopted wholeheartedly one of American popular music's genres, in the process losing their Canadian identity.'[34] As with Potter's argument, Rice and Gutnik make assertions as to an innate and pre-existing 'Canadian identity' being lost by the adoption of a similarly unqualified Americanism. Not only is the dichotomy jarring but the explanation as to why Mitchell and Young left for the United States is prejudicial and incorrect; the two barely subsisted in Toronto and had almost no popularity to 'cash in on,' their economic hardship leaving them little choice but to relocate to the United States in order to access industry hubs (that Mitchell got married and her new husband was popular on the Michigan folk circuit was, of course, also a factor that went unnoted). Mitchell and Young, unlike Cockburn, did not have a well-connected manager like Bernie Finkelstein and the benefit of Canadian content regulations. Rice and Gutnik's nationalistic intent is made more than clear when they warn readers that 'there is a whole world out there, and Canada must relate to it to reduce her dependence on the United States, both culturally and economically.'[35] Just as notable is that this nationalistic viewpoint did not prevent the article from being published in an academic Festchrift.

Nor did a nationalistic agenda prevent the inclusion of John Lehr's 'As Canadian as Possible … Under the Circumstances: Regional Myths, Images of Place and National Identity in Canadian Country Music' in the scholarly *Canadian Music: Issues of Hegemony and Identity*, an edited collection that spanned a century of music in Canada. Lehr's look at country music in Canada acted as a platform for arguing, with little evidence and very incorrectly, that the Canadian content regulation was legislated in order to make a qualitative contribution to national identity and, consequently, is flawed for allowing the inclusion of songs that reference the United States.[36] This skewed approach allows Lehr to inform readers that the 'ineffective … controlling [of] the substance of the material broadcast within the nation' has led to 'the failure of the CRTC regulations to actively promote the building of a Canadian identity of place' and that correcting it requires a 'rewording of Canadian content criteria to acknowledge the significance of lyric material treating a subject in Canadian terms.'[37] Lehr does not offer a look at country music in Canada, then, so much as advocate on the behalf of what he calls 'the cause of Canadian identity.'[38]

The relatively recent release of musicologist Elaine Keillor's *Music in Canada: Capturing Landscape and Diversity* inadvertently raises warning signs as to how reductionist narratives are becoming enshrined as analysis without any scholarly assessment or critique.[39] Keillor presents Fetherling's assertion that Neil Young's voice 'sounds like the wind on the Prairies' and that Canadian music is epitomized by 'a sincere gentleness' that, in paraphrasing Fetherling's argument, 'gets its true flavour when combined with a sense of isolation, reflecting the loneliness of the landscape.'[40] Rice and Gutnik's assessment of Bruce Cockburn is similarly restated as a given.[41] This problematic situation is compounded when Keillor maintains the 'us' and 'them' dichotomy, rhetorically asking if 'the difficulty of finding a Canadian identity [is] due in part to the fact that we do not recognize our sound when non-Canadians use it?'[42] (an assertion harking back, and contrary to, Fetherling's claim of being able to detect the innate Canadianness within 'Some Day Soon' even when performed by an American). Barriers to identifying Canadianness are further attributed by Keillor to the possibility 'that as Canadian musicians become more successful in the international music industry, they may be influenced by demands of their non-Canadian record managers,' overlooking how no manager has done more to tailor musical acts to international audiences than Canadian-born Bruce Allen (Loverboy, Bryan Adams, and Michael Bublé being among the bigger acts on his roster).[43] If anything, history reveals the opposite: Canadian managers have long focused on the international market, both in terms of securing airplay and exporting acts, while the foreign-owned subsidiaries of multinational labels have done much to develop, via their distribution systems, opportunities for domestic acts of limited interest abroad.

To find authors and even academic scholars who present popular music as something innately national is of little surprise. Much like the population as a whole, they have 'read' the cultural texts within the contexts in which they live. What Cecily Devereux has noted about *Anne of Green Gables* in the national literary canon can also be applied to popular music. It is

a discursive site for what can be understood in ideological terms as the interpellation of national identity: 'we' read *Anne* as part of being 'Canadian';

'we' recognize in Anne signs of 'our' shared 'Canadianness,' and in that process recognize (or constitute) ourselves as national subjects. Because these terms are ideological they are not necessarily articulated or even apparent, but circulate in representations of the national community as identifying claims: Anne is 'our Anne'; she is part of 'us.' The attributes of this community identity are largely indeterminate (they are part of a national 'essence,' and they are also the shared 'values' that underpin nationalism).[44]

Any innateness disappears when the musical text is placed in a different context and interpreted within other ideological and discursive parameters. Much as how Devereux found that '*Akage no An* is a Japanese national figure; Anne Shirley in the United States is an American girl,' musicians and songs commonly identified in Canada as being quintessentially Canadian are commonly interpreted by audiences elsewhere as being North American, if not, by default, American.[45] This is especially the case for Americans, who, raised with the likes of Joni Mitchell rallying them 'back to the garden' in 'Woodstock,' Neil Young decrying a national tragedy in 'Ohio,' and the Band giving voice to historic America in 'Up on Cripple Creek' and 'The Night they Drove Old Dixie Down,' understood these musicians to be American.

With the musical paradigm shift, songwriters and musicians joined a long list of cultural icons around which Canadians could rally and share a national sense of self. At the turn of the twentieth century, Canadians praised painters, poets, authors, playwrights, and other cultural producers for their supposed ability to reveal the essence of the nation within the recently confederated colonies. The ways in which the work of Tom Thomson and the Group of Seven became more important in national than artistic terms is an obvious example. Robert Wright of Trent University is correct in noting that 'if landscape painting provided the first pretext for aggressive cultural nationalism in modern English Canada, then pop music provided the last.'[46] Yet, and tellingly, both the Group of Seven and such revered songwriters as Gordon Lightfoot and Joni Mitchell drew heavily upon non-Canadian influences and resources; their work did not emerge in isolation.[47] As well, there is a significant difference between these two groups in terms of nationalist intent. Whereas the Group of Seven intentionally used their craft to promote nationhood among the general population, in what was an art for nation's sake rather than an art for art's sake, this was not the case among songwriters who felt it necessary to maintain a distance from nationalist ideologies. 'There is no Group of Seven among us,' as Bruce Cockburn put it to Myrna Kostash in a 1972 interview for *Saturday Night*.[48] Between the desire for artistic freedom and, in the wake of the Canadian content regulation, a need to prevent their work from seeming popular due to nationalism or legislated airplay, let alone the frustration that came with having radio stations overplay established hits, musicians have been much less interested in connecting their music to the nation than have fans who use music to mediate a connection to the nation.

What then does the survey of existing literature on music in Canada disclose? It reveals a continuation of a long-standing nation-building discourse that uses selectivity and established identifiers along the lines of what sociologist Anthony D. Smith has called a myth-symbol complex, an interconnection of 'myths and symbols' that includes people, places, events, and other elements commonly identified as national in nature, essence, or affiliation.[49] From famous military battles and war heroes to television shows and musical celebrities, the myth-symbol complex offers a means for the citizenry to communally engage in a sense of what it means to be not only citizens of a country but members of a nation. The myth-symbol complex is made possible by systems of communication that allow citizens to share an experience despite having met relatively few of their fellow members. As Benedict Anderson has famously discussed, the rise of print and literacy made possible the modern nation-state as an 'imagined community' in which, 'regardless of the actual inequality and exploitation that may prevail in each, the nation is always conceived as a deep, horizontal comradeship.'[50] The proliferation of communicative commodities in the wake of modernity, particularly feature films, radio programs, pulp press, and, as of the mid-century, television, furthered the ability for individuals to mediate a connection to the nation.

Musicians of the folk and folk rock veins have been identified more than any others because their work is so easily connected to a myth-symbol complex that upholds an anti-modern, romanticized, outdoors image of Canada that dates back to the Group of Seven and even much earlier. The vastness of the prairies, the rawness of the Precambrian Shield, the grit of the lumber camp, the earthiness of the habitant, the simplicity of the east coast folk: these often 'identified' essences of Canada are in keeping with a heartwarming and celebratory narrative that, in reality, overlooks related issues of class struggle, racial oppression, industrial imbalance, let alone the urbanity in which so many Canadians live.[51] Still, by no means do musicians have to be of folk or folk rock to be revered as artists able to speak for the national experience. Rock and roll has proven a fertile site for national identity because it operates on highly

empowered *'in' and 'out' groups:* teenagers versus parents, alternative lif-
ers versus the mainstream, freedom lovers versus button-down authorities, and so forth. At the turn of the 1970s this came to include the
nation with the juxtaposition of a 'Canadian' versus 'American' music.
That Canadian music is shaped within an international musical ebb and
flow underwritten by multinational media conglomerates matters not.
'Rock and roll locates its fans as different even while they exist within the
hegemony,' Lawrence Grossberg has noted.[52]

The catch-22 is that those who can be connected to pre-existing elements are inherently 'authenticated' while, conversely, those who challenge the norm are revered as innovators who take Canadian music to
new areas – all the more so when the narrative employs literary tropes
and situates the contemporary scene within a lineage spanning from a
nostalgic past to an inevitably successful future.[53] The situation allows the
likes of Lee Silversides, president of the Canadian Academy of Recording Arts and Sciences, to declare in the forward to a history of the Juno
Awards that 'our artists have never been more creative and our music has
never sounded better. Enjoy this historical salute that allows us to reflect
on our cultural heritage while moving forward with confidence through
the next phase of our country's musical evolution.'[54] Given that it is 'our'
music, one does not even have to be a fan in order to feel a sense of
pride in a highly acclaimed act. Few observers have touched on this issue
better than music journalist Larry LeBlanc, who, in the autumn of 1974,
noted that 'just as many Canadians are against foreign investment *on
principle*, without any clear idea of what resources are being taken over
by whom, many Canadians love Anne Murray *on principle*, without knowing or even caring much about her music.'[55] LeBlanc was certainly being
a bit facetious given Murray's multiple Juno Awards, but the gist stands.
(Reverence for Anne Murray similarly prompted John Macfarlane, associate editor of *Maclean's*, to argue a few years later that 'if you like Anne
Murray, I hope you like her not because she's Canadian but because she
is good').[56]

For musicians to write themselves into or at least sanction the discursive and emotional mediation of music as essentialistically national
makes sense, whether they are devotees or simply those who understand
the value of national acclaim. Common are such exclamations as Joni
Mitchell telling *Maclean's* that there is 'a lot of Prairie in my music and
in Neil Young's music' and Burton Cummings remarking that the Guess
Who and Wide Mouth Mason both possess 'wheatfield soul.'[57] Confessions to the contrary, on the other hand, offer a window into music as a

contested ideological terrain. Many people would be surprised to hear Ian Tyson, commonly identified as a quintessentially Canadian songwriter (his 'Four Strong Winds' was selected as the top Canadian song by the Canadian Broadcasting Corporation's *50 Tracks: The Canadian Version* in 2005), situating himself within an American musical experience. 'We imitate American music forms,' Tyson argued in his autobiography *I Never Sold My Saddle.* 'If you remove the basic American guitar forms, you'd remove everything. A lot of people say I'm American, that I sound American. Well, I probably do. I've lived down there a long time, and every singer that has ever influenced me has been American.'[58] For others, a desire for artistic freedom and concerns about the subsuming power of nationalism often meant a distancing from the national imperative. Although Rice and Gutnik identified Bruce Cockburn as the quintessential Canadian songwriter, he has long self-identified first and foremost as a member of the global community and has expressed discomfort with nationalism.[59] Or, as Jane Siberry once explained about being labelled Canadian, 'I've always resented any kind of arbitrary boundary ... I mean, the borders to countries were articulated by men, and they're not natural boundaries between people. And so I don't think that way, and think of myself not as a Canadian but just as a type of being, and think of other people that way.'[60]

Just what is Canadian music, in particular rock and roll, then? As soon as music is spoken of as 'Canadian' it is being made subject to categorization and external considerations; lines are drawn that sever, or at least attempt to, the experience along geographical, national, political, and ideological lines. It becomes defined by the parameters of those who seek to categorize it, whether the CRTC's citizenship criteria for measuring Canadian content or popular assertions of essentialistic Canadianness tied to the myth-symbol complex. Some might say that the Tragically Hip are more Canadian than Paul Anka because their lyrics identify with specific geo-historical events and have maintained their residency whereas Anka left Canada as a teenager and has rarely returned to the country.[61] Yet Anka is the recipient of numerous national awards and honours. For Stompin' Tom Connors, who sparked a controversy in 1978 over the Juno Awards being given to 'border jumpers,' Canadian music entailed residency and making a domestic contribution. At the other extreme is Bryan Adams, who, as seen in the controversy that arose when *Waking Up the Neighbours* did not qualify to be counted towards Canadian content airtime, viewed Canadian music as requiring nothing more than citizenship if even that. The paradigm is so encompassing that it even stretches to John Kay, who, despite not being a citizen and only living in Canada for only a few years, has been inducted into the Juno Awards Hall of Fame for his work in the California-based Steppenwolf.

Such broadness has become a necessity among an increasingly urban and multicultural population that does not share with earlier generations a rural ancestry evoked by folk and folk rock. The spaciousness of the Prairies is a far cry from Toronto's Jane and Finch; the gentle timbres of an acoustic guitar that dominated radio decades earlier now share the airwaves with abrupt vocals and synthetic beats.[62] Raw nationalism has helped to ease the transition, or perhaps even acted as a counterforce. Academic Will Straw offered thoughts along these lines back in 2000: 'The rowdy nationalism that now marks concerts by Sloan, the Tragically Hip or the reconstituted Guess Who works to paper over the fractures that more and more (amidst the Canadian explosions of club music, Canto-pop, bhangra and hip-hop) disrupt notions of a singular Canadian popular music tradition.'[63]

The contentious terrain on which Canadian music is debated, negotiated, and reified reveals as much about the subjectivity of 'Canadian' as it does about the inability to come to a specific definition. The category is as much about the people who engage in it as it is about the conclusions arrived at. *Canuck Rock*, then, does not attempt to identify an ideologically or aesthetically 'true' Canadian music or rank some musicians over others. Instead, this book explores how and why Canadian popular music evolved and examines the questions, controversies, and problems that have arisen. A few academics have started to take steps in this direction. Douglas Ivison of Lakehead University has insightfully argued that any attempt to identify, isolate, or essentialize Canadianness is, in his words, 'not only ultimately untenable and unproductive but dangerously reductive.'[64] Ivison points out how

it is presumed that the Scots-Irish musical traditions are specific to Atlantic-Canadian music, when they are also a significant presence in certain regions of the United States; a vision of the 'true' Canada as a rural nation of small towns is privileged over the largely urban country in which most of us live; and, the authentic Canada is nostalgically situated in the past: a past in which Canada was largely British and rural, a time in which things were simpler ... Having lived my life in Ottawa, Hamilton, and Montreal, I do not recognize my Canada in this 'Canadian' sound, nor, I imagine, do many urban Canadians or those Canadians from different cultural backgrounds.[65]

Ivison instead asks how musicians 'mark themselves as "Canadian" in the local marketplace. In such a context, the point is not to "discover" themes of images or sounds that can be claimed as essentially Canadian, but to examine the ways in which English-Canadian rock performers deploy and construct "Canadianness" (which is not an essential quality but something that is always partial and contested, and always already in transition) as a means of differentiating themselves from their largely American and British models.'[66] This focus would apply to such performers as Stompin' Tom Connors and the Tragically Hip, acts that incorporate specific, ideologically loaded identifiers in their work.

Examining how national identity has been 'emplotted' in popular music is but one approach. For Bart Testa and Jim Shedden, understanding the national music experience requires looking at the regional ebb and flows that span the continent. 'Rock sub-genres,' they argue,

> arise simultaneously but heterogeneously in numerous North American regions – regions that often cross national boundaries in terms of musical styles and their popularity ... Hence, for a Canadian example, in the 1950s and 1960s, Toronto can be seen as part of the North American middle-west and was a city receptive to R&B, not unlike other Great Lakes industrial cities, e.g., Chicago or Detroit. R&B cover groups made up of white Canadian musicians, like the Diamonds and the Crew Cuts, were successfully launched from Toronto into the U.S. market in that era.[67]

Testa and Shedden are correct in noting how 'connections are more often drawn between regions than countries.'[68] Don DiNovo of the band Lighthouse experienced this first-hand, telling the Canadian Radio and Television Commission during the 1970 hearings into the proposed Canadian content quota that 'you can have a hit record in Toronto sometimes and they won't know who you are in Winnipeg.'[69] Although the regulation helped to break down the isolation of regional music scenes by prompting stations into using hits from other areas and, in time, regional playlists would give way to pan-national ones, regionalism would continue to prevail to a significant degree. As Testa and Shedden noted in their study, 'the triumphs of Canadian rock in the 1970s arose from, and traveled through, regional scenes, and ... musicians linked up, again region by region, *across* the national border with the U.S., most significantly with other places in the Great Lakes area – with, in other words, the great industrial middle west of the continent.'[70] Needless to say, at the very least, such academic explorations are contributing much to our understanding of the Canadian musical experience. Recently, Larry Starr, Christopher Waterman, and Jay Hodgson have even produced a university survey textbook that discusses the Canadian music scene within the evolution of North American rock and roll. *Rock: A Canadian Perspective*, designed for introductory-level music courses, is important for not letting the border divide the study of popular music.[71]

Identity, national and otherwise, in popular music has tended to be a problematic area of academic study. Sociologist and music theorist Simon Frith complained over a decade ago that scholarship has

> been limited by the assumption that the sounds must somehow 'reflect' or 'represent' the people. The analytic problem has been to trace the connections back, from the work (the score, the song, the beat) to the social groups who produce and consume it. What's been at issue is homology, some sort of structural relationship between material and musical forms ... the issue is not how a particular piece of music or a performance reflects the people, but how it produces them, how it creates and constructs an experience – a musical experience, an aesthetic experience – that one can only make sense of by taking on both a subjective and collective identity.[72]

To these ends, Frith had previously recommended that 'what we should be examining is not how true a piece of music is to something else, but how it sets up the idea of "truth" in the first place.'[73] Fortunately, international scholarship has begun to unravel the relationships between music and national identity. Peter Symon, for example, has shown how folk musicians in the 1970s and 1980s reworked earlier musical styles into a selectively formed music deemed to be representative of Scottish identity.[74] Noel McLauchlin and Martin McLoone have similarly pointed out that musicians in Ireland have privileged some elements over others in order to mark their work with national difference.[75] A case study on New Zealand revealed much the same.[76] Christian Lahusen showed how punk music was used to mediate national identity in the Basque country. Likewise, David Treece revealed how different ideas of nationalness were being contested by competing music in Brazil and Peter Manuel has explored the mediation of national identity through music selection in Cuba.[77] Sometimes, as Edward Larkey reveals in 'Just for Fun? Language Choice in German Popular Music,' it is the political state that deploys selective identifiers, as in the German Democratic Republic's creation of a Soviet-friendly rock and roll song and dance called the 'Lipsi.'[78]

Canuck Rock builds upon these academic inroads by exploring the evolution of the Canadian music scene and the multifaceted ideological, legislative, geographical, and industrial process by which the experience became a means of interpreting, negotiating, and encoding national identity. How and why did a socio-economic entertainment that transcended borders and threatened social stability become virtually inseparable from nationhood? What does this tell us about the ways in which people mediate their identities? And just how and why has nationalization managed to take place and even thrive during a time in which industry resources became increasingly centralized under a few multinational entertainment conglomerates? Answers require digging through the relationships between the people who make music, the industries that produce and sell the recordings, the radio stations and government legislation that determine availability, the fans who listen to the songs, and the myriad sites and ways in which they interact. From that day in 1956 when Les Vogt and the Prowlers shared a Vancouver stage with Bill Haley to the House of Commons debates about Canadian content to the contemporary workings of the multinational recording industry, the relationship between people and music has been changing. *Canuck Rock* offers a history of the people, places, industries, organizations, legislation, and songs that fostered and shaped music as a postwar entertainment and, in time, a means for the citizenry of a country to view themselves as members of a nation.

1

Lonely Boys and Wild Girls: Rock and Roll in Canada in the 1950s

They didn't care a hoot about his singing, don't kid yourself. The supersonic screams came when he jiggled, and joggled, and worked his knees and his hips, and slipped his hands, as though burned, and when he just stood there, legs astraddle, and shook. 'Love me!' he shouted in one song.

Mac Reynolds, *Vancouver Sun*, 1957[1]

The people are really friendly, but it's a little cool outside.

Elvis Presley, 1957[2]

I was 15 at the time. At my age, there was nothing political about music, or geographical, it was just music.

Norm Sherratt, Little Caesar and the Consuls, 2008[3]

'Rock 'n' roll, a jarring, jolting combination of primitive jungle rhythm and hillbilly blues struck like a discordant cyclone blowing in from across the border in the shape of Bill Haley and his Comets.' John Kirkwood of the *Vancouver Sun* did not have much good to report about the deranged new music group that performed at Vancouver's Kerrisdale Arena on 27 June 1956, that city's first major rock and roll concert and one of the earliest in Canada:

> This is the eight-man group who invented the craze that has barnstormed its way across a continent in less than two years. Exactly what it is and how it weaves its hypnotic spell over addicted juveniles has never been accurately determined. But to the 4,630 delirious teen-agers who jived, stomped, kicked and shrieked their way through Haley's three-hour Wednesday night concert at Kerrisdale Arena, the answers didn't matter ... With the first honking bars of 'Rock Around the Clock,' the teen-agers rushed the floor.

Boys danced with girls; girls danced with girls; boys danced with boys; boys and girls danced with themselves, on the seats, up and down the aisles, into a conga line and out again. By the time 'See You Later Alligator' arrived, sanity had departed. The law surrendered the floor to the twitching, gyrating youngsters. The hall became a seething mass of flashing arms and legs, twisting torsos – loud with noise, sticky with heat. Faces were contorted, eyes glazed, mouths open. Mass hypnosis was in evidence.[4]

Canadians were more than merely audience members: the Prowlers, a Vancouver-based teenage rock and roll band headed by Les Vogt, shared the stage that day with Haley and His Comets.

Rock and roll, the latest musical fad to be given significant airtime, was intertwined with the just as recent socio-demographic phenomenon of being a teenager. A passage between adolescence and adulthood was itself nothing new, but as Doug Owram describes in *Born at the Right Time: A History of the Baby Boom Generation*, 'the arrival of urbanization and industrialization in Western society initiated long-term and fundamental changes to the concept of youth … when the baby-boomers arrived at adolescence, they did so not only as a group of children who had always been treated as important, but in a society that gave youth culture a distinct and important position.'[5] Teenagers in Canada thrived amid a strong continental economy and an abundance of leisure time that pegged them, in the mid to late 1950s, as a consumer group valued at over $100 million a year. 'For all their strange talk and outlandish clothes teenagers are as welcome as a couple of Grey Cup tickets these days,' *Maclean's* noted in the autumn of 1957.[6] Fortunately for the recording industry, technological advances meant that expensive and fragile shellac recordings were replaced by inexpensive vinyl records, teenagers making up approximately 60 per cent of the market.[7]

Many parents, having been adolescents but not teenagers, struggled to understand their offspring. Not surprisingly, the popular press found this generation gap to be a valuable site to probe, with *Maclean's* offering such partially tongue-in-cheek articles as Robert Thomas Allen's 'How to Live with a Teen-age Daughter,' published in 1957:

A teen-age daughter is something between a child and a young woman in ten petticoats, bare feet and crooked lipstick. Her main drive in life is to wear spike heels and My Downfall perfume, dress like a $25,000-a-year fashion model out of *Seventeen* magazine, give as much lip as the traffic will bear, stay up until midnight, which she claims every child of normal parents is allowed to do, and to avoid all work, which she claims all normal parents do themselves. She's never chilly; she's frozen. She's never warm; she's burning. She never dislikes things; she loathes it – and this sometimes includes her father and mother, who, she thinks, won't face the facts of life.[8]

'How to Endure a Father,' a rebuttal by Robert Thomas Allen's teenage daughters Jane and Mary, offered the other side of the equation:

> He won't listen to rock 'n' roll. He says it's not music, it's an excuse for not learning how to play an instrument, a symptom of what's happening to the world, and that it could only be taken seriously by a generation that doesn't know any better. He evidently doesn't apply any of this to the songs he plays when he sits down at the piano. Some of this favorites are: 'Jada, Jada, Jada Jing'; 'Yes, We Have No Bananas'; 'I Want Some Sea Food, Mama'; 'Doodle De Doo,' and 'It Must Be Jelly 'Cause Jam Don't Shake Like That.'[9]

Musical tastes, the exchange between Allen and his daughters makes clear, distinguished – and separated – the generations. During the early 1950s there had been plenty of musical overlap as listeners of various ages shared a single household radio, but with the mass production of inexpensive transistor sets and record players, youths could listen to recordings of their choice on their own devices. Record companies in turn began treating teenagers as a group with its own genres, artists, sounds, and marketing campaigns. Doug Owram has gone so far as to argue that 'in 1950 there was no teenage music – period. Individual artists like Frank Sinatra could and did attract an adolescent audience, but Sinatra's crooning did not distinguish him in form or content from artists appealing to adults.'[10] The same was true for such solo acts as Bing Crosby ('Swinging on a Star'), Patti Page ('Confess,' 'All My Love,' and 'The Tennessee Waltz'), Rosemary Clooney ('Come on a My House' and 'Mambo Italiano'), Eddie Fisher ('I Love You'), Nat King Cole ('Nature Boy,' 'Mona Lisa,' and 'Too Young'), and clean cut vocal-harmony groups such as the Four Aces ('[It's No] Sin') and the Four Freshmen ('It's a Blue World').

For aspiring Canadian and American performers alike, the best chance at 'making it' meant relocating to hubs of the recording industry – managers, studios, labels, pressing plants, and access to major media outlets – in the United States, particularly New York City, Philadelphia, Chicago, Nashville, and Los Angeles. The Four Lads, a group of ex–choir boys from St Michael's Cathedral Choir School in Toronto, achieved stardom by building on local success and landing a long-term gig at Le Ruban Bleu nightclub in New York. With these credentials the group secured work doing background harmonies for Columbia Records on Johnnie Ray's 'Cry' and 'The Little White Cloud that Cried' and, following the success of the former, recorded and released their own single, 'Mocking Bird.' The group, harmonious on follow-up singles 'Moments to Remember' and 'Standing on the Corner,' offered Columbia Records a very sellable quartet.

That the Four Lads came from Toronto while the Four Aces were from Pennsylvania and the Four Freshmen from Indiana mattered not; they sounded and looked similar, were young, energetic, clean cut, and, just as importantly, white. The recording industry had little interest in groups that fell outside of this template because the big money came from white performers recording the songs of marginalized black performers. 'Whitewashing' worked just as well for the Crew Cuts, who, like the Four Lads, had their roots within the St Michael's Cathedral Choir. Although the Crew Cuts had a bit of a hit with their self-penned 'Crazy 'bout You Baby,' their label built upon this promise by having them record 'Sh-Boom' (originally performed by the Chords), 'Earth Angel' (the Penguins), 'Gum Drop' (the Charms), 'Don't Be Angry' (Nappy Brown), and 'Young Love' (Sonny James), among others. For their part, the Diamonds, also originally from Toronto, charted with covers of 'Why Do Fools Fall in Love?' (Frankie Lymon and the Teenagers), 'Church Bells May Ring' (the Willows), 'Little Darlin'' (the Gladiolas), and 'The Stroll' (Clyde Otis and Nancy Lee). The whitewashing of R&B included such famed American acts as the McGuire Sisters, who had hits with 'Sincerely' (the Moonglows), 'Shake, Rattle, and Roll' (Joe Turner), and 'Goodnight Sweetheart, Goodnight' (the Spaniels); Perry Como, with his notable cover of 'Kokomo' (Gene and Eunice); and Pat Boone, who had hits with 'I Almost Lost My Mind' (the Harptones), 'Two Hearts' (the Charms), 'Ain't That a Shame' (Fats Domino), and 'Tutti Frutti' and 'Long Tall Sally' (Little Richard), to name but a few. Paul Friedlander, author of *Rock and Roll: A Social History*, has argued that the practice of white groups recording songs written by black artists 'had the effect of smothering the original black versions. The indies simply could not press enough records and lacked the network to distribute them nationwide – and they did not have the necessary friendly relations with radio station personnel to ensure radio exposure.'[11]

Few black performers made it into the mainstream. The barrier they faced is perhaps no better displayed than in the case of Nat 'King' Cole.

Cole was a popular guest on variety shows hosted by Perry Como and Ed Sullivan, yet when NBC gave him a show of his own in 1956, the first of such shows to be hosted by a non-white performer, many advertisers withdrew their sponsorship dollars out of fear that white audiences would steer away from products associated with a black host. *The Nat King Cole Show* lasted for only one season.[12] Despite being a top recording star, Cole was excluded from opportunities given to his white counterparts. Nicholas Jennings has written about Cole's difficult time in Canada: 'When Cole arrived to perform in Toronto for the week of November 13, 1950, at the Loew's Uptown theatre, Capitol Canada's Ken Kerr greeted him and arranged to book him into a hotel. But the "finer" establishments in Toronto turned him down. "We wanted to put Cole up at either the Royal York or the King Edward," recalls Kerr, "but they wouldn't take him. We wound up having to go to the St. Regis Hotel over on Sherbourne Street, which was a bit of a dump."'[13]

Cole's success, limited as it was, was an abnormality. Careers for black musicians were primarily limited to live performances and recordings made by entrepreneurs sold through specialty retail outlets. Sam Phillips of the Memphis Recording Service stands out as a seminal figure in recording the likes of Ike Turner and B.B. King. Similarly, the duo of Phil and Leonard Chess of Chess Records in Chicago helped establish Muddy Waters, Little Walter, and Howlin' Wolf. Separate industries for white and black performers existed not only in terms of recordings and sales but radio stations and even jukeboxes.[14] Tellingly, *Billboard* tracked the music in a separate 'race records' chart.

Crossovers between the two industries began to appear in the early 1950s as white youths started to dial into radio stations that broadcasted to predominantly black audiences. Detecting a growing audience for the recordings, a few disc jockeys at white-focused stations risked controversy by spinning some of the singles. Dewey Phillips at WHBQ-Memphis, who would later go on to be among the first to give airtime to Elvis Presley, offered one of the first mixed formats when his 'Red Hot and Blue' radio show was launched in 1952. Perhaps more famously, Alan Freed at WJW-Cleveland hosted the 'Moondog Rock and Roll House Party,' airing from 11:45 p.m. to 2:30 a.m. on Saturday nights, and is widely considered not only to have popularized the phrase 'rock 'n' roll' but also to have organized and hosted the first rock and roll concert, 'The Moondog Coronation Ball,' held on 21 March 1952 at Cleveland's municipal arena (an event featuring the Orioles, the Dominoes, and the Moonglows). This first rock and roll concert is remembered as well for having the first rock and roll riot; Freed reportedly allowed tickets to be oversold, resulting in a crowd of youths erupting in frustration outside of the arena after being denied entrance.[15] Nor was this the only controversy Freed would face. His dedication to playing the original recordings of black performers instead of the white covers angered many people in the general public and recording industry alike. Wes Smith, in *The Pied Pipers of Rock 'n' Roll: Radio Deejays of the 50s and 60s*, has noted that

> repeated news photos of white teenage girls dancing with black teenage boys or white teens in adulatory poses around black performers at Freed's concerts increased the racial tension. Because Freed was popularizing music and musicians traditionally relegated to the far reaches of the radio dial and the back bins of record stores, the entrenched powers of the music business were also alarmed. The American Society of Composers, Authors, and Publishers was the established music-licensing organization that oversaw royalty payments to those who created music, at least to those whites who created music. ASCAP had traditionally excluded black, Hispanic, and hillbilly performers.[16]

Broadcasting signals did not care about national borders. American stations, with the likes of George 'Hound Dog' Lorenz at WKBW in Buffalo and Alan Freed at WINS-New York (having relocated from WJW-Cleveland in September 1954), sent hits into the bedrooms of Canadian youths. Dov Ivry, of the teenage rock band the Asteroids in Saint John, New Brunswick, was one of those who lucked into hearing what rock and roll disc jockeys had to offer.[17] 'Late in 1954 as I was turning the dial,' Ivry recalls, 'I heard it for the first time and sat ramrod straight up in my bed. This incredible music. "What in %@*/^& is this?," I asked. And the guy on the radio was good enough to answer. "This is Alan Freed from WINS-New York and we're playing rock 'n' roll music." For the next months I listened every night, but it turned into a sort of a secret vice. You couldn't hear any of that music on the air locally and I really felt I was in a world of my own.'[18]

On the other side of the country, teenagers in Vancouver could pick up not only signals from American stations but also the musically adventurous offerings of local disc jockeys Jack Cullen, host of CKNW's *Owl Prowl*, and Red Robinson, a high school student who helped out around CJOR and, upon graduating in September 1953, took over the reigns of the station's *Theme for Teens*.[19] Bruce Allen, Canada's most famous (and infamous) of music managers, has credited local airplay with introducing him to black performers. 'I have Red Robinson to thank for that,' Allen explained to the *Vancouver Courier* in 2004: 'His play list was so wide and he was colourblind. So when I heard rock 'n' roll for the first time it was both dangerous and exciting. I was drawn to it like a moth to the flame.'[20] His encounters with rock and roll were made all the more exciting by the lack of segregation in local venues. According to Allen, 'people like Little Richard, James Brown, the Ike and Tina Turner Review etc. performed here to an integrated audience where they couldn't do that in some states. Those audiences had to content themselves with "whitenized" versions of black songs sung by clean cut cutouts like Ricky Nelson, Pat Boone and Patti Page.'[21]

Yet Allen was only partially correct in his assessment of authenticity. Black artists were able to perform in front of white audiences in Vancouver, but, more critically, the shows were racially skewed in a different way. The music industry sought black performers who sang, danced, and acted in accordance with stereotypes held by white audiences. Music theorist Simon Frith, in noting this element of caricature, points out that 'the racism endemic to rock 'n' roll ... was not that white musicians stole from black culture but that they burlesqued it. The issue is not how "raw" and "earthy" and "authentic" African-American sounds were "diluted" or "whitened" for mass consumption, but the opposite process: how gospel and r&b and doo-wop were *blacked-up*.'[22] Stage theatrics became requisite manifestations of a supposed 'primal' essence.

The shift from R&B to rock and roll as a 'crossover' music is often attributed to the success of Bill Haley and the Comets' 'Rock around the Clock.' Haley, a white performer who combined a percussive country strumming with the upbeat horns of R&B, recorded the track in 1954 but had little success with it until it was featured in the MGM film *Blackboard Jungle* (1955), a cinematic tale of conflict between a teacher and students at an inner-city high school. For Ivry of the Asteroids, and many youths who attended the film, the exposure to the song was a pivotal moment in their engagement with rock and roll. 'Most of the audience in the theatre where I was that afternoon were teenagers and I remember being part of a crowd that flowed down from the theatre to the nearest record store. The guy was standing outside beside a bin of "Rock around the Clock" records. He was selling them like the proverbial hotcakes.'[23]

For many youths and adults alike, 1955 was the year in which they became aware of rock and roll. In April, *Time* offered its first, and far from encouraging, report on the phenomenon:

> The pop-music business, having scraped the hillbilly barrel and blown the froth off the mambo craze, has taken over r. and b., known to the teenage public as 'cat music' or 'rock 'n' roll.' (So stimulating that Bridgeport, Conn. police last week banned teen-age rock-'n'-roll dance parties because the dancers 'got out of hand'). The commercial product, whether by Negros or whites, only superficially resembles its prototype. It has a clanking, socked-out beat, a braying, honking saxophone, a belted vocal, and, too often, suggestive lyrics.[24]

A year later, with rock and roll showing no signs of going away, *Time* used plentiful metaphors and similes to explain to readers just what the music entailed:

> The fad began to flame a couple years ago, when pop music was so languid and soupy that kids could no longer dance to it – and jazz headed farther out. Rock 'n' roll got its name, as it got some of its lyrics, from Negro popular music, which used 'rock' and 'roll' as sexy euphemisms … Rock 'n' roll is based on Negro blues, but in a self-conscious style which underlines the primitive qualities of the blues with malice afterthought. Characteristics: an unrelenting, socking syncopation that sounds like a bull whip; a choleric saxophone honking mating-call sounds; an electric guitar turned up so loud that its sound shatters and splits; a vocal group that shudders and exercises violently to the beat while roughly chanting either a near-nonsense phrase or a moronic lyric in hillbilly idiom. Samples:
>
>   My love is so hot / My love is hotter than a hot-rod / My love is hotter than that / My love is hotter than a pistol / Cause, Baby, I've got you.
>   or
>   Long tall Sally has a lot on the ball / Nobody cares if she is long and tall / Oh, Baby! Yeh-heh-heh-hes, Baby / Whoo-oo-oo-oo, Baby! I'm havin' me some fun tonight, yeah.[25]

Not only were the lyrics considered morally questionable but, *Time* further explained, the experience was socially disruptive. Boston Roman Catholic leaders called for a boycott of the music; Hartford officials considered banning rock and roll after an energetic show; a brawl almost broke out at a concert at the National Guard Armory in Washington; a Minneapolis theatre pulled a film featuring the music after youths left the theatre and 'snake-danced around town and smashed windows'; four youngsters were arrested after a fight broke out at a show at an Atlanta baseball park; San Antonio banned rock and roll from city swimming pool juke boxes because of kids 'practicing their spastic gyrations in abbreviated bathing suits'; and white supremacists in Birmingham labelled the music a plot by blacks against whites and called for it to be banned for the sake of racial purity.[26]

The warning was timely. Just over a week later, on 27 June 1956, Vancouver was to host an appearance by Bill Haley and His Comets. The newspaper reports that followed typified the sensationalized take on rock and roll that was pitched at adult – and parental – readers who lacked knowledge let alone understanding of the music. 'The Comets, who evolved the controversial phenomenon which has been called degraded, play at Kerrisdale Arena tonight,' warned the *Vancouver Sun* on the day of the show. 'Five thousand teen-agers are expected to pack the house, and police will be on hand to keep an eye on things.'[27] Bill Williamson, guitarist for Bill Haley and His Comets, made the case for the band: 'Just let anyone who thinks our music is immoral come out tonight, they'll go home thinking otherwise.'[28] As noted in the epigraph to this chapter, reporters for the *Sun* did not leave the concert 'thinking otherwise.' The following day, the newspaper told of chaos and immorality as boys and girls danced with members of both sexes in a trance of sights and sounds that was no less than mass hypnotism. 'Dancing was taboo but the youngsters persisted in spite of police efforts to stop them. Said maestro Haley: "The kids shouldn't have danced, but, man, with this kind of beat who can stop 'em."'[29] Stanley Bligh, the newspaper's music critic, was one of many adults who wanted to stop the kids:

This was my first exposure to the rock 'n' roll medium of expression. I came away with the feeling that I had witnessed the ultimate in musical depravity. It has nothing of social value. On the contrary it is exhausting both mentally and physically. With measured beat it dulls the perceptions of the listeners; then gradually works them into a frenzy which could easily produce a form of hypnosis. This monotonous rhythm is occasionally relieved by a short and often unmelodic line based on a crude inharmonic accompaniment. The result is a cacophonous noise that might cause permanent harm to not fully developed adolescent minds. One can scarcely conceive that adult entertainers could lower themselves to perform such weird contortions and degrading movements to a so-called musical background as those presented Wednesday evening. Good clowning or harmless slapstick comedy can be very enjoyable but the abasing actions used in rock 'n' roll have a decidedly nauseating effect.[30]

The apparent chaos and immorality that took place in Vancouver were not enough to prompt Toronto's city council to cancel a show scheduled for the following week at Maple Leaf Gardens, a massive spectacle involving Bill Haley and His Comets plus eleven other acts and attended by 12,000 youths and a few adults. Unlike the Vancouver concert and the limitations of a local press, the Maple Leaf Gardens show received coast-to-coast coverage by Barbara Moon in *Maclean's*. 'What You Don't Need to Know about Rock 'n' Roll,' a rather sympathetic article published on 7 July 1956, attempted to inform readers about the essence of this controversial music phenomenon:

1. Few rock 'n' roll records are purely instrumental; almost all have some sort of accompanying chant.
2. Most of these chants are crude, in the sense of wanting finish. Almost the entire burden of Tutti Frutti, for instance, consists of the curious phrase 'tutti frutti, all rooty.'
3. Many of the lyrics are crude in the other sense. One exhibit: 'Somebody Touched me in the Dark Last Night.'
4. A lot of vocalists seem able to get from one syllable to the next only by a series of shunts, as in 'hi luh-huh-huh-huv you-hou.'
5. I had played 'Rock-a-Beat-in-Boogie,' and 'See you Later, Alligator' was on the turntable when I discovered I was beating out a solid background on my notebook with my pencil.[31]

Was the morality of Canadian youths at risk? Moon had no trouble finding people who called for rock and roll to be banned. 'It isn't like the old revivalist music where people were moved upon by the spirit of the Lord,' argued Reverend W.G. McPherson of the Evangel Temple in Toronto in an interview with Moon. 'This music works on a man's emotions like the music of the heathen in Africa.'[32] His assertion was accompanied by a reprint of a piece by *Toronto Telegram* religious columnist Jane Scott in which she informed readers about the sin of rock and roll: 'I have met a lot of young people, and older people too, who have learned the three Rs – Rock, Roll and Regret ... Have you ever felt that way after a session of rock 'n' roll? When you tried to get to sleep, you couldn't because deep down in your heart you felt that the whole business of pleasure-seeking and self-indulgence was a mockery and a sham ... Sorry, young reader, I can't promise you that there is any easy way out of this situation.'[33] Rock and roll, it seemed, was on a par with masturbation when it came to self-harm. Moon, however, was not taken in by such foreboding. The combination of dancing and music was nothing new, from the 'salomé' and 'shimmy shewabble' to jazz and swing dancing controversies.[34] Rock and roll was simply the latest trend, she argued. The difference now was the scale, age grouping, and the displacement from 'gin joints' and dance-halls and into the arenas, community clubs, and even – via the radio and record player – the bedrooms of adolescents.

The baby boom generation had dialled into a new music outlet for emotional and physical expression as well as social and gender identity negotiation and cohesion. This was particularly true for teenage boys, who had limited peer status opportunities outside of sports at this time. According to William T. Bielby in his 2003 presidential address to the American Sociological Association, 'to teens of [this] era, demonstrating competence in rock and roll performance was seen as a potential means of gaining the same kind of peer acceptance as one does from being athletically competent ... in the socially and culturally segregated milieu of the late 1950s, this role could give him standing not just with his male peers, but with girls too.'[35] Bielby has further noted that the visual identifiers – particularly fashionable clothing – were affordable and easy to access. 'For example, white bucks, rolled up jeans or polished cotton pants with a buckle on the back, sleeves rolled up two turns on a short-sleeved shirt, and a skinny belt buckled on the side would make a teenage boy immediately recognizable as part of teen music subculture.'[36] Add to this basic guitar skills and the ability to replicate popular songs and one could change his (or in much rarer cases her) participation from that of audience member to performer, a higher rank within the rock and roll – and peer group – hierarchy. Although girls were largely excluded from the act of performance at this time, something that would change at the turn of the decade with the coming of 'girl groups,' dancing provided an important opportunity for identity negotiation and consolidation. For Susan J. Douglas of *Where the Girls Are: Growing Up Female with the Mass Media*, 'dancing to this music together created a powerful sense of unity, of commonality of spirit, since we were all feeling, with our minds and our bodies, the same enhanced emotions at the same moment.'[37] What Douglas recalled as a positive experience was at the time treated by many in the mainstream press as a mysterious and socially detrimental phenomenon. In 1956 *Time* informed readers that 'psychologists feel that rock 'n' roll's deepest appeal is to the teen-ers' need to belong; the results bear passing resemblance to Hitler mass meetings.'[38]

Bill Haley was only the first of the rock and rollers to be accused of threatening public morality and youthful innocence. Elvis Presley, a truck driver from Memphis, Tennessee, melded the sexuality of rhythm and blues with the country and western styles enjoyed by many white audiences. In the summer of 1953 Presley first paid to record an acetate at Sam Phillip's Sun Records, hoping that he would attract attention, but it took almost a year of dropping by the studio to see if any bands were looking for a singer before it came to any fruition. Guitarist Scotty Moore and bassist Bill Black were in need of a singer, and Phillips pointed them towards Presley. After a few false starts, the trio fused with a cover of blues singer Arthur Crudup's 'That's Alright Mama,' and with support from Phillips the group began touring, garnering media attention, and managed to put four songs on the *Billboard* charts in 1956: 'Heartbreak Hotel,' 'Don't Be Cruel/Hound Dog,' 'I Want You, I Need You, I Love You,' and 'Love Me Tender.'[39] One would not know that these songs were on the chart by listening to CJCH-Halifax, however. The station, like many others, banned Presley's music.[40]

Bans did only so much to limit access to the music. For those who wanted to hear the singles, the best bet was to buy the record or share it with friends. Fortunately for many teens, vinyl discs were within their economic grasp. As famed guitarist and songwriter Randy Bachman has recalled about the times, 'I was transfixed. I saved up my money and bought that first Elvis Presley album ... That was my first record album ... There was a wildness to the music – the singing, the rhythm, and playing – that leapt off the grooves.'[41]

Elvis was not the first rock and roller, but he did manage to bring R&B and country music together with a compelling and rhythmic style that attracted industry and media attention. Substantial airplay for his singles opened the door to television appearances over the course of 1956, on *The Dorsey Brothers Stage Show*, *The Milton Berle Show*, and *The Steve Allen Show*, leading up to his famed performance on the *Ed Sullivan Show* on 9 September 1956 to an audience of approximately 60 million (the largest television audience up to that time). Unlike the pudgy, aging Bill Haley, Elvis offered a strikingly youthful and charismatic image in the television age. His appearance on television meant publicity and sales and, importantly, conveyed a sense of what it meant to attend a rock and roll show: rabid screaming and shaking among audiences were not only permitted but expected.

The following year Elvis swung through the (relatively) northern part of the continent with concerts in Toronto, Ottawa, and Vancouver in what would be the only shows he ever performed outside the United States. On 2 April 1957, seven months after appearing on the *Ed Sullivan Show*, Elvis arrived in Toronto to an audience of 23,000 fans over the course of afternoon and evening appearances at Maple Leaf Gardens. 'The much publicized pelvis was plainly in action,' Joe Scalion reported in the *Toronto Daily Star*. 'Elvis rocks his hips back and forth. He shakes his knees and wobbles his legs and bumps like a fan dancer.'[42] Photos of screaming girls drove the point home to the readers. Apparently the screaming was so loud that no one could actually hear Elvis sing, the concert being an opportunity for adolescents to engage in a shared episode of emotional release and expression; it was a visual show with a high-pitched adolescent soundtrack. Still, according to the *Toronto Daily Star*, the spectacle was relatively sedate, if only because of the police presence. 'Whenever a youngster bounced up in his seat a policeman would reach over and plunk him down again ... Two women fans were ejected late in the second performance when they tried to break through 20 policemen and as many Maple Leaf Gardens' attendants to reach the stage.'[43]

The situation was much the same the next day in Ottawa. Elvis arrived on the train from Toronto at eight o'clock in the morning, surrounded by police officers, one of whom carried his guitar and another a brown and yellow teddy bear. Dispelling the idea that only prepubescent girls were interested in Elvis, the *Ottawa Citizen* reported that at the train station 'there were perhaps a half-dozen youngsters who obviously were waiting for him, but passers-by began to gather around when they noticed something was up, and a small but feverish group of middle-aged women suddenly appeared out of nowhere and began jumping up and down and shoving each other.'[44] A few hours later word spread that Elvis might be making an appearance at journalist Norman MacLeod's luncheon on Parliament Hill after a place card bearing Elvis's name was seen on one of the tables, but this turned out to be a hoax.[45] Elvis did show up, though, at the Ottawa Auditorium for an afternoon show for approximately 3,000 people and an evening appearance for 9,000. Many of the attendees had come from Montreal, as the city council there had bowed to the requests of the Catholic clergy and concerned citizens to cancel the show that had been scheduled for the next day. Clergy in Montreal were not the only ones expressing concern: Notre Dame Convent in Ottawa condemned Elvis Presley and banned students from attending the concert. Elvis, apparently a little distressed at the ban, told the press that he would 'like to invite whoever did this to come and see the show. If he still thinks it is harmful to kids after that, okay.'[46]

As for the concert itself? The *Ottawa Citizen* offered contradictory coverage.[47] 'It Was Sheer Pandemonium,' exclaimed a headline, while the one next to it read 'The Police Kept It Peaceful.' Greg Connolley and Gerry Mulligan regaled readers with tales of emotional chaos similar to those of Elvis's performances elsewhere: 'Girls burst into tears. Girls covered their faces, overcome with emotion. Girls and boys shrieked, exulting in this tremendous experience. One girl screamed: "He looked right at me." Then she started crying.'[48] Yet these reporters also told of how 'generally it was a peaceful Presley program.'[49] The chaos escalated when 'Elvis turned on the steam and gyrated like a Minsky burlesque graduate,' but 'Presley seemed to sense when things might get out-of-hand and would halt his wiggling, temporarily.'[50] The only real violence was attributed to leather-clad youths, apparently from Montreal, who tried to crash the gates, but that was quickly handled. Able to predict the sort of ruckus that would come with the concert, the Ottawa police department had assigned fifty officers to the event.[51]

Reports in the *Toronto Daily Star* and *Ottawa Citizen* were certainly tame compared with the sensationalism offered by the *Vancouver Sun*. Similar to the coverage given to the Bill Haley concert of the previous year, the *Sun* portrayed rock and roll as an all-out threat to public morality. Even the lead-up to the concert was hostile – and not only towards Elvis: 'Daughter Wants to See Elvis?: "Kick Her in the Teeth!"' boldly stated a headline on the front page. Writing from Spokane, Washington, staff reporter Mac Reynolds had attended an Elvis concert the previous night, and now not only warned Vancouver and the surrounding communities about the threat posed for that evening at Empire Stadium but offered a solution:

It's hardly original, but if any daughter of mine broke out of the woodshed tonight to see Elvis Presley in Empire Stadium, I'd kick her teeth in. On his Friday night show he didn't say a dirty word. He didn't sing a dirty song. His bumps and grinds, coming from a man, were in themselves no more erotic than half-witted scribblings on a fence. Yet from his tawdry green stage on the 50-yard line of Spokane's Memorial Stadium, an obscenity penetrated the crowd, like an electric spark jumping a gap. When he shook one pant leg, they screamed like jets, these fresh-faced girls of this pleasant wheatland city. When he shook both pant legs, they screamed, and quivered, and shut their eyes. And when he did the most grotesque and imbecilic things with his body, they screamed, and quivered, and shut their eyes, and reached out their hands to him as for salvation. It is a frightening thing for a man to watch his women debase themselves.

Elvis was portrayed as a deviant, one who during his pre-concert press conference in Spokane posed with girls from his fan club and took 'make believe snaps with his teeth at their fingers.' The victims 'were all children, and most of the children were female,' innocents who fell under his power and 'looked demented.[52]

Perhaps it is no coincidence that a few pages into the paper one finds an article that praised square dancing as a socially positive music activity. 'Square Dancers Have Lots of Fun,' the title of a report by Martha Robinson stated. 'Polite as a waltz, intricate as a tango and pretty as a Renoir pastel, today's four-couple "square" has shed the last rowdy traces of its chuck-wagon ancestry. It's fast making history as a new dance art. And it's more fun than a picnic.'[53] Having shed its 'rustic' character, the music and dance now offered wholesome refinement and intricate patterning – an alternative to the teenage desire for rock and roll.

Teenagers were not swayed by the recommendation. Nor did Mac Reynolds's warnings about the predatory nature of Elvis prevent 16,000 fans from attending the concert. Still, the *Vancouver Sun* was able to justify its words of warning after the police told Elvis to leave the stage after performing only four songs. The fact that the show's abrupt end contributed to, if not precipitated, the chaos that followed went unnoted by the *Sun*. Supported by front-page photos showing rows of teenagers apparently running amok, reporter John Kirkwood described 'the wild mob scene ... when frantic, frenzied teen-agers stormed police lines at the riotous Elvis Presley show.' Kirkwood, the same reporter who a year earlier had condemned Bill Haley and His Comets, offered an even more scathing portrayal of rock and roll:

Vancouver teen-agers [were] transformed into writhing, frenzied idiots of delight by the savage jungle beat music. And by a hard, bitter core of teenage troublemakers who turned Elvis Presley's one-night stand at Empire Stadium into the most disgusting exhibition of mass hysteria and lunacy this city has ever witnessed ... With something over 16,000 at the stadium, it was billed as the largest theatrical entertainment attraction in Western Canada. Don't kid yourself. This was not entertainment. Not when children as young as nine, 10 years, glaze their eyes, unhinge their hips and fling themselves into wild orgies of lunatic ecstasy. Not when they grovel like animals on

the ground where Elvis had stood. Not when six louts attack one police
sergeant for no apparent reason. Not when boys and girls alike spit into policemen's faces for the sheer thrill of defying law and order. Entertainment?
These kids were out for blood – anyone's.

Presley himself was presented as the manipulative ringmaster of the
chaos: 'He glazed his eyes, twisted his youthful face in a sullen sneer,
swiveled his hips, dropped drunkenly to his knees and threw himself into
more bumps and grinds than the PNE girly show has seen for years. He
made love to the microphone and teen-age girls in the crowd reached
out to touch him.' Dancing turned into intoxication and sexual exhi-
bitionism. The microphone became every girl in the audience as they
longingly sacrificed themselves to Elvis's wanton lust. The climax came
with equal deviousness. Elvis, having 'staggered across the stage … like
a drunk picking his way home on New Year's morning,' slipped away in
a black Cadillac 'through a rear exit like a bank bandit's get-away car.'
    Elvis having left the building, the event reportedly went from orgias-
tic debauchery to brute violence as, in Kirkwood's words, 'the hoodlum
patrol engaged in open warfare with the police near the stage.' The
description certainly struck fear into parents who read the account.
'Girls crawled through policemen's legs then were dragged screaming off the field on all fours; several fainted in the crush; the backs
of angry policemen's hands rattled smartly across the pouting faces
of hysterical hoods.' Girls on all fours like sexual beasts. The policemen's punches were 'smart' while the agitators 'pouted.' And Elvis's
management team behind the scenes? Apparently Colonel Tom Parker
smoked a cigar and ducked a flying bottle while proclaiming the chaos
to be harmless.[54]
    Bill Haley and Elvis Presley were at the forefront of a multi-faceted
music movement that offered a number of outlandish performers. Jerry
Lee Lewis and Little Richard provided fanatical performances in which
the piano became as much a prop as an instrument. Chuck Berry created a wild stage show that included a dancing and guitar-slinging style
that kept kids jumping with such hits as 'Maybellene,' 'Thirty Days,'
'Roll Over Beethoven,' 'Too Much Monkey Business,' 'School Days,'
'Rock and Roll Music,' 'Sweet Sixteen,' and 'Johnny B. Goode.' Johnny
Cash, Carl Perkins, and Eddie Cochran ensured themselves an audience among cautious white teens by keeping rock and roll closer to the
country and western side in a so-called rockabilly. Busloads of musicians
toured major cities in caravans advertised under such banners as 'Show

of Stars.' A 1956 tour included Fats Domino, Chuck Berry, and LaVerne Baker. The following year, Buddy Holly, Eddie Cochran, Fats Domino, and the Everly Brothers, among others, were part of a travelling show that included a swing through Vancouver, Calgary, Edmonton, and Regina.[55] Living in Canada, or at least the major cities, meant opportunities to catch big names as they made their way across the continent.

The tour circuit even brought to Canada a performer who would go on to become a centrepiece of the domestic music scene. 'I was lucky,' 'Rompin' Ronnie 'the Hawk' Hawkins recalled in his autobiography. 'I was real lucky that when I arrived in Canada, everything was changing; everything was happening. To a musician, man, it was as if the streets were covered in gold ... There were so many of those damn baby-boom kids coming along right after the war, and they wanted to do things. They wanted to get out and *do something*.'[56] The Arkansas rockabilly singer arrived in Canada in 1958, bringing with him a backing band, the Hawks, consisting of Levon Helm, Jimmy Ray 'Luke' Paulman, and Will 'Pop' Jones. Hawkins and the Hawks had made their way northward on what he has called 'the Eskimo tour, though I gotta tell – I ain't never seen an Eskimo, or a Mountie in red either,' a series of clubs in southern Ontario that operated as an extension of scenes in New York State and Michigan.[57] The bandleader has recalled, with characteristic panache, how he expected the sort of 'wild frontier' presented in Hollywood-produced Canuck exploitation films: 'Going to Canada, at first we thought we were going to run into igloos, Eskimos and dogsleds. It's the north pole, that's what we thought. Levon's dad even made it worse. He said, "Those goddamn Canadians up there in Canadia" – that's what he called it, "Canadia" – "they're worse than the Mexicans. They'll stick a goddamn knife in ya for a nickel, never mind a dime." He'd never been out of his own country but that's how he was ... he sure was against us going. He said that in "Canadia" there's ten months of winter and two months of bad sledding.'[58]

The first sweep through southern Ontario included the Golden Rail Tavern (Hamilton), the Brass Rail (London), and Le Coq d'Or (Toronto), although the band then had to return to the United States to fulfil previously scheduled dates. Still, Hawkins was so taken with Ontario that after completing the contracts, he and the Hawks – now including Jimmy Evans – returned and made a home in Toronto. Here Hawkins found a market for rock and roll in which he could be a big fish in a relatively small pond. Together he and his band offered audiences a ferocious show that blended camel walks and back-flips with a fierce, guttural vocal style and a tight backing band that had cut its teeth in Arkansas honky-tonks.

The impact of Hawkins on the Toronto music scene cannot be over-emphasized. 'Ronnie's band became very popular in Ontario clubs,' Peter De Remigis, founding member of Little Caesar and the Consuls, has recalled. 'We Toronto musicians wanted some of that popularity, so we copied Ronnie's rockabilly style until we had lost most of our earlier swing, R&B, and rock and roll style.'[59] Hawkins's influence grew even more as he began to take local musicians directly under his wing. With members of the Hawks becoming homesick and returning to Arkansas – with the exception of drummer Levon Helms – Hawkins had little choice but to seek out and train local talent to back him at Le Coq d'Or and its upstairs venue, appropriately named the 'Hawk's Nest.' Some replace-ments stayed on for short stints, like pianist Stan Szelest and legendary guitarist Roy Buchanan, but among the others were four musicians who would go on to form, along with Helms, the Band. Robbie Robertson, a teenager who had been in such local bands as Robbie and the Robots, Thumper and the Trambones, and Little Caesar and the Consuls, applied for a position with Hawkins in early 1960, but to no avail. Yet instead of rejecting the aspiring guitarist, Hawkins opted to take him onboard as an apprentice, setting him up as an understudy with guitarist Fred Carter, Jr. Along with Robertson, the Hawks came to include bassist Rick Danko, drummer Richard Manuel of the Rockin' Revols, and keyboardist Garth Hudson, all from southern Ontario.

Working with Hawkins meant succumbing to rigorous training sched-ules and monitoring extracurricular activities, including fines when one stepped out of line. 'They were boys when they started,' Hawkins told *Rolling Stone* in a 1969 feature about the Band, 'but they were men when they finished. They'd seen damn near everythin' there is to see. They practiced, played and fucked in every town you care to name. Real dudes, man.'[60] When this generation of Canadian-born Hawks left for the United States in 1964, picked up by Bob Dylan to be his backing band on his first electric tour, Hawkins took on Robbie Lane and the Dis-ciples as replacements, and later the trios of John Till, Richard Bell, and Larry Atamniuk, and Richard 'King Biscuit Boy' Newell, Roly Greenway, and John Gibbard. (These latter three would eventually set out on their own until Newell went solo and the others helped form the notable rock band Crowbar.)

Although Hawkins was a fan of Canadian musicians, many venues had little interest in anything other than big-name bands, and that, by default, meant visiting American acts. The rationale was simple enough: venue owners wanted to draw as big a crowd as possible, and with the tour circuit acting as a pipeline for American talent, there was a solid supply of skilled acts. For Hawkins, the lack of support for local talent was infuriating, and although his stories need to be taken with a grain of salt given his well-earned and legendary bravado, they offer a colourful first-hand account. For instance, as he told *Canadian Musician* in 1981 about the struggle faced by domestic bands, 'I used to lend them my car with the Tennessee plates and tell the club owners that a hot new band from Memphis or Nashville was in town. They'd get hired and half way through the week the truth would come out that they were from Ottawa or Peterborough but by then the club was full, but listen, it was uphill all the way.'[61]

The situation was not completely black and white, of course. American rock and rollers drew crowds that filled clubs, but the combination of teenage thirst for rock and roll, an entrepreneurial desire to cash in on the fad, and the inability of youths to get into many of the drinking-age venues meant that there were opportunities on the 'sock hop' circuit. This was the route for such aspiring performers as Denny Doherty, later of the Mamas and the Papas, as a member of the Hepcats in Halifax, Gordon Lightfoot in the quartet/barbershop groups the Collegiate Four and the Teen-Timers in Orillia, Little Caesar and the Consuls and Robbie Lane and the Disciples in Toronto, the Beau-Marks and Leonard Cohen's country-rock band the Buckskin Boys in Montreal, Wes Dakus and the Club 93 Rebels in Edmonton, and the Chessmen and the Prowlers in Vancouver.[62] 'I was trying to sing a little rockabilly, and we were starving,' Ian Tyson recalled about the days when his band the Sensational Stripes performed Elvis Presley and Buddy Holly songs around Vancouver (including a regular stint at a Chinese restaurant).[63] Nicholas Jennings, in his detailed and anecdotally engaging *Before the Gold Rush: Flashbacks to the Dawn of the Canadian Sound*, has told of how 'the city's suburbs were full of teenagers with raging hormones, all desperately craving the latest sounds. Teen dances were the obvious solution. Held at high schools, community centres and hockey arenas around town, these sock hops not only satisfied pubescent urges for mixed company, they provided aspiring bands with much-needed stages to perform on. Where else did a group go once it had graduated from the garage or the rec room?'[64]

For the Prowlers, a telephone call to Jack Cullen's *Owl Prowl* led to airplay and recordings. In an interview with the *Vancouver Sun*, band leader

Les Vogt recalled how 'one of our girlfriends called Jack Cullen's radio program … We didn't even know she did this. She phoned from the rec room phone in the house we were playing in, and he put it on the air. The phone was just being held up in the room – the sound must have been completely awful. We were rehearsing Elvis tunes, and I was trying to sound as much like Elvis as I could, as everybody did at the time. He got so many calls on it, he called us in the studio and he recorded six songs.'[65] The Prowlers became a top draw in the city thanks to radio support, singles, and an opening slot for Bill Haley and His Comets. Their single, 'The Blamers,' even managed to rank number one on CFUN-Vancouver in August 1960 – the first local band to top the station's chart.[66]

The single, although a hit in Vancouver and the surrounding area, did not go much farther than that. This was a time of isolated regional music scenes when it came to domestic releases (American releases were, of course, aired throughout Canada). A strong local following was often enough to secure airplay at a station because programmers knew that there would be an audience, but to spin an album from a different market was a separate matter. Dov Ivry has spoken about how his local Saint John, New Brunswick, station was willing to spin the Asteroids' 1957 single 'I'm Your Satellite' because of public interest in the recent launch of Russia's Sputnik satellite, and the singles of a few prominent regional acts, but otherwise there was little other than American imports.[67] Says Ivry: 'One thing I remember about that time was the disconnect between the Maritimes and the rest of country. We had no idea what was happening beyond the Quebec border.'[68]

Radio station programmers did not have to think too much about which singles should be aired: American trade periodicals such as *Billboard* and the domestically produced CHUM Chart offered lists of songs already proven to be popular in other markets. The CHUM Chart, issued by CHUM-Toronto, a station that shifted to a Top 40 rock and roll format in 1957, not only reflected the station's reliance upon American trade papers and industry consultants but compounded the situation by informing others stations and retailers as to the 'hottest' tracks.[69] Department stores Eaton's and Simpsons in fact only stocked the singles that were on the chart.[70] Tellingly, no Canadian act, including those that had relocated to the United States, made it in the Top 10 of the first CHUM chart, published on 27 May 1957, although the Diamonds' cover of 'Little Darlin'' did rank eleventh.[71] And, just as telling, the chart reveals a pattern of sticking to proven songs as recorded by different acts, with multiple versions of 'Party Doll,' 'I'm Walkin',' 'Butterfly,' 'Four Walls,'

'Sittin' in the Balcony,' 'Rosie Lee,' 'Marianne,' 'Empty Arms,' and 'Pledge of Love.'[72]

With little in the way of radio airplay to encourage the domestic recording industry, the major labels, whose primary purpose was to distribute singles recorded abroad, had no reason to invest in aspiring acts. Picking up a Canadian band could mean investing a lot of money in singles that sat in a warehouse without any airplay. Ronnie Hawkins has painted a pretty bleak image of the times and recalls warning Levon Helm and the other ex-Hawks that it was in their best interest not to go out on their own under the name the Canadian Squires: 'You're going to have to forget this Canadian Squires thing ... because [record labels] won't touch a Canadian group. Take my word for it. They know the Canadian market is so small they won't get their money back.'[73] Some groups, albeit usually with non-nationally specific names, did manage to record at this time, usually thanks more to eager entrepreneurs and the domestically owned Quality Records than to the major labels. The Prowlers' 'The Blamers' is an example of this. So are Wes Dakus and Club 93 Rebels' 'El Ringo' and the Del-Tones' 'Rockin' Blues' and 'Moonlight Party' and, following a name change to the Beau-marks, 'Clap Your Hands.' In the Maritimes, the Asteroids were among the first to record rock and roll, making a trip in 1957 from their homes in Saint John, New Brunswick, to Rodeo Records, a country music recording studio in Halifax, Nova Scotia. 'The only [recording studio] we were aware of in the Maritimes was Rodeo in Halifax,' Dov Ivry has explained. 'I think when we recorded we had two mikes. Get it right, and get out.'[74] The recording session resulted in two singles, 'Shhhhh Blast Off' and 'Don't Dig This Algebra,' although the band did not get much further than that. The Asteroids' venture into the world of semi-professional rock and roll was, given the newness of the music and the band's relatively remote location, rather isolated, with little direction that they could turn to for insight and guidance let alone management and career development. 'There was no one among the senior musicians in Saint John to talk to. They were either straight pop musicians, rooted in the 40s, or country. No one had any experience in rock 'n' roll and could offer advice. We were just kids, two [Don Ivry and Alan Reid] at 16, Mel [Clark] at 15, and Bob [Seely] at 17 ... No one out of high school was interested, except for professional musicians, music store merchants, or those in radio who wanted to know what was going on.'[75]

Canadians, it seems, experienced specific challenges in terms of recording and airtime opportunities and the level of success that opened doors to the bigger venues, but drummer Peter De Remigis, who was in both the Suedes and Little Caesar and the Consuls, does not recall having realized it at the time. Although access to industry resources usually meant heading south, this was simply par for the course, and the closeness of Toronto to New York City, and the track record of successful Canadians abroad, made it seem a non-issue.

> Until we, the Suedes, met Ronnie [Hawkins] in the early 1960's we did not think much about 'systemic' disadvantages hampering Canadian performers. When the Consuls began playing in 1957 our main concern was attracting a larger following than other Toronto groups, one of these being the Blue Bops, a rockabilly group that performed on Queen Street at Dufferin long before I knew there was a Ronnie Hawkins.
>
> The Consuls, then together about a year, recorded at Bell Sound in New York City in 1958. Although we were surprised at the ease with which we recorded at Bell Sound where Elvis Presley, Buddy Holly, Dion and the Belmonts, and other rock and rollers were said to have recorded, we did not feel we were at a disadvantage because we were Canadian. Indeed when a meeting between us and Dick Clark was arranged that winter evening at the Little Garden Theatre in New York, I assumed it was because the Consuls' recording earlier that day had put us in the big time with all the other recording artists Clark was promoting. Perhaps our confidence arose from our awareness of the international recording notoriety of the Four Lads, the Crew Cuts, and Diamonds of Toronto. We were all familiar with Paul Anka of Ottawa's hits 'Diana' and 'Put Your Head on My Shoulder.' A vocalist friend of mine, Judi Jansen, who knew Paul and had known Alan Freed since she was very young made it seem as though the big time/the Big Apple was attached in some way to Toronto because she seemed to be always travelling from Toronto to New York to visit Alan.[76]

The rock and roll paradigm, De Remigis has testified, was much more regional than pan-Canadian let alone national. 'In a sense we had been thriving in our own little show-biz world stretching from the Hank Noble Show on CHUM in Toronto to the Hound Dog show in Buffalo, and the recording and promotional facilities of the Big Apple.'[77] His bandmate Norm Sherratt has recalled the situation to be much the same: 'We had enough success that we were recording in Toronto and New York, and felt all we needed was a hit record, the same as any American musician would feel.'[78]

Doug Owram has argued that 'rock and roll overwhelmed national boundaries ... It erected generational differences in the same way that it ignored national ones.'[79] This is certainly true to an extent: even though the music was understood as being derived from elements of American society, particularly African-American and southern cowboy lifestyles and songs, Canadians showed few signs of filtering and idealizing the music as an example of the 'American way of life'; there was not enough isolation and societal difference. Rather, rock and roll thrived as a result of continental socio-political demographics, postwar economic abundance, and a recording industry interested in the teenage dollar. In ideological terms, the rock and roll experience was not essentialistically national, with youths viewing themselves as Canadians attempting to engage in an American phenomenon; it was, rather, a socio-economic paradigm of entertainment commodities whose meanings were debated by those who produced them, the social forces that attempted to relabel (and suppress) them, and the youths who reconfigured them for their own individual and collective gender, class, and generational meanings. It was not so much the music but the blurring of racial divisions and sexual regulation that worried social patriarchs; it was not that the recordings were American but that they were essentially hedonistic, regressive, and morally deprived and corroded social, religious, moral, and national stability. The music may have originated from points within the United States, but not even the Americans wanted to lay ideological claim to this passing, and apparently detrimental, musical fad as their own.

Canadians experienced rock and roll much in the same way as their American counterparts, unlike many non-North Americans who not only filtered the music through significant linguistic and sociocultural differences but idealized rock and roll as representing the modernity, freedom, and consumer abundance for which they longed.[80] In Britain, Bill Haley and His Comets placed several singles on the charts for months at a time, and over the next few years the rock and roll imports, mixed with postwar impoverishment and strong class distinctions, produced a 'skiffle' style that would underwrite the sounds of the British Invasion in the mid-1960s.[81] For German youths the music offered a much-desired escape from socio-economic conditions, and they embraced the songs of a country that their parents had been at war with only a decade earlier. 'Those are our voices,' explained one German youth to *Time*. 'In Germany all the elders work, work, work. Makes it kind of lonely for us. But there's always Elvis Presley and Wild Bill Haley. It gets you; it lifts you. Soon you believe you can do it too.'[82] The same was true for Japan, where imitators such as Masaaki Hirao and Keijiro Yamashita dressed in Elvis-style garb and sang translated lyrics for massive crowds of screaming boys and girls who were enthralled with Americana.[83]

A quick look elsewhere in the world reveals much the same. 'Rock around the Clock' entered the Finnish music charts in second position at the end of 1955.[84] A 1959 poll conducted by the *Sunday Times* in Johannesburg, South Africa, ranked Elvis as the top male vocalist of all time, a status backed by over 2 million records sold and characterized by the standard public outcry against rock and roll.[85] In New Zealand, teenagers listened to the latest hits on the *Lifebuoy Hit Parade*, a weekly half-hour program of rock and roll aired on the state-owned ZB radio network (the only radio network until the start of private-sector broadcasting in 1968). David Eggleton, author of *Ready to Fly: The Story of New Zealand Rock Music*, has explained that 'the authorities looked on nervously as the specter of juvenile delinquency loomed in the shape of youth cults: the bodgies, widgies, motorcycle cowboys and milkshake-slurping teeny-boppers.'[86] Across the Tasman Sea, Festival Records in Sydney, Australia, had to set up a nightshift in order to meet the demand for 'Rock around the Clock.' The music was performed by such bands as Alan Dale and the Houserockers, and the outcome, reported the *Sydney Morning Herald*, was 'Rock 'n' Roll Rioting in Brisbane.'[87]

Governments behind the Iron Curtain, on the other hand, were not so willing to let their eager youths access records that seemed to glamourize Western society. The German Democratic Republic (GDR) asserted its control over popular music by limiting record production to a state-owned label, permitting discussions of music to take place only in state-owned newspapers and magazines, and requiring that musicians of both amateur and professional status obtain a state licence to perform in public.[88] A further clampdown on rock and roll in the GDR took place in 1958, with an increase in prosecutions against venues offering Western rock and roll and the passing of legislation banning couples from dancing apart in popular 'jitterbug' styles. Since it was impossible to purge rock and roll completely, the GDR ministry of culture created and attempted to popularize the Lipsi, a state-approved song and dance with pro-socialist lyrics. Denying the music had the result of turning it into a tool of protest, and East German performers turned to rock and roll as a means of asserting their dissatisfaction with the government and the times in which they lived. As Edward Larkey explains, East German rock and roll not only employed 'figurative language' but also used English 'as an oppositional identity-marker in order to subvert censorship aimed at achieving conformity to socialist ideology and as a way to repudiate and actively withdraw from the official institutionalized context and discourse of what the government popularized as "GDR Rock."[89]

The Soviet Union adopted an even harsher position than the GDR, including two-year jail sentences for a pair of entrepreneurs who established the country's largest underground record distribution business and a one-year sentence of hard labour for their financier.[90] Members of the Communist Youth League differed from Western teenagers by monitoring venues and reporting on those that offered foreign music.[91] Despite crackdowns, Eastern Europe was not free from rock and roll imports, although the Soviets did suppress Western rock and roll to a greater extent than the border countries of Poland, Hungary, and Czechoslovakia.[92] The popularity of jazz music in Hungry and Poland helped to facilitate the emergence of rock and roll, if only at first as a jazz-rock hybrid, in such venues as the Non-Stop Club in the town of Sopot, Poland.[93] Hungarian authorities, for their part, generally opted to turn a blind eye to places that offered rock and roll as there was a need to placate youths in the wake of the 1956 Soviet invasion. Timothy W. Ryback explains that 'the governments preferred that the young people vent their frustrations in cafes and clubs with "wild dancing" rather than in the streets with rocks and guns.'[94] By the end of the decade, rock and roll would take hold even in Romania and Bulgaria, two countries that Ryback describes as being 'bastions of authoritarian rule.'[95]

Rock and roll thrived around the world, incorporated into different countries' social, economic, and political situations, yet the music's longevity was far from ensured. As early as the autumn of 1957 some disc jockeys were pointing to the wane of rock and roll in favour of calypso and Hawaiian music as the next music fads.[96] For disc jockey Marty Faye of Chicago, 'the kids have accepted this twanging guitar, this nasal, unintelligible sound, this irritating sameness of lyrics, this lamentable croak. They've picked a sound all their own, apart from anything the adults like. Rock 'n' roll is still as strong as ever, and we'll have to live with it until the kids find a new sound.'[97] Bill Marlowe of WBZ-Boston was more direct: 'Rock 'n' roll has had it. The teen-agers are beginning to look to better music.'[98] Rock and roll's vitality was reduced by several major events. In December 1957, Jerry Lee Lewis came under fire for marrying a teenage girl: 'I can assure you that my wife is all woman, even though she looks kinda young,' Lewis defensively told the British press during a tour with his new wife.[99] She was, he explained, fifteen. Yet word soon leaked that not only was she thirteen but, adding to the scandal, the couple were first cousins. A media hellstorm erupted and Lewis became

labelled an immoral, inbred baby-snatcher. British audiences rejected
Lewis, the tour was cancelled, and Terry Wayne took over the scheduled dates under the slogan 'He's good! He's clean! He's wholesome!'[100]
Three months later, in March 1958, Elvis reported for a two-year tour of
duty after being drafted by the U.S. Army. Soon after, he would be living
in Germany. The next year, Chuck Berry drove across the state line with
an underage girl supposedly involved in prostitution; after being arrested
and found guilty of this illegal activity, he spent two years in prison. The
final nail in rock and roll's coffin seemed to come on 3 February 1959,
when the Beech-Craft Bonanza carrying Charles 'Buddy Holly' Hólley,
Ritchie Valens, disc jockey J.P. 'Big Bopper' Richardson, and pilot Roger
Peterson lifted off a strip of snowy tarmac in Clear Lake, Iowa, towards
Fargo, North Dakota, only to crash and be found ten hours later with no
survivors.

The loss of important performers was compounded by sensationalized
media reports of continued violence at rock and roll concerts. A riot at
a show in Boston in May 1958, an event organized by famed disc jockey
Allan Freed, led to a massive crackdown. *Time* reported as to how 'all
around the Arena common citizens were set upon, robbed and sometimes
beaten. A young sailor caught a knife in the belly, and two girls with him
were thrashed. In all, nine men and six women were roughed up enough
to require hospital treatment. Boston police blamed Freed and his fre-
netic fans, but could not prove it, since they nabbed nobody.'[101] Despite
an apparent lack of evidence as to liability, the mayor used the episode
as justification for banning rock and roll concerts. As for Freed, he was
indicted for inciting 'the unlawful destruction of property,' his concerts
scheduled for New Haven and Newark were cancelled, and he eventually
quit his job at WINS-New York in protest of the station's lack of support.[102]
This was the start of the end for Freed, who soon became entangled in a
payola scandal in which radio programmers and disc jockeys were alleged
to have accepted payments from record companies in exchange for airing specific records. Federal hearings into payola, initiated in 1958, were
about much more than paying for airtime, however. Here was an opportunity for the U.S. Congress to reify norms of public morality and hope-
fully purge American society of rock and roll. To this end crooner Frank
Sinatra was called upon to testify not only about payola but rock and roll
as a music genre. Given that Sinatra was competing against the popular
rock and rollers of the day, it is little wonder that he told the members of
the hearings that 'rock 'n' roll is the most brutal, ugly, desperate, vicious
form of expression it has been my misfortune to hear.'[103]

The stage was set for a new era of conservatism among the radio broadcasting and recording industries. Performers such as Perry Como and the Crew Cuts had done well in the early 1950s with their whitewashed R&B sound, and now record labels and radio stations attempted to do something similar by replacing tainted performers with a set of celebrities who were youthful but clean cut and presentable enough to placate worried parents. Record companies found no lack of boys and girls next door to be fashioned into cults of personality complete with records and other consumer goods. Over the past few years, companies had learned much about producing and selling extra-musical commodities. In 1957 the *New York Times* estimated sales of non-music Elvis products, ranging from embroidered shirts and bobby socks to charm bracelets and lipstick with such shades as 'Hound Dog Orange,' at $20 million.[104] The music industry now had an entire mass marketing infrastructure at its disposal. Dick Clark and *American Bandstand* offered a platform for fandom; Hollywood took singers and put them on beaches with bikinis and surfboards; and *16* magazine and other pulp idol periodicals turned singers into 'dreamboat' pin-up fantasies within the reach of hormonal adolescents. Music theorist Simon Frith was certainly correct in asserting that 'the music business doesn't only turn music into commodities as records, it also turns musicians into commodities, as stars,' but one can go even further in arguing that media outlets turn audiences into commodities to be sold to the advertisers buying commercial space on radio and television programs and in teeny-bopper magazines.[105]

While record labels and radio stations in 1958 had made hits out of singles by Jerry Lee Lewis, Chuck Berry, and Elvis, in 1959 the chart was given over to the youthful crooning of Bobby Darin ('Mack the Knife'), Frankie Avalon ('Venus'), Fabian ('Tiger'), Annette Funicello ('Tall Paul'), and the Canadian-born Paul Anka. Much like the Crew Cuts, the Diamonds, and other wholesome quartets of the early to mid-1950s that made their way from Canada to the hubs of the North American music industry, in 1956 Anka headed from Ottawa to New York City in hopes of making a career. After finding himself unable to get his foot in the door, the aspiring singer-songwriter lucked out by running into the Rover Boys, a Toronto-based quartet that he had befriended following one of their shows in Ottawa. This fortuitous meeting led to the Rover Boys getting Anka an appointment at ABC-Paramount; in turn, the singer-songwriter wowed the record executives with his self-penned song 'Diana.' Anka offered the label an act with a soft crooning voice, boy-next-door vulnerability, and the ability to distil teenage emotions into catchy, commercially friendly lyrics. When the record label cracked the charts with the song, Anka was well on his way to international fame as the next big heartthrob.

For Anka, the decision to remain in the United States came quite easily. In a 1958 interview with *Maclean's*, the singer-songwriter aired his grievances about the lack of a recording industry in Canada: 'I tried my songs on Canadian publishers with no results,' he complained. 'The CBC did nothing but hold me back; but I could see no future here except very slowly. I figured I'd make it faster in the States.'[106] A few years later, in the same magazine, Anka expressed his disinterest, if not disdain, for Canada. 'For three years running I've turned down offers to headline the Canadian National Exhibition grandstand show,' Anka explained. 'The O'Keefe Centre in Toronto wants me and so does the Central Canadian Exhibition in Ottawa ... They're not going to get me now.'[107] The Canadian market was simply not adoring enough for Anka. As the article put it, 'Anka's standards of "acceptance" are high. In Japan two thousand youngsters stood in a typhoon to get tickets for his show. In San Juan, crowds at a department store where he was signing autographs became so dense he left via the roof in a helicopter. In Algiers, a dozen paratroopers with machine guns made a way for him through the crowds.'[108]

Although heading to Tin Pan Alley in New York City greatly eased Anka's odds of making it big as a pop crooner, occasionally a domestic recording would slip onto the charts. Bobby Curtola, a sixteen-year-old from Port Arthur, Ontario, was one of the lucky few, having a hit with 'Hand in Hand With You,' a song written, recorded, and released in 1960 by Basil and Dyer Hurdon of Tartan Records. Not only did the disc combine the recording quality and catchy lyrics and melody that typified the teenage heartthrob genre, but, even more important, it was given airtime by several influential disc jockeys. After making a name with this single, Curtola had a follow-up hit with 'Fortune Teller.'[109] It is perhaps not a coincidence that Anka eventually enjoyed years of fame as a songwriter in the United States, whereas Curtola went no further, at least not significantly, in his recording career. Port Arthur was no New York City.

'The first rock and rollers really got to me,' Burton Cummings, singer for the Guess Who, explained in a 1979 interview. 'I still have all the Little Richard records on Specialty [Records]; Fats Domino blew me away. Early Elvis Presley was amazing.'[110] Cummings was one of a generation of Canadians who turned to the excitement offered by rock and roll, whose sounds and movements offered opportunities for negotiating gender and group identities with a particular flair. For youths listening to rock and roll in their bedrooms or in local arenas, the music existed in the here and now, a sensual and social experience that belonged to them alone. Disc jockeys in Canada – and American ones within broadcasting range – spun hits while girls and boys screamed, danced, and became dishevelled at concerts by the likes of Bill Haley and Elvis Presley. Aspiring rock and rollers picked up guitars and formed groups for local sock hops, although, for the more career minded, access to material resources meant relocation and integration into industry hubs in the United States.

For parents, clergy, city councils, and critics at large, rock and roll was commonly thought of as the latest gimmick from a recording industry that was interested only in the teenage pocketbook. The music had it origins in the United States, critics noted, but not in the good parts – the use of 'jungle' and 'hillbilly' more than speak to that. Neither the Americans who initially produced the music, nor the Canadians who listened to it, thought of the music as essentialistically or ideologically American. Rock and roll was considered by the mainstream not as a point of national pride but as a debasement of the moral structure upon which the nation rested – at best a trick being played on naive youths and at worst a sickness needing to be purged.[111]

Canadians shared in a music experience that originated in the United States and spread quickly across the continent along demographic, racial, and consumer lines. There was no significant linguistic difference, at least not in English-speaking Canada. The shared postwar economic prosperity, similar socio-economic systems, and geographical proximity of the two countries meant that the music was more of a continental than a national phenomenon. Although Canadians were not at ground zero of rock and roll, they did live in its blast radius. 'Rock around the Clock' came to Canada, while 'Hand in Hand with You' was a hit south of the border; Ronnie Hawkins fit perfectly into the Yonge Street strip, while Paul Anka seemed born for Tin Pan Alley. Still, the flow was more often than not northwards, as Canadians responded to the sounds and styles that they were being given by disc jockeys and record promoters. Material resources and systems of distribution were centralized in pockets of the United States that then went on to shape the musical experience within both countries. To the youths themselves, though, industrial paradigms did not matter. The music seemed to be theirs. Although they took to it with much passion, rock and roll seemed to have a limited shelf life, just like any other fad, and by the end of the decade, as rock and rollers fell away in favour of pleasant boys and girls with soft, crooning voices, the predictions were coming true. Riots in arenas gave way to beach parties, and sexuality lost out to puppy love. Rock and roll, at least its raucous vein, seemed to be over.

2

Guess Who?: Beatlemania and the Race to Be British

Take the frolics that go with the Grey Cup and add an Elvis Presley appearance – and you have a Beatle performance.

– Mike Cobb, *Vancouver Sun*, 1964[1]

One Saturday night in 1965, Chad Allan and the Expressions managed to access CJAY-Winnipeg TV's one-track Ampex recording machine, a rare opportunity to record in a time when facilities were few and far between. As legend goes, after setting up their gear in the concrete studio, the band launched into a cover of 'Shakin' All Over,' a song taken from a recording by Britain's Johnny Kidd and the Pirates.[2] After each attempt they repositioned the cables in order to hear it play back, until one time, when they failed to return the cables to their proper positions, the recording was accidentally cloaked in a 7 1/2 ips 'slap echo.' This technical glitch gave the track a great sound that the band decided to keep for their final recording.[3] Laying down a track was only one hurdle, however. Radio stations had a well-earned reputation for dismissing anything made in Canada. A promotional stunt seemed necessary, so the band teamed up with Quality Records (and American distributor Scepter Records) and in January 1965 sent a pressing of the single to stations under the name 'Guess Who?' Along with the single, a rumour was spread that the single was produced by a famous British act, or combination of musicians, who wanted to remain anonymous, with the plan being that the label would eventually reveal to everyone that it was Winnipeg's own Chad Allan and the Expressions.[4]

The single was a massive hit as deejays and curious fans debated whether the song was by the Beatles, the Rolling Stones, or some sort of celebrity hybrid band made up of popular 'British Invasion' musicians. But the publicity stunt did not unfold exactly as hoped. 'I'd hear deejays saying, "Here's the latest from England, the Guess Who with 'Shakin' All Over'!,"' Randy Bachman, guitarist for the band, recalled. 'I'd phone the radio station and say "That's me, that's us, that's our band," and they'd say, "No." We had this number one record in Winnipeg and nobody believed it was us.'[5] The reason was simple. Bachman and his bandmates, having taken sounds from British records for their own style, came off sounding like a British band, and the confusion was all the more so because the 'Guess Who?' moniker was easily confused with that of the British group the Who. Recognition came in time but, in order for Chad Allan and the Expressions to cash in on the fame, they had to adopt the name which had come out of the gimmick: the Guess Who? (the question mark would be dropped in time).

The incident typified how Canadians interacted with the British Invasion of the 1960s, a phenomenon that reinvigorated the guitar-based rock and roll that had declined at the turn of the decade in favour of the softly crooning boys and girls next door. The British Invasion took over where the rock and roll stars of the late 1950s, many of whom were still around, had left off. Elvis, returning from the army in March 1960, revived his fame with the release of 'Stuck on You,' 'It's Now or Never,' and 'Are You Lonesome Tonight?' but his earlier, threatening pelvis was replaced by homogenized appearances in Hollywood films and Las Vegas nightclubs. Chuck Berry, returning to life outside of jail, never recaptured the intensity of his early career, nor would the minor-marrying Jerry Lee Lewis and his flaming piano. Little Richard had become a preacher. And Buddy Holly, Ritchie Valens, and Eddie Cochran were dead. Although record labels and radio stations had largely retreated from rock and roll excesses and payola scandals, filling the airwaves with the soft crooning of non-threatening teenagers, earlier rock and roll songs nonetheless continued among teenage bands performing in dance halls, community centres, and clubs. In the Vancouver area, the Hollywood Bowl (renamed the Grooveyard in 1965) in New Westminster joined with clubs in the bustling Gastown district in giving over their stages to local rock and roll and R&B bands such as the Prowlers, the Night Train Review, the Shantelles, the Classics (founded by Bill Henderson and later reworked into the Collectors and then Chilliwack), and the Chessmen (fronted by singer and guitarist Terry Jacks, who formed the Poppy Family in 1968). In Toronto, Ronnie Hawkins and the Hawks dominated the scene, followed by the likes of Ritchie Knight and the

Midnights, Robbie Lane and the Disciples, Little Caesar and the Consuls, and David Clayton-Thomas and the Shays. Although the venues on
Yonge Street were usually reserved in the evenings for the 21-and-over
crowds, Saturday afternoon matinees brought in younger audiences,
as did the many performances held in high schools, community halls,
church basements, and restaurants. There was also a new generation of
venues offering a grittier atmosphere attuned to rock and roll. For audiences in Winnipeg, teenagers had the Cellar, a club frequented by Bachman and his bandmates. According to music historian John Einarson,
'what the Cellar offered that was different was its atmosphere: it was the
antithesis of the community clubs. Whereas the community clubs epitomized innocent fun, the Cellar was a forbidden place that you dare not
tell your Mom you went to.'[6]

The Cellar was also the place where many Winnipeggers first heard
the sounds of the British Invasion before the albums were released in
Canada. Einarson has documented a trans-Atlantic musical pipeline that
existed between Winnipeg and Britain, or more specifically, between
local teenage performer Allan Kobel – aka Chad Allan – and a friend
in England. With access to a large selection of British singles that had
yet to be released in Canada, Chad Allan and his band the Silvertones
had an edge over their local competition. When teenage guitar phenomenon Randy Bachman joined Chad Allan's group in 1961, the band
was renamed Chad Allan and the Reflections as a play upon the British
group the Shadows (the 'Reflections' was later changed to 'the Expressions' after a Detroit band by that name had a Top 10 hit).[7] Bachman
has been very forthcoming as to the importance of the British groups
in his early years: 'We took anything British and did it. We were like the
ultimate British copy band. We still did Bobby Vee, Chuck Berry, Little
Richard and a lot of Buddy Holly, but we would also do British songs
like Shane Fenton and the Fentones, Billy Furry, Marty Wilde, and Mike
Berry and the Outlaws. We just got all these records and said "This is it,
this is our source of material."'[8] When the band got hold of songs by the
Beatles previous to their official release in Canada, they incorporated
the songs into their setlists and, it has been said, many Winnipeggers
first heard the songs of the 'Fab Four' in versions offered by Chad Allan
and the Expressions at the Cellar.[9] As Bachman told Einarson, 'we had
been so in love with England we just latched onto the Beatles as another
cool English group. "Wow, a whole new British music to capitalize on!"
That was a year before they debuted on Ed Sullivan. Winnipeggers heard
those songs first from us. Neil Young's introduction to Beatles songs

came from us. Months later when Beatles records began being played on local radio, some kids actually thought it was us.'[10] (The band would experience the reverse situation when they managed to get their recording of 'Shakin' All Over' on the radio.)

Canadians started to hear about the Beatles in late 1963 or so. In that November, almost three months before the Beatles made their legendary arrival at New York City's Kennedy airport, *Time* magazine first reported: 'The raucous, big-beat sound they achieve by electric amplification of all their instruments makes a Beatle performance slightly orgiastic. But the boys are the very spirit of good clean fun. They look like shaggy Peter Pans, with their mushroom haircuts and high white shirt collars, and onstage they clown around endlessly.'[11] At first glance, the Beatles seemed to be yet another soft-rock band not too different from those who were already on the radio. Clean-cut, humorous, and even sweetly wry, these Liverpudlians were non-threatening with their songs about hand-holding and unrequited love. But there was a grittiness hidden behind their charm. John Lennon, Paul McCartney, and George Harrison, along with their first drummer, Pete Best, had refined their techniques while playing dives in the notorious red-light district of Hamburg during trips from 1960 to 1962. To find British-born musicians performing songs copped from American recordings in German clubs – 'Roll over Beethoven' (Chuck Berry), 'Be-Bop-a-Lula' (Gene Vincent), and 'Long Tall Sally' (Little Richard), among others –speaks loudly as to rock and roll's international ebb and flow. This tough learning curve meant that on the band's return to Liverpool, and with Best replaced by Ringo Starr, they could offer tight and energetic performances at the likes of the Cavern Club. It was there that music store operator Brian Epstein met the Beatles, eventually becoming their manager and using his business expertise to shape and market them at home and abroad. Ethnomusicologist Laurel Sercombe was on the mark in noting that the Beatles owed a sizeable degree of their success to a manager well acquainted with music as a commodity that could be packaged and sold.[12]

On 7 February 1964, the Beatles landed at John F. Kennedy airport in New York City in what was not only an arrival but a media spectacle.[13] Two days later the band made its appearance on *The Ed Sullivan Show* to an audience of approximately 70 million viewers in the United States alone (over half of the total television viewing audience). New York City was merely one of many beachheads for Beatlemania. Ian Inglis, a sociologist and theorist of popular music, has summarized how international media picked up on the sensational phenomenon: 'Beatlemania quickly spread around the world. In June, more than 100,000 people thronged the streets of Amsterdam to see them. In Australia, where they had in March held the top six positions in the singles charts, with a total of ten in the Top 20, 300,000 fans surrounded their hotel in Adelaide, 250,000 in Melbourne.'[14]

Canada experienced the phenomenon in much the same way. In March 1964 the Beatles charted six of the Top 10 singles in Canada, the same number as in Australia and one more than in the United States.[15] Beatlemania arrived in full force in Canada five months later with the band's appearance at Vancouver's Empire Stadium. Just as Bill Haley and Elvis Presley had stirred up the city years earlier, the Beatles attracted frantic audiences and sensationalized media coverage. The timing was all the more perfect given that the 22 August performance coincided with the opening day of the Pacific National Exhibition (PNE). Scream-ing fans converged on the hotel that was rumoured to be hosting the Beatles; the downtown core filled with revelling fans co-opting the PNE opening ceremonies into a celebration of all things Beatles; and the stadium was surrounded by youths hoping to catch a glimpse of their beloved musicians.[16] The excitement was so great that the concert had only been on for about half an hour when the police signalled the band members to drop their instruments and leave the stage, a scenario that was by this point routine for the Beatles. In the words of William Littler, the *Vancouver Sun*'s music critic, 'seldom in Vancouver's entertainment history have so many (20,2761) paid so much ($5.25 top price) for so little (27 minutes).' Not that there was apparently much in the way of quality to miss out on:

> The stuff shouted by these Liverpudlian tonsorial horrors left me particu-larly unimpressed ... aside from their haircuts (or lack of them) and Mer-sey-side accents, I perceived nothing that made them better or worse than any number of less ballyhooed groups, either as vocalists or instrumental-ists. They sounded just as loud, just as monotonous, and just as unmusi-cal ... I do not know how it came, why it came and when it will go way. But go away the Beatle phenomenon will, and with it will go The Beatles. The day has yet to come. When it does, music lovers everywhere can rejoice – yeah, yeah, yeah.[17]

After the show was cut short, jubilance turned into disappointment and the chaos increased. The *Vancouver Sun*, much as it had done with the Bill Haley and Elvis Presley concerts, offered a sensationalized report:

the front-page story told of how 'time and again officers fought their way into the crowd to rescue youngsters from almost certain death under the feet of their co-howlers.'[18] According to interviewee Police Inspector F.C. (Bud) Errington, 'there's no comparison with any other crowd I've seen – at least the others still could think to some degree. These people have lost all ability to think ... one hundred policemen were there – that's all that stood between the way it wound up and a national tragedy.'[19] At the first aid station alone, Shillington reported, he found 'dozens of girls slumped in chairs, or corners, or anywhere out of the way, sobbing uncontrollably. Many had been vomiting. Hair that had been carefully combed now drooped in stringy shambles. Pretty, and often expensive, clothes were ripped.'[20] A car apparently transporting a member of the Beatles drove by the band's hotel and, in the ensuing chaos, a youth attempted to grab a police officer's gun; a girl, getting too close to the car, required medical treatment; a police dog was needed at the stadium to hold back the fans; and a gate was supposedly smashed and two others stormed. Photos published by the *Sun* showed the police apparently buckling against crowds of teenagers who were trying to squeeze through the lines and lunge over gates.[21]

It is worth noting the report of famed columnist Allan Fotheringham in what was his first article for *Maclean's*. Intended as a warning about what to expect at the upcoming Toronto and Montreal shows, the article is valuable because, unlike the *Vancouver Sun*, *Maclean's* was read from coast to coast. The article told readers about how the Vancouver airport was mobbed by 3,000 screaming fans; a riot broke out at the Beatles' hotel after Vancouver disc jockey Red Robinson had a Ringo Starr impersonator drive by and, during the melee, revolvers were swiped from the holsters of two police officers (a more detailed, and somewhat differing, account than that offered by the *Vancouver Sun*); the concert was a chaotic event characterized by girls and boys screaming, passing out, crying, and vomiting from over-excitement; and rough-housing youths knocked down a stadium barricade before the police held them back with German shepherds. 'The Beatle invasion of Vancouver was more than an orgiastic experience for the 20,621 fans who assembled in Empire Stadium on the sultry Saturday night of August 22,' reported Fotheringham. 'For law enforcement authorities it was also a deadly serious exercise in crowd control, civil defense, and the protection of several hundred youngsters who literally risked their lives trying to get close to their idols.'[22] The outcome of the concert was summarized numerically with an eye to shock and awe: 'For twenty-eight minutes of admittedly dangerous work, the

Beatles had collected $48,000, caused almost two hundred casualties and frightened the daylights out of several hundred policemen and several thousand parents.'[23]

In the same issue as Fotheringham's warning to fearful parents, reviews of *Viva Las Vegas*, Elvis Presley's latest film, and the Beatles' big-screen hit *A Hard Day's Night* made it clear that rock and roll had entered a new phase. Wendy Michener, a respected arts and entertainment critic, noted that 'the offending sideburns and gyrations have gone the way of all fads, and The Pelvis has become a clean-cut commercial personality like Annette Funicello, Frankie Avalon, and all the rest of the beach-party swimming-surfing crowd.'[24] Elvis had left the building and the Beatles had taken the stage.

Despite the warnings published in *Maclean's*, or perhaps because of them, waves of youths descended upon shows in Toronto and Montreal. On 7 September 1964, the Beatles held court at Maple Leaf Gardens with all of the expected fanfare and sensationalism. Paul McCartney had his shirt ripped during one of the many chases between the airport, hotel, and concert venue; a police paddy wagon was used to get the band members safely to the gig; approximately 33,000 fans attended the two concerts performed that day (total); over 200 girls reportedly fainted; and the Beatles netted $93,000 (total) for two gigs of thirty minutes each.[25] The following day the group performed a show in Montreal with a similar outcome. Approximately 3000–5000 youths greeted the Beatles at the airport, and after a raucous performance, the band left behind what the *Montreal Star* identified as 'one case of hysteria at Montreal Children's Hospital and 210 cases of fainting, exhaustion, and overexcitement.'[26]

With the success of the Beatles, the multinational recording industry had managed to open markets for other bands that could be sold as part of a British fad, including the Kinks ('You Really Got Me'), the Animals ('House of the Rising Sun,' 'Don't Let Me Be Misunderstood,' and 'We've Got to Get Out of this Place'), and the Who ('I Can't Explain,' 'My Generation,' and 'Substitute'). Still, no rival, or at least carefully marketed antithesis, to the Beatles stood out more than the Rolling Stones. The self-appointed bad boys of rock and roll, the Rolling Stones emphasized libido over love, sex over sweetness, and hedonism over the heart. 'I Just Want to Make Love to You,' their cover of a song written by Willie Dixon and first recorded by Muddy Waters, was a dirty declaration far removed from the Beatles' 'I Want to Hold Your Hand.' Marketing campaigns, the most famous being 'Would you let *your* daughter marry a

Rolling Stone?' were part of a self-fostered 'demonology' undertaken by Stones' music publicist Connie De Nave.[27]

Press conferences, used by the Beatles as opportunities to construct a media image of themselves as witty jokers, provided the Rolling Stones with a chance to affirm a rebellious image. A report of the 23 April 1965 press conference in Montreal, the first stop on the Canadian leg of their tour, told of how Brian Jones 'sneered' when complaining that the band had earlier been denied entrance into Canada after a show in Detroit, punctuating his condescension with the remark 'We couldn't understand it. We thought Canada was our colony. How could they have stopped us from coming in?'[28] The terse language of the press conference was heightened by Mick Jagger's remark about trying to speak French while in Quebec: 'Well, all French Canadians speak English, so there's no point in exercising our mental capabilities in speaking French.'[29] The press conference in Toronto two days later led to a similar report. 'Typical of the Stones vulgarity,' the *Toronto Daily Star* told readers, 'was the way drummer Charlie Watts treated a high school student reporter at the hot sweaty press conference preceding the show. He told her she was stupid in answer to a number of her questions. And larded his remarks with a strong four-letter word.'[30]

The Rolling Stones concerts in Montreal (23 April), Ottawa (24 April), Toronto (25 April), and London (26 April) offered the media more than enough fodder for sensationalized reports. At the show of 12,000 in Ottawa, reported on by the *Citizen*, 'girls shook with delight and trembled at each contortion of the frenzied performers, who in turn went into even greater gyrations. Teenage boys – many barely recognizable as such with their long hair – shook and stomped at the rhythm and heat and themselves went into frenzied dances on the fringes of the mass around the stage … Was this fun? Was this entertainment? It was mob hysteria. It was mass mesmerization.'[31] The *Toronto Daily Star* focused less on sexuality and more on disorder and injuries: 'It had to be one of the worst managed crowds in the history of Toronto rock 'n' roll shows. Those on the ground floor stood atop their rickety folding chairs throughout. One girl fell and cut a deep gash in her leg and had to be taken to hospital on a stretcher … two dozen girls shrieked themselves into hysteria and had to be treated by St. John ambulance staff … one girl was dragged out by her hair.'[32] Upon finishing their set, the Rolling Stones jumped into a car and reportedly 'charged full tilt into the crowd,' knocking over kids and pushing one girl up onto the windshield.[33]

Such antics and reportage became commonplace for the Rolling Stones. When they reappeared in Montreal in October of that year, six months after their first appearance, the *Montreal Star* reported that

> all control was lost. A sea of teenagers knocked down the thin blue line like tin soldiers. Ushers and St. John Ambulance men were sent in to help. Ushers, guards and first aid men were atop the stage bodily throwing teenagers off. The Stones rolled on. An usher at one point couldn't prevent five teenagers from getting on stage. He picked up a chair and raised it over his head threateningly. Rolling Stone Nick [*sic*] Jagger grabbed it from his hand and casually threw it over his shoulder, with a Henry VIII flair. This aroused the teenagers to more action. It was a go-ahead from the Stones.[34]

Coverage of the Vancouver show just over a month later focused on the same elements. Over thirty girls passed out, reported the *Vancouver Sun*, and there were 'many evictions (police lost count) of rowdies, including five thrown into horse boxes beneath the Agrodome to cool off before being set free.'[35] When the Rolling Stones returned the next summer for a show at the PNE Forum, the *Sun* told of how

> thirty-six screaming, hysterical teen-agers were carried bodily from the PNE Forum Tuesday night during a frenzied performance by the Rolling Stones. Two youths were arrested on drunk charges during the rock 'n' roll show, and a juvenile was arrested and may be charged later today with stealing a policeman's hat. Eleven youngsters were taken into custody during the performance and held in a detention room in the Forum until the show had ended. They were then released. A reserve police officer was kicked in the groin; an usher suffered a concussion when struck on the head by a youth; a policeman collapsed from exhaustion; and one juvenile suffered a fractured ankle.[36]

Police Inspector F.C. (Bud) Errington, the same officer interviewed by the newspaper at the Beatles concert two years earlier, explained that he and his fellow officers had apparently been the victim of what the *Sun* called 'offensive remarks and rude gestures' – including Mick Jagger reportedly pointing his finger at Errington and then thumbing his nose in a sign of disrespect.[37] The entire episode was worse than that of the Beatles, opined Errington, with the previous crowd of bawling girls now replaced by brawling boys. There had even been a bomb threat. The Rolling Stones, the Vancouver city council decided, would not be allowed to return. The move echoed that of such far-off places as the German Democratic Republic, which the previous autumn had banned the Rolling Stones after a show at the Waldbüne, on the other side of the Berlin Wall, resulted in a crowd of approximately 21,000 leaving the venue in ruins.[38]

Of course, all of this sensationalism needs to be taken with reservation. A decade had past since rock and roll first emerged, and over the years it had been increasingly integrated into daily life. No longer did youths have to covertly tune their transistor radios into stations offering forbidden sounds. Rock and roll was found not only on the radio but in movie theatres and magazines. There were even clubs dedicated to it, such as Ronnie Hawkins's 'Hawk's Nest' on Yonge Street, where, as *Maclean's* explained in a March 1965 cover story, 'parents are invited ... for a check-up-on-your-kids visit, but, apart from the fun of seeing young people have fun, it's an unnecessary trip. The dress-up rule keeps out the motorcycle hoods and the tough guys. Apparently the drinkers aren't frequenting the Nest either.'[39] Just as telling, only two months later *Time* magazine published a cover story titled 'Rock 'n' Roll: The Sound of the Sixties' that explored the rise of the 'discotheque,' the popularity of rock and roll among twenty- to forty-year-olds, and how rock and roll radio shows even attracted advertisers for soap and household goods to cater to the housewives who tuned in.[40] As one teenager complained in the article, 'nothing is sacred anymore. I mean, we no sooner develop a new dance or something and our parents are doing it.'[41]

Nonetheless, the British Invasion was a strong reminder of just how chaotic rock and roll could be. Although the arrival of the Beatles at John F. Kennedy airport is often identified as the start of the British Invasion, it is worth noting that the band had already had significant success in Canada. As of 1963, Capitol Canada, a subsidiary of the British-based EMI Records, began building on the success of Cliff Richards and the Shadows by importing the singles of other British acts, including the Beatles. According to Nicholas Jennings, 'the British Invasion had established a North American beachhead in Canada first, months before it was able to move into the United States. Capitol Canada had released more Beatles singles than any other country, and in the process [Capitol Canada executive/record promoter/A&R director Paul] White had helped to fill the company's coffers with consecutive hits by other English acts as well, especially the Dave Clark Five and Gerry and the Pacemakers.'[42]

Both Jennings and White have linked the success of British imports in Canada with the decision to sign some Canadian acts, leading to deals with the Esquires, Wes Dakus and the Rebels, Robbie Lane and the Disciples, David Clayton-Thomas and the Shays, the Staccatos, and Jack London and the Sparrows. 'That was a major fringe benefit,' White recalled, although, as he further noted, 'the challenge was to get our salesmen to push the stuff. They'd say "why do I have to go out and promote the Esquires when all I have to do is walk into Sam's and sell 500 copies of Beatlemania?"'[43] At the very least, it is telling that profits from imports were being used to help foster the anemic domestic industry.

For fans of rock and roll, the British Invasion was an exciting change from the status quo, a refreshing option after years of the whitewashed sounds of Fabian, Frankie Avalon, Paul Anka, and Annette Funicello. Musicians cast off the old in favour of the new, with mohair suits and leather greaser jackets replaced by shaggy combed-down 'Beatle cut' hair and whatever clothing resembled the mod styles seen on the covers of British records and magazines. 'The British Invasion gave all the bands more options,' Burton Cummings has recalled about the new sounds and their impact. 'There were infinitely more styles to emulate ... Oh, what England did for the local bands of the world back then ...!!'[44] Cummings was one of a legion of Winnipeggers who turned to the new music and adopted such British-sounding names as the Wellingtons, the Viscounts, London Fog, King's Row, the Cavaliers, the Quid, and the Chancellors.[45] David Downing has noted that 'in Winnipeg, anyone with any pretensions to being hip was trying to write songs like "Do You Want to Know a Secret?" and learning how to play "She Loves You."'[46] Neil Young's first public performance, reportedly in the cafeteria of Winnipeg's Kelvin High School, entailed the Beatles singles 'It Won't Be Long' and 'Money' (the latter written by Barrett Strong).[47] His mother, Edna Young, has told of how 'Neiler and [his friend] Ken Koblun would stand in our living room and play those darn Beatle albums and try to copy them.'[48] Together as the Squires, Young and Koblun joined bandmates in regaling audiences with a combination of American and British hits, apparently wearing Beatles wigs at times, at least until their hair was long enough to be shaggy on its own.[49]

For some Canadians, the Beatles were too similar to the heartthrobs who were already dominating the Top 40, and it was the sound and attitude offered by the likes of the Rolling Stones and the Kinks that really caught their attention. For Dave Bingham of the Ugly Ducklings, a band that would go on to be a gritty Canadian precursor to hard rock and punk, that moment came when he first heard the Rolling Stones' 'It's All Over Now' in 1964:

I was studying for a math exam or some such, cloistered away in my parents' basement. I had an old big-box magic-eye tuner unit with a 15 inch powered speaker. It had its own built-in compressor. When the opening chords of that tune boomed out of the speaker I was blown away! No one had ever recorded at that volume before. It was a preview of what was to come. Two days later I had the single and would play it over and over every night down in the basement marveling at the intensity of feeling and the exuberance in their playing. When I played it for Roger [Mayne, the band's guitarist] he felt it too.[50]

Bingham and Mayne, initially taking the name the Strolling Bones as a play on the Rolling Stones, soon rechristened themselves the Ugly Ducklings, went on to captivate Toronto teenagers, and even managed to sign with Yorktown and have a local hit with 'Nothin'' in early 1966.[51] Soon after, they were asked to open for the Rolling Stones at Maple Leaf Gardens on 29 June that year.[52] According to Tim Perlich in a 1999 retrospective, the concert involved 'the group's resident Brian Jones double, Glynn Bell, accidentally wearing the exact same sweater and cords ensemble as [Brian] Jones … And if you think Jones was pissed, imagine Mick Jagger's reaction when the Ducklings kicked off the night with Solomon Burke's "Everybody Needs Somebody to Love" – precisely what the Stones planned to crank as their set-starter.'[53]

Bands commonly followed the lead of established British groups, adopting Beatles suits, Rolling Stones attitudes, Mersey Beat pants, and shaggy hairstyles. Yet Canadian acts were not just mimicking musical elements but adapting to and appropriating aspects from a geographically, and to a degree nationally, situated music genre. The need to respond to the public's interest in the British Invasion meant going beyond music and fashion styles; the need to assert 'authenticity' led to a wide-scale appropriation of British-sounding names and, in some cases, even fake accents and background stories about having recently arrived from England. Those bands that were capable of representing themselves as part of the British Invasion stood the best chance of accessing the industry's material resources. As Jennings has explained in his history of Capitol-EMI, 'with the arrival of the British Invasion in 1964, Canadian record labels were quick to sign any local group that exhibited an English pop sound of mop-top image. Columbia boasted the Mersey beat-like Liverpool Set, while Red Leaf touted the Union Jack-sporting British Mod-beats. Few bands were more successful in adopting English affections than the [Capitol Canada–signed] Jack London and the Sparrows.'[54]

In their quest for authenticity and the desire to attract the attention of industry and audience alike, many bands ended up virtually 'out-Britishing' the British. The top British Invasion band names – the Beatles, the Rolling Stones, Herman's Hermits, the Dave Clark Five, the Hollies, the Yardbirds, the Who, the Kinks – were not identifiably British. British bands had been influenced by American imports, drawing upon established rock and roll acts. The name 'Beatles' was a play on Buddy Holly's 'Crickets,' with the spelling of 'beetles' altered to reflect the 'beat' of the music. The Rolling Stones took their name from a song by Muddy Waters.[55] Even their singing voices, although betraying an accent at times, were adaptations of rock and roll voices extracted from imported albums, particularly blues and R&B singers: Mick Jagger's raspy inflection comes immediately to mind. Now that the British Invasion was the latest musical fad, many Canadian groups were doing something similar, not simply latching onto rock and roll musical identifiers but appropriating national ones, with little being left to chance.

Jack London and the Sparrows were among the more popular of British-styled acts on the Toronto scene and one of the most blatant when it came to co-opting British elements. Although the 'Sparrows' was a play upon Ronnie Hawkins's 'Hawks,' everything else was seeped in Britishness, with singer and frontman Dave Marden changing his name to 'Jack London,' guitarist and drummer Dennis and Jerry McCrohan swapping theirs to Edmonton (as it was thought to sound more British), and the full band faking British accents.[56] Jerry Edmonton has explained that

> when the British Invasion thing took off we jumped on the bandwagon, especially Dave Marden. Whenever I'd go over to his house, he'd be talking with this English accent. Then I'd hear him talking to his Mom in a normal accent. When people were around he went into this thing about how he was from Liverpool. Strange guy. Then we all had to put on these fake British accents. Once when we went to Niagara Falls and were eating roast beef in this restaurant, a very British place, the waiter came up and asked us what we would like for dessert. So Dave, or Jack London, in his best fake British accent says, 'Yorkshire Pudding.' The waiter just stared at him in amazement. Then Jack caught on and went, 'Ha, ha, just joking.'[57]

Despite such occasional missteps in asserting their Britishness, Jack London and the Sparrows epitomized the ways in which Canadian acts changed with the times in order to break into the market. Jack London and the Sparrows were picked up by Capitol and charted with 'If You

Don't Want My Love' and 'Our Love Has Passed.' The similarly inspired Lords of London, formed in a Toronto suburb and reminiscent of the Monkees, had a number one hit on CHUM in the summer of 1967 with 'Corn Flakes and Ice Cream,' the first domestic single to hit number one on the chart in four years (Ritchie Knight and the Midnights had done so previously).[58] The British Modbeats out of St Catherines, Ontario, failed to chart with their offerings, but it was not for a lack of trying: the band not only took a blatantly British-sounding name but went so far as to put a Union Jack on the cover of their album *Mod ... Is the British Modbeats*.

In French-speaking Canada, the British Invasion was incorporated into the popular 'yé-yé' movement, which took its name from the lyrics 'yeah, yeah' of the Beatles' 'She Loves You' and fused early rock and roll and R&B styles with the British Invasion. Robert Giroux, in *Le guide de la chanson québécoise*, has described (somewhat critically) how yé-yé singers engaged adolescents through versions of American songs dealing largely with such youthful preoccupations as school life, going to the movies, and dancing.[59] The more popular of these groups included les Beatlettes, les Baronets (with hits 'Twiste et chante' ['Twist and Shout'] and 'C'est fou mais c'est tout' ['Hold Me Tight']), les Sinners ('Penny Lane'), and les Sultans ('Va t'en' and 'À toi que je pense'). As in English-speaking Canada, Beatles-style suits and bobbed hair were common.[60]

Groups who managed to attract record labels and radio stations by dressing in clothes embellished with the Union Jack and by speaking with Liverpool accents angered some musicians, who felt themselves to be more serious and talented. Jurgen Peter, guitarist for the seminal 1960s Montreal rock group the Haunted, looks back at the period with a degree of contempt:

> During that time, MANY bands surfaced attempting to plug in and ride the import tsunami and most trying desperately to copy their visual presentation ... they called themselves British names and used phony accents. Even some of the local French bands had a go at it ... The Haunted were never in the same league with bands such as Jack London and the Sparrows, the Mod Beats, the Merseys, the Penny Lanes, the Strawberry Fields ... It still makes the back of my hair stand up when I hear my name mentioned along with these bands in the same sentence!!

The abundance of British-styled groups did not result in an increase in songwriting; bands were commonly little more than human jukeboxes offering renditions of popular songs. Musicians were thought of as entertainers more than as artists. Even serious bands like the Haunted could not escape the need to offer popular hits. As Peter has recalled, 'local bands that had no material of their own available and asked for by their fans had to play the songs that were being hyped on the radios just like all the similar bands in the rest of the world did and still are.' When the Haunted did offer originals, he says, fans typically went wild when they heard something new. 'They took us under their wings and cheered when we played our original songs like '1-2-5' and "Searching for My Baby."'[61]

Although the domestic music scene was highly adaptive to the British Invasion, there were also non-British factors at play. After all, American rock and roll hits were still high on the charts. As Jeffrey Ridley of the United Empire Loyalists has explained, although his group was into the Rolling Stones and the Kinks, they also performed singles by the Kingsmen and Young Rascals, among others.[62] Further, many of the bands that have been thought of as simply British copycats were in fact drawing from the same well of earlier American R&B and rock and roll. The Haunted, Jurgen Peter has argued, was one of those bands that had learned from the same recordings as their British counterparts and as such needs to be thought of as running along the same general path:

> Most of us learned to play our instruments by listening to and emulating the sound of the older black blues artists in the US; as did all of the British bands including the Beatles that spearheaded the 'new' sound coming from England. In other words, we learned to play, listening to the same records, at around the same time as the musicians of the yet to become 'British sound' did. As a result, the Haunted sounded and were already of the same caliber as the newly arriving import bands. We were, at will, able to play any song that was being played by the local radio stations, as good, if not often better than the record itself simply because we had the same mentors as they had.[63]

Dave Bingham, vocalist for the Ugly Ducklings, has said much the same, citing the formative influence of Bo Diddley, Chuck Berry, Marvin Gaye, James Brown, and Ronnie Hawkins. What the British rockers did, Bingham explains, was offer a direction in which to take their musical influences:

> The emergence of the Stones, Kinks, Yardbirds, and Them (with Van 'the

man' [Morrison]) was an affirmation for us. It gave us the impetus to break away from the standard music-biz mold of clean-cut model teenagers playing watered down impressions of black R&B. We wanted to go for the jugular. Mick and Keith, Clapton and Van showed us it could be done and we jumped right in … We wanted to be wild and rough and they paved the way … When the Brit-Invasion hit we were already firing on all eight cylinders and ready to launch.[64]

Consideration also needs to be given to the significant use of domestic material resources. Will Straw, a cultural theorist and music industry expert at McGill University, has asserted that the supposedly imitative groups used numerous local resources and, in doing so, existed in a paradigm that was in some ways more national than the ideologically national but industrially multinational one that emerged in the early 1970s. His argument is worth offering at length:

Typically, the history of postwar popular music in countries outside the U.S.-U.K. axis is imagined as a set of national struggles to break free of blatantly imitative forms and to find national, musical voices. In dozens of different countries, this is a story which takes us from cover bands of the early to mid-1960s (who covered Anglo-American hits in local languages) to those practices of the 1970s in which rock was articulated to indigenous national traditions (such as Mexican rock or the Québécois chanson). What is often overlooked in this narrative is the uprooting of local musical cultures which this struggle for respectability and distinctiveness entailed. In Quebec, for example, the early and mid-1960s saw the production of hundreds of records covering Anglo-American hits; dozens of studio albums in which U.S. film hits were covered, with cha-cha or Tijuana rhythms, by local studio orchestras; and innumerable recordings in which local singers sang versions of Burt Bacharach or Simon and Garfunkel compositions. Abject as these practices came to seem, they were rooted in local and national practices of collaboration, venues of live performance, and, much of the time, the commercial activities of independently owned record companies. By the time these practices had withered, giving way to the music of rock groups engaged in reclaiming national traditions and musical languages, the most successful performers were on the Canadian subsidiaries of multinational labels (or, at least, distributed by such labels). Paradoxically, music taken to possess enhanced local credibility and integrity was now much more firmly integrated within multinational corporate structures. The music of a

few years earlier, easily dismissed as shamelessly imitative, nevertheless had
been produced in contexts in which rich networks of local practices and
institutions served to mediate the assimilation of musics from elsewhere.[65]

For Straw the involvement of domestic, predominantly local, resources
meant that this period of creation and consumption cannot be easily
dismissed and, in fact, contains elements missing in later periods.

Finally, it is worth noting that in the same way as Canadians shared
a continent with the Americans when it came to the first wave of rock
and roll, they shared an empire with the British when it came to the
latest musical trends. British royalty appeared on the currency with
which Canadian teenagers purchased records after walking down streets
adorned with mailboxes sporting the British crown and flagpoles draped
with the Red Ensign. Canada's connection to the British Empire was
a hot topic of public debate, particularly during the discussions about
replacing the Red Ensign with a new flag in 1965.[66] One has only to look
at the United Empire Loyalists in Vancouver and Paul Revere and the
Raiders out of Boise, Idaho, two popular acts that, as their names display, were situated within different historical connections to Britain. For
the teenaged United Empire Loyalists, the name had its origins in the
Canadian history component of band member Anton 'Tony' Kolstee's
grade 11 social studies class, with the group going so far as having Union
Jack–patterned jackets made by the owner of a head shop on Fourth
Avenue in Vancouver's Kitsilano.[67] The Raiders, on the other hand, having hits with 'Steppin' Out' and 'Kicks' and appearing on a series of Dick
Clark television shows, became known for wearing colonial-style tricorn
hats, jackets, ruffled shirts, and on occasion draping their backdrop in
stars and stripes.[68] In appropriating British identifiers, groups were, con-
sciously or not, affirming a connection that was not only familiar but
familial.

'Prairie Town,' an autobiographical tune released by Randy Bachman in
1993, hearkens back to the days of Chad Allan and the Expressions and
their hit 'Shakin' All Over.' The lyrics tell about being a kid who starts
up a band in the cold of winter and learns songs from singles imported
from Liverpool. Bachman certainly was not alone in such a recollection.
The British Invasion inspired potential, aspiring, and professional musicians alike, who extracted and interpreted a new musical paradigm from
records, media outlets, and concerts. This phenomenon came complete
with British-sounding monikers, 'mod beat' clothing and shaggy hair,

and outfits and album covers adorned with the Union Jack. Nor was this phenomenon confined to Canada. In New Zealand, for example, the Mods and St Paul offered sounds and performances patterned on British acts and recordings.[69] In Germany, bands used not only the sounds and sights but also the key phrasing of English songs, just as the yé-yé movement did in Quebec and France.[70]

Why did a large part of the Canadian rock and roll scene take on the appearance of an overeager cover band? Musicians, excited by the new musical genre and having little in the way of domestic resources, found that their best shot at success was to incorporate, if not become fully immersed in, the musical and national identifiers of the British Invasion. In doing so the groups offered a domestic twist on the fad. Whereas British groups had reconfigured rock and roll within their socio-economic spaces, adopting accents and styles thought to best represent American rock and roll 'authenticity,' Canadians co-opted not only musical but national identifiers that would give them British Invasion capital. What started as an exciting new genre soon became a category to which many performers felt they had to conform, and bands had good reason for casting themselves in the British Invasion mould. The subsidiaries of multinational record labels, radio stations looking for economic gain in fads, and teenagers eager to be a part of what was hip, combined to entrench the British Invasion paradigm. Capitol Records set the trend by popularizing their roster of British artists and then signing the likes of Jack London and the Sparrows, and other labels, detecting a swelling of radio industry and consumer interest, were quick to follow suit.

Not everyone was a copycat, though. Canada had a bevy of up-and-coming acts that devoured American tunes, including the same ones that had inspired British bands. By the time the British Invasion took root, many domestic rockers were already exploring their own scenes, only to find in the British Invasion like-minded musicians. 'When Keith Richards picks up his guitar and plays "Oh Carol" or "Route 66" or "Little Red Rooster,"' Jurgen Peter has argued, 'he would be playing it exactly as I would. For the same reason: we both learned them off the same records.'[71] Other musicians have testified along the same lines. To some musicians the British Invasion was a source of inspiration, guidance, or simply a sign that there was hope for grittier rock and roll at a time of sickly sweet ballads offered by the *Beach Blanket Bingo* set. As Peter has put it, at least in regard to his own musical experience, 'I believe that the word "Invasion" is used incorrectly and has caused much confusion ... I would have labelled it the "British Awareness."'[72]

At the very least, the British Invasion, and the Canadian acts participating in it, thrived in the absence of any substantive notions of a 'Canadian' rock and roll. The new fad was unhindered by nationalist sentiments because rock and roll was still considered to be an entertainment of relatively little, if any, redeeming social value, let alone reflective of the nation and needing to be empowered as a national paradigm. What would it matter that musicians were singing in bands named after British cities and adorning themselves and their record albums with the Union Jack? It was only rock and roll. Not even in Britain was the British Invasion widely revered as something national in value and essence, as displayed in the protest that followed the government's 1965 decision to make the Beatles Members of the Order of the British Empire (MBE) in recognition of their international sales. As Linda Martin and Kerry Segrave explain the controversy, 'the furor over the award showed that even such a "good" rock group as the Beatles would never really be accepted by the adult establishment ... What the Labour government failed to take into account was that, at the bottom, the Beatles were still a rock group. And rock groups and music were, after all, "bad."'[73] Over the next few years, however, a 'songwriting turn' would take place in which the maturing baby boom generation began to address socio-political elements of everyday life and, within this new discourse, create a musical experience deemed ideologically valuable in national terms. Rock and rollers would go from being a social threat to an artistic avant garde and achieve privileged and highly celebrated positions as spokespeople for the nation. The germination of this process can be traced, at least in part, to the folk music revival of the 1960s.

3

From 'Tom Dooley' to 'Mon Pays': Folk Music and the Nation

We're from Canada. We have about eight anthems up there, but hardly any love songs. So I wrote a ballad, 'Four Strong Winds.' Actually it's a combination love ballad and winter weather report.
> – Ian Tyson, to a Greenwich Village audience, 1965[1]

I've written only one protest song. That was 'Urge for Going,' which was a protest against winter. And it certainly isn't going to stop winter.
> – Joni Mitchell, 1968[2]

Quebec's politically conscious pop singers sound like a well-rehearsed chorus of anti-federalists.
> – 'Maclean's Reports,' *Maclean's*, 1969[3]

'It is not absolutely essential to have hair hanging to the waist – but it helps. Other aids: no lipstick, flat shoes, a guitar. So equipped, almost any enterprising girl can begin a career as a folksinger.'[4] *Time* was being playful but not completely off the mark when it typecast the latest musical fad in the summer of 1962. Over the previous few years folk music, which had once been looked upon as a relic of the Depression and dust-bowl years, had become hip among politically aware young people. The anti-modernism of folk music flourished among those who wanted to escape the looming nuclear apocalypse, among musicians interested in hearty styles and sounds after years of commercial hits, and among record labels and radio stations recovering from rock and roll excesses. When *Time* magazine declared that 'anything called a hootenanny ought to be shot on sight, but the whole country is having one,' the sentiment was just as true for Canada.[5]

Folk music was the latest fad, but as a genre it was certainly not new. Many of the songs sung by aspiring folkies hearkened back to such nineteenth- and early twentieth-century folklorists as Francis Child, a collector of Anglo-Celtic ballads who had done much to catalogue works that he feared would otherwise soon disappear. 'By correspondence, and by an extensive diffusion of printed circulars,' explained Child in *The English and Scottish Popular Ballads*, a multivolume set published in 1882, 'I have tried to stimulate collection from tradition in Scotland, Canada, and the United States, and no becoming means has been left unemployed to obtain possession of unsunned treasures locked up in writing.'[6] Child, a professor of English at Harvard, did much to track down, document, categorize, and canonize ballads. In doing so he helped to set the tone for a reverential and essentialistic treatment of the 'folk' as a simple pre-modern people. According to historian Ian McKay, 'because of his implicit stress on ballads originating in non-literate societies, Child's legacy was an exaggerated tendency among ballad collectors and others to equate change with corruption, in pursuit of the *authentic* and *original*.'[7] In the opinion of University of Bristol sociologist Lee Marshall, this treatment meant 'a certain fetishizing of the "folk song," which became an artifact, cast in stone, to be revered as the true representation of the folk.'[8] Among those who followed in Child's folklorist footsteps was Cecil Sharp, a Cambridge-educated music composer who documented folk songs and dances in England and the United States (notably the Appalachian mountains), and, in Canada, folklorists John Murray Gibbon, Marius Barbeau, and Helen Creighton, among others.[9] Out of this international compilation of the folk emerged what McKay has called a 'complex and powerful Anglo-American folklore matrix, a common trans-Atlantic entropic sensibility that structured assumptions and methods of study of the Folk and their supposed lore.'[10]

During the 1920s in the United States, the Anglo-Celtic ballads became accompanied, if not supplanted, by a politicization of 'worker songs' as an essentialized voice of the American proletariat. Many of these tunes initially came from musicians who were also labourers and those who made an income by performing for labourers in live venues and on radio broadcasts. Sociologists Vincent J. Roscigno, William F. Danaher, and Erika Summers-Effler have explained that 'some of these songs, set to traditional southern folk and gospel tunes, were written by the musicians themselves. Others, written by mill workers, were picked up, polished, and sung by the musicians as they traveled into and between mill villages ... These songs employed a collective sense of experience, using the words "we," "us," and "our," and communicated anxieties specific to the experiences of most mill workers.'[11] The threat seemed more than real to some mill owners, who responded by banning songs deemed to be subversive to workplace harmony and production.[12]

Other socio-economic groups in American society took to, and used, folk music for their own interests. McKay has offered an insightful summary as to the ebb and flow of folk music in early twentieth-century America:

> The United States was too heterogeneous and too nationalist to permit so heavy an emphasis on a construction of the American Folk as the passive bearers of the British Ballad. Gradually a broader category of 'folk song' – characterized by oral transmission, constant formal changes, 'vitality' over a 'fair period of time,' and the loss of all sense of individual authorship and provenance – came to supplement the narrower category of the Child Ballad. Right-wing industrialists and racists, worried about the popular spread of black music in the 1920s, were significant for this emergent concept of folksong. In the 1930s and 1940s the Left, no less essentialist in its cultural politics, championed the folksong within an aesthetic united front, and the Folk were vaguely defined as the 'working class' or 'ordinary people,' whose songs were invariably expressed inchoate longings for a society of justice and freedom ... Communist enthusiasm for the Folk in the 1940s and 1950s might also have reflected many of the same antimodernist impulses that can be documented in other aspects of cultural life.[13]

As McKay notes, the worker song was of great value to leftist political organizations, all the more so because of the ease with which its members could participate in the music. It was with no small degree of irony, music theorist Simon Frith has noted, that the Communist Party 'adopted rural music as the most suitable expression for the urban worker; the party's intellectuals became "people's artists" by singing folk songs dressed in Oakie clothes ... the authenticity of the music was, despite the folk language, still being judged by its effects rather than its sources.'[14]

Although worker songs involving blacks were viewed with unease by some advocates of the folk, they were slowly incorporated through the efforts of such musicologists and folklorists as John Lomax and his son Alan. Songs of the country blues style, typified by field singers who were exposed to both southern country and delta blues music, came to be of particular interest among the political left. Martha Bayles has pointed out that 'the left embraced the blues largely because of Lomax's tireless showcasing of such masters as Huddie "Leadbelly" Ledbetter. But here the rejection of commercial music played a role, as many people on the left, taking their cues from Lomax, found only one type of blues acceptable: the "country blues," played by solo acoustic guitarist-singers and focusing on hard times – or better still, on protest.'[15] Much like Child, Sharp, Creighton, and others who selectively documented their conception of what constituted 'true' folk, John and Alan Lomax hunted out singers and, thanks to technology, made acetate recordings of performances and interviews.[16] Many of the recordings took place during the 1930s as the duo travelled the southern United States on behalf of the Library of Congress Archive of American Folksong (and with economic help from the Carnegie and Rockefeller foundations). Prisons were of particular interest, given their relative isolation from radio airplay and developments in musical styles, offering sites in which 'authentic' songs had supposedly been preserved, not unlike Cecil Sharp's treatment of the isolated populations of the Appalachian mountains. It was at a prison in Dallas that the Lomaxes discovered the aforementioned Leadbelly and subsequently formed a close relationship that led to his eventual release and relocation to New York City with Alan Lomax in the winter of 1940 – as his house servant and reportedly, under Lomax's guidance, occasionally performing for local folkies while wearing prison garb as a sign of his authenticity.[17]

Lomax headed to New York City in order to take up a position at the Archive of American Folksong, yet even here, in perhaps the most cosmopolitan city in the United States, the musicologist discovered folk gold. Greenwich Village was fast becoming a hub for leftists and assorted bohemians with a tremendous interest in folklife and lore. Among those who made their way to the scene was Woody Guthrie, a folksinger whose work drew upon personal experiences with poverty, the dustbowl, and workers' movements and union drives.[18] Guthrie ended up not only recording for Lomax as part of the Library of Congress's Archive of American Folk Songs but also released *Dust Bowl Ballads* on Victor Records and *Deep Sea Chanteys and Whaling Ballads* and *Sod-Buster Ballads* as a member of the Almanac Singers on General Records. Among the other Almanac Singers was Pete Seeger, a musician (and son of a musicologist) who dropped out of Harvard and ended up playing banjo in Greenwich Village. Seeger's time spent with the Almanac Singers was followed by fame as a member of the Weavers, a folk group formed in 1947, that charted 'Tzena, Tzena, Tzena,' 'Goodnight Irene' (written by Leadbelly), 'On Top of Old Smokey,' 'Kisses Sweeter than Wine,' and

'So Long It's Been Good to Know You' (recorded on the Decca Records label), selling over 5 million records between 1950 and 1952.[19]

Unfortunately for Seeger and his compatriots, their socialist ideology made them targets of Senator Joe McCarthy's witch-hunt of communists, socialists, leftists, and various sympathizers. Seeger was subpoenaed to testify in front of the House Committee on Un-American Activities on 18 August 1955 and, after choosing not to directly answer questions about his connection to socialist activities, was handed a jail sentence for contempt.[20] Although the sentence was later dropped, it had not only hindered his domestic recording career but also led to him to back out of a plan to host a folk music show in the works with the Canadian Broadcasting Corporation, *Singalong Jubilee*, that eventually came to air in 1961.[21]

Nonetheless, the banjo player continued to write songs unabated, including 'Turn, Turn, Turn' (later made into a hit by the Byrds), 'If I Had a Hammer,' 'Where Have All the Flowers Gone,' and wrote a book on how to play the banjo (from which Joni Mitchell would later teach herself to form chords on a ukulele). When the Weavers performed at Carnegie Hall in December 1955 the fans and media attention that surrounded the event signified a growing commercial market for folk music. The concert, released as *The Weavers at Carnegie Hall*, inspired many aspiring performers, including Gordon Lightfoot, who, according to Nicholas Jennings, from that point began to take folk music more seriously and to blend it with his love of country and western.[22]

Although *The Weavers at Carnegie Hall* was a success, the start of the commercial folk period is commonly identified as being the 1958 release of the Kingston Trio's version of the folk standard 'Tom Dooley.'[23] Jennings has stated that 'it's difficult to overstate the influence of "Tom Dooley." Across North America, coffeehouses like the Inquisition in Vancouver, the Gate of Horn in Chicago and Gerde's Folk City in New York began springing up in the wake of the song's success, presenting hootenannies and a host of folksingers. And record companies, from independents like Vanguard to majors like Capitol, began scouting for the next major folk stars.'[24] The Kingston Trio were themselves signed with Capitol, accounting for approximately 12 per cent of the label's sales.[25]

By the turn of the decade folk music was in full swing. Banjo sales increased 500 per cent between 1957 and 1959.[26] The advertising industry, particularly those involved with television, began to latch on to the latest musical sounds as a means of selling their goods.[27] This commercialization of folk music ran counter to the very elements that had initially made it popular among so-called 'purists,' but there was little that could be done to prevent entrepreneurs from cashing in on the next big thing.

The appeal of folk music is certainly understandable. Children who had been brought up with fears of a nuclear attack were now young adults turning to a musical reprieve from the world they stood to inherit, a genre that offered an escape from commercialization, consumerism, and an impending nuclear holocaust.

With the popularity of folk music came a new generation of festivals, something common earlier in the century but now undergoing a revival. In 1959, George Wean and Albert Grossman founded the Newport Folk Festival, and two years later the Mariposa Folk Festival began in Orillia, Ontario, its name taken from the fictional town in Stephen Leacock's *Sunshine Sketches of a Little Town* (and one rumoured to be based on Orillia).[28] Although Mariposa would favour Canadian acts, Gillian Mitchell explains that any desire to 'Canadianize' the festival was held only by 'a small faction within the organizing committee and audience.'[29] Even when steps were taken in the direction of Canadianization, the emphasis was on creating opportunities for citizens rather than favouring acts that performed songs that identified Canadian locations or themes that could be commonly thought of as national.[30] Although folk songs often celebrated elements of heritage, many performers resisted attempts to exploit their music for nationalist ends. Instead, they intended their songs to promote pluralism and inclusiveness irregardless of citizenship. Gillian Mitchell tells of how 'former revivalist musicians in Canada are frequently, and justifiably, baffled, even irritated, by the contention that they were victims of cultural imperialism; they will often respond to the effect that, although the music they played was, indeed, American in origin, they did not see it that way – it was "just music," not to be dissected or separated so arbitrarily.'[31]

On 18 and 19 August 1961, Mariposa presented its first lineup, headlined by the popular Toronto-based duo of Ian Tyson and Sylvia Fricker. Born and raised in British Columbia, Tyson hitchhiked across Canada and into the United States before ending up in Toronto. There, in 1958, he met Sylvia Fricker, a singer who had arrived from her home in Chatham, Ontario, only a few hours away. She brought to the duo not only standard folk, country, and blues songs but also lesser-known Anglo-Celtic ballads and hymns, the sorts of works catalogued by Child and Sharp.[32] These ballads, Sylvia explained in an interview with *Chatelaine* in January 1976, allowed the duo to stand out from their peers. 'The folksingers here all worked from the same basic repertoire, because they had all bought the same Pete Seeger and Woody Guthrie albums, and there was limited material, and they were not aware of my source from books.'[33] Ian and Sylvia did so well in Toronto, in fact, that Pete Seeger pulled them onto stage during his 1961 appearance at Massey Hall and requested that they perform a few songs.[34] The event certainly gave the duo significant credibility among local folkies.

Sylvia was not alone in turning to folk ballads and hymns. Joan Baez, a singer who performed in coffee houses to folkies, beatniks, and those who, in her words, had 'the bomb on their minds,' mixed established worker songs and folk standards with ballads catalogued by Child and other folklorists.[35] When *Time* published a cover story on her in 1962, the article went so far as to include a picture of Child and an explanation as to how his work was 'still the definitive anthology in its field.'[36] Baez's male counterpart, and a close friend, was introduced to the readers in that same issue. Bob Dylan was 'a promising young hobo' who 'delivers his songs in a studied nasal that has just the right clothespin-on-the-nose honesty to appeal to those who most deeply care.'[37] Dylan had arrived in New York City from Minnesota in January 1961 and had taken to performing in the cafes and 'basket' houses. His self-titled album, recorded in November 1961 and released in March 1962, presented a powerful selection of traditional blues and folk songs with two original compositions. By the spring of 1963, *Time* was describing him as 'the newest hero of an art that has made a fetish out of authenticity,' noting that this bohemian with a hillbilly voice fared well at the Monterey Folk Festival, an event started that year, alongside established acts like the Weavers and Peter, Paul and Mary.[38]

At about that time Dylan made a foray northwards and ended up in one of Toronto's trendy European-style coffee houses, the Bohemian Embassy, on the night of a poetry reading. According to Nicholas Jennings, Dylan was recognized by some attendees and overlooked or ignored by others, and he either did not want, or was denied a chance, to get on stage. As the story goes, Dylan apparently became agitated that the coffee shop had planned a poetry contest – a competition being quite different than a reading – for the next week.[39]

Coffee houses were becoming all the rage in major cities across Canada. In Montreal there were many along Stanley Street. In Vancouver the more popular places were on Fourth Avenue. Ottawa had Le Hibou. Calgary had the Dimension. Winnipeg had the Java Shoppe and the Fourth Dimension. Toronto's coffee houses were described by *Maclean's* columnist McKenzie Porter in 1963 as 'cellars and garrets, cluttered with broken furniture, festooned with cobwebs and registered by such Left-Bankish names as the Womb, Dante's Inferno and the Tender Trap.' Porter took readers on a voyeuristic excursion of these new sites of bohemian indulgence:

> The interior of a typical coffee house, the Purple Onion on Avenue Road in Toronto, suggests a Victorian parlor that was blown up by a gas explosion during a whist drive. The customers sit at rickety card tables and look at the remains of a fretwork-fronted upright piano, fragments of bombazine sofas and aspidistra pots, fractured specimens of spelterware and bits of stuffed birds. Beyond the wreckage is a tiny kitchen painted indoor-swimming-pool green, and in the most prominent position is a shaky dais, so littered with microphones, record players and dusty loud-speakers that it looks like the backroom workshop of a bankrupt radio repairman. Yet the Purple Onion is packed every night by patrons between the ages of fifteen and fifty. They enjoy sandwiches and coffee, exchanges of jazz jargon, table hopping and unrestrained flirtation.

At the Purple Onion, Porter took in performances by Eon Henstridge and jazz singer Don Francks backed by guitarist Lenny Breau. Then, at the Fifth Peg, he attended a show by nineteen-year-old folksinger Bob Grossman. Finally, at the Bohemian Embassy, which Dylan had visited and Porter described as 'a dark barn-like room which, save for some interesting abstract paintings and slightly bawdy notices around the walls, resembles the sort of weaving shed in which despots of the industrial revolution chained child labor to the looms,' he encountered a 'Happening,' a semi-spontaneous, participatory, improvised performance that came off as 'a highly bewildering antic.'[40]

The bulk of the Toronto cafes, at least the ones of any notoriety, were in the Yorkville Village, an area nestled between Avenue Road and Bay Street and running a few blocks north of Bloor Street. The 'village' gained prominence for its folk cafes, beat poetry, and old ballads sung by candlelight in rooms with mismatched furniture. Here one could mingle with folkies, bohemians, political activists, and wannabes of various sorts while sharing ideas, music, poetry, and political cacophony. The streets of Yorkville, Nicholas Jennings has written, brought forth 'a strange mixture of scents: rich coffee, pungent marijuana and anxious automobile exhaust.'[41] For those who lived there and those who passed through, it became 'a cultural crossroads, a musical mecca where talented guitarists, singers and songwriters from across Canada gathered.

With its greasy spoons and crash pads, Yorkville was also becoming a haven for drop-outs and draft dodgers, artists and eccentrics, a place where you could work, live and play, largely outside the conventions of straight society.'[42] With its proximity to New York, Yorkville attracted the likes of Tom Rush, Sonny Terry and Brownie McGee, Phil Ochs, Son House, John Lee Hooker, and, notably, Buffy Sainte-Marie, the Saskatchewan-born, Massachusetts-raised, Cree singer-songwriter who followed her undergraduate degree at the University of Massachusetts with a career in Greenwich Village and the influential 1962 release *It's My Way* on Vanguard Records.[43]

Joan Anderson (later Joni Mitchell) would eventually get a big break in New York City thanks to Saint-Marie, but her early years were spent trying to make a name for herself in Canada. Born in Fort Macleod and raised in Saskatoon, Anderson began studying fine art at the Southern Alberta Institute of Technology in the fall of 1963 but ended up spending much of her time performing in the region's coffee houses, notably at the Depression in Calgary and the Yardbird Suite in Edmonton.[44] In 1965 she made the decision to drop out of art school in order to pursue a music career in Toronto. Anderson, initially unable to afford the musicians' union dues, eventually obtained gigs at such venues as the Village Corner, the Purple Onion, the Half Beat, the Penny Farthing, the Underground, the Bohemian Embassy, and the renowned Riverboat, although the Riverboat originally would only hire her as kitchen help. Still, the appearances that she stitched together helped her to land a spot at Mariposa in 1965 alongside Ian and Sylvia. Soon after, she married fellow folksinger Chuck Mitchell, changed her name, and moved to the United States.[45]

Although Yorkville was the focal point of the folk scene, the bars and taverns dotting the downtown core offered overlapping opportunities, particularly for performers who were not so much socialist 'longhairs' as country-influenced balladeers. For Gordon Lightfoot, who combined country and western with folk music, gigs at the working-class Steele's Tavern suited him just as much as those at the folksy Riverboat. By the time Lightfoot began making a name for himself in Toronto, he was already a bit of a veteran: he had performed on the CBC's *Country Hoedown* from 1958 to 1961 (his lack of dancing skills leading to the nickname 'Leadfoot'), was a member of vocal harmony-folk groups the Gino Silvi Singers and the Two Tones, and hosted the 1963–4 season of the British Broadcasting Corporation's *Country and Western Show*. A successful appearance at Mariposa in 1964 ensured that he would not lack opportunities around town. Ian and Sylvia, impressed by Lightfoot, recommended him to their manager Albert Grossman – who also managed Bob Dylan, Joan Baez, and Peter, Paul and Mary –who took him on not as a performer but as a songwriter. Peter, Paul and Mary, among many others, went on to have major hits with Lightfoot's 'That's What You Get (For Lovin' Me)' and 'Early Morning Rain.'[46]

Folk music dominated Yorkville but the scene was far from a purist's dream. Sylvia Tyson has explained that country musicians and other non-folk acts were often unable to afford a backing band and simply performed stripped-down renditions of songs, and people in turn labelled the music as folk. 'Sure, a lot of it was folk-influenced, but they weren't folk per se.'[47] Further, with Yorkville catering not only to folkies but to jazz, blues, country, rock, and R&B, there was a lot of blending. As Ian Tyson explained to *Maclean's* magazine: 'What actually is happening to popular music is that everything's coming together. Jazz, rock, folk, we're all meeting. We listen to each other, we use each other's material, and a lot of guys move back and forth across the different styles.'[48]

Moving across styles was something that Neil Young knew well. Young arrived in Yorkville in the summer of 1965, having travelled from Winnipeg via a stint in Thunder Bay with his British Invasion–era group the Squires. When the remaining band members failed to make a mark in Yorkville under the moniker Four to Go, Young decided to try it on his own as a solo folksinger.[49] When this too failed to pan out, Young accepted an offer to join the Mynah Birds, a band that already had a position in the village. Jennings describes Young's meeting with bassist Bruce Palmer in early 1966: 'Palmer spotted him walking along Yorkville Avenue carrying a guitar and balancing an amp on his head like an African tribeswoman,' the two struck up a conversation, and Palmer invited Young to be the band's new guitarist.[50] Although Young's twelve-string acoustic guitar was much more appropriate for folk than the rock and R&B of the Mynah Birds, he could not turn down the prospect of a paying gig. The group, headed by singer and future 'super freak' Rick James (at that time AWOL from the U.S. Navy) and bankrolled by department store heir John 'Craig' Eaton, was the house band for a venue that was home to an actual mynah bird.[51] 'What a scene,' Young recalled in a 1971 interview. 'There was every vice you can think of. One night while everybody was playing a guy crashed and died. I was using speed. I'd wander around Toronto until three or four in the morning.'[52]

Folk, rock, R&B, and blues came together in a Yorkville scene that offered musicians and bands an opportunity to not only fuse elements together but also reinvent themselves. That was the case for the British Invasion–era Jack London and the Sparrows. In September 1965, Jack London, having fallen out with the other band members after hogging their recording royalties, was replaced by the East Prussia–born Joachim Krauledat, also known as John Kay. With Kay in the band, and shortening their name to the Sparrow, the group shifted from its British Invasion origins – and fake accents – into an amalgam of the blues and rock loved by Kay. He had immigrated to Canada in March 1958, finished school in 1963, and soon after moved to Buffalo with his family before making his way to music scenes in Santa Monica, San Francisco, and Los Angeles. Returning to Toronto in mid-1965, he billed himself as 'John Kay from California' and secured a gig at the Half Beat.[53] It is a testament to Yorkville as a musical crossroads to find a European-born musician using an American moniker and injecting styles picked up in California into a British Invasion–era band in a Canadian city.

By the time Kay arrived in Yorkville, the folk music scene was rather different than the one that had nurtured Ian and Sylvia. A turning point took place in May 1963 with the release of *The Freewheelin' Bob Dylan*, a sophomore album that, instead of reworking established folk songs as was the norm, contained original pieces that challenged the socio-political status quo. Written in the wake of the October 1962 Cuban missile crisis, the album critiqued the military-industrial complex ('Blowin' in the Wind,' 'Masters of War,' 'A Hard Rain's a-Gonna Fall,' and 'Talkin' World War III Blues') and civil rights injustices ('Oxford Town,' written about the riots and deaths that followed the controversial integration of African-American James Meredith into the University of Minnesota). Two months after the release of *The Freewheelin' Bob Dylan*, *Time* reported that

> all over the U.S., folksingers are doing what folksingers are classically supposed to do – sing about current crises. Not since the Civil War era have they done so in such numbers or with such intensity. Instead of keening over the poor old cowpoke who died in the streets of Laredo or chronicling the life cycle of the blue-tailed fly (the sort of thing that fired the great postwar revival of folk song), they are singing with hot-eyed fervor about police dogs and racial murder ... The done-in and dying cowboy has been replaced by victims of racial violence.[54]

Dylan had set a precedent for others to follow. Sylvia Tyson has testified as to how Dylan 'began to write his own music, and that was a revelation to everyone. We began to think, "Hey, we can do that too!"'[55] For Ian Tyson the idea was so remarkable that, the day after hearing 'Blowin' in the Wind,' he penned 'Four Strong Winds,' copying the metaphor from the original song.[56] Joni Mitchell too has credited Dylan for her approach to songwriting: 'Bob Dylan inspired me with the idea of the personal narrative, he'd speak as if to one person in a song ... I mean, nobody had ever written anything like that in song form, you know, such a personal, strong statement, and his influence was to personalize my work, "I feel this for you," or "from you," or "because of you" ... that was the key, okay now this opens all the doors, now we can write about anything.'[57] And it goes without saying that one did not have to be a folkie to appreciate the impact of the album. As Burton Cummings, still in his teenage rock band the Deverons at the time of *The Freewheelin' Bob Dylan*, later explained, 'Dylan, of course, was very important to me – he made it possible for songwriters to work in a completely different dimension.'[58]

Folk music not only took on a contemporary edge but also blended with rock and roll guitar styles into a so-called 'folk rock,' a new genre that thrived on an intellectual desire for political songs and the aural pleasure of rock and roll. Not only would youths use popular music to mediate their gender and group identities as they had with earlier rock and roll, but now, realizing that they were cogs in systems of inequality, economic imperialism, and militaristic aggression, they increasingly did the same with their political identities. Musically, Donovan rocked a hit out of Buffy Sainte-Marie's 'Universal Soldier,' while Barry McGuire put folk lyrics to a rock and roll beat in 'Eve of Destruction.'[59] A listener did not even have to care too much about the politics in order to enjoy folk rock. Historian Jerome L. Rodnitzky has noted how 'teenagers were now dancing the latest steps to the newest folk-rock, topical songs, and listening to equally new and frantic folk-rock groups such as the Byrds ('Turn, Turn, Turn').'[60] Even non-political folk songs attracted such interest, as when We Five reworked Ian and Sylvia's 'You Were On My Mind.'[61]

While folk and folk rock were being used in the West to address the excesses of capitalism and, to some degree, to promote socialist values, in the Soviet Union popular music was being used to critique the excesses of the socialist state. Nikita Khrushchev's move towards de-Stalinization in 1956 led to the freeing of prisoners from Stalin's camps and the rise of songs telling of their struggle. Timothy W. Ryback, a specialist in European cultural and political history, has pointed out that 'at the same time that Joan Baez and Bob Dylan were condemning racism and injustice in coffeehouses across the United States, Soviet-bloc folknics were singing about the crimes of Stalin, the abuses of the Communist leadership, and the shortcomings of the socialist system.'[62]

In Canada, the children who had been weaned on Bill Haley and the Beatles were now politically aware young adults exploring, and becoming anxious about, the world in which they lived. Across the country there was a growth in political activism. When the first batch of Bomarc nuclear warheads came up from the United States to Canada in August 1964, a blockade was established at the air force base in La Marcaza, Quebec, with protesters lying on the road and singing 'We Shall Overcome.'[63] The Combined Universities Campaign for Nuclear Disarmament morphed in 1964 into the Student Union for Peace Action as a major player in the 'new left' politics.[64] In October of the following year, in what was but one of many gatherings on university campuses, the University of Toronto held an International Teach-In that included radio-telephone hookups with over forty Canadian and American university campuses and speeches ranging from those of U.S. state department adviser Adolf Berle to Cambodian cabinet secretary General Phuong Margain.[65] Women's rights movements similarly thrived, not only at universities but also within the working-class labour movement and culminating in the Royal Commission on the Status of Women in 1967.[66] Groups such as the Voice of Women, formed in 1960, brought a feminist edge to political issues. Among its activities was a defiance of militarism and an attempt to overcome the segregation of women along national lines by inviting and touring across Canada with women from Vietnam, Russia, and China.[67] Experiments in communalism and alternative living took hold in such venues as Rochdale College in Toronto where, *Rolling Stone* Canadian correspondent Ritchie Yorke reported, the occupants were keen to undertake such adventures as 'a sympathy bed-in' along with John Lennon and Yoko Ono. 'One student said: "We'd be willing to go even further with a nude-in. We would not only strip our bodies, we would strip our souls."'[68] And, adding much to the feeling of the times, many Canadians opened their homes to American draft dodgers and deserters; as of 1968 there were over twenty supportive organizations, such as the Toronto Anti-Draft Committee and its *Manual for Draft-Age Immigrants to Canada*, to help them become integrated into Canadian life.[69] In the words of Doug Owram, 'here was the most privileged generation in history, in one of the most affluent Canadian economies ever, out to destroy everything that earlier generations had built. Movements rose and fell, and protests erupted instantaneously. Campus life ... seemed a tinder-box of radicalism.'[70]

Youthful critiques of society were accompanied by, and often interwoven into, a Canadian nationalism that emerged by the mid-1960s, fuelled by the belief that foreign economic investment and the importation of cultural and entertainment goods had led to a loss of national sovereignty. A so-called new nationalism, which contained a strong vein of anti-Americanism, flourished as artists, academics, authors, poets, filmmakers, publishers, economists, and others began to critique the concept of continentalism that had apparently tied the country to, and opened it to exploitation by, an American society that was wracked by civil rights protests, the Vietnam conflict, and an aggressive military-industrial complex. Canada, argued nationalists, should be an alternative to the United States, a 'peaceable kingdom' of social equality, multiculturalism, and a welfare state benefiting all citizens.[71] The optimism of the times was buoyed by such events as the adoption of a new national flag in 1965, the 1967 Centennial and Expo 67 celebrations, and the election of Pierre Trudeau in 1968. Authors wrote monographs and edited collections designed to unveil and detail the impact of the United States on Canadian sovereignty, published in large part by nationalistic grassroots presses like Coach House Press and Hurtig Publishers. Artists formed alternative venues to put on Canadian-authored works, particularly those which addressed American imperialism, as in the case of the Factory Theatre Lab's staging of *Branch Plant* and discussion afterwards about the problems of American branch plants. Such groups as the Committee to Strengthen Canadian Culture and Canadian Artists Representation were formed in order to organize protests and rallies in hopes of dislodging Americans from positions in Canadian art galleries and institutions. Filmmakers called on the government to institute quotas in theatres to ensure screen time for domestic films. The Association of Canadian Television and Radio Artists pushed for greater domestic programming in the broadcasting sector. And academics fought for employment opportunities and Canadian content in universities dominated by American professors.[72]

In almost all of the arts and entertainment sectors concerned citizens used their skills to fight on behalf of the new nationalism; this was not the case with folksingers, however. There are several reasons for this. First, many folk musicians viewed themselves as operating outside of national considerations. Gillian Mitchell explains:

As folk revival participant Brian Walsh remarked, when asked if there was a 'distinctly Canadian' quality to the music of Canadian folk musicians, responded [*sic*] that he preferred to consider music as 'the individual's own voice. And I think that's the way to put it – it's the individual artist's own voice. It's not like the Group of Seven. The Group of Seven tried to have the Canadian artistic voice in the early part of the century; now these folks weren't doing that. They were just doing their thing.'[73]

Second, although a lot of folk music offered a sense of community and evoked a romanticized past, sharing with nationalism the celebration of roots, the musicians tended to be ethnically and culturally open and lacking in exclusive connections to national projects. This is not surprising given the fact that political nation-states had placed the world on the brink of destruction in the first place; by no means did folksingers, at least those who felt themselves to be true to the music and lifestyle, want to join in on the side of the 'establishment.' Participants in the movement, Mitchell reveals, 'adhered to a very loose definition of nation which embraced and celebrated many diverse kinds of music and cultures. "Nation" in the folk "boom" was a secondary concern; when defined, it was defined, basically, as a collection of varied peoples whose collective music styles were embraced by the revival.'[74] In Canadian terms, the wide-ranging and eclectic collection of ethnic folksongs on display at folk festivals defied the tendency to slot them into the dominant 'two solitudes' narrative of Canada, thereby requiring and facilitating an inclusiveness broader than that of the national narrative. This was all the more so given that, for their part, hootenanny tunes like 'She'll Be Coming 'round the Mountain,' 'He's Got the Whole World in His Hands,' 'Barbara Allen,' and even the politically charged 'We Shall Overcome' offered little to a civic nationalism concerned with foreign economic investment and a lack of opportunities for domestic cultural producers.

Further, in terms of material resources, a domestic music industry did not exist that could support, to what little extent they may have existed, the authors of original works that addressed contemporary issues. The lack of airtime and recording opportunities for the most part inhibited the ability to sustain, or even establish, careers and contributed to an exodus to the United States at the time that the new nationalism was just getting underway. Simply put, Canada lacked the necessary recording industry infrastructure and domestic airplay for a musical component of the new nationalism. It was the case for folkies and rockers alike. Ian and Sylvia were among the first of the Yorkville generation to leave, moving to New York City in 1961. Then, in the middle of the decade, there was a rapid succession of songwriters who would go on to make a significant contribution in the United States. Robbie Robertson and his bandmates in the Hawks left in September 1965, picked up by Bob Dylan as his backing band for his infamous electrified tour. That same year Joni Mitchell and her new husband Chuck moved to Detroit (by 1967 she would be single and living in New York City before making her way to California arm in arm with David Crosby). Neil Young and Bruce Palmer piled their gear into a hearse and departed for California in March 1966. In the summer of that same year the Sparrow, fronted by John Kay, relocated to New York City, although they only stayed for a few months before moving to Los Angeles and being reinvented as Steppenwolf. And these were only but a few of a generational musical exodus that included the likes of Denny Doherty, Zal Yanovsky, and Leonard Cohen.

With few opportunities for a career in Canada, performers found that they had little choice but to emigrate to the industry hubs in the United States. Much of the reason for this rests with radio stations, gatekeepers of the airwaves that to a large degree defined popular music. Station programmers do not simply play popular songs so much as they make songs popular; they select the tracks to air and through repetition create a familiarity that creates hits. As Bob McAdorey, CHUM's most influential disc jockey, noted in a July 1966 interview, 'if CHUM was playing the record a group could sing "God Save the Queen" and the kids would buy it.'[75] Even after Ian Tyson was well known across the continent with a number of commercial radio hits, he still felt it necessary to go to CHUM and promote his latest album. 'Bob McAdorey is Mr. Music in Canada,' he explained to *Maclean's* in February of 1968. 'When Sylvia and I made *Lovin' Feeling* early last year, I took the first tape to McAdorey because I know if he plays a song, every rock station from Newfoundland to the Rockies will fall in line.'[76]

Despite the fact that stations are granted privileged access to the publicly owned airwaves and governed by a Broadcasting Act that requires the promotion of domestic programming, station owners are not patriots but business people and have little economic reason to air untested domestic recordings. It makes no business sense to give airtime to unproven singles when there are many profit-proven albums in the American market. Simply stating a responsibility, as the Broadcasting Act did in this period before Canadian content regulations, was not enough to motivate stations. Disc jockey John Loweth of CHNO-Sudbury admitted this reality in an interview with the *Toronto Telegram* in July 1967: 'Ninety percent of Canadian radio stations refuse to play an unproven record, whether it's from Czechoslovakia or Tillsonburg. They don't feel they have an obligation to prove themselves heroes.'[77] Or, as disc jockey Tom Fulton of Top 40 station CKFH-AM Toronto stated that same summer, 'One region will not try another region's talent. Sure, they'll play the monster hits from another area, but they won't take a chance on the unknowns.'[78] Money, not patriotism or even a legislated responsibility, determined the operations of radio broadcasting and in turn the state of the music industry as a whole.

Radio, although not the sole source of shaping public taste for music at this time, was the most important, all the more so because of the lack of other outlets. Academics Bart Testa and Jim Shedden have noted that

> first, in general, radio is historically rock's premier delivery system. Second, radio has played an even more critical role in Canadian rock, often a matter of life and death for basic economic reasons. The population of Canada is so small and distances between population centres so great that musicians must generate a market base for record sales quickly to support concert tours, which by themselves cannot usually sustain even a low-cost rock outfit. Until very recently, in the absence of secondary supports, like a viable rock press or television exposure, radio was the only medium available to Canadian bands.[79]

This lack of support from other outlets frustrated music journalist Ritchie Yorke, an Australian who immigrated to Canada in 1967 and became one of the most ardent proponents of a domestic music scene. In his 1971 book *Axes, Chops, and Hot Licks: The Canadian Music Scene*, Yorke complained that

> many newspapers employed rock writers on a freelance basis, dropping a vague story or two into the weekend entertainment sections as an ad hoc method of covering all potential age groups, even young people. These writers, with very few exceptions such as Dave Bist of the *Montreal Gazette*, and Jim Smith of the *Hamilton Spectator*, either didn't appreciate Canadian music or were overwhelmed by U.S. chart domination. If any of these journalists had built up any sort of a readership with Canadian youth and had seen potential in Canadian music, the chances were good that they could have stirred up a lot of interest in local talent.[80]

Gordon Lightfoot used an interview with *Maclean's* in 1971 to similarly complain about this problem. 'I *do* this country. I go to the Maritimes. The money isn't that good, man. And it's hard to get there. The concerts are packed. The local paper sends no one, *no* one to cover the concert. That turns me off. The sounds are going down. There's good times, *good*. It should be covered. Don't take me for granted.'[81] Although the *Toronto Telegram*'s 'After Four' section catered to the musical interests of teeny-boppers, this was a far distance from serious, or even significantly pro-motional, journalism.

Joni Mitchell has not surprisingly identified the lack of airtime and exposure as a key reason for her departure. In a 1971 interview with Yorke, she opined that 'the masses receive their information through American newspapers, magazines, radio and television. In Canada, there were only three major centres – Vancouver, Toronto and Montreal – and that's just not enough publicity. Exposure is vital to success. Nightclub owners wouldn't hire you unless you had a name to guarantee a full house. So I packed my bags and went where I could get a name.'[82] Like-wise, as Neil Young recalled in a 1975 interview with Cameron Crowe of *Rolling Stone*, 'I couldn't wait to get out of there because I knew my only chance to be heard was in the United States.'[83] Or, as he told biographer Jimmy McDonough, 'first I wanted to quit school and go to L.A. Then I modified my plan – quit school, go to Toronto. I thought that if I made it in Toronto, it would be easier to make it in L.A. So I went to Toronto and I couldn't make it. So I said, "Fuck Toronto – I'll go to L.A. and make it. If I make it in Toronto, all I am is big in Toronto. If I go to L.A. and make it, then I'm big in the fuckin' WORLD." Then I'm talkin' to more people – I got a bigger audience, and an audience is where it's at.'[84]

The few prominent songwriters who remained in Canada did little to engage in the new nationalism or advocate on the behalf of the nation. The biggest name in English-language folk music still around at the time of the new nationalism was Gordon Lightfoot, his ability to live in Canada made possible by American management that ensured touring opportunities and songwriting royalties. Yet, despite having significant access to the airwaves, Lightfoot had no interest in political issues – Canadian, American, or otherwise. Although Lightfoot would often draw inspiration from newspaper and magazine stories, he thrived by feeling a personal connection to the subject matter, and politics rarely crossed into his sphere. 'Everything I've written,' he explained in a 1966 interview with the *Globe and Mail*, 'has come from something that's hap-pened to me, something I've seen, something that's impressed me. Take a song like "Talkin' High Steel." I spent some time with the high-riggers at the Toronto Dominion Centre. They were on about the 48th floor at that time. Anyway, I got to know them, I got to understand what they're

all about, how they think, so I could write about them.'[85] The lack of
songs dealing with civil rights and militarism, the newspaper noted, was
because 'Selma, Alabama and the war in Vietnam are outside his orbit.'[86]
Although he penned 'Black Day in July,' about the racially fuelled riot in
Detroit in 1967, this was influenced by his experiences in the city and the
tensions that led to the riots, not by a desire to be a political or protest
songwriter. As he later explained, 'I felt it was kind of silly for me to write
protest songs, being a Canadian. After all, people could say, "What the
hell is a Canadian doing protesting against an American problem?" It's
tantamount to cashing in on a sensitive American situation.'[87]

Although as a Canadian he could have easily commented on domestic
issues, these too were outside of his orbit. Lightfoot was, at root, apolitical and uninterested in dealing with nationalism. What did attract
him was commercial success, women, and alcohol. By 1968, at the age
of twenty-eight, he had built himself a small empire taking in approximately a quarter of a million dollars a year, a lot of it from songwriting
royalties (by the mid-1970s his income had increased to almost half a
million dollars a year in songwriting royalties alone).[88] He chose to live in
a seventeen-room house in Toronto's Rosedale neighbourhood among
the nouveau riche, not with the folkies and beatniks on Queen Street
or in a Yorkville communal house.[89] This was not a bohemian, activist,
or nationalist, but a businessman and songwriter who kept tight control
over his media image and binged on women and drink. Tom Hopkins
of *Maclean's* was not off the mark in noting that 'offstage, the stories of
depressions, hard wenching and even harder drinking are endemic …
There is hardly a veteran fan in the vast legion who has not been physically stung in the middle of a concert or a club appearance by a petulant
Gordon Lightfoot obscenity flung at a hapless sound man or been hurt
by a disparaging comment when a cherished early tune is shouted out
in request.'[90] Although Lightfoot would go on to temper his relationship
with alcohol and infidelity, his early career is rife with difficulties and
struggles. Making light of his lifestyle in a 1976 interview with *Maclean's*,
Lightfoot talked of how he was 'a good Canadian drinker. I've been
drinkin' a bottle a day [of Canadian Club] for the last three years.'[91]

Lightfoot's lifestyle and interests came across in his song topics. One
needs to keep in mind that the highly praised 'Canadian Railroad Trilogy' was not an act of nationalistic prerogative but a made-to-order song
about the railway commissioned by the Canadian Broadcasting Corporation for *100 Years Young*, a television special celebrating the Canadian
centennial. For this song Lightfoot took the triptych framework used

by Bob Gibson in the similarly historical 'Civil War Trilogy,' going so far as to use a parallel name (including use of the American 'railroad' rather than Canadian 'railway'). His other hits from the era, the ones that he chose to write of his own volition, are much more indicative of a commercial imperative seeped in a lifestyle of rough living, booze, and women. 'That's What You Get (For Lovin' Me)' tells of using women and leaving them broken-hearted with no regrets or intent to stop. 'I'm Not Sayin'' similarly presents a man with no qualms as to cheating on someone who loves him. 'Go Go Round' tells of a girl who falls for a charming man at a go-go club only to end up mistreated. And 'Early Morning Rain' expresses a sad state of impoverished travel and homesickness made bright only by whisky and fast women.[92]

Yet authorial intent is not a prerequisite for music to act as a catalyst for national identity. In the case of Lightfoot, it was not necessary for him to become involved in nationalist issues in order for his songs to act as a rallying point. It was not simply that Lightfoot was tremendously popular and respected abroad, although that certainly helped. It was the ability of Canadians to read into his songs Canada as they wished to see it. In other words, Lightfoot's tie to nationhood came about by the ways in which his songs contained elements that were already thought of as being quintessentially Canadian rather than addressing issues of nationalist concern. Lightfoot's penchant for songs related to wilderness, train travel, and a general sense of spaciousness, elements that were entrenched in the national myth-symbol complex, left him open to being read as a channeller of what it means to be Canadian. These themes are found in the likes of 'Early Morning Rain,' 'Steel Rail Blues,' 'Sixteen Miles (To Seven Lakes),' 'Changes,' 'Peaceful Waters,' 'Long River,' and 'The Way I Feel,' all of which appeared on his 1966 debut album *Lightfoot*. Such songs countered post–Second World War urban and suburban expansion, and the growing distance and alienation from agricultural and 'small town' life it entailed, if only within one's imagination. Daniel Francis, author of *National Dreams: Myth, Memory, and Canadian History*, has noted that Canadians commonly turn to nature as something 'our own,' its strength and appeal being that it 'imparts to us a unique set of characteristics,' as opposed to Canadian cities, which are 'indistinguishable from cities anywhere.'[93] As Francis notes about Canadians' imagined connection to 'the North,' few have actually travelled there, and for most people it exists as 'a north of the mind.'[94] That many of Lightfoot's songs were hits south of the border is telling of their universality or, at the very least, a shared North American romanticized anti-modernism and connection to rurality, land, and a pioneering spirit.

Further along these lines, there is nothing inherent in Lightfoot's 'Black Day in July' to identify the song as being penned by a Canadian, but knowledge of the author's citizenship allows the song to be used as a means of reinforcing national dichotomies; the author's citizenship, not the song's lyrics, allows it to become a commentary of 'us' observing 'them.' 'Black Day in July' certainly took on such an interpretation for Gordon Sinclair of the Tragically Hip, who, as a fourth-year history student at Queen's University, wrote a paper on the song. This application of a nationalist prerogative upon the song is made clear in Sinclair's description as to 'the images he evokes from literally across the river; you're watching Detroit burn – I always loved the concept that here, literally a stone's throw away, while we have tons of social problems that are uniquely Canadian, that we don't have this one, clearly nagging, monstrous problem that the United States have.'[95]

More generally in terms of folk music and Canadian identity, there is also something to be said about the genre attracting those who seek to identify an 'authentic' Canadian music. Softer vocal deliveries and instrumental choices can be easily connected to the 'prairies' and 'open landscapes' and act as evidence of Canadians as kind, gentle, and in tune with nature (juxtaposed against 'brash' and 'loud' Americans). 'Vague as it is,' Gillian Mitchell noted in her survey of folk music in Canada and the United States, 'the notion that folk music provides the best mouthpiece for the Canadian experience, born during the period of Centennial nationalism, has persisted even to this day.'[96]

By offering commercial songs that could be identified with popular conceptions of what it meant to be Canadian, Lightfoot reified an idea of Canada and set himself up for being identified as a 'voice' of the nation.[97] There is a truth to singer-songwriter Matthew Good's assertion that 'Lightfoot is the Emily Carr of Canadian songwriting,' insofar as Canadians have vested national value within the work of Lightfoot and Carr based on the production of goods tied to a naturalness popularly deemed essentialistically Canadian.[98] Lighfoot's status as a national bard was affirmed in 1970, when he became the first English-speaking 'popular' musician to be awarded the Order of Canada.[99] 'How it's explained I can't recall exactly, but it's for a general contribution to the overall good of the country,' he remarked about the award to the *Canadian Composer* in the fall of 1970.[100]

Whereas folk music and nationalism in English-speaking Canada had a tenuous relationship at best, as of the early 1960s Québécois chansonniers (folksingers) like Félix Leclerc, Gilles Vigneault, Raymond Lévesque, Pauline Julien, and Claude Léveillée had been actively using chansons (folk songs) to contribute to their community's dream of nation, supported not only by audiences but venue owners, record labels, and radio and other media outlets. The Québécois were years ahead of English-speaking Canadians in turning to and treating musicians and their songs as ideologically national. Chansonniers had a privileged position and respectability, owing much to the 'genuineness' and 'authenticity' read into songs of the folk idiom, a position denied to participants in such 'pop' genres as yé-yé (the fusion of American and British rock and roll discussed in the previous chapter). French studies and communications expert Robert Giroux has noted that chansonniers differ from their yé-yé (pop music) peers not simply in style but also in topics and interests, with chansonniers often using songs about nature, land, and habitant lifestyles to explore issues of identity and freedom among individuals and the collective.[101] The political climate in Quebec made possible a tremendous cultural contribution by chansonniers as purveyors of what it meant to be Québécois.

Quebec had a long tradition of chansonniers, although before the 1960s they were a relatively small part of the music industry, often having to first achieve acclaim in France. Chansonnier Gilles Vigneault, in a 1974 interview with *Canadian Composer*, reflected on how a change in the political climate in Quebec led to the rise of the chansonnier:

> The mass of Quebeckers wasn't ready [previous to the 1960s] to recognize itself in la chanson. It does today, in Félix Leclerc, but we had to make this enormous mistake of asking Paris for its seal of approval – that ultimate alienation – for us to decide, finally, to consecrate our own chansonniers, ourselves. That was in 1960, when I, along with a lot of others, came on the scene, but it wasn't my doing. It coincided with an election that opened a lot of doors, that opened up the floodgates. That was … the time of de-Duplessification that started the big thaw, a sort of great awakening, when we decided to recognize everything and everyone, and give letters of credit to our own people. The chansonnier phenomenon wouldn't make any sense at all if there hadn't been a political upheaval.[102]

Vigneault was speaking of the provincial election of 1960 in which the Liberal Party, led by Jean Lesage, replaced the Union Nationale government of Maurice Duplessis and marked the start of the Quiet Revolution. Duplessis's premiership, characterized by political corruption and Catholic conservatism, was followed by an overhauling of Quebec society that saw the decline of Catholicism, the provincialization of resources and industries (including hydro-electricity), and an anti-British sentiment most violently undertaken by the loosely knit Front de Libération du Québec (FLQ). Anti-British sentiment was strong enough that Paul McCartney, set to perform with the Beatles in Montreal on 8 September 1964, worried that the concert might be a target.[103] (Interestingly, the Beatles shared the cover of the *Toronto Telegram* that day with the article 'Separatists Burn Flags').[104]

Beatlemania and the yé-yé fad helped youths to swing their hips, but the chansonniers offered an affirmation of Québécois nationhood. Félix Leclerc has recalled how 'for me, Quebec used to be like a huge black mountain. And then I lit a small fire with my songs, in my way, in my corner. Vigneault lit another fire with Natashquan in his corner of the mountain, [Jean-Pierre] Ferland with Pleine Ville lit his small light, Claude Gauthier, his ... and small fires were lit all over Quebec. The people felt that something was happening.'[105] The 'fire' lit by Vigneault most famously includes 'Mon Pays,' a song that Pierre Nadeau of *L'Actualité* has called 'un hymne national pour un Québec souverain.'[106] 'Mon Pays' had its roots in a National Film Board production cast in wintertime, the lyrics fitting with the Québécois habitant legacy strongly situated within the Québécois myth-symbol complex and manifested in such works as the paintings of Cornelius Krieghoff and Claude Jutra's classic Québécois coming-of-age film *Mon oncle Antoine*. For his part, Vigneault has attempted to downplay his position within the movement, although such modesty should not be taken as fact.

The power of the chansonnier was enhanced by their ability to engage with audiences in live music venues; communalism thrived within the walls of cafes and clubs. Among the more notable was Le Patriote on St Catherine Street East. 'You had to be crazy, back in the Quebec of 1964, to baptize a club "Le Patriote,"' journalist Georges-Hébert Germain of *La Presse* and contributor to the *Canadian Composer* noted a decade after the club had been founded. But, as Yves Blais, co-founder and director of Le Patriote explained to Germain, 'we did want our independentist and nationalist ideals to be made perfectly clear. What we were interested in was to help Quebec culture bloom, to find an identity for ourselves, and to express ourselves. We chose these means, rather than weapons and violence, to help bring about the revolution.'[107] By the end of the 1960s, Blais and like-minded venue owners were valuable members of the push for Québécois nationhood in an increasingly polarized country. Blais told *Maclean's* in 1969 that, as a venue owner, 'we couldn't have Lightfoot here. Nobody would come. You have your own places.'[108]

Popular media also made a significant contribution to the idea of a Québécois nation and helped performers make a living at their craft. For Ritchie Yorke, the rest of Canada had much to learn from Quebec's support of its artists, as he told *Canadian Composer* in 1976: 'Take a look at Quebec. People will tell you that it's the language situation, but it's not just that; it's a whole attitude of caring about who they are. We need everything they have, and we need it here in the rest of Canada: television that promotes Canadian artists, newspapers and magazines that continually stress Canadian performers, a media that believes.'[109]

Québécois patriotism and a sense of isolation made the rise of the chansonnier all the more powerful. *Maclean's* staff writer Jon Ruddy, although being overly dramatic, was not totally off the mark in telling readers in June 1969 that 'the chansonniers have been leading the province Pied Piper–like towards separation because we have never given a damn about them.'[110] This sentiment extended to the performers themselves, national icons to the Québécois yet overlooked or ignored by the rest of Canada. An anonymous letter to the editors of *Maclean's* in early 1969 made this point clear: '[French-speaking performer Robert] Charlebois is so damned talented, yet his French-Canadianism automatically disqualifies him from becoming a personality in the rest of Canada. You have to explode a bomb or spit on the Queen of England for English Canadians to recognize you.'[111] Such animosity makes clear that the divide was about more than mere disinterest. Many Québécois had a valid sense of being subjected to hostility, both in Quebec, with its powerful English-speaking business interests, and outside the province, with talk of the 'Quebec problem.' Pierre Trudeau, after all, had come to power in the 1968 federal election as someone, many voters hoped, who would put Quebec in its place. Chansonnier Tex Lecor has identified such hostility and discrimination as being at the root of his own support for a separate Québécois state: 'I have hitchhiked all over Canada,' Lecor explained. 'I love the plains and the Rockies and I know our country is more beautiful than France or Sweden. I stood at Lake Louise and I thought, "I don't want to be a separatist. This is my country." But people put you down. In Hamilton I was talking French to a friend in a bar and they said, "If you can't talk so we can understand you, get out." And it wasn't my country any more.'[112]

'Song for Canada,' written by Ian Tyson and famed reporter and person-ality Peter Gzowski, stands out as an anomaly in the field of folk song, a commentary by a commercially successful performer on an issue of national pertinence. The lyrics, a call for national unity subtly framed as a torn but supportive relationship between two people, suited the times but ended up being, both then and now, largely overlooked (it is per-haps best known for its inclusion on Bob Dylan and the Band's 1967 *Basement Tapes* bootleg).

Tyson, as discussed in the next chapter, did not see himself as a politi-cal songwriter. He spoke openly of his political apathy and in later life went on to decry Pierre Trudeau's bilingual policy and federal attempts to incorporate French-speaking Canadians into national life, sharing with many other western Canadians a frustration at what was seen as a Liberal policy of appeasement if not favouritism. Perhaps the audience reactions to this song played a role in ensuring that Tyson did not make any more attempts to address national problems. 'We've sung "Song for Canada" in Canada four times and we've gotten four weird reactions,' Tyson told *Maclean's* in the summer of 1965 from Ian and Sylvia's home base of Greenwich Village:

> The first time was last winter at Massey Hall in Toronto. I introduced it wrong and gave the impression that the song was a kind of 'Spring Thaw' satire. The audience laughed at first, but then they listened and by the end they were taking it very seriously. We sang it at the University of Ottawa where the kids were half English and half French and afterwards the French kids came on very strong. They told us, 'Thanks, but you're five years too late.' The audience at McGill were all English and they had to be the squar-est audience we've ever played. I came away figuring that a lot of the trouble in Quebec is that all the hip people of Montreal are French. We sang the song at a Liberal Party dinner in Toronto and the politicians there were puzzled. Man, they didn't know how to react. They kept looking at [prime minister] Lester [B. Pearson] and he kept looking at his watch.
>
> At first when we did 'Song for Canada' in the U.S., I used to try to explain a little of the background to the song, but I don't anymore. Now I just say, here's a song about Canada. They've got too many of their own problems down here. I mean, they're uptight over Vietnam and the South.[113]

'Song for Canada' was an abnormality not only for Tyson but for Eng-lish-speaking songwriters as a whole. Despite the tremendous nationalism permeating Canada by the mid-1960s, there was little in the way of music that addressed national issues. Canada possessed the requisite audiences, as the fervour of nationalist activity in other sectors displayed, but lacked an industry and career opportunities; an exodus of talented songwriters occurred during the years in which the new nationalism was starting to gain momentum. By the mid-1960s it was more than common for musicians to be drawn to Yorkville only to treat it as a stopover to meet others, mingle in the clubs and share songs, and then leave in favour of resources in the United States. Once south of the border, many of them went on to address the issues of their times alongside like-minded American songwriters. With few folk songs, and even fewer songwriters, to be turned to as rallying points, the music offered at most a minor means for emboldening the nation.

Québécois nationalists were years ahead of their English-speaking counterparts when it came to mediating a national sense of self through popular music, with folksinger-songwriters on the ground floor of a musical empowerment that celebrated and romanticized the past while laying a blueprint for the future. Félix Leclerc and Gilles Vigneault, among others, offered audiences comfortable, sentimental, anti-modern songs that offered not only a shared sense of heritage, but, in linking the past to the present, a path to political sovereignty as a Québécois people and nation. Tyson's 'Song for Canada' was not about to change anything.

4

'California Dreamin'': Why Canadian Musicians Were Not 'Helpless' in the United States, 1965–1970

Personally, I regret very much that I can't go ahead and join up with people like Leonard Cohen, Gordon Lightfoot, Joni Mitchell. Many of those people had to go to the States to make a name for themselves, to get their letters of credit, in the same way that Félix Leclerc, the first chansonnier (who started it all here), had to go to Paris for his reference letters before he was permitted to sing about his own country.

– Gilles Vigneault, 1974[1]

I talk about American cities, about Paris, about Greece, I talk about the places where I am.

– Joni Mitchell, 1974[2]

Quoi? Il est canadien? Moi, je pensais qu'il était américain.

– An attendee at a Leonard Cohen performance in Paris, 1969[3]

'Those songs,' observed Ralph J. Gleason of *Rolling Stone* in reviewing a show by the Band in May 1969, 'are part of the American heritage now as much as any others and the audience, even on Thursday night, knew them so well they sang along with "The Weight."'[4] Robbie Robertson, Levon Helm, Rick Danko, Richard Manuel, and Garth Hudson had, with the recent release of *Music from Big Pink*, spoken for a generation:

The truth is that this is a remarkable, deeply important group of artists whose music is now firmly imbedded in the American consciousness, the fruits of which are yet to be seen. Somehow, four Canadians and an Arkansas country boy … found it in themselves to express part of where all of us are at now while expressing where they are at themselves in language and metaphor that can ignite explosive trains of thought inside your head.[5]

The Band, nestled away in New York State, embraced an idea of America at a time when that country's youths had rejected America in favour of, as Joni Mitchell voiced in 'Woodstock,' getting 'back to the garden.' Now the Band stepped in and articulated a return to romanticized, salt-of-the-earth values, leading the way for a disillusioned, and aging, generation to deal with the excesses of the 1960s youthquake. For Greil Marcus, famed music critic and author of the seminal *Mystery Train*, the reason for the Band's appeal was clear:

> Many young Americans had spent the best part of the decade teaching themselves to feel like exiles in their own country; the Band, particularly songwriters Robbie Robertson and Richard Manuel, understood this, and were sure it was a mistake. They had come here by choice, after all. They had fallen in love with the music, first as they sought it out on the radio and on records, later as they learned to play it, and, wonder of wonders, define it. Coming out of Canada into the land that had kicked up the blues, jazz, church music, country and western, and a score of authentic rock 'n' roll heroes, they fell in love with the place itself.
>
> They felt more alive in America. They came to be on good terms with its violence and its warmth; they were attracted by the neon grab for pleasure on the face of the American night, and by the inscrutable spookiness behind that face. American contradictions demanded a fine energy, because no one could miss them; the stakes were higher, but the rewards seemed limitless. The Band's first songs were a subtle, seductive attempt to get this sense of life across. Their music was fashioned as a way back into America, and it worked.[6]

The Band made themselves members of America as they imagined it and, in doing so, invited back a generation that had walked away from the nation in favour of alternative communities found in such locales as Greenwich Village in New York City and, especially as of the mid-1960s, sunny California. Greenwich Village was the hub of the American folk music scene attracting, much like Yorkville in Toronto, like-minded people who shared a thirst for the folk ideology as well as those with professional music aspirations. Beatniks, folkies, and various hangers-on came to the scene, checked out the offerings of the Folklore Centre, caught performances at Cafe Wha? and Gerde's Folk City, and gathered at Washington Square, where performers shared songs and busked for pocket change. Their presence as outsiders drew scorn from many local inhabitants, however, and police harassment at the cafes and Washington Square, justified as crackdowns on those who performed without a licence, created a sense of community among the participants.[7]

Greenwich Village, like Yorkville, was carved out as an alternative to the mainstream by laying claim to territory and asserting difference through dress, song and dance, and idealized, egalitarian values. The 'villages' were made all the more autonomous through a combination of ideology and sustainability that allowed their participants to live, literally, in a village.[8] According to Gillian Mitchell, Greenwich Village and Yorkville

> represented an attempt to manifest the myth of utopia in daily life. Both districts became residential centres for artists, musicians and refugees from conventional society, and developed distinct identities as alternative, 'beloved communities' of young people linked by their ideals and their love of the contemporary arts and music; and, at least for the first half of the 1960s, folk revival music was at the artistic and ideological centre of the utopian experiment.[9]

To live in one of the villages was to experience an empowered communalism that made possible ways of life otherwise shunned by mainstream society.

For Ian and Sylvia Tyson, the decision to move to Greenwich Village in 1961 was not so much ideological as it was professional. As Sylvia later told *Chatelaine*, it was 'a natural thing – New York was where the action was.'[10] The city did not fail to live up to expectations with its abundant music venues, high-profile management, and record labels. By the following year they had signed with Albert Grossman, co-founder of the Newport Folk Festival and manager of Bob Gibson, Bob Dylan, and Peter, Paul and Mary, among others, and recorded *Ian and Sylvia* on the revered folk label Vanguard Records, a debut album of established folk, ballad, and spiritual songs. Their follow-up, *Four Strong Winds*, released that same year, also consisted of traditional songs with the exception of the title track and a cover of Dylan's 'Tomorrow Is a Long Time.'

The duo had little interest in the village's political ideas, and, when folk music took on a more political role following the release of *The Freewheelin' Bob Dylan*, they found themselves increasingly out of sorts. 'There was a pressure on us to write or perform political songs,' Ian explained in his autobiography *I Never Sold My Saddle*:

> We were almost ostracized for not doing political stuff, anti-Vietnam stuff.

I was almost non-political in those days ... I just didn't relate then. In true
cowboy fashion I just didn't relate, and it got us shut out of a lot of stuff. We
did one tour in 1964 for Lady Bird Johnson with Faron Young of all people.
It was a lot of fun ... We were living in the States, and I had a draft card, and
I guess I would have gone, but I was 4-F because of the shattered ankle. I just
had no concept of what Vietnam was.[11]

The situation was a bit more complex for Sylvia because she had dual
citizenship.[12]

Four Strong Winds was the pinnacle of their career in Greenwich Village,
and they had enough commercial success with 'Four Strong Winds,' 'You
Were On My Mind,' and 'Some Day Soon' to ensure a steady income of
royalties. 'Even when we started trailing off, I wasn't hurting,' Ian has
explained. 'I got the first big "Four Strong Winds" check some time in
1963, and I went out and bought a big cattle farm east of Toronto. No
one had a real big hit with the song, but everybody covered it.'[13] Then,
when Judy Collins had a hit with 'Some Day Soon,' Ian increased the
size of his ranch, the number of cattle, and the amount of time spent
living his dream as a rancher.[14] With their position in Greenwich Village
slipping, Ian and Sylvia returned to Canada and, when not spending
time on the ranch, bought a home in Toronto's posh Rosedale neighbourhood. Although Ian would return to the United States to record
in Nashville and considered the possibility of being a rancher in Texas,
a drug bust kept him out of the United States long enough for him to
establish roots in Alberta.[15] Still, as recently as his 1994 autobiography,
Ian talked of leaving Canada behind for the lifestyle and music industry
offered in Nashville. 'I've put as much into Canadian music as I've taken
out,' Tyson opined with characteristic bravado. 'Maybe more. So I don't
owe anything. And that's why I can go to Nashville and maybe never
come back.'[16]

Greenwich Village's folksy heyday spanned from the late 1950s until
the early to mid-1960s, by which point the community had become a
stopover for aspiring acts who were lured by talk of vibrant communities and better weather in California, particularly Haight-Ashbury in
San Francisco, the Sunset Strip in Los Angeles, and the city of Berkeley,
home to a campus of the University of California. The 'golden state'
had been idealized at the turn of the 1960s as a teenage playground of
beach blanket bingo, surfboards, and hot rods, but by mid-decade it had
become home to alternative lifestyle enthusiasts. 'Counterculture hippies emerged on the horizon, a wide cultural leap from Mouseketeers,

Gidget, and the Beach Boys,' as Krise Granat May describes in *Golden State, Golden Youth.* 'The hippies shared attributes of the Beats but broadened their influence. Modeling a "counterculture," played out in defiance of earlier images, the hippies represented mainstream America's worst fears: sexual freedom, dangerous rock and roll, and drug use.'[17]

Berkeley, situated not too far from San Francisco and Los Angeles, became a hotbed of radicalism thanks to the University of California. The university attracted international attention in 1964 when the Free Speech Movement called upon administrators to allow unrestricted political discussions on campus. The following year the campus was immobilized by a massive sit-in.[18] Activism spread throughout the city as optimistic youths sought to create a utopia. The Berkeley Liberation Program, one of its pamphlets explained, was willing to go to forceful ends to bring this about. 'The people of Berkeley must arm themselves and learn the basic skills and tactics of self-defense and street-fighting ... We will expand and protect our drug culture ... We will break the power of the landlord and provide beautiful living for everyone ... We will create a soulful Socialism in Berkeley.'[19] Land appropriation for the betterment of their utopia included getting 'back to the garden,' rather literally, with the seizing of a vacant university-owned lot that was then turned into the 'People's Park,' a combination of garden, park, and community hub.[20]

Denny Doherty, formerly of Halifax, Nova Scotia, helped to establish California as the place to be. Like a plethora of other musicians, Doherty arrived in California after a stint in New York City, his earlier attempts at rock music in Montreal and Toronto having led him to a partnership with guitarist Zal Yanovsky in the folksy Halifax Three, a group that, despite a deal signed with Columbia Records, fell apart. The two ended up in Greenwich Village, where they met Cass Elliot of the Big Three and formed the Mugwumps before splitting up, although Doherty and his friends John and Michelle Phillips of the Journeymen would convene with Cass in California and form the Mamas and the Papas. Their 1965 song 'California Dreamin'' was a continental hit and acted as an invitation for like-minded youths seeking music, freedom, drugs, and a warm climate.[21] 'They managed to exemplify an image of California hippiedom to millions of buyers,' Nathan Rubin has pointed out.[22] Yanovsky, now with John Sebastian in the folk-jug band the Lovin' Spoonful, further contributed to the feel of the times with their single 'Do You Believe In Magic?' Peter Gzowski, in a 1966 article for *Maclean's*, singled out the Lovin' Spoonful as 'one group that typifies the New Music ... They are not nearly as poetic as Dylan and not nearly as crass as Bill Haley; they make, with their rock-and-roll, amplified instruments, one of the most vital, joyous, pleasant sounds I heard.'[23] Yanovsky's stature came to an end in 1967 when he was arrested for marijuana possession; he avoided jail time and returned to Canada.[24]

Few southern California–based songwriters had as much success within the youth movement as did Neil Young. In the late 1960s, Young began his legacy of engaging in American society, bringing others along with him through his music. Academic William Echard, author of *Neil Young and the Poetics of Energy*, has noted that a 'constant yet often subtle remobilization of Americana was one factor placing Young among artists like the Band and Bob Dylan, who made American histories and identities a key part of their work. By contrast, despite his early years as a Canadian and occasionally passing reference to Canadian places, Canadian identity has never been a central theme in Young's work.'[25] Young and bassist Bruce Palmer had said goodbye to Canada in February 1966; following the break up of the Yorkville-based Mynah Birds, they sold some of the band's gear to buy a hearse and head towards Los Angeles. Unlike many others, the duo travelled to southern California without first stopping over in New York City, as Young intended to visit Stephen Stills (the two met when their earlier bands – the Squires and the Company – performed in Fort William, Ontario). It just so happened that Young had also owned a hearse when he was in Fort William, and it was the sight of this rather rare vehicle with Ontario licence plates crawling along Sunset Boulevard (soon after Young had arrived in the city) that caught the attention of Stills and Richie Furay. An impromptu reunion was held in a parking lot and the celebration of good luck turned into talk of music and the decision to form a group. Initially toying with the name the Herd, they instead opted to go with a moniker seen adorning the side of a steamroller parked outside of where Furay was staying: the Buffalo Springfield Roller Company.[26] Another Canadian, drummer Dewey Martin, was soon brought on board, with the group now made up of three Canadians and two Americans. Buffalo Springfield made its first appearance in early April and then scored a house gig at the Whisky a Go Go on the Sunset Strip from the start of May until mid-June.[27] Before disbanding a couple of years later, Buffalo Springfield released such Young-penned tracks as 'Nowadays Clancy Can't Even Sing,' 'Mr. Soul,' 'Broken Arrow,' and 'Flying on the Ground Is Wrong,' as well as Stills's seminal 'For What It's Worth,' written in the wake of a riot between the police and club-goers on the Sunset Strip.[28]

Young too would express outrage at a moment of violence against members of his generation, but this occurred a couple of years later when he was part of Crosby, Stills, Nash, and Young. On 4 May 1970, Ohio National Guardsmen opened fire on a gathering of protesters at Kent State University, killing four and wounding nine others. Young, moved by a news story about the event, sat down and wrote no-holds-barred lyrics about the shootings. Mainstream radio stations were afraid to touch the single and, noted David Downing in his biography of Young, 'Vice-President Agnew was moved by it to denounce rock music as anti-American, but you could still buy the record at the local store – and who cared what Spiro Agnew thought about anything anyway.'[29] The single hit no. 14 on the *Billboard* charts thanks to sales and airplay on college and 'underground' radio stations. Young crafted an ideologically loaded musical statement out of a tragic incident, but any personal gain that came from doing so was more than forgiven by audiences who felt that the lyrics spoke for them; the song was a powerful rebuke of the state and of the irrationality of the militarism of the times.

'Ohio' was written in the small coastal town of Pescadero, located between San Francisco and Santa Cruise and about two dozen miles from Young's 'Broken Arrow Ranch.' On an isolated piece of land nestled into the hills of Woodside, the ranch offered Young self-imposed isolation in the wake of a broken marriage and the strangers who treated his previous home in the Topanga Canyon as a communal flophouse. A few years of the intensity offered by Los Angeles had been enough. As a songwriter he found a need for quiet and solitude in which to think and write, yet the ranch was close enough to the city when he desired stimulation or musical collaborations. From here Young would go on to collaborate with Crosby, Stills, and Nash, front the energetic Crazy Horse (*Everybody Knows This Is Nowhere*, released in May 1969), and establish a solo career with a self-titled album in November 1968 (remixed and rereleased in January 1969).

Like Young, Joni Mitchell thrived on the energies offered by Los Angeles but sought the relative seclusion offered by Laurel Canyon, a few minutes away from the Sunset Strip and home to members of the Mamas and the Papas, the Byrds, the Buffalo Springfield, the Monkees, and the Doors, among others.[30] Mitchell had left Toronto in September 1965 with her new husband and fellow folksinger Chuck Mitchell, but as of early 1967 was single and living in New York City. There she attracted the attention of Buffy Sainte-Marie and her manager Elliot Roberts. The latter, captivated by Mitchell's performance, took her on and arranged numerous club shows along the east coast. In Florida she was seen by

David Crosby, ex of the Byrds, with whom Mitchell headed to California in the autumn of 1967. With Crosby as producer, she recorded her first album, *Joni Mitchell* (also known as *Song to a Seagull*), released in March 1968. Her reputation buoyed by Judy Collins's hit recording of her song 'Both Sides Now' and Tom Rush's version of 'Urge for Going,' Mitchell spent the rest of the year touring. By the following spring, with the release of her second album, *Clouds*, she had made it onto the cover of *Rolling Stone* and had established a persona as an archetypal sensitive confessor.

Mitchell's constitution and songwriting skills came through as she struggled with the intensity of the world around her and, in particular, the issues of the counterculture and protest movements. At times this proved to be overpowering. 'I can't help but know what's happening,' she explained to *Rolling Stone* in the spring of 1969, 'but I also know that I can't do a thing about it. It's good to be exposed to politics and what's going down here, but it does damage to me. Too much of it can cripple me. And if I really let myself think about it – the violence, the sickness, all of it – I think I'd flip out.'[31] Her desire to speak on a pressing issue took shape as 'The Fiddle and the Drum,' a vocal lament of the American government's violence against its own people, but her biggest contributions were lyrical celebrations of her community in songs like 'California' and, perhaps most significantly, 'Woodstock.' 'Woodstock' was inspired by the Woodstock Music and Art Fair held in upper New York State on 15–18 August 1969. Although scheduled to appear at Woodstock, Mitchell was advised to cancel her appearance due to reports about traffic congestion and worries that she could not return in time to perform on *The Dick Cavett Show*. The lyrics were based upon news reports she saw on television. Crosby and Stills, having used a helicopter to get in and out of the festival, joined Mitchell on *The Dick Cavett Show*, and together they turned the television appearance into an opportunity to discuss the event and what it meant to their generation. The following month, Mitchell introduced a new song, 'Woodstock,' as a testament to the community she viewed as, in her words, a 'nation' of youths that needed to 'get back to the garden.'[32]

Having rapidly risen to the forefront of American singer-songwriters, Mitchell found the pressure hard to handle, and at the end of 1969, after touring in support of *Clouds* – praised by *Melody Maker* as 'a superb second album from one of America's best singer-songwriters' – she needed a break.[33] On 13 December 1969, a mere seven months after it had placed her on the cover, *Rolling Stone* reported that Mitchell had announced her retirement.[34] Although the report was a bit overblown, Mitchell did drastically reduce her schedule to only a handful of dates over the next two years, taking time to travel through Europe and building a house at Half Moon Bay on British Columbia's Sunshine Coast. Mitchell found it impossible to stay away from the spotlight, however. 'California,' released on the 1971 album *Blue*, described her longing to return to California. Conversely, 'River,' on that same album, expressed disillusionment with California and a desire to skate away on a frozen river. A year later, 'For the Roses' found her in her cabin away from it all but longing to return to performing, the rustling of the wilderness sounding like applause and the moon beaming down like a spotlight. Mitchell would spend the rest of her life repeating this pattern, drawing upon the intensity of her community until she felt it necessary to find solitude. As Mitchell told Penny Valentine of *Sounds* in the summer of 1972, she needed 'the stimulation of the scene in Los Angeles,' yet, when things became too much, she headed to the cabin, 'a solitary station … I mean, it's by the sea and has enough physical beauty and change of mood so that I can spend two or three weeks there alone.'[35] Moving back and forth between the United States and Canada became a lifestyle requisite for the songwriter.

Songs like the Mamas and the Papas' 'California Dreamin'' and Mitchell's 'Woodstock' offered rallying points for a generation who were seeking a fraternalism based not on political citizenship but a shared desire for peace, love, freedom, sexual liberation, and egalitarianism. For some people, their disenfranchisement from the world they stood to inherit led them towards communities that advocated the positive benefits of mind-altering drugs and offered opportunities to, as famously put by Timothy Leary, 'turn on, tune in, drop out.' Musically, this entailed a 'psychedelia' that began to emerge among sounds shaped by such musical devices as wah-wah pedals and tape loops that blended well with the experience of being on drugs. In its original genesis, psychedelic music shared much with folk. As ethnomusicologist Craig Morrison has well summarized, the lineage can be seen 'in its ideology, repertoire, instrumental techniques, vocal harmonies, critique of politics and society, inclusion of female vocalists, penchant for playacting, and its approach to learning music, rehearsing, and performing. Psychedelic bands found their material in folksong books, field recordings, the Harry Smith Anthology, any number of other records, or from the playing of another singer.'[36] Politicized lyrics, however, were abandoned in favour of aural stimulation. Jerome L. Rodnitzky has pointed out that 'the protest flavour was still there, and if anything the fervor had increased, yet the

lyrics were now less important and often could not be heard clearly over
the music anyway. This new psychedelic music registered a protest of
form rather than substance. The music often featured sexually explicit
lyrics, high creativity, and nonconformist delivery. It presented a hazy
but direct protest to white, middle-class America.'[37]

The psychedelic sounds resonating in California were epitomized in
the work of such bands as Grateful Dead, Big Brother and the Holding
Company, the Doors, Quicksilver Messenger Service, the Jimi Hendrix
Experience, Janis Joplin and the Full Tilt Boogie Band, and, among
the top acts, Jefferson Airplane, a group that featured drummer Alex
'Skip' Spence of Windsor, Ontario. Although Spence was with the band
for only a short time, he penned 'My Best Friend,' a track included on
the band's second album, *Surrealistic Pillow* (more notable for the hits
'White Rabbit' and 'Somebody to Love'). By the time *Surrealistic Pillow*
was released in early 1967, Spence had co-founded seminal psychedelic
band Moby Grape. 'Hey Grandma' and 'Omaha' from the band's 1967
self-titled album drew much attention, but, as was the case for so many of
his peers, Spence's career was derailed by drugs and a declining mental
state. After using an axe to break into a bandmate's hotel room, he was
ejected from the band and went on to a life wracked by drugs, alcohol,
and psychological problems.

Much of the California scene distilled down to a sense of freedom:
freedom from exploitive capitalism, restrictive social norms, imbalanced
gender roles, and the monotonous suburban lifestyle of their parents.
The sentiment was perhaps no better epitomized than by 'Born to Be
Wild,' Steppenwolf's contribution to the counterculture film *Easy Rider*.
The song resonated within an American myth-symbol complex that trumpeted individualism and open spaces.[38] Although Steppenwolf, formed
in Los Angeles in 1967, has been consecrated as a voice of America, John
Kay and the band have been just as commonly claimed by Canadians,
with Kay even inducted into the Juno Awards Hall of Fame in 1996.[39] His
value as a national rallying point is contested territory. The Canadian
hold upon Steppenwolf has been based not on the band's citizenship
or ideology so much as the earlier residency of some of its members in
Yorkville as the Sparrow (and, before that, Jack London and the Sparrows). Of the members making up Steppenwolf, however, only two,
drummer Jerry McCrohan (i.e., Jerry Edmonton) and keyboardist Goldy
McJohn were Canadian citizens, although bassist Nick St Nicholas had
an on-and-off position in the group. Kay immigrated to Canada from
Europe in March 1958 at the age of fourteen and did not take up citizen-

ship before moving to the United States five years later, at which point his family became American citizens.[40] 'I'm grateful to Canada because of what it taught me,' he explained less than a decade after his departure, 'but I didn't really care when we went to the States. I'd left my home years before. Canada was just another stop.'[41]

Kay's participation in Yorkville came after he had moved to the United States and became an American. After living for a time in Buffalo with his family, he took off to immerse himself in the burgeoning California music scene, eventually returning home for a visit and then for a brief stint in Toronto. At this point Kay took over for Jack London and, with the group renamed the Sparrow, worked the circuit for a few months For Kay, though, the goal was to return to California. 'I had been hyping the guys about California,' he recalled in his autobiography. 'Though I enjoyed the companionship of people in the Village and playing with the Sparrow was fun, I really felt during the winter months that I had had enough of cold weather. I still considered California my home and had every intention of returning, but I wanted to bring the band with me.'[42]

Heading first to New York City in June 1966, where they worked the scene and even recorded with Columbia, a few months later they continued on to California, splitting their time between clubs in West Hollywood and Los Angeles. The departures of guitarist Dennis Edmonton (who renamed himself 'Mars Bonfire') and bassist Nick St Nicholas, and then Edmonton's replacement Michael Monarch, brought the band to an end. Steppenwolf, the name taken from the title of a Hermann Hesse book popular among the counterculture, was formed out of the remnants by original the Sparrow members Kay, McJohn, and the remaining Edmonton brother, with the replacement musicians.

Steppenwolf not only popularized 'Born to Be Wild' as an anthem of Americana but also had such topical hits as 'Magic Carpet Ride,' 'Don't Step on the Grass, Sam,' and 'Monster.' Kay later told *Canadian Musician* that 'the '60s, especially the late '60s, were highly political and since we (Steppenwolf) were really just reflecting a lot of existing viewpoints and opinions of our listeners (on albums like *Monster*), it was second nature to me.'[43] A highly politicized childhood in Europe, musical apprenticeship in the clubs of Buffalo, Los Angeles, and Toronto, and an interest in lyrical protest, all ensured that he was set to contribute to the 1960s youthquake. Yet this internationalism also made him uncomfortable with being exclusive to one national project. Of East Prussian birth and claimed by Americans and Canadians alike, Kay has explained that he is not interested in being slotted into any of them. 'I just consider myself a citizen of the world because I've lived in three or four different countries and I've seen all their good and bad points. I just don't believe in boundaries and nationalism and all those things. I think that it's just a way of hyping your own inadequacies and fostering jealousies for other countries, so I don't really go into that.'[44]

For Kay, nations had little ideological appeal. He had lived in too many of them to align himself to a single one. Mobility had also shaped the world view of Leonard Cohen, a burgeoning poet from Montreal who lived on the Greek island of Hydra before making his way to the United States. The sunny communes of California did not appeal to Cohen, and unlike those who only stayed briefly in New York City before moving on, his trip in the autumn of 1966 went from an intended stopover to a couple of years of residency. Nashville, the centre of the country music that he loved, had been his planned destination as he hoped to make the jump from poet to performer. Cohen had carved out a name for himself in the area of literature, publishing *The Spice Box of Earth* (1961), *The Favourite Game* (1963), *Flowers for Hitler* (1964), *Beautiful Losers* (1966), and *Parasites of Heaven* (1966), and had been profiled in the National Film Board of Canada documentary *Ladies and Gentlemen ... Mr. Leonard Cohen* (1965). A traditional literary career, or the possibility of teaching at a university, did not appeal to him, though. Being a songwriter, on the other hand, was a definite possibility. 'I've always felt very different from other poets I've met,' he explained to *Maclean's* in 1966, just before departing for the United States. 'I never felt too much at home with those kinds of people. I always felt more at home with musicians. I like to write songs and sing and that kind of stuff.'[45]

Cohen headed not to the Greenwich Village folk music scene but to the bohemian Chelsea district. He took a room at the Chelsea Hotel on West 23rd Street, a hotspot of artistic decadence and debauchery that for years had attracted a mélange of artists, poets, and musicians. It was here that Dylan Thomas died and Sid Vicious killed Nancy, William Burroughs wrote *Naked Lunch* and Andy Warhol held court and made a film, and Cohen, as rather brutally addressed in 'Chelsea Hotel No. 2,' had sex with Janis Joplin.[46] Chelsea fed his interests, not only personal but musical. Although he would perform traditional folk songs penned by others, including 'The Partisan' and Pete Seeger's 'Banks of Marble,' neither his choice of songs nor those that he wrote were overtly political.[47] He was not concerned with 'the people' so much as simply 'people,' particularly women. As David Boucher puts it in *Dylan and Cohen: Poets of Rock and Roll*, 'Cohen was much more concerned with the politics of the personal ... than with the assorted movements that were popular then. For him, that meant an obsession with women and his relations with them.'[48]

It was folksinger Judy Collins who helped popularize Cohen's work, recording 'Suzanne' on her album *In My Life* and 'Sisters of Mercy,' 'Priests,' and 'Hey That's No Way to Say Goodbye' (as well as Joni Mitchell's 'Both Sides Now' and 'Michael from the Mountains') on *Wildflowers*. The strength of his songwriting and the uniqueness of his voice led to a meeting with John Hammond of Columbia Records, the producer who had given Dylan his first recording opportunity despite the disapproval of his label, and who would once again record an artist against the wishes of the company. Cohen was, after all, relatively old to be a pop star, and there was good reason to question the commercial appeal of his droning, monotonous voice.

Songs of Leonard Cohen, issued in early 1968, was not a top seller in the United States, but it did attract enough attention on image alone to warrant label support. Columbia Records certainly understood that Cohen needed to be sold as much on his persona as on his music, and they did so with such pieces as a character-driven, half-page advertisement in *Rolling Stone* for his sophomore album *Songs from a Room*:

'Is your name Leonard Cohen?' From time to time you get the feeling that you want to disengage yourself from your life. Because you're no different from anyone else. And because your life is filled with the same love and the same hate and the same beauty and the same ugliness as everyone else's. You want to withdraw into some kind of solitary contemplation – a locked room or a quiet corner of your mind just to think about everything for a while. You. Her. It. That. Them. If you put it all down on paper according to a form of meter and line, you're called a poet. And if you're a poet who sets it all to music, then your name is Leonard Cohen. And this is your second album of – for want of a better word – songs. And these are your songs from a room. On Columbia Records.[49]

Cohen established himself as a blend of poet and musician, influenced by the chansonniers of Quebec, the country swing of Hank Williams, jazz vocals, and the music of Bob Dylan, the latter looked to by Cohen as an example of how a poet with an unusual voice could become a successful performer. Cohen was living in Greece during the first stages of Dylan's career but upon returning had become enraptured with *Bringing It All Back Home* and *Highway 61 Revisited*. David Boucher is correct in noting how 'it was not that Dylan influenced Leonard Cohen's songs, although Cohen recognized his genius. Instead, it was Dylan's role that Cohen wanted to emulate, the voice and icon of an age.'[50] Or, as Cohen said about Dylan in a December 1967 interview with Richard Goldstein of *The Village Voice*, 'it wasn't his originality which first impressed me, but his familiarity. He was like a person out of my books, singing to the real guitar. Dylan was what I'd always meant by the poet – someone about whom the word was never used.'[51] The difference was that Dylan was a lyricist who became a poet while Cohen was a poet who became a lyricist. Their approaches were also significantly different, with the former caustic and the latter self-deprecating. The *New York Times*'s review of *Songs of Leonard Cohen* summarized this well: 'Whereas Mr. Dylan is alienated from society and mad about it, Mr. Cohen is alienated and merely sad about it.'[52]

Just as Cohen had fit in with the post-bohemian New York City scene, so too did David Clayton-Thomas, a Torontonian who had spent his teenage years as a runaway living on the streets and in reformatories before making his way onto stages on Yonge Street alongside the likes of Ronnie Hawkins. Clayton-Thomas and his band first travelled to New York City in 1964 on the wave of their regional hits 'Boom Boom' (a John Lee Hooker cover) and 'Walk That Walk,' having been noticed by Paul Anka, who was working for NBC's *Hullabaloo* at the time. Their television appearance was all the more memorable, Nicholas Jennings has noted, thanks to the accompanying go-go girls. 'As Clayton-Thomas and the Shays did their best to impress, viewers were treated to the bewildering sight of girls in hockey uniforms, brandishing sticks and helmets in an unfortunate fit of patriotism.'[53] Clayton-Thomas would return to Toronto and make his way from Yonge Street to the Yorkville Village, from the rock and roll strip to the folk and blues cafes, now incorporating a horn section into his band the Bossmen. Even with another hit, 'Brainwashed,' added to the list, he had little money to support his musical career, and one night in 1966, after sitting in with his idol John Lee Hooker at a club in Yorkville, Clayton-Thomas accepted an offer to accompany the bluesman to New York City.

Time spent in Greenwich Village, living off the 'basket circuit,' earned Clayton-Thomas some important connections that led, in 1968, to a position as front man for the New York City–based Blood, Sweat and Tears following the departure of their original singer, Al Kooper. BST possessed the sort of jazz-rock fusion that Clayton-Thomas had been developing during his time with the Bossmen, and in New York City the band had a solid audience. 'New York kids identify themselves with our sound,' as he remarked in a 1969 interview with *Melody Maker*.[54] This was especially true with 'Spinning Wheel,' a song that Clayton-Thomas carried over from his time with the Bossmen. Not only was the scene in New York City more in line with his goals, surrounded by like-minded musicians influenced by the same blues and jazz greats (many of whom still performed in the city), but his prospects were greater than they had been in Toronto. In a 1971 interview, riding high with BST, Clayton-Thomas painted a rather bleak picture of his Toronto years: 'I worked for ten years in Toronto, and I had hit records – five of them. But I didn't make any money and I wasn't able to make any sort of a living. I was lucky to pull in $125 a week, and that doesn't give you much incentive. Scuffling around the country like starving rats, begging agents for an extra fifty bucks a week so that we could get some new strings for the bass guitar, or a new drum skin.'[55] In the United States, a single hit like 'Spinning Wheel' could do more than multiple hits in Canada ever could.

Doherty, Yanovsky, Young, Mitchell, the Sparrow, Cohen, Clayton-Thomas – for them to be so successful among their American peers was of little surprise given their shared musical and generational experience. Historian Robert Wright has already pointed out that Canadian folk musicians thrived because the music they offered preserved a folk paradigm that had been extracted from American recordings.[56] Just as important was that citizens of various countries were setting aside their national birthrights in order to create a world without military-industrial, exploitive capitalist, and unequal racial and gender problems. Gillian Mitchell was correct in noting that when Young and Mitchell rejected the America in which they now lived,

> they did not only do so as Canadians, but also in company with their American peers, who now wished, especially considering the current political climate, that their music move beyond all such considerations and associations ... songs such as 'Woodstock,' which proclaimed that 'we've got to get ourselves back to the garden,' and 'Helpless,' which was full of natural imagery, were as much a part of an American, or even international, 'return to nature' as they were part of any Canadian expressions of this impulse.[57]

In time, those who remained in the United States would come to accept America as their home and become members, if not citizens, of that national project. When rock journalist Cameron Crowe titled a February 1979 *Rolling Stone* article on Neil Young 'The Last American Hero,' the identification was not simply ironic. The songwriter's early years in Toronto and Winnipeg seemed less relevant than the period in which he lived and matured as a songwriter in the United States. Little surprise, then, when asked by Bill Flanagan two decades after leaving Canada if he felt 'like a citizen of the United States,' Young responded:

> Yeah. I'm proud to be living in the United States. I'm proud of what this country is doing. Not every little nuance, everything isn't right, but I am behind it. I've been all over the world and I feel at home here ... I just can't say that I hate Reagan. I'm proud of the way he's handled himself. I don't agree with everything he's done, but I'm proud of him as a leader of our country.[58]

For the Band, an embrace of America came much earlier, and their music in the late 1960s would act as a return to the nation for many of those who had previously abandoned it in favour of making their way 'back to the garden.' The sense of community and the dream of crafting a nation of peace and love peaked with Woodstock before giving way to negative undercurrents that became increasingly pronounced. Hard drugs, bikers, a general malaise with the lifestyle, and the aging of the baby boom generation had begun to disillusion its members and leave them searching for something more rooted and tranquil. A mere four months after Woodstock, the Altamont Speedway Free Festival took place on 6 December 1969, headlined by the Rolling Stones and featuring such acts as Santana, Jefferson Airplane, and Crosby, Stills, Nash, and Young. The event was marred by violence and three deaths, including the stabbing of an audience member by the Hells Angels, the biker gang hired to provide security.

Music from Big Pink, the Band's 1968 debut, was a declaration of love for America, or at least the America they envisioned, by a group that was four-fifths Canadian, had apprenticed with Ronnie Hawkins and Bob Dylan, and had been seeped in Americana. 'Tears of Rage,' the first track on the album, has been passionately described by Greil Marcus as a commentary on an

> America betrayed by those who would no longer be part of it. The Band made a claim to an identity others no longer wanted, and the album opened up from there ... The songs captured the yearning for home and the fact of displacement that ruled our lives; we thought that the Band's music was the most natural parallel to our hopes, ambitions, and doubts, and we were

right to think so. Flowing through their music were spirits of acceptance and desire, rebellion and awe, raw excitement, good sex, open humor, a magic feel for history – a determination to find plurality and drama in an America we had met too often as a monolith.[59]

It had been almost a decade since the members had come together as Ronnie Hawkins's backing band and only a few years since they went out on their own for the first time, achieving minimal success despite their popularity on the southern Ontario circuit and the release of the singles 'Leave Me Alone' and 'Uh-Uh-Uh' on Ware (a New York label) in 1964 as the Canadian Squires and, as Levon and the Hawks, 'The Stones I Throw' and 'He Don't Love You (And He'll Break Your Heart)' on Atco in 1965. Teaming up with Bob Dylan came about thanks to Toronto-born Mary Martin, a fan of the band who also happened to be the secretary for Dylan's manager Albert Grossman. Dylan, Martin told the Hawks, had gone electric and was in need of a backing band after his initial one dissolved. On 20 July 1965, Dylan had released the raucous *Highway 61 Revisited* with its single 'Like a Rolling Stone' and, less than a week later, on 25 July 1965, performed at the Newport Folk Festival backed by organist Al Kooper and the Paul Butterfield Blues Band. The electrified combination famously horrified audience members and led to collective booing; instead of challenging the social status quo through folk music, Dylan flipped the paradigm and challenged the crowd through folk rock. A combination of other commitments and discomfort with the abuse, however, forced the Paul Butterfield Blues Band to leave and Dylan to seek replacements.

Dylan met with Robbie Robertson in New York City in mid-August and, when the two hit it off, flew to Toronto a few weeks later to hear the band in action. After the show, at the Friar's Tavern on the corner of Yonge and Dundas Streets (now the location of the Hard Rock Cafe), they all jammed late into the evening.[60] That night led to an eight-month world tour. When they showed up in Toronto for a performance at Massey Hall, Peter Gzowski of *Maclean's* was more than a little overwhelmed but nonetheless impressed. 'At Dylan's signal,' Gzowski reported, 'Levon and the Hawks exploded into sound like a squadron of jet planes, a leaping, rising, crushing wave of sound that pulled the air and rocked the floor. In the balcony, I could feel the bass notes through the soles of my shoes.'[61] Too often, however, audiences simply booed and catcalled, prompting Levon Helm to walk away during an American stop on the tour; he would spend the next couple of years drifting between jobs, including a stint on an oil rig, before reuniting with the musicians to form the Band.[62]

What was to be a brief reprieve from the tour at Dylan's home in Woodstock, New York, was sidelined after he crashed his Triumph motorcycle. The backing band, residing in the picturesque landscape of Woodstock, and with the return of Levon Helm, recorded an album of their own, affectionately called 'Big Pink' after the house in which they rehearsed. Although they had apprenticed under Hawkins and Dylan, *Music from Big Pink* was not simply rock and roll by a band that had been moulded by Americans: the album was America as envisioned by musicians who had lived the rock and roll experience. The Band used a combination of American geography, history, and mythology to reinvigorate an earlier anti-modern, nostalgic folk sentimentality and blend it with a down-home feel that soothed the psyches of people dealing with the excesses of the youthquake. For Greil Marcus, this first release made it clear that the Band had the ability to 'dramatize a sense of what it is to be an American; what it means, what it's worth, what the stakes of life in America might be … In their music and in their careers, they share a range and depth that seem to crystallize naturally in visions and versions of America: its possibilities, limits, openings, traps … It was obvious they were committed to the very idea of America: complicated, dangerous, and alive.'[63] More critically, in a phrase offered by Gillian Mitchell, they used 'traditions to create countries of the imagination,' putting forth an America that could appeal to a variety of people who were able to write themselves into the emotive narrative.[64]

The Band, their self-titled sophomore album released the following year, was a carefully constructed piece of American anti-modernism, seeped in the past but resonating within the present, playing upon deeply seated sentiments of patriotism and identity. The album's cover photo showed the musicians bearded and in wool overcoats; as described by Bart Testa and Jim Shedden, 'the members looked and dressed in photographs like well-worn homesteaders who had wagoned in from a winter's solitude to kick up their heels a bit at a church social.'[65] The songs more than matched the album sleeve. Levon Helm has talked of going with Robbie Robertson to the library to read up on American history and heroes; the outcome was such compelling stories as 'The Night They Drove Old Dixie Down,' about the aftermath of the American Civil War presented from the viewpoint of Virgil Cain, a southerner who recounts his life of chopping wood and tilling the soil in Tennessee, his excitement at an appearance by Robert E. Lee, the loss of his brother in the war, and the ruthless destruction caused by the Union 'Yankee' Army under General George Stoneman.[66]

Bohemian and hippy communities, notably those in New York City and California, had provided kinship for a generation seeking an alternative to a world on the brink of self-destruction, but, with the collapse of urban utopias and the maturation of flower children who were now starting to bear children of their own, the Band stepped in and helped them to come to terms with the nation, and nations, they had rejected. The America of their parents did not have to be their America, and under the inequality, strife, and superficiality was a hearty foundation upon which to build something better. Ralph J. Gleason of *Rolling Stone* picked up on this in his review of *The Band*, pointing out to readers that 'we live in these cities and forget that there is more than 3000 miles between New York and the smog of Los Angeles and those 3000 miles are deeply rooted to another world in another time and with another set of values.' The song 'King Harvest,' Gleason opined, 'takes us there,' not only Americans but Canadians as well, the song speaking 'for the continent' and a generation turning towards the familial stability and heartiness of ruralism, even if it existed more in the imagination than in reality.[67]

'Down to Old Dixie and Back,' *Time*'s 1970 cover story on the Band and the magazine's first on a rock and roll group, explained to its international readership that 'what the Band has worked out is something that countless other Americans hope for, a sort of watchful, self-protective truce with the encroaching world of noisy commerce.'[68] In this the group was part of the new 'country rock … a symptom of a general cultural reaction to the most unsettling decade the U.S. has yet endured. The yen to escape the corrupt present by returning to the virtuous past – real or imagined – has haunted Americans, never more so than today. A nostalgic country twang resounds all up and down the pop charts.'[69]

The cocaine canyons of California and psychedelia of Haight-Ashbury had taken their toll. Peace and love were wonderful ideals, but consolidating them into urban utopias had resulted in a generation that was fraying at the seams. Throughout it all, musicians held privileged positions by articulating the sentiments felt by many of their peers. 'Rock around the Clock' and 'I Wanna Hold Your Hand' seemed prehistoric, if not juvenile and naive, compared with 'Ohio' and 'The Weight.' Canadians and Americans collaborated, recorded, and performed within a shared musical matrix located in a 'nation' of youth; Canadians were not so much national outsiders 'looking in' as they were compatriots carving out alternatives to the world they stood to inherit.

Back in Canada, however, the growing notoriety of musical expatriates was beginning to draw the attention of nationalists, who thought that their brethren should be holding these highly regarded positions at 'home.' Whereas *Time* and *Rolling Stone* pointed to the Band as a manifestation of an American society in transition, the Canadian music industry trade paper *RPM*, in its review of *Music from Big Pink*, complained that 'what isn't happening at home for Canadians IS, on a large scale, in the U.S. Americans are becoming more familiar with Canadian artists, groups, actors, etc., much sooner than those in the "just society."'[70] With popular music growing in social capital, the exodus of talent became identified as a tragic drain and raised questions as to the lack of opportunities for citizens to develop a career without going abroad. The answer, as will be explored in chapter six, would lead to the Canadian content regulation. First, though, it is necessary to explore how regionalism shaped the Canadian counterparts to California's psychedelic scenes.

Rock and rollers Les Vogt (top) and the Prowlers and Wes Dakus & the Rebels (bottom).

Paul Anka did it 'his way' by heading to the United States.

Folk singer Ian Tyson at the Village Corner Club, Toronto.

Gordon Lightfoot at the Riverboat in the Yorkville Village.

Félix Leclerc: revered chansonnier.

Joni Mitchell during a visit back to Canada. Photo taken in Fort Macleod, Alberta, in January 1969.

Buffy Sainte-Marie: still active on the folk circuit forty years later.

Ronnie Hawkins and Robbie Robertson on stage at the Le Coq D'Or Tavern, 1963. Robertson would go on to fame as a member of the Band.

The Staccatos (later the Five Man Electrical Band) performing for Queen
Elizabeth II at a 1967 Centennial concert (top). J.B. and the Playboys (bottom).

Clockwise from top left: Neil Young with the Squires; The Lords of London; Advertisement for the Canadian Broadcasting Corporation's *Let's Go* featuring the Guess Who.

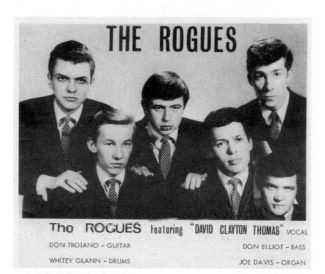

THE ROGUES

The ROGUES featuring "DAVID CLAYTON THOMAS" VOCAL

DON TROIANO – GUITAR   DON ELLIOT – BASS

WHITEY GLANN – DRUMS   JOE DAVIS – ORGAN

TICKET
TICKET

"WHERE THE SOUND IS IN AND THE MUSIC IS WAY OUT"

SUNDAY, OCTOBER 9

PRESENTING

THE ROGUES

APPEARING FOR THE FIRST TIME AS

THE MANDALA

WORLD PREMIERE OF THEIR NEW RECORDING
'OPPORTUNITY'

2 BIG DANCES EVERY SUNDAY

THE TICKET IS YOUR TICKET TO WHAT'S HAPPENING

THE TICKET FEATURES		HOME OF THE TICKET
• Top recording artists from around the world	2 p.m. to 5.30 p.m.	8.00 to 11.30 – Nite Club Atmosphere	CLUB KINGSWAY
• Nite Club atmosphere	AFTERNOON DANCE	EVENING DANCE	100 THE QUEENSWAY
• Non-stop entertainment			
• Largest dance floor in town	• THE ROGUES • THE MAJESTICS • SHAWN JACKSON • THE SECRETS	• THE ROGUES • THE MAJESTICS • SHAWN JACKSON	
• Club memberships available $1.00		JAX JACKSON	
• MC — "The Pres" Brian Skinner		• THE TRIP	
COMING	ADMISSION — $2.00 DRESS — Casual	ADMISSION — $2.50 Jackets and Ties and Dresses	
OCT 14— Neil Diamond			
	Advanced Ticket Sales – ASA RECORD BAR	NOTE — All members will be on advanced mailing list.	
	RECORD WORLD		
	CLUB KINGSWAY		
		GO GO GIRLS	
BOOKED THROUGH THE WILLON AGENCY		Produced by Entertainment Productions	

Mandala
1st U. S. TOUR
ENGLAND'S NUMBER 1 GROUP

THE FARM at THE MONROE COUNTY FAIRGROUNDS

Friday, June 16, 1967	Saturday, June 17, 1967
TEEN SHOW	*BEER BLAST*
8 P. M. UNTIL 11:30 P. M.	9 P. M. UNTIL 1 A. M.
$2.00 Advance Sale	$2.00 Proof of Age Required

TICKETS MAY BE OBTAINED BY WRITING OR CALLING
CHARTER HOUSE ASSOCIATES
1265 CALKINS ROAD • PITTSFORD, N.Y. 14534 • PHONE 334-6312

The Rogues (for a brief period featuring David Clayton-Thomas) and later as the Mandala, featuring guitarist Domenic Troiano. Note their billing as 'England's #1 Group' during a U.S. tour.

The United Empire Loyalists, cornerstones of Vancouver's psychedelic scene (top). The Haunted at the Montreal Forum (bottom).

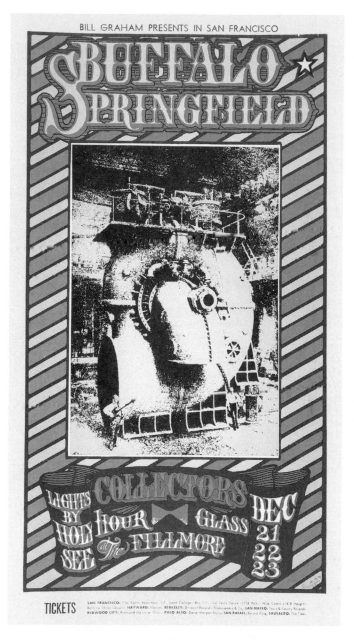

Concert poster for the Buffalo Springfield (featuring Neil Young) and the Collectors (later Chilliwack) at the legendary Fillmore Auditorium in San Francisco.

The Ugly Ducklings: proto-punk rockers.

McKenna Mendelson Mainline.

Kelly Jay of Crowbar shaking hands with Pierre Trudeau. Crowbar's 'Oh What a Feeling' was the first big hit following the Canadian content regulation.

A Foot in Coldwater: '(Make Me Do) Anything You Want' (top). The Stampeders of 'Sweet City Woman' fame (bottom).

Trooper made their mark with such hits as 'We're Here for a Good Time (Not a Long Time)' and 'Raise a Little Hell.'

Stompin' Tom Connors: figurehead of musical patriotism.

Bruce Cockburn offered an international viewpoint to an increasingly nationalistic music scene.

Northern Lights for Africa: 'Tears Are Not Enough' (top). A young Colin James and Sarah McLachlan (bottom).

Honeymoon Suite's hit 'New Girl Now' helped establish them among the forefront of 'hair bands.'

Corey Hart complete with sunglasses.

Born in Kingston, Ontario, to English parents and living in five countries by his teenage years, Bryan Adams eventually took up residence in London, England.

Tom Cochrane's hit 'Big League,' about the dream of becoming a hockey player, resonated among many Canadians.

Gord Downie of the Tragically Hip: that the band has had tremendous domestic success but attracted little attention abroad acts to reify their Canadianness among fans.

Ed Robertson and Barenaked Ladies went from the 'independent' 1990s scene to become a multinational sensation.

Folk rocker Hayden (top). Gordie Johnson of Big Sugar showing off his skills (bottom).

Joel Plaskett has won many fans by situating his lyrics within Canadian locations.

Jill Barber: among the forefront of a new generation of crooning folksy songstresses.

The success of Stars (top) and Broken Social Scene (bottom) helped to make Arts & Crafts a major player in the industry.

Canadian Musician: thirty years of advice and reviews for aspiring and established performers alike.

5

'Turn On, Tune In, Drop Out': Psychedelia, Regionalism, and How a Band from the Prairies Had Wheatfield Soul

What is happening is that the folk-rock movement, heady with the success of its big-message-with-a-big-beat songs, has been prompted to try racier, more exciting themes. It is no longer down with the P.T.A. and conformism, but – whee! – onward with LSD and lechery.

– *Time*, 1966[1]

'It's still a cowtown, but the cows are starting to get groovy.'
– An unnamed American 'hippie' visiting an Edmonton love-in, 1967[2]

'We were known up and down the coast from Vancouver to Tijuana, but Toronto didn't have a clue who we were. In all fairness, I'd have to say that Vancouver didn't know who the Toronto groups were, either.'[3] For Bill Henderson of the Collectors, and other bands of the psychedelic scenes on Canada's west coast, any place east of the Rockies was pretty much off the musical map. The Collectors regularly shared stages with the likes of trippy California bands Jefferson Airplane, Grateful Dead, and Country Joe and the Fish, as did Toronto-based groups like Luke and the Apostles in Toronto, but it was rare for Canadian acts of different regions to appear on the same bill. Although the Collectors did venture across the country to perform in Toronto, after coast-to-coast exposure on the CBC teen music show *Let's Go*, Henderson has explained that 'it was and really still is mostly a matter of the expense of travelling 2000+ miles. Air travel in those days was far more unusual than it is now. Plus, the emerging psychedelic scene was coming from San Francisco. So our attention was focused quite a bit on that scene.'[4]

What was happening in Vancouver, Toronto, and in other cities across Canada was a new musical component of a social paradigm in which youths were getting 'groovy,' immersing themselves in love-ins, wearing flowers in their long hair, adopting Indian garb and spiritualism, and, of course, making songs and sounds inspired by ideas, acid, and sexual freedom. Their alternative lifestyles stressed freer and more coopera-tive living while the music blended rock and folk into swirling sounds (thanks to the likes of wah-wah pedals and tape loop machines) that fed into, and were often fed by, drug trips – particularly amphetamines, marijuana, and LSD. The outcome was commonly called 'psychedelic' or 'acid' rock.

Beat, folk, jazz, and blues cafes and clubs were retailored to appeal to the new clientele, while 'head shops' offering drug paraphernalia and psychedelic clothing, music, and decorations, began to sprout up. Public spaces where you could hang out and pass around a guitar were just as popular as any cafe, particularly among those with little money to spend. From coast to coast, Ron Verzuh notes, people could light up a joint and join in on the communalism:

> In Vancouver, Fourth Avenue was the place to get stoned and groove on the stars out over English Bay or catch a gig at the Village Bistro. The waiters at the Alcazar Hotel would sell you a joint with your twenty-cent glass of draft. In Calgary, hips congregated at Riley Park. In Edmonton, it was the Middle Earth coffee house. Saskatoon offered the Ritz and the Senator hotels. Win-nipeg had the Experiment head shop and 655 Broadway, the biggest dope house west of Toronto. Yorkville, Baldwin Street and Sullivan Street were the main stops in T.O., and in Montreal, Mountain and Crescent Streets were key points on any hipster's city tour. In Halifax, Victoria Park was a must. And wherever they went, the music played.[5]

Vancouver's Kitsilano and Toronto's Yorkville Village were the two most popular options, particularly if you were an aspiring musician. Just up the sunny Pacific coast from California, Kitsilano was an ideal com-munity for those who wanted a temperate climate, access to nature, the learned hotspots of the University of British Columbia and Simon Fra-ser University, and relatively close proximity to the psychedelic scenes in Los Angeles and San Francisco. The Afterthought, Dante's Inferno, and the Retinal Circus were hubs for the psychedelically minded, the latter described by Bill Henderson as 'the focal point in Vancouver for the entire rock scene.'[6] Or, as put more colourfully by Ron Verzuh, the Retinal Circus was seen by the mainstream as 'a concentration camp for teen-agers; the teen-agers themselves saw it as a heaven on earth with

tons of good dope, the best music and much love being shared around.'[7]
There was even a weekly alternative newspaper, the *Georgia Straight*,
that discussed community issues and informed readers about concerts
and events. To Jack Wasserman of the conservative *Vancouver Sun*, the
'*Straight*' was 'an inept attempt to duplicate the even more pungent (and
better written) underground papers of San Francisco and Los Angeles.'[8]
The first issue was published on 5 May 1967, starting what would become
years of incendiary columns and lawsuits.

Although Vancouver has been mythologized as a vibrant site of hippy
and psychedelic communalism, in actuality many Vancouverites were
disgusted with what they saw as an invasion by undesirable outsiders. In
a 1967 interview with *Maclean's*, Warren Tallman, professor of English
at the University of British Columbia, told of how 'the hippies are, of
course, from outside as a movement. In many cases, they're from outside as individuals too. By resisting the hippies, the Vancouver people
are simply acting to protect their home town.'[9] There was an eerie similarity between their reactions and those taken against earlier undesired
immigrants. *Maclean's* noted that the 'reactions range from a laborious-
ly hand-printed note Scotch-taped to the door of the Arbutus Café at
West 4th and Arbutus – "No hippies allowed" – to the recent proposal of
Alderman Halford Wilson that the entire hippie population be relocated, ghetto-style, in a crummy but easily policeable district in downtown
Vancouver.'[10] Even those who set about establishing themselves as busi-
nesspeople to serve like-minded clientele found themselves under harassment by a police force that wanted them out of the city. An undesired
outside group would in time become integrated and romanticized as
part of Vancouver's identity, but in 1967 these transients were regarded
with disdain.

Vancouver, isolated by the mountains yet in easy access of the thriving
west coast psychedelic scene, became a place where local bands shared
stages, sounds, ideas, and dope with acts from California. When the likes
of Jefferson Airplane, Grateful Dead, the Doors, and the Steve Miller
Blues Band arrived in town, they shared the stage with such acts as
the Collectors, the Hydro Electric Streetcar, Mother Tucker's Yellow
Duck, Seeds of Time, Papa Bear's Medicine Show, Painted Ship, and
the United Empire Loyalists. To them the music scene ran up and down
the coast. For the Collectors, their closeness to California, and the lack
of domestic recording studios, led to them recording the single 'Looking at a Baby' in Los Angeles with Valiant Records; when the label was
subsequently bought, they found themselves on Warner. With a big label

came access to high-profile studio talent, notably producer David Has-singer, who had worked with the Rolling Stones, Grateful Dead, and Jefferson Airplane. In the lead-up to the album's release the band spent a significant amount of time in California but ended up returning to Canada and missing out on the darker period of psychedelic excess that claimed the likes of Jim Morrison, Jimi Hendrix, and Janis Joplin. As Henderson has recalled,

> we basically lived down there from our first single to the release of our first album. That was at least a year probably a year and a half. By the end of that period I for one, wanted nothing more than to come back to my wife and daughter and to stay with them. We decided to base ourselves back in Vancouver and try to reach across the country and then roll our success down into the states. Wrong move career wise. Right for the family though. I quite possibly wouldn't be alive right now if I'd made the other choice. So I don't regret it.[11]

Despite being a major Vancouver act with a successful single to its credit and an album backed by a major label, the Collectors experienced first-hand just how difficult it was to manage a successful career in Canada without having already broken into the United States.

The pull of geography down to California was not matched within Canada; coast-to-coast interaction required the sort of exposure made possible through pan-Canadian airplay, media coverage, and affordable touring circuits. Consequently, acts in Canada shared more with visiting American acts than they did with their Canadian counterparts. For Jeffrey Ridley of the United Empire Loyalists, this meant a lot of time spent with bands from California, including 'the Grateful Dead whenever they came to Vancouver; likewise Country Joe and the Fish. The Haight-Ashbury scene was a big influence ... We had heard vaguely of a Yorkville scene in Toronto but couldn't name any bands, and our unawareness of scenes in other Canadian cities was total ... Nor would we have had any interest in them; we were totally absorbed in our own burgeoning scene – our mecca – fuelled as it was by the visiting San Francisco bands and tales of Haight-Ashbury.'[12] The United Empire Loyalists did make one exception, however: they made their way to Edmonton and Calgary, where they had a small group of fans, and mingled with local acts Willy and the Walkers and David Wilkie.[13]

There was a lot going on in Toronto, but there was little reason to expect the west coasters to know much about it. Toronto had not only clubs but large auditoriums and stadiums that hosted such spectacles as the fourteen-hour Toronto Sound concert at Maple Leaf Gardens in September 1966, the Toronto Pop Festival of June 1969 that mixed the Band with the Velvet Underground and Robert Charlebois, and the Rock and Roll Revival in September of that same year, bringing John Lennon and the Doors together with such childhood rock and roll heroes as Jerry Lee Lewis and Chuck Berry. Such concerts and festivals were organized by savvy baby boomers, who combined their love of music with their business skills; 'hipsters' and 'suits,' the identities sometimes overlapping, were finding peace and love to be profitable. Bob Bossin of Stringband, reporting on this trend in *Maclean's*, observed how 'in the Woodstock Nation, the Establishment had its best, if unlikeliest, ally in years. And a number of sharp, hip young entrepreneurs had the material and the market for a quick, peacefully earned fortune.'[14] John Browser of Karma Productions was one of these entrepreneurs, responsible for the Toronto Pop Festival and the Toronto Rock and Roll Revival. Having hit it off with John Lennon, the two set about putting together the Toronto Peace Festival for the long weekend of 4–6 July 1970. Problems with securing a site (Mosport Raceway and the farming community of Park Hill both backed out after the Ontario Provincial Police reportedly scared the town council with edited film footage of the chaos at Woodstock), and a conflict between Browser and Lennon over ticket costs, led to the collapse of what would likely have been the largest rock and roll concert in Canada up to that time.[15]

Perhaps no Toronto concert, or in this case series of concerts, was more significant for psychedelic music than one given by Jefferson Airplane and Grateful Dead, with local opening act Luke and the Apostles, at the O'Keefe Centre from 31 July to 5 August 1967. The lead-up to the series involved a free concert at Nathan Phillips Square featuring the Jefferson Airplane and Luke and the Apostles, an event that, according to Nicholas Jennings, attracted more than 50,000 people and marked what he has called the transition from the city's 'love affair with r and b' to the 'the kaleidoscopic sounds of acid-rock.'[16] The O'Keefe Centre series drew enough public interest that the CBC televised one of the performances in a broadcast that, in the words of music industry trade paper *RPM*, had 'enough drawing power to attract thousands of young viewers, who have read much about but seen little of the sounds that rocked San Francisco and Toronto. If they have colour television they'll be that much better informed.'[17]

For those who wanted to wade deeper into Toronto's psychedelia,

Yorkville was the place to be, with hipsters and assorted hangers-on enjoying a chance to smoke dope, listen to music, and maybe luck into a sexual indulgence. Nicholas Jennings was one of the curious teenagers who explored the village from a safe distance. 'To suburban kids like us … it was the forbidden zone, strictly off-limits as decreed by our parents because of the sensational news accounts of free love and drugs. But as soon as I was able to borrow the family car … [we] snuck down to the village – as spectators, not participants. We did the Yorkville Crawl in bumper-to-bumper traffic, gawking like every other tourist at the kaleidoscopic sights and sounds.'[18] With the village's shift from beat, folk, and R&B to psychedelia came a new atmosphere that required existing venues to either change with the times or fold up. The closure of the Bohemian Embassy in the summer of 1966 was a sign of this transition. As *Maclean's* noted, 'in six cyclonic years of evolving coffee-set fashions, the Bohemian Embassy changed from being off-beat and far out to being square and *passé*. It was conceived in the Kingston Trio era; it began to fade with the dawning of the Beatles. In an age of such in-places as the Mousehole and the Purple Onion, the very adjective "Bohemian" sounds quaint.'[19]

Folk balladeers and British mods had turned into psychedelic hipsters, soaking up the California sounds and creating drawn-out, swirling jams of their own. The Paupers emerged at the forefront of the Toronto scene, managed by Bernie Finkelstein, and developed a strong following. The band managed to record a few singles – 'Never Send You Flowers' and 'If I Told My Baby' on Toronto-based record label Red Leaf, and 'For What I Am' and 'Long Tall Sally' on Roman Records – and even secured a deal with MGM in 1966.[20] Their big break came in early 1967 with a two-week gig at the Cafe Au Go Go in New York City. Although the Cafe Au Go Go had initially raised the idea of the band opening for Ian and Sylvia as part of a 'Canada' night, Finkelstein knew that the pairing was musically out of synch and instead managed to book them on a bill with up-and-coming psychedelic act Jefferson Airplane, a band which, by the time the show took place, had become one of the biggest on the continent. Yet by some accounts the Paupers stole the spotlight from the darlings of the California scene. 'There is this incredible group from Toronto called the Paupers,' reported Richard Goldstein of the influential *Village Voice* after one of the Cafe Au Go Go shows. 'They swooped out of nowhere, from a scene nobody knew about, and suddenly they were playing real electronic music with a teenage audience screaming allegiance in the background.'[21] Or, as in *Crawdaddy*'s review, the band 'managed to shake up New York City more than any other group in months. Not because they were the best New York's seen, exactly, but because they have a fantastic impact on an audience, a real ability to get tired people out of their seats and screaming. The group comes from Toronto, and bases itself around fantastic breaks in which three of the four members will be playing drums at once, while the fourth goes through strange and lovely guitar changes.'[22] The industry press was not alone in being enthralled with the Paupers. Musical powerbroker Albert Grossman, the manager behind such acts as Bob Dylan, Joan Baez, Ian and Sylvia, and Gordon Lightfoot, convinced Finkelstein to let him co-manage the group, and soon after Finkelstein found himself sidelined, selling his stake, and returning to Yorkville.

The Paupers had much to gain from Grossman; this manager to the stars was able to set the Paupers up on dozens of high-profile concerts during 1967 and 1968, including opening for Jefferson Airplane and Grateful Dead at the Fillmore Auditorium in San Francisco, an appearance at the Monterey Pop Festival, opening for Eric Clapton and Cream at the Cafe Au Go Go, and, in February 1968, opening for Jimi Hendrix back in Toronto. They even managed to record two albums during this short period, *Magic People* and *Ellis Island*, on MGM's Verve Forecast label. Despite high-profile gigs and multiple albums, though, the band was coming apart at the seams, wracked by debts and the toll of too much acid. Drug-addled bass prodigy Denny Gerrard departed in early 1968, only a year after first opening for the Jefferson Airplane at the Cafe Au Go Go, and, soon after, so too did restless drummer Skip Prokop.

Finkelstein emerged from the deal with Grossman with a big chunk of money and, just as important, experience, industry connections, and a knowledge of how to launch a band in the United States. Now back in Yorkville, he and singer Keith McKie assembled Kensington Market, the band's name taken from an ethnically and artistically eclectic neighbourhood in Toronto, and groomed them into a tight group in six weeks of rehearsal in a waterfront warehouse.[23] This was no lackadaisical acid rock jam-band but a professional unit being groomed for commercial success. To his credit, Finkelstein signed a deal with Bell Records and secured famed record producer Felix Pappalardi (whose credits included Joan Baez and Cream).[24] This sort of managerial skill led to a *Saturday Night* magazine cover story in May 1968 that referred to Finkelstein as 'a kind of Canadian Brian Epstein or Albert Grossman.'[25] The big break came that same spring, a mere one year into the band's existence: a contract with Warner Brothers for six records (two albums and four singles) with $100,000 towards recording and $210,000 for promotion.[26] This was an unparalleled agreement between a U.S. record label and a Canadian-based band. *Time* predicted that it 'will probably give them the loudest hearing and promotional hoopla a Canadian group has ever had in the vast North American market.'[27] That was true, but, just as significantly, the deal revealed an early, and rather exploratory, interest among the multinationals in supporting talent in Canada, or, at the very least, to cherry pick an act with an eye to international sales. In this case, the band was being handled by Warner Reprise Canada, the domestic subsidiary of the major U.S. label, and one established the previous year with the primary purpose of pressing and distributing foreign releases.

The deal with Warner brought with it the attention of influential rock and roll trade papers and the popular press. Things looked good when Dave Butcher of *Rolling Stone* called *Avenue Road* 'a much-better-than-average first album ... the arrangements are interesting and polished. The level of musicianship is high throughout ... Overall, *Avenue Road* is exceptionally easy listening music by a talented group.'[28] The sophomore album, *Aardvark*, released the next year, had promise as well, but as with many of their peers, the band was falling apart due to the excesses of the psychedelic lifestyle. 'We all started going a little crazy,' Luke Gibson said in an interview with Jennings. 'There was a lot of paranoia, mostly drug related. In the end, all that tension simply blew the band apart.'[29]

Not just the band, but Yorkville itself was collapsing, giving way to hard drugs, biker gangs, pressure from city council, speculative real estate developers, and a citizenry wanting to purge the blight of psychedelic hedonism. *Rolling Stone* went so far as to connect Jimi Hendrix's drug bust at the Toronto airport on 3 May 1969, to civic pressures and the police crackdown on the community:

> The Mounties do not typically lie in wait at the airport, ready to pounce. Toronto authorities have been getting rough on the free-living hippie community of Yorkville, more or less Toronto's version of the Haight-Ashbury, in recent months, and there is the possibility that Hendrix may have been caught in the squeeze.
>
> The populace of Toronto are a very conservative lot, and tend to look with suspicion upon anybody who looks and dresses a little different from themselves. Hendrix looks a lot different. Make an example of this freaky, frizzy-haired psychedelic spade (if you go by this reasoning) and maybe you can scare the freaks out of Yorkville.[30]

The police did not have to do much to chase the hippies out of Yorkville: real estate developers had the blessing of City Hall to move in, scoop up the cheap property, and gentrify it into something more commercial. By 1973 the Yorkville of the beats, folkies, hippies, and psychedelic youths had been wiped off the map. Melinda McCracken of *Maclean's* offered readers a stark image of the transition from bohemian to bourgeois: 'the colorful ticky-tacky houses, full of hippies, head shops, coffee houses, outdoor cafés, kids and music are empty, their windows blank with new plate glass, their new facades a trim grey-pink, waiting to be filled with expensive objects to attract the [new Hyatt Regency] hotel's clientele, nothing special to go there for anymore. Nothing happening.'[31]

By 1969 the scene had pretty much collapsed. Although the infamous Altamont Speedway Free Festival in December of that year is commonly pointed to as the end of the hippy period, a similar moment of chaos took place earlier that year at a music festival on 17–19 May in Aldergrove, British Columbia. According to *Rolling Stone*, several hundred 'outlaw bikers' ran amok among the approximately 27,000 attendees; guns were waved at the crowd; guy wires were cut and scaffolding fell onto the stage, almost hitting Guitar Shorty and the Mark V; bikers repeatedly made their way on stage before being forced off; a girl was injured when bikers jumped on her while she was in her sleeping bag; and, most horribly, six bikers stood accused of gang-raping a fourteen year-old girl. Only after the promoters brought in the Royal Canadian Mounted Police did the bikers leave.[32]

For the Guess Who, living on the prairies, far from the communities of free love, copious drugs, and psychedelic musical jams, was a mixed blessing. Based in Winnipeg, the group had made a minor name for itself during the British Invasion era with 'Shakin All Over'; their follow-up singles 'Hey Ho (What You Do To Me)' and 'Hurting Each Other' were not top charters, but were strong enough to be picked up for international distribution and to be mentioned in *Billboard*.[33] In early 1966, with the departure of keyboardist Bob Ashley and founding member Chad Allan, Randy Bachman took over the band's leadership and singer/keyboardist Burton Cummings was recruited from the local group the Deverons.[34] Winnipeg continued to be their base of operations, although they did not lack for opportunities to head south. In a June 1979 interview with *Canadian Musician*, Randy Bachman told of how Neil Young, visiting his mother for Christmas in 1966, met up with Bachman and Jim Kale and invited them to join him down in California.[35] The duo, needless to say, passed.

A few months after that meeting the Guess Who did head abroad, but not to the United States. The band's relative isolation meant that their first encounter with psychedelic music took place during a trip to England in February 1967. Although their time abroad was economically disastrous – they returned with approximately $25,000 in debt – they came back with new sounds and styles copped from bands like the Who and the Jimi Hendrix Experience.[36] This experience gave the Guess Who an edge in a city that had little experience with psychedelia. As Bachman recalled in an interview with John Einarson, 'we were hip again because, like years before in the Silvertones and the Reflections, we were ahead of the pack [in] having access to English music before it hit these shores. Burton back-combed his hair like Hendrix, I had my whammy bar on my guitar sustaining and bending feedback notes, and all of a sudden we were heavy. Winnipeg had yet to witness any psychedelic music. Once again we were trendsetters.'[37] The new sounds came in handy later that year when Chad Allan, now hosting the Thursday segment of the CBC-TV music show *Let's Go*, a program broadcast from a different major city each weekday, hired the Guess Who as the house band.[38] *Let's Go* was a lifesaver. Einarson has credited it with helping the band to offset their economic debt, achieve coast-to-coast exposure, establish connections and experience with recording studio and other music industry folks, and prompt them into writing original pieces (up until that time they had, like most bands of the era, primarily performed popular radio hits).[39]

The CBC was not the only corporation that benefited the Guess Who. Although the band would later disparage the United States in 'American Woman,' in 1967 they teamed up with that icon of Americana, Coca-Cola, to record an advertising jingle. Coca-Cola's first significant use of Canadian popular music had taken place in 1964 when the company hired heart-throb Bobby Curtola to record the 'Things Go Better with Coke' jingle and to make public appearances.[40] Over the next few years the jingle campaign was extended to various regions and the jingle was recorded by the likes of J.B. and the Playboys, Jack London and the Sparrows, David Clayton-Thomas, the Collectors, the Mighty Preachers, and the Staccatos in English-speaking markets and Petula Clark, Cesar and the Romains, les Baronets, and les Cailloux in French-speaking Canada.[41] The producer of the commercials, Jack Richardson, first saw the Guess Who on *Let's Go*, and soon after the band was brought on for the campaign.[42] 'Across Canada, young people heard their favourite groups singing the story line jingles for Coke,' noted music trade paper *RPM* in

1967 about the advertisements.[43] Reflecting the largely one-way flow of music into Canada, though, the domestically recorded jingles were limited to the Canadian market and supplemented by those of such American acts as Roy Orbison, the Four Seasons, and Jan and Dean.[44]

Coca-Cola's decision to follow up the jingle campaign of 1967 with a promotional 45 record featuring two bands led to additional exposure. Jack Richardson, whose responsibility it was to choose the two groups, opted for the Guess Who and the Staccatos, the latter having had a hit with 'Half Past Midnight' (and, later as the Five Man Electrical Band, 'Signs' and 'Absolutely Right'). Each group was to record five tracks for A Wild Pair, with the Guess Who including the original composition 'Mr. Nothin',' mailed out to almost 90,000 people who sent in ten bottle cap liners and one dollar.[45] According to Richardson, Coca-Cola did much to buoy the cash flow of these two groups in an industry that otherwise offered few economic opportunities: 'Coke was very generous to both groups. They gave them a fair royalty and didn't deduct the recording costs. I guess the two groups wound up making about $40,000 between them. And in those days, that was a small fortune.'[46] The Guess Who and Richardson got along so well that they formed a partnership; the record producer and his business partners in Nimbus 9 Productions signed the band and purchased their existing tracks from Quality Records for a mere $1,000.

Together the Guess Who and Nimbus 9 Productions set out to make a full-length LP, but both parties had enough experience in the industry to know that it made little sense to focus on the Canadian marketplace. Even if a single was aired by a station in response to a band's strong local following, there was little reason to expect other stations to follow suit. Nor did it make sense for a band to focus on breaking itself in other Canadian markets. Making it in Toronto offered minimal awards and little chance at career longevity. In focusing on the American market, the Guess Who sidestepped the struggle experienced by such bands as Witness Inc. of Saskatoon. Witness Inc. used the strength of their regional hits 'I'll Forget Her Tomorrow,' 'Jezebel,' and 'Harlem Lady' to make a move into the Toronto market, but even with plenty of shows around the city they found themselves unable to garner airplay. Toronto stations were simply unwilling to deal with a non-local act despite their popularity.[47] Still, the band seemed determined to make it in Toronto and use the city to establish itself across Canada. As lead singer Kenny Shields explained in 1969, 'I've always said that we're going to make it here first because we're Canadians, even although it seems that our groups will continue to leave until Canada no longer has the potential to compete in the international market.'[48] After two years and several personnel changes, the band folded. A decade later, Shields, now the singer for Streetheart, had seen the light: 'Let's face it, as lovely as this Canadian thing is, this country is about 2% of the world rock market. The U.S. is about 50%, so we want to go for some of those big zeros in America while we've got a shot. That's what it's all about, right?'[49]

Understanding the highly fragmented and regional nature of popular music in Canada, the Guess Who headed to New York City to record *Wheatfield Soul.* A distribution contract was secured with RCA and everyone pooled their money – Richardson took out a second mortgage on his home and Bachman sold his car – to pay for an independent promoter to push the single 'These Eyes' in several major American cities.[50] The gamble worked. 'These Eyes' broke first in Detroit, and then other stations followed, pushing the single to no. 6 in *Billboard* (the album reached no. 45).[51] Canadian stations, Bachman has recalled rather bitterly, finally came on board. 'When "These Eyes" first came out in Canada, it didn't do well. CHUM radio in Toronto and some of the other so-called Canadian supporters wouldn't play it ... CHUM and other influential Canadian markets didn't pick up on the record until the momentum had already gathered steam in the U.S. Then they jumped on the bandwagon.'[52] Likewise, bassist Jim Kale told music journalist Ritchie Yorke that 'when it started to move in the U.S., CHUM went right on it, and even claimed they'd broken the record, made the first release. Like hell they did.'[53]

For Nancy Edmons of *Rolling Stone*, *Wheatfield Soul* was a testament to a supposed 'midwestern' tendency to appropriate commercially established sounds; the album was thought of in regional, not national, terms: 'If the Guess Who's music is too derivative to get full credit as their own (and it is, it is), call it the major problem of midwestern music: the distillation of accepted influences from all over into something you'd swear you've heard before.'[54] *Canned Wheat*, released less than a year later, not only again had a name situated in the prairie wheat fields but, according to famed *Rolling Stone* columnist Lester Bangs, continued to suffer from the midwest's imitative complex.

With a fine hit single, 'Undun,' behind them, they're quite refreshing in the wake of all the heavy metal robots of the year past, and would be even more pleasurable if they didn't sound a mite too much like the [Jefferson] Airplane (instrumentally) and the [Buffalo] Springfield (vocally and often instrumentally). 'No Time' is a soaring riff with all of the Airplane's drive and none of their pretensions, but songs like 'Minstrel Boy' sound so much like the Springfield's brand of the sad bittersweet ballad it's almost embarrassing. Still, in the absence of their great inspiration, the Guess Who carry the torch admirably. Digging it is, I suppose, a matter of personal taste and morality. I'll take it and be satisfied – they have the musical accomplishments to let us hope that the next album might find them singing their very own song.[55]

Critics at *Rolling Stone* may not have been the biggest of fans but *Canned Wheat*'s 'Laughing' hit no. 10 and the B-side 'Undun' was a surprise success, rising to no. 22 (the same position achieved by 'Shakin' All Over' four years earlier).[56] However, the audience for the band, much to their chagrin, seemed to be composed of lovers of what was derisively called 'bubblegum' and 'shlock rock.' In trying to crack the market the Guess Who had issued the most commercially friendly of singles, their initial target audience being not rock and rollers but radio stations. It was an image that RCA found necessary to counter by taking out a full-page advertisement in the 13 December 1969 issue of *Rolling Stone*:

The next guy who puts down The Guess Who as a mushy Top-40 group ought to be made to spend a night with their albums. You people who are ashamed to walk into a folk/rock department and ask for 'Canned Wheat' or 'Wheatfield Soul' better wake up. And you heads who sell their albums and Stereo 8 tapes and hide them back in some dusty bin better listen, too. The Guess Who gets on a different kind of music on 33s than they do on 45s. You take 'Canned Wheat.' Have you ever listened to Randy Bachman and Burton Cummings' 11-minute 'Key'? It's one of the most original hard rock compositions around. Sure you've heard Cummings sing 'Laughing' and 'These Eyes.' But have you *listened* to his flute, organ, and guitar work? Or Jim Kale's bass? Or Bachman's lead guitar? Or Garry Peterson's drumming? They're a very cohesive, together band. You really ought to give a serious listen to Guess Who music. And since most record stores won't let you listen, and since we don't expect you to lay out all that bread on our say alone, maybe you FM-radio cats can help out a little. How about it, *all* of you?[57]

If *Wheatfield Soul* and *Canned Wheat* were most identifiable by their regionalism, notably a midwest tendency to replicate rather than innovate, the next release was much more blatantly national, at least in ideological terms. *American Woman*, with a self-titled single that gendered and rebuffed the United States, utilized national paradigms and played upon deep-seated emotions. For the Guess Who, the song was culled from experiences of touring in the United States and the band's penchant for creating simple, catchy phrases. It had been back in the mid-1960s that they made their first trip south of the border, the success of 'Shakin' All Over' leading to dates with the Kingsmen, Dion and the Belmonts, the Turtles, and as a backing band for the Shirelles and the Crystals. In his autobiography, Bachman spoke of this tour as having a substantial impact on his sense of the United States:

> We had no idea we were walking into the 1965 race riots. We played places where there was blood on the floor. It was unbelievable for us, white kids from Canada. We drove through Georgia and saw the ghettoes, and that was quite an eye-opener. We would go to gas stations with everyone in the same vehicle and guys would greet us with shotguns. 'You can't come in here with those niggers,' and calling us 'Nigger lovers.' It was scary.[58]

Subsequent trips during the Vietnam conflict added to a growing repository of negative experiences that were eventually vented during a performance at a hockey rink in Kitchener, Ontario, soon after they had returned from a tour in the U.S.[59]

The story behind the song, as documented by band's biographer John Einarson, is that during a break Bachman was restringing his guitar and, in the midst of doing so, worked out the riff that would later be used in 'American Woman.' Everyone else assembled back on stage and jammed, and when Cummings exhausted his use of harmonica and flute, he improvised the lyrics that set the foundation for the song. If an audience member had not recorded the show and given the tape to the band afterwards, the song, Cummings has speculated, likely would have been forgotten. With a recording to work from, they set about putting pen to paper in a lyrical disemboweling of a 'straw woman' of American society by playing upon negative elements and stereotypes.[60]

Although the song's blatant anti-Americanism owed much to their time spent touring the United States, the lyrics employed characterizations and a national juxtaposition that played into, if not pandered to, an anti-Americanism that was permeating Canada at that time. That the band, by request, did not perform the song during their appearance at the White House in the summer of 1970, testifies to the song being more about commercialism than a political stance.[61] Nonetheless, the song resonated with a population caught up in a widespread nationalism that rejected continentalism and sought to reassert Canadian sovereignty in the face of American imperialism. The nationalism of the period was spurred all the more by the 1967 Centennial celebrations. Canadians were primed for a song along the lines of 'American Woman,' although not everyone, such as Juan Rodriguez of the Canadian leftist intellectual newsmagazine *Last Post*, was ready to buy into it: '"American Woman" is merely a silly, but "hip," song capitalizing on pointless anti-Americanism. It has no relevance to the reality of what is going on in America these days and it implies (if only from the fact that the Guess Who have kept their Canadian identity – smart move: being Canadian is "in" these days) that the same things don't happen in Canada.'[62] This, of course, is the song's strength: it emotionally charges individuals within a collectivity while asserting difference and distinction from the United States, a foil against which one can rally a national sense of self. At issue is not Canadian identity as it exists but, more simply, what Canada is not. In asserting what Canada is not, they are encouraged to rally together in a way that is just as, if not more, effective than asserting specific ideas of Canadianness (ideas that might not speak for all of the members of a highly regionalized and politically, economically, and socially heterogeneous country). As theorist Simon Frith has pointed out, music is used not only to assert what one is but what one is not: 'We use pop songs to create for ourselves a particular sort of self-definition, a particular place in society. The pleasure that pop music produces is a pleasure of identification – with the music we like, with the performers of that music, with the other people who like it. And it is important to note that the production of identity is also a production of non-identity – it is a process of inclusion and exclusion.'[63] This is just as true in national, gender, and socio-economic terms.

Paradoxically, 'American Woman' pitted Canadians against Americans yet became the first single by a Canadian group to hit number one in both countries. The reasons for its success were different in the United States than in Canada, however, as the song corresponded with the widespread rejection of that country's 'war machines' and 'ghetto scenes' by its own citizenry. After all, there was nothing in 'American Woman' that gave the song an exclusively Canadian viewpoint. The 'American Woman' was the America of their parents, of Nixon and the White House, of the military-industrial complex, racism, poverty, and empty consumerism. 'American Woman' was open to multiple mediations and narratives. It is worth noting that the song's lack of an exclusively identifiable Canadian position allowed it to be used successfully three decades later in *Austin Power: The Spy That Shagged Me* as a means of depicting a male British super-spy's distress and anger towards a female American spy who betrayed him.[64]

The Guess Who rejected the violence and racial problems that characterized the United States but, except for Randy Bachman, had no qualms with wholeheartedly accepting the rock and roll lifestyle offered within its major cities. Life in Winnipeg had sheltered the band from the excesses of the psychedelic drug culture, yet fame and touring across the continent changed all of that. Bachman has explained that

> Winnipeg wasn't much of a drug city then but we would go to Vancouver or San Francisco on tours and you would shake someone's hand and when you took your hand back there would be a joint in your palm or some purple capsules or a chunk of hash. 'What's this? This guy put a piece of rabbit droppings in my hand.' There was a prevailing belief at that time that you had to take drugs to be creative. That was the sentiment put forth by the subculture of the San Francisco bands like the Grateful Dead and Jefferson Airplane, and the British bands picked up on that.[65]

Bachman, a Mormon who abstained from alcohol and drugs, did not buy into that belief. His bandmates, on the other hand, proved more than keen to enjoy the fruits of their success, and Bachman, the level-headed businessman, dynamic guitarist, and half of a prolific songwriting duo, departed after a show at the Fillmore East in May 1970. Cummings, Kale, and Peterson have long said that they fired Bachman, while the latter has claimed that he had been about to quit the band, not only because of the partying but due to a chronic medical problem that often left him hospitalized after a performance. Either way, Bachman fell out with the band, and two guitarists from the Winnipeg scene, Kurt Winter and Greg Leskiw, were brought on as replacements.

With Bachman's moderation and guidance out of the way, and stuck with a 'soft rock' image that needed to be corrected, the Guess Who went about indulging in the benefits of rock and roll with little qualms about doing it in the public eye. Their antics received widespread coverage, among the most memorable being Jack Batten's account of the time he spent with them during a 1971 tour. This included, Batten told *Maclean's* readers, a particularly questionable encounter between the band and a groupie:

'Hey, we got a chick in there who'll do anything,' [roadie Jim] Martin says.

Inside, a small, pale, blond girl is sitting on a bench smoking a cigarette. She has a wistful, spaniel face and the unfinished body of a 13-year-old, though she's probably closer to 20 … 'Hey, come here.' [Roadie Jim] Kirby motions to the girl. He takes her down the hall off the dressing room. Cummings ambles behind and all three turn into the shower room. 'Only one day on the road,' [road manager Jim] Millican says, 'and already there's a bad case of animalism going on.'[66]

Although the psychedelic drug period had pretty much ended by the time the Guess Who hit its stride, there was nonetheless plenty of booze, pot, and, the drug of choice in the 1970s, cocaine. The Guess Who's reputation for boozing was so great that it was mentioned in the 2000 film *Almost Famous*, directed by former music journalist Cameron Crowe. In the film, *Rolling Stone* writer Lester Bangs is shown having a conversation with radio disc jockey Alice Wisdom, during which he dismisses Jim Morrison of the Doors as 'a drunken buffoon posing as a poet' in favour of the Guess Who: 'They've got the courage to be drunken buffoons, which makes them poetic.'

For west coast bands like the Collectors and the United Empire Loyalists, regionalism meant remoteness from the Toronto scene and interaction with the California psychedelic bands; for Toronto bands the Paupers and Kensington Market, their location led to drug-fuelled musical experiments in Yorkville and a launching pad into deals with major American labels; and for the Guess Who, life in the prairies shielded them from the heavier elements of psychedelia and helped to keep them on an even keel as they built a career that allowed them to rally attention south of the border. In each case the bands were tied to a continental ebb and flow that ran north-south, and had little contact, even in terms of airplay, with Canadian groups outside their region. They were much more likely to share a bill with Jefferson Airplane, Grateful Dead, Country Joe and the Fish, or the Doors than with a Canadian band from a different region. Often enough they also shared management and record labels with their American counterparts, having focused on, if not relocated to, the United States. Staying in Canada offered little more than, at best, regional success.

The Guess Who started out as a regional band but became – and were perhaps the first rock and roll group in Canada to be treated as such – archetypically national. It was not just that they went on to achieve substantial coast-to-coast airplay in the face of regional divides, as that was not completely unheard of, nor that their affiliation with the prairies played into the national myth-symbol complex, nor even that they tied into the anti-Americanism of the time, although those elements certainly endeared them to many Canadians. The band came to prominence at a time when rock and roll was undergoing a major shift in which the citizenry started to use 'pop' music to mediate a national sense of self, and, in turn, musicians became exalted as representatives of the national community. With the Canadian government about to pass a broadcasting regulation that required radio stations to air a minimum level of domestic programming, the Guess Who's numerous commercial singles received extensive airplay across the country. A combination of ideology and legislation would help to make the Guess Who not only a rock and roll band but also 'Canadian content.'

6

'Legislated Radio': Industry, Identity, and the Canadian Content Regulations

What can you do when radio stations just aren't interested in Canadian discs? Unless you have a U.S. chart listing, the Toronto stations couldn't care less whether you're Canadian or Calathumpian. We just wouldn't bother to make another disc for the local market; it's a waste of money, talent and energy. Forget it.
— Brian Pombiere, manager of the Lords of London, 1968[1]

The stock answer is 'We play what the listeners want to hear' and the phrase 'according to their popularity outside Canada' is omitted.
— *RPM*, 'Legislated Radio: Americanized Radio,' 1968[2]

We seriously believe that today Canadian radio is, in fact, as Canadian as the Maple Leaf. Music, on the other hand, is truly international.
— W.D. Whitaker, Station Representatives Association of Canada, 1970[3]

What Canadian broadcasters have done so well for over half-a-century in promoting to Canadians the talent of foreign countries, the CRTC contends can now be directed towards selling Canadian artists to Canadians.
— Lynman Porrs, President of Standard Broadcast Productions and General Manager of the Canadian Talent Library, 1970[4]

'The trouble with the music that Canadian teenagers listen to, if you believe a thirty-five-year-old Toronto music publisher named Walt Grealis, isn't that it's rock 'n' roll; the trouble is that it is *foreign* rock 'n' roll.'[5] Jack Batten of *Maclean's* was reporting on an idea that many readers in 1964 would have found to be rather strange. Why did the origins of this guitar-strumming, drum-clanging, sometimes foolish, sometimes debauched, music matter? For Grealis, the origins mattered because the airwaves were publicly owned yet radio stations were airing little other than recordings that were already popular in the United States. Domestic talent was thus being shut out of its own marketplace. How could a recording industry come into existence when airtime was not being used for domestic releases? Frustrated with the status quo, Grealis launched an industry trade paper, *RPM*, in February 1964. Such an undertaking for an industry that barely existed certainly took determination. Grealis, an ex-member of the Royal Canadian Mounted Police and a former record promoter, faced an uphill battle. Fortunately for Grealis, he was supported by record promoter and friend Stan Klees, who joined the magazine as a columnist and helped out behind the scenes. Klees has told of how they 'weren't journalists and didn't realize that every word in *RPM* would be scrutinized. As years went on and we got staff, they really educated us and we became better at what we did. No trained journalist would have been foolish enough to have launched something like *RPM*.'[6] An anemic industry and a lack of journalistic experience were only two of the many hurdles the duo faced. It turned out that the lack of airplay for domestic singles was not simply the result of radio stations being in the dark. As Grealis described to music journalist Ritchie Yorke at the turn of the 1970s, 'the majority of people told me to get lost.'[7] The biggest problem facing the development of a music scene was what Grealis called the 'apathy of broadcasters. A promotion man would take in a Canadian record and they'd throw it into the garbage right in front of him. Those things actually happened.'[8]

For Yorke, Grealis was not saying anything new. The music journalist, an Australian by birth, had only been in Canada for a few years but had already made his way to the forefront by writing a music column that was published in approximately 150 newspapers and holding the position as Canadian correspondent for *Rolling Stone* and *Billboard*.[9] Frustrated at the lack of opportunities for domestic talent, Yorke would eventually join *RPM* as a columnist. Together these three people – an ex-Mountie, a record producer, and a recent immigrant – would do more than any Canadian musician to bring about legislation designed to ensure opportunities for Canadians to access their own airwaves.

Fortunately for the trio, they had allies among like-minded entrepreneurs, particularly grassroots record labels that were run more out of passion than for profit. Stan Klees had himself started off as a teenage disc jockey at CHUM and gone on to work at London and Astral Records before forming his own label, Tamarac Records, in 1963, followed the next year by the all-Canadian Bigland label. Similarly, entrepreneurs Duff and Danny Roman created David G Records and Roman

Records, releasing singles by David Clayton-Thomas and his Quintet. Art Sniderman launched Chateau, Canatal, and in the fall of 1964 created ACT (All Canadian Talent). In January 1965 Art Sniderman, Dave Pears, Stan Klees, and Duff and Danny Roman teamed up to create Red Leaf, a musical collective in which each component operated independently but benefited from the strength of name recognition and industry presence that came with an umbrella company.[10] Later that year, Quality Records, which had distributed the Beau-Marks and the Guess Who, got on the Canadian content bandwagon by creating Can Cut, a label dedicated to Canadian music.[11]

Multinational record labels, with branch plants in Canada for distributing foreign records, even began taking a chance on Canadian-produced singles. RCA Victor, which possessed one of the two main recording studios in Toronto at the time, created the 'Canada-International' label in 1964 to export Canadian artists to the United States, Britain, Europe, Australia, and even South America. Likewise, Capitol and Columbia began picking up singles for distribution in the United States.[12] Among the exports were the Esquires' 'Love Made a Fool of You,' the Big Town Boys' 'It Was I,' Little Caesar and the Consuls' 'You've Got a Hold on Me' and 'It's So Easy,' and the Guess Who's 'Shakin' All Over,' 'Hey Ho (What You Do to Me),' and 'Hurting Each Other.'[13]

The surge of activity seemed to signify the genesis of a domestic recording industry. '"Stop the world, we want to get on" just about sums up the spirit of 1965 within the recording industry in Canada,' Kit Morgan reported to readers of *Billboard* in January 1965.[14] 'Enthusiasm and optimism about Canadian production keynotes the forecast for 1965 from both major companies and smaller independent companies, promising that this will be the breakthrough year, the year in which Canadian records will make their first strong impact on the national and international markets.'[15] Although celebratory, Morgan was nonetheless quick to remind readers that the major labels were primarily in Canada to press and distribute foreign recordings, so such moves were to be taken with a grain of salt.[16] This was less the case in French-speaking Canada, with its gushing of Québécois nationalism. Morgan explained to the international readership of *Billboard* that 'the French-speaking people have a spirit of togetherness, a pride in being French Canadian, that leads them to support French-Canadian artists and make "stars" out of them to an extent that is envied in English-speaking Canada.'[17] There were enough labels, musicians, entrepreneurs, and consumers in Quebec for a five-day event, Festival du Disque and Grand Prix du Disque, to be held in

Montreal in 1965. Together they celebrated not only industry but identity. The economic potential in the French-speaking market was so great, in fact, that investors often bypassed the English-speaking market.[18]

Morgan was right to temper his enthusiasm. The industry splurge in the English-speaking market did not pan out; there was no reason for radio station programmers to take a chance on unproven domestic singles when they could turn to *Billboard* to find out which singles were already profitable elsewhere. Not surprisingly, then, it has been estimated that only 200 or so singles were recorded and pressed by Canadian acts in 1966.[19] The failure of the prospective investment boom was more than clear by 1968. In April of that year Stan Klees offered readers of *RPM* a gloomy perspective on the prospects of the recording industry: 'Today the American and British A&R man casts a wary eye at Canada and asks himself if it is worth the trouble. He can also sit back in confidence knowing that not one of the groups could be worth two cents of promotion when they haven't been able to prove their point in Canada.'[20]

Klees and Grealis could not let the situation continue unabated. Two weeks after Klees's complaint about the state of the industry, *RPM* launched what became the most important and influential campaign for Canadian content in radio broadcasting. On 20 April 1968, the trade paper published the first of a ten-part 'Legislated Radio' series that called upon the federal government to legislate a minimum amount of Canadian content on the radio airwaves. '"Legislated Radio" hung around for a few weeks before Walt [Grealis] decided to risk publishing it,' Klees has recalled. 'It had many rewrites and still has many errors (as did *RPM* and I constantly apologize that we were not journalists). Running the series put the future of *RPM* at risk. Neither the multinationals nor the broadcasters wanted to see that in print.'[21] The tremendously provocative series was left unsigned, but Klees has recently claimed authorship while explaining that Grealis 'heavily edited' the pieces.[22] Officially at *RPM* as the contributor of 'Music Biz,' a column about the industry side of things, Klees was sure to distance himself from the series. For instance, he remarked in the 22 June issue that 'like so many in the music industry, I read the current series of articles in *RPM* on "Legislated Radio" with great interest.'[23] Klees had good reason for taking such measures given that he was a record producer and could not risk souring his relationship with labels and stations further; he had already been tied up in a libel suit against Robert McAdorey and CHUM.[24] That he was actually doing more than merely writing a column, given his friendship with Grealis, though, would have certainly come as no surprise to many people in the industry.

'Legislated Radio: A License to Make Money?' the first instalment of the series, held little back. Combining a nationalistic angst with the belief that, as a publicly owned resource, the airwaves should be opened to use by performance and recording talent alike, *RPM* made clear its support for Canadian content regulations:

Nationalism is non-profit so advertising revenue is the chief concern of most programmers. We have often been reminded, by holders of licenses to make money, that as much as 85% of their programming is Canadian in content. It's quite obvious that they also have a license which allow them to exaggerate. Canadian content on any radio station or television station could never tally up to 85%, even if you considered dead air as being of domestic content. Stations have low costs for acquiring albums, either getting them at discount prices or, often the case, free from labels seeking an audience for their 'canned goods.' It is quite unlike television in this way. Too often they hide behind the excuse, particularly border stations, that they must present the same content as American stations in order to hold listeners, and, just as popular a defense, the ease by which they defend radio broadcasting as a 'free enterprise' irregardless of the fact that airwaves are limited and, in getting to use them to make money, an obligation is owed to the audiences. What is the worst that could happen to the Canadian programmer if 'legislated radio' came about? It would force him to program for Canada, regardless of any foreign competition. It would also make his license forcibly Canadian causing the station to serve Canada as a good citizen; and the Americanized programming could then become the spice that would add to the inventiveness that Canadian content would demand and in fact is presently in need of.[25]

Airwaves as a publicly owned resource; regulations a sign of good corporate citizenship; a level playing field between the few stations that aired Canadian records and those that operated for maximum profit; the creation of a star system essential to attracting industry investment; opportunities for talent otherwise lured to the United States and England – these were just a few of the justifications for a legislated, minimum amount of domestic airplay that *RPM* presented over the course of its ten-part series.[26] Further, *RPM* took great offence at the claim that radio stations were already providing 85 per cent Canadian content. According to statistics compiled by the trade paper, apparently less than 6 per cent of radio airplay went to songs involving any Canadian talent, and of that 6 per cent a mere 17 per cent of it was 'wholly Canadian,' including performer, recording talent, record company, and so on, while the other 83 per cent had on average only one Canadian component, usually the performer. Out of these statistics, *RPM* assessed that 'less than one half of one percent are completely Canadian in content.'[27]

Given the ways in which the television industry played freely with its Canadian content quota, claiming dubious programs and airtime, any regulations for radio broadcasting needed to be free from loopholes. 'Canadian content must be emphatically defined,' *RPM* argued to its readers. 'We might endanger the future of the Canadian industry in Canada if we legislated Canadian content too loosely. The only answer is a definitely defined percentage of records, totally Canadian. We would be an industry that would export Canadian music, not Canada's talented people.'[28] Instead of putting the level at 55 per cent as in television, a regulation that had been in place since 1961, *RPM* suggested that 25 per cent was sufficient but that the components should be 100 per cent Canadian in origin in order to ensure that the industry as a whole had opportunities to access the airwaves.[29] Only then would the industry escape the self-defeating loophole of radio stations airing records that *RPM* described as 'a Canadian artist produced in a foreign country singing a foreign song and under contract to a foreign record company.'[30] The need to prevent a loose definition of Canadian content was reiterated by Klees in his 'Music Biz' column later that year: 'If Canadian content is to encourage a Canadian record industry, then there are certain things we can assume. We can immediately regard any production made outside Canada as NOT Canadian content or not sufficiently Canadian content to create a Canadian record industry. Obviously it is (in fact) a production that is supporting a foreign record industry.'[31] The recording industry, then, was deemed just as important as songwriters and musicians; without material resources there would be few opportunities for performers other than those who were able to attract attention outside of Canada.

On 6 July 1968, after ten persuasive segments, the 'Legislated Radio' series came to an end. In a final pièce de résistance, *RPM* provided readers with the mailing address for Pierre Juneau, the recently appointed chairman of the Canadian Radio and Television Commission, and the battle was turned over to the energies of others:

We have started the ball rolling for the industry. It is now up to the music industry to see to it that this Legislation is not shelved. It is up to the music industry to lobby harder than the Broadcasters to make sure that the Legislation is thorough enough to guarantee progress in the Canadian industry …

Canadian content is NOT the broadcasting of expatriated Canadians who have prospered in other parts of the world and are Canadians by name only. Canadian television is not shows that are broadcast in Canada but have originated elsewhere. Canadian motion pictures should be made in Canada by Canadians and should star Canadian actors. A Canadian trade magazine is not a magazine that contains 85% foreign news because the Canadian industry has little to offer.

Our responsibility to the industry as crusaders for this cause ends here. What happens now is in the hands of the industry, the Canadian Radio and Television Commission and the Secretary of State.[32]

Of course, this was not the end of it, and *RPM* kept the issue alive. Among the most notable pieces was written by Yorke (by now a regulator contributor to *RPM*) two months after the series had wrapped up. In 'Can a Law Put Canada on the Hit Parade?' he opened the issue to people on both sides of the debate. Garry Ferrier, program director for CHUM-FM, reportedly told Yorke that the complaints were 'like a broken record. A lot of garbage.' Ferrier went so far as to claim that 'we listen to every Canadian record and play it if it's good. We've been a leader in promoting Canadian talent.' Yet he then dismissed the possibility of actually having to account for the number of singles being played, telling Yorke, 'you can't shove Canadianism down people's throats.' When Yorke gave Klees a chance at a rebuttal in the article, the same analogy was used but with a different onus: 'Our stations are followers, not innovators. If a disc makes it in the United States we get it shoved down our throats too. Now and then Toronto stations will play a local disc but it's very rare. I figure that of every 100 good local records, maybe 10 get a chance at exposure.' Klees made his point clear. Radio programming was by nature a selective process, and by relying upon foreign recordings proven abroad radio stations were regulating the airwaves as much, if not more, than any legislation would.[33]

With pressure building against the broadcasters, a number of major stations mobilized against a quota. In June 1969 the Maple Leaf System (MLS) was formed by CKLG-Vancouver, CKXL-Calgary, CHED-Edmonton, CKOM-Saskatoon, CKCK-Regina, CHLO-St. Thomas, CKOC-Hamilton, CHUM-Toronto, CKPT-Peterborough, CFRA-Ottawa, CFOX-Montreal, and CJCH-Halifax as the twelve voting members and CJVI-Victoria and CKLC-Kingston as non-voting associate members. The

MLS, in its own words, was established 'to create an environment for encouraging the development of Canadian talent by establishing an association of radio stations which will, as a group, lend their facilities for the greater exposure of Canadian artists on a regular and continuing and simultaneous basis.'[34] But truer to the reason for its formation, CHUM admitted in an interview with the trade paper *Music Scene*, 'it is hoped that this success will eliminate some of the severe criticism leveled against private broadcasters over the years for what was deemed to be their lack of interest in fostering Canadian talent.'[35] As put more forthrightly by Yorke, 'the real reason for the formation of the MLS was to try to throw the [broadcasting regulator] off the track, to demonstrate a sincere effort among broadcasters to expose Canadian artists on domestic airwaves, to dismiss the need for legislation.'[36] Whereas for the first six months stations said they would give a minimum of two weeks over to three albums agreed upon by the members, the system was then changed to a point system in which stations ranked albums and airplay was not compulsory. In the end the system came down to member willingness.[37] Thus, radio stations could publicly say they were part of a system giving airtime to Canadian records, but there was no actual requirement for member stations to do so. The MLS achieved a coup by convincing Walt Grealis to come on-board as a coordinator, bringing with him tremendous credibility. 'At first I was suspicious,' Grealis explained to Yorke in 1971, 'but I decided to help wherever I could. They appointed me MLS coordinator. They thought they had silenced one of their noisiest critics.'[38] After only a few months in the position, though, he resigned in frustration.

The idea of instituting a Canadian content regulation for radio airwaves was nothing new. Television had a 55 per cent quota as of 1961, the result of a federal decision to end the Canadian Broadcasting Corporation's reign as the country's sole television network and to allow privately owned stations to create an independent network not required to carry CBC programming. When radio broadcasting underwent a similar but only partial denationalization a couple of years later, the Board of Broadcast Governors (the regulator at the time) was still busy sorting out the television sector yet talked about similar regulations for radio to come in time.[39] Years passed, however, and the radio issue languished. A beacon of change came with the election of Pierre Trudeau in 1968 and the replacement of the Tory-leaning Board of Broadcast Governors with the more Liberal-friendly Canadian Radio and Television Commission.

Trudeau selected Pierre Juneau, an old friend who had worked at the National Film Board and the Board of Broadcast Governors, to chair the CRTC. Although the new broadcasting regulator had a lot of tasks to be sorted out and undertaken, *RPM* made sure that the Canadian content issue was at the forefront. 'We had stacks of reprints at the office and handed it out to anyone who would write to the CRTC and further the cause,' Klees has recalled.[40] The CRTC also received a petition for a 50 per cent quota from the Canadian Council of Performing Arts Union, representing the American Federation of Musicians (Canada), ACTRA, AGVA, and Actors Equity, among others.[41]

On 12 February 1970, just under two years after *RPM* launched 'Legislated Radio,' the CRTC proposed increasing Canadian content on television from 55 to 60 per cent and initiating a 30 per cent quota for AM-band radio broadcasting.[42] The proposed criteria for what constituted Canadian content in radio was much looser than hoped for by *RPM*. The CRTC only required that two of four points be met in order for a song to be quantified – a word used here because the criteria are a tabulation of citizenship and location rather than a qualitative assessment of character – as Canadian content. The categories were as follows:

M (music) – the music is composed entirely by a Canadian;
A (artist) – the music is, or the lyrics are, performed principally by a Canadian;
P (production) – the musical selection consists of a live performance that is (i) recorded wholly in Canada, or, (ii) performed wholly in Canada and broadcast live in Canada;
L (lyrics) – the lyrics are written entirely by a Canadian.[43]

The so-called MAPL system was to start one year from the date of the proposal, with only one of four points being required during the first year and, as of the third year, a minimum of 5 per cent of the airtime entailing the musical composition component. A Canadian was defined as a citizen, landed immigrant, or someone who was a resident for at least six months before their participation in the act of creation. Canadian citizens living abroad were included but only releases produced up to the date that they took American citizenship (if this became the case).

The CRTC followed the Canadian content proposal with a week of hearings starting on 16 April 1970. At the first day of the hearings the Canadian Association of Broadcasters (CAB), representing the privately

owned broadcasters, launched a presentation designed to convince the
regulator that broadcasters were community-builders doing their best
to offer Canadian content despite their access to little other than sub-
par singles. Economic interests were easily, but not always convincingly,
guised within rhetoric of good corporate citizenship. 'Broadcasters are
just as Canadian, just as interested in developing Canada and in strength-
ening the total Canadian fabric as anyone else,' argued Don Hamilton,
vice-president of the CAB, to the commissioners.[44]

> If truly 'Canadian' music of a usable nature existed in any large quantity,
> broadcasters of course would be using it. Most broadcasters are right now
> employing the usable music that can be defined as Canadian. Some of them
> have gone out of their way to broadcast now and then 'Canadian' music
> simply because it appeared to be Canadian, at the double risk of adverse au-
> dience reaction and of equating 'Canadian' with mediocrity. No regulation
> is necessary to require Canadian broadcasters to utilize Canadian music;
> and no regulation can succeed in compelling them to use raw material that
> is simply not available.[45]

The CRTC was told to stop blaming broadcasters, drop the proposed
quota, and instead push the government to institute new copyright legislation, anti-dumping and tariff legislation, import duties or excise taxes,
and/or withhold a percentage of foreign record sales and divert it to the
recording industry.[46]

This dodging of responsibility and obligation was backed by the well-
worn argument that regulations were a form of censorship and a limi-
tation on consumer choice. John Funston of CKSL-London, Ontario,
another representative of the CAB, took the liberty of speaking on behalf
of the 'average' Canadian in praising the existing relationship between
broadcasters, airwaves, and audiences:

> We believe one of the most overlooked facts about radio and television is
> that they are essentially media of entertainment. Canadians spend millions
> of dollars each year to provide entertainment in their homes and in their
> automobiles. The purchasers are not interested in Government bodies reg-
> ulating their entertainment or their culture. In a free society, an individual
> is free to see the movie of his choice, read the newspaper of his choice, the
> book or magazine of his choice, listen to the record of his choice, or listen
> to the radio station of his choice. That is what the individual in Canada has
> been doing ... We oppose the suggestion of regulating broadcast music be-

cause it is censorship. It is an inhibiting factor in programming. We reject
the concept of programming by regulation because it is contrary to the
democratic way of life.[47]

Yet an educated observer would have no trouble pointing out the flaws in
the arguments. Broadcasting was not 'essentially' an entertainment but
a limited, publicly owned natural resource regulated by the government
on behalf of the population as a whole. This had been recommended by
the 1929 Royal Commission on Radio Broadcasting and affirmed by the
1932 Radio Broadcasting Act (and subsequently in the 1958 and 1968
Broadcasting Acts). Station owners were granted a privilege over other
citizens to use the airwaves to make money but, in exchange for doing
so, the Broadcasting Act required that the programming entail 'predominantly Canadian creative and other resources.'[48] As to the CAB's second
argument, freedom of choice did not come into play because radio stations acted as filters offering audiences content from which to choose.
Canadians were not free to access domestic recordings on the airwaves
because they were not provided as an option. In critical terms, radio stations were the censors; they were the 'inhibiting factor in programming,'
as Funston had put it, in selecting what was and was not broadcast. It
is no coincidence that the supposed freedom station owners rallied to
protect also happened to be the process by which the most profit could
be had.

The Association of Canadian Television and Radio Artists, representing domestic talent, was more than familiar with CAB smokescreens.
The day after the CAB made its case, ACTRA arrived with a delegation
that included three prominent CBC figures (Warren Davis, Fred Davis,
and Adrienne Clarkson) and two popular authors and public commen-
tators (Pierre Berton and Farley Mowat). Whereas the CAB identified
itself as the protector of freedom of speech, ACTRA argued that freedom of speech only existed insofar as there was diversity in offerings
and access. The problem, Warren Davis argued, was the 'lack of access
to the public. Too few opportunities to say what needs to be said. There
are just too few programs; too few places that books can be published or
sold; too few radio shows; too few films; too few film companies making
films so that these stories can be told. It is a lack of access to the public.'[49] Whereas Davis spoke moderately, the acerbic Farley Mowat, true to
form, derided the private sector for its willingness to sacrifice domestic
talent for the sake of money. 'I think, essentially, the way I feel about
the whole problem that faces us today is that the little money grubbers

in the communications media who seem to think we have nothing of worth here to sell outside of the country, and that they must go outside the country and buy what they have and bring it back, I think they are absolutely wrong. I think they are liars.'[50] Still, the most poignant insight of the day seemed to come from Pierre Berton, who argued that because the airwaves belong to all Canadians the programming should serve a breadth of interests, including the desire for Canadian content. 'Surely part of the public broadcasting philosophy of this country,' he stated to the members of the hearing, 'must be to give not just the majority of people what they want, but a minority of people what they want.'[51] Both the CAB and ACTRA were protecting the economic interests of their members; only ACTRA, however, did so with arguments in line with the Broadcasting Act.

Ritchie Yorke certainly agreed with ACTRA. On 20 April, five days into the hearings, the committee called upon the long-haired, hippy-looking music journalist to offer his insights into the industries in Canada and abroad. Yorke had only been in Canada for three years, having arrived after time spent in Britain, but he had a lot to say: 'My reason for being here is that I honestly believe it is a tragedy, an incredible lack of awareness that Canada has gone through allowing broadcasters to use a segregationist policy against young Canadians.'[52] Yorke told of how, soon after arriving in Canada, he

turned on the radio and television and was astonished at the complete lack of anything Canadian apart from the news. I talked to a few young Canadians at random and asked them if they had anything against Canadian Talent. 'No,' they said, the trouble was they never heard any Canadian talent, all they ever heard was U.S. or English acts and the occasional transplanted Canadian band living in America. Three years later I am firmly convinced the lack of a Canadian music industry is the direct result of the lack of exposure of the Canadian product. Despite what our broadcasters might think, there is absolutely nothing wrong with Canadian talent. In fact as far as talent goes, this country is among the top five in the world.[53]

Not only were radio stations doing little to support domestic talent, Yorke argued, but programmers were not experts when it came to quality; they had regularly aired poor singles simply because they were of American origin, singles that nonetheless sold because with enough exposure any release will sell.[54] 'Any broadcaster who played "Yummy, Yummy, Yummy, I've Got Love in My Tummy," that memorable American hit by the Ohio

Express should never get himself involved in a discussion on quality.'[55] At the same time, stations routinely rejected domestic singles that went on to success in the United States. Yorke pointed to the Guess Who as an example of a group that was continually overlooked until its singles broke south of the border.[56] In the end, he offered a position not unlike the one presented by ACTRA several days earlier: 'What [a Canadian content regulation for radio] will do is give young Canadians a choice, a chance to stay in their own country, the land they were born in and offer their artistic talents to their fellow Canadians. That surely is not too much to ask.'[57]

Yorke was not the only 'longhair' to testify in front of the committee. The next day Skip Prokop and Don DiNovo of Lighthouse, a group that melded rock and roll with brass and strings to create a 'rock and roll orchestra' of over a dozen pieces, made what was certainly one of the most memorable appearances. Called to the hearings as representatives of the music scene and asked about their employment and lifestyle – 'I was going to say "bag," but I promise not to,' joked one commissioner – the duo explained that they were musicians who had been performing in Canada for years.[58] Prokop had been part of the Paupers, one of the biggest acts of the late 1960s, before moving on to session work for the likes of Peter, Paul and Mary and Janis Joplin, and had most recently joined with keyboardist Paul Hoffer and guitarist Ralph Cole to form Lighthouse. His experience with the domestic scene, particularly the ways in which audiences went out of their way to support the performers, led him to the conclusion that Canadians wanted to hear the works of other Canadians. Although Prokop did not phrase it in nationalist terms, the implication was there: youths were starting to take to music as a national component of their identities. Prokop emphasized this by telling of how the previous year at the Atlantic City Pop Festival, Lighthouse had to stall for time by talking with the audience when the venue's equipment was not working, only to find themselves experiencing an unexpected moment of national pride. 'We were not aware of the fact that there was about 200 Canadian kids who had gone down to support us,' Prokop explained to the commissioners. 'About halfway through this talk to the audience, they broke out a Canadian flag and got a standing ovation from, like, 70,000 people. This led to a lot of questions after the Festival about what is happening in Canada. It also led me to believe that there is a certain kind of admiration for the Canadian people and the Canadian musicians and an interest in why there aren't more Canadian groups making it today.'[59]

Prokop did not finish his appearance with that anecdote. Much like ACTRA and Yorke, he told the commission that in order to have a domestic music scene one needed an industry, and that meant overhauling the broadcasting system in order to allow for performers and audiences to interact. His prediction as to what could happen if a change was made turned out to be rather accurate:

If Canada can get behind this whole thing, there will be a lot more kids who will so-called 'make it' worldwide. I feel it will be a chain reaction. A chain reaction could be set off. I do not think that any D.J. should be forced to, you know, have a piece of garbage stuffed down his throat – 'there it is buddy, and you play it because it is Canadian.' What I do feel, although, that, like, there are a lot of records around right now sitting in libraries and sitting in kids' houses that you never hear on a Canadian radio station.

Now, if we can start getting good Canadian airplay of Canadian artists, what happens are several things. The kids who are trying to make it and who are recording will start getting hit records, obviously. The next that will happen is that Canadian kids will start paying a certain amount of money to go and see them in concert. This also creates – it is the beginning of an industry. Then, the third thing that happens is that you start creating – I hate to use the term again – but, like, 'stars' within your own country and this is something that Canada has never really had.

Now, when that happens, you will start getting, like, worldwide interest in what is happening in Canada and I think what is happening, in general, throughout the United States and throughout England and Europe now, people are wondering – you know, they have heard a little bit about different groups; they know that the band, a group called the Band, who now lives and resides in the United States, you know, who is like one of the top record sellers, were all from Canada. A group called Steppenwolf, which was formerly called the Sparrow – I hung out with all these people. They were good friends of mine. They were from Canada, and in order to make it they had to go to the United States. So, because of these things happening, people around the world are aware of Canadian talent.[60]

Prokop found himself in a tougher position when asked to comment on the activities of radio stations, since, unlike Yorke, his band relied upon airplay. Still, he did not hold back in his assessment:

I hate to say this, but I will go ahead and say it, you know. I could make some enemies through this. There is a magazine called *RPM*. And I think the people from that magazine have tried very hard and seem to be very dedicated to the Canadian music thing, probably more so than most people would like to admit. In some stations it is considered, like you know, the Canadian version of the Bible as far as Canadian music is concerned, you know. But in most stations they say, 'Oh what is that?' They find out and they say, 'Oh, right. 'r-r-r-i-p-p-p." And it is filed under the trash, you know. I mean, I really mean that. That is the kind of thing that is going down.

In other words, it is really based on what is happening in the United States. Now, Lighthouse and a few other groups, Edward Bear, for example, signed with Capitol Canada. They are starting to get a big record in the United States. There are Canadian groups making it now in the United States and the reason why we would probably get a lot of airplay in Canada is because, you know, we have that thing – 'oh, they went to the States and made it.'[61]

Grealis and Klees had an ally in Prokop, and on that day the commission was offered an insightful view from the trenches of the performing industry.

The week of hearings was wrapped up on 22 April with a noteworthy appearance by the Canadian Musician Publishers Association. Allan Meyer, manager of Gordon Lightfoot's Early Morning Productions and a member of the association, added to the chorus of voices that argued on the behalf of Canadian content. One had only to look at the number of Canadians succeeding abroad to see that it was not an issue of talent, he argued:

While I was waiting I just went through the new issue of *Cash Box* magazine, an American trade paper. I noticed that the number 4 song is a Canadian composition performed by a Canadian group, the Guess Who. The number 17 song is a song recorded by a Canadian of sorts, Joni Mitchell who is one of the people whom you would have to decide would still qualify. The number 27 song was recorded in Canada by a Canadian group and written by Canadians, the Poppy Family from Vancouver. As well there are other selections chosen by various American recording artists. There is a Leonard Cohen composition and a Gordon Lightfoot composition.[62]

For Mitchell to be identified as 'a Canadian of sorts' was telling of the times; in the eyes of many people, holding Canadian citizenship was not sufficient for inclusion in a measure designed to ensure a self-sufficient domestic industry. There could be no clearer sign that the Canadian content regulation had its genesis more in industrial than ideological terms. Meyer certainly felt this way, arguing that any possible regulation should exclude citizens who had not been residents for over a year and, conversely, should include non-Canadians who lived in the country for more than a year.[63] That way the Canadian content regulation would support those who contributed to the domestic scene and prevent radio stations from relying on musicians who were famous enough to live and record abroad and as such likely to receive airplay anyway.

To this argument T. St Clair Low, a fellow member of the association, added the idea that by keeping the regulation domestically focused the industry would be more likely to attract foreign investment, much as the Beatles had done for England.[64] Over the course of the next two decades, the industry did indeed become economically viable and did attract large amounts of foreign investment – although not necessarily in line with what St Clair Low might have imagined. As will be examined in chapter eight, the money would come, but instead of being direct economic investment in Canadian-owned companies, multinational music and media conglomerates would expand their branch plants, acquire small domestic labels, and secure a monopoly over record distribution, thereby reaping the economic bounty sowed by the regulation.

The Canadian content hearings were brought to a close, but this was not the end of it all for Pierre Juneau. The Canadian Association of Broadcasters had followed their appearance at the hearings by taking their case to the federal government's Standing Committee on Broadcasting, Film and Assistance to the Arts, and on 5 May, only two weeks after Juneau had wrapped up the earlier hearings, he was called upon to address station grievances and defend the CRTC proposals. A very tough day awaited him. Stan McDowell of the *Toronto Daily Star* described Juneau's appearance in front of the committee as 'a stormy 3 1/2-hour grilling.'[65] Private-sector interests had plenty of support among committee members who agreed with the CAB that music was first and foremost a form of entertainment, not something of national concern but a mass commodity best left to the industries themselves. Besides, to MPs who likely had little knowledge of the industry outside of what they had been told by the Canadian Association of Broadcasters, Canada lacked available music and radio stations would be forced to air songs of little or no interest to audiences. No moment at the tense meeting more typified the lack of knowledge, arrogance, and support for the private sector than when an MP told Juneau that Canadians did not want to hear songs 'like

"Squaws along the Yukon" and "The Log Driver's Song" by Mac Beattie and the Ottawa Valley Melodiers.'[66]

The recent success of Canadian acts in the United States, though, meant that Juneau could offer a solid rebuttal. 'I have before me here the top record on the American market this week [and it] is called *American Woman*.'[67] After clarifying to the MPs that, although the name implied otherwise, the release was indeed by a band from Canada, Juneau rallied for a change to the radio sector status quo. 'There are a lot of singers in Canada, there are composers in Canada who have things to say, and we think we have got to make a little bit more room for them to be heard on the air. We say 30 per cent, that is all.'[68]

Broadcasters, musicians, journalists, managers, and assorted industry talent had left the CRTC with much to ponder. On 20 May, three weeks after the initial hearings had come to an end and two weeks after Juneau's appearance in front of the standing committee, the CRTC announced that the MAPL system would be implemented.[69] True to the proposal, stations would only have to use music that met one of the four criteria during the first year and two of the four as of the second year; the 30 per cent would have to be aired between 6:00 a.m. and 12:00 midnight; 'Canadian' included citizens, landed immigrants, and special cases of residency; and, as the MAPL criteria made clear, the system was to be extended equally to the main components of the musical process. Recording studios and composers were treated on a par with performers because they had just as much right to access the airwaves as did those who sang the songs, and, it almost goes without saying, a strong domestic recording industry was a prerequisite to ensuring these opportunities. The MAPL system was certainly weaker than hoped for by *RPM* and like-minded industry-builders, but it was an improvement. The Canadian content issue would be revisited in 1975 with much less fanfare, when the regulation was extended to the FM band (in this case with amounts tailored to station formats).[70]

Before concluding, it is worth noting that the Canadian content regulation has been treated as a case study by other countries. New Zealand stands out as a prime example of a country that not only had to contend with American records but also those of close-to-home competition. Much like the musicians born in Canada who relocated to the United States and became famous, many New Zealanders routinely moved to Australia because their domestic broadcasting industry relied largely on imports from Australia. In turn, musicians from New Zealand commonly became incorporated into Australian society, winning awards and coming to be regarded as Australian musicians.[71] The situation was not curbed in the slightest by New Zealand broadcasting regulations that merely required station owners to make a promise to support domestic talent, with no actual system for measuring or counting the amount of airplay.[72] Roy Shuker and Michael Pickering have explained that a vein of political conservatism meant that talk of a quota did not come about until the mid-1980s, at which time the Royal Commission into Broadcasting and Related Telecommunications (1986) recommended that the state institute a 10 per cent quota.[73] Musicians and industry entrepreneurs had been hoping for a 20 per cent quota, commonly pointing to the effectiveness of quotas in Canada, France, Sweden, Israel, Jamaica, Tanzania, and even neighbouring (and talent-attracting) Australia. The quota in Australia, in fact, had been established back in the 1970s and was credited with helping to develop a $1.5 billion music industry employing over 70,000 people by the mid-1990s.[74] Station owners in New Zealand, on the other hand, employed well-worn arguments against a quota system: audiences preferred foreign music; domestic recordings were sub-par; stations were already serving the public interest; regulations were a form of censorship, and so forth. The issue dragged on for another decade before the government began to show serious interest in a quota, leading radio stations to try to defuse the situation by adopting a voluntary 10 per cent quota (not unlike radio stations in Canada with the MLS system). New Zealand broadcasting and recording industry expert Rocky Douché, in a report for the government's Industry New Zealand, found that the voluntary quota, as a self-monitored commitment, only reached about half the promised level, and, making the situation worse, stations tended to relegate the music to the midnight to 6 a.m. slot when listener levels were at their lowest.[75] Not until the election of the Labour government in 1999 was a move made towards a mandated quota, although even this was reduced to a voluntary 20 per cent quota in the face of obstinate radio stations and, quite tellingly, warnings from the United States government that the General Agreement on Tariffs and Services might not be ratified if New Zealand went ahead with a mandated quota.[76]

Skip Prokop, having served in the trenches of Yorkville as a member of the Paupers and then as Lighthouse, knew that musicians did not necessarily want to move away from Canada but that the lack of industry left them little choice. 'A lot of kids are very interested in cutting albums and signing with managers, but they are very afraid to sign or to record in Canada because there is no industry,' he explained to the CRTC, 'so they go to the United States.'[77] Up to this point acts had often made demos using mono- or duo-track equipment and without the aid of properly appointed studios let alone trained producers and engineers. Only on rare occasions did this lead to success, as with Chad Allan and the Expressions (later the Guess Who), who recorded their hit 'Shakin' All Over' on a single-track Ampex recording machine in a concrete room at CJAY-TV in Winnipeg. They had little option at the time. Allan, in a 1968 article for *Music Scene*, told of how 'there are no professional recording studios in Winnipeg ... Many local groups do manage to record their own material, but they are forced to travel to such places as Minneapolis, Toronto, Edmonton or anywhere else that can assure them of a good, clean sound. Those who cannot afford the expense of recording away from home have the doubtful alternative of trying their luck in local makeshift studios.'[78] As of 1968 only a few studios of significant quality existed in Canada, notably RCA Victor, Bay (ARC), Sound Canada, and Hallmark.[79]

RPM and others in the industry were helping to change the situation, but doing so did not come without a fight. The trade paper was not exaggerating when it told readers that 'no music industry organization has lobbied as heavily for legislation as the broadcasters have worked to suppress it ... While most industries have organizations working to make their needs known to the government, the music industry has been completely lax in this area.'[80] After all, by this point the Association of Canadian Television and Radio Artists had successfully rallied for a television Canadian content regulation, the periodical sector had pushed the federal government into passing the Paperback and Periodical Distributors Act (1964), and feature-film makers had achieved a $10 million investment fund administered by the Canadian Film Development Corporation (1968). As the Broadcasting Act made clear, federal intervention on behalf of the music industry was just as justifiable as any of the other initiatives because the airwaves were a publicly owned natural resource to be used to promote interaction – including musical – among the citizenry. Station owners had a long track record of using the airwaves to make money by importing low-cost, highly profitable content; in exchange for this privilege, logic seemed to dictate, stations should have to provide a minimum amount of domestic talent on the publicly owned airwaves.

Fortunately for the advocates of Canadian content, Pierre Trudeau valued culture and communications as tools of nation-building. Over the course of the next decade his administration launched funding programs and citizenship and ownership regulations designed to encourage the production of domestic cultural goods.[81] The CRTC, for its part, made it clear that the privilege of making money from the publicly owned airwaves came with the obligation of allocating a relatively small amount of the airtime – less than a third – to domestic talent. The fact that the MAPL criteria gave equal weight to the four main components of a recording reveals the degree to which the regulation was designed to ensure a breadth of opportunities.

During the hearings popular music was not yet thought to be a component of nationhood. There were no grandiose statements about songwriters being essentialistic providers of a nation's voice; in fact, quite the opposite was the case: there were calls to exclude certain expatriates who would later be elevated to the status of national icons. The ideological fusion of music and national identity was still in its genesis. The Canadian content regulation made sense because, even putting aside the convincing industrial arguments, the Broadcasting Act declared that the airwaves were a publicly owned resource to be used to facilitate exchanges among the citizenry. Yet, although the CRTC hearings on Canadian content did not stray from talk of industry and opportunity, the act of state involvement inherently meant, if only to a limited extent, a conflation of industry with identity and the possibility that music existed to some degree in national terms. Further, although the MAPL criteria measured a musical commodity in industrial terms, the term 'Canadian content' could easily be twisted into a decree of Canadianness. Whether the participants realized it or not, the Canadian content regulation, in coinciding with a maturation in songwriting and a greater sense of popular culture as tied to the national identity, would contribute to a paradigm shift in which music in Canada would become 'Canadian music.'

7

'Oh What a Feeling': Canadian Content and Identity Politics in the 1970s

Across the nation, deejays were ringing the changes on the Maple Leaf theme, dusting off old Lorne Greene and Gisele MacKenzie records, figuring whether Paul Anka and Robert Goulet hold Canadian passports, and discovering with delight that *The Darktown Strutters' Ball* and *K-K-K-Katy* are legitimately part of the Canadian cultural heritage.

– *Time*, 1971[1]

Songs have always enjoyed a somewhat privileged position as the mouthpiece for nationalist feelings.

– Michel Rivard, Beau Dommage, 1977[2]

'Opportunity,' a single by the Toronto-based rock band Mandala, promised to be a breakthrough. That is, if they could get it aired. Much like their compatriots, Mandala ended up butting heads with the most influential radio station in the country. The band's guitarist Domenic Troiano has informed Ritchie Yorke that

> when CHUM refused to play ['Opportunity'], almost two hundred Mandala freaks picketed the station. It shocked the hell out of them. You wouldn't believe the kind of things Randy [Martin of the band] had to do to get CHUM to play our records ... We were desperately keen to do our number as a Canadian thing. But you got tired of that when everybody in the media was trying to screw you. We couldn't get any space in any of the papers except with sensational stuff, like girls ripping off their clothes or fainting at our gigs. Nobody would write about our music – they refused to believe that a Canadian band could actually make music.[3]

The lack of an industry through which to be heard had previously prompted Mandala to head south of the border in hopes of making it big. Shows at the Whisky A Go Go and Hullabaloo in Hollywood, and the recording of 'Opportunity' in Chicago with the famed Chess Records, were turned into larger concerts with the likes of Wilson Picket, Cream, and Mitch Ryder and the Detroit Wheels and eventually a record deal with Atlantic Records that resulted in *Soul Crusade* and the single 'Love It-Is.'[4] Airplay, not talent, was now the issue.

Opportunity was what Mandala needed. It was also the reason for establishing the Canadian content regulation on the publicly owned but largely privately controlled airwaves. The grandiose rhetoric about popular music as a cornerstone of national identity had yet to be applied to this sector of the entertainment industry. Even ardent advocates like Walt Grealis, Stan Klees, and Ritchie Yorke discussed the quota in terms of ensuring that domestic talent, both creative and industrial, had an opportunity to access the airwaves in the face of radio stations that relied on imported singles.

An opportunity was not the same as a guarantee, of course. The Canadian content regulation only ensured that a minimum amount of airtime was set aside for domestic recordings; the decision as to what to air came down to radio stations. As Larry Evoy, drummer and singer-songwriter for Edward Bear, pointed out to the *Georgia Straight*, 'We're not guaranteed airplay, [but] when you've done reasonably well, you've got a really good chance of getting airplay again. I think it's helped the average band, because it's increased record production and helped to make better quality records ... If bands can't record, if there's no industry, then they can't improve, write all kinds of original material, get new ideas for recording because there's no impetus for it.'[5] Edward Bear, taking its moniker from the real name of the bear made famous as Winnie the Pooh, was good enough to be backed by Capitol for the release of *Bearings* in 1969. A single from this album, 'You, Me and Mexico,' cracked the charts, although it was 'Last Song' on their third and self-titled album that gave the band a number one hit in Canada and even ranked high south of the border.[6]

The Canadian content regulation was welcomed by many aspiring musicians. For Murray McLauchlan, who had moved to New York City before a lack of funds, homesickness, and medical issues prompted his return to Canada, the recently minted regulation meant that he could try a career from home. Its importance was made clear in his autobiography *Getting Out of Here Alive: The Ballad of Murray McLauchlan*:

There was no CRTC back then, no content regulations and no level of support in Canada for homegrown music. You could walk into a top-forty radio
station with a Canadian record and it didn't matter how good it was, they'd
file it in the garbage. All the Canadian artists who'd made an impact had
done so by going to the U.S. I was beginning to bump my head on the ceil-
ing in Canada. Yes, I'd made it to a major festival and had a string of mid- to
top-line clubs I could play, but that wouldn't translate into getting a record
out and actually making some money.[7]

Pierre Senecal of Mashmakhan, another to benefit from the regulation,
similarly stated that he did not think that 'any of us are going to have
to move away anymore.'[8] Indeed, his band managed to stay in Canada,
secure a deal with Columbia, and release the highly successful 'As the
Years Go By' (a song perhaps most notable for being a massive hit in
Japan, where the band performed in a Tokyo baseball stadium).

Although many musicians were appreciative of the new regulation,
they also expressed caution towards, and even a distancing from, the
nationalism of the period and the role that the government had in passing the regulation. 'Canadian musicians,' Robert Wright has noted, 'did
not want their success to appear to be due solely to the meddling of the
government. Musicians of every stripe attempted to dispel the percep-
tion that they had a nationalist axe to grind or, worse, that their work was
officially sanctioned.'[9] Bruce Cockburn was among those who felt ill at
ease with nationalism.[10] In a conversation with Ritchie Yorke, Cockburn
supported the regulation but noted that he did so on a pragmatic level:
'I'm a Canadian, true,' Cockburn explained, 'but in a sense it's more or
less by default. Canada is the country I dislike the least at the moment.
But I'm not really into nationalism – I prefer to think of myself as being
a member of the world.'[11] Thirty-five years later he still held onto that
belief, telling Sue Carter Flinn of the *Coast*: 'I identify myself [as a Cana-
dian], inwardly as well as outwardly, but I feel like a citizen of the planet
as much as I am a Canadian.'[12] To think of oneself as anything but an artist first and foremost was detrimental to the creative process, Cockburn
has opined. 'If one is a Christian artist, one has to be a good artist first
or sell nothing. It's the same if one is a Marxist artist. If he's a Marxist
first, he's limiting his artistic range.'[13] Similarly, Anne Murray, who had
success with her recording of Gene MacLellan's 'Snowbird,' credited the
regulation with making her career possible, but at the same time, she
explained to Yorke, she wanted to be thought of more as an 'artist' than
as a 'Canadian artist.'[14]

On the other side of the spectrum, Kelly Jay of Crowbar ardently self-identified as Canadian, yet he too made reference to the regulation in terms of opportunity. Jay's patriotism, and that of the band as a whole, is legendary; their stage show featured Canadian flags and even an amplifier stack painted red and white with a red maple leaf. 'Anyone who saw Kelly Jay standing atop a concert grand piano,' Richard Flohil reminisced in 1988, 'resplendent in high-heeled leather boots emblazoned with maple leaves and a swirling cape made from the then, still-new Canadian flag will always remember the sight.'[15] Crowbar even managed to perform for Pierre and Margaret Trudeau in Perth, Ontario, presenting them with a plaque and offering thanks for the regulation: 'To Pierre Elliot Trudeau, for making it possible through the CRTC for Canadians to be heard in their own country.'[16]

The regulation certainly worked for Crowbar: their song 'Oh What a Feeling' became the first single to be a hit after the start of the regulation. The tightness of the track owed much to their years as a backing band for Ronnie Hawkins. Famed disk jockey, music correspondent, and actor Terry David Mulligan, at this time program director at CKVN-Vancouver, had nothing but praise for Crowbar, the single, and the regulation: 'Crowbar have left a good impression on Vancouver audiences,' Mulligan noted in March 1971, two months into the regulation. 'The single is THE most requested single CKVN currently plays. AKLG likewise. The record is a bitch ... just never lets down. If this is the end result of Canadian content then maybe it's worth it.'[17] That Crowbar was based in Hamilton and CKVN was in Vancouver was a sign of how the regulation was already helping to break down regional isolation.

While Crowbar was being given a chance on some stations, others, most notably the more conservative AM stations, operated on rigid formats with little room for experimentation. 'You'd hardly know that Canadian groups such as Lighthouse, Mainline, Crowbar, Chilliwack, and the Perth County Conspiracy existed if you listened only to AM radio,' Roy MacGregor of *Maclean's* complained. 'These groups have loyal followings, but they refuse to compromise their standards by adhering to a two-minute deadline when they record.'[18]

Radio stations also had little interest in singles tailored to the Canadian market. Border stations, competing against American broadcasters for audiences in both countries, were particularly disinterested. For Bob Bossin of Stringband, a group that released such singles as 'Maple Leaf Dog' and 'Dief Will Be the Chief Again,' what Canadians needed was a regulation that promoted the national identity. It was not opportunity but nation-building that Bossin sought:

> The CRTC as far as I know has never helped Stringband in any way and has probably hurt it. The form of Canadian content that they encourage has nothing to do with *content*; it results in the production of American-style music, made in Canada or American style music produced in the States that has a couple of Canadians in it. Radio stations do exactly what they have done for years – play the grooves off Anne Murray or Paul Anka.[19]

Bossin shared this frustration with Stompin' Tom Connors, a performer who managed to develop a strong grass-roots following despite being overlooked by the major record labels and urban radio stations. Connors explained to *Maclean's* that, when it came to those in the industry who rejected his work,

> their attitude was, who in hell in his right mind is going to write a song with a first line that goes, 'Just a little bit west of Kapuskasing,' or a song about 'Movin' on to Rouyn.' Well, the people there in the Travel Host Lounge in Timmins, they loved it. I guess they were tired of hearing about the stars falling on Alabama and about people waltzing in Tennessee. They wanted to hear some songs about the north country. Their country.[20]

The ability of stations to easily dismiss Connors's straightforward lyrics and simple rhymes was made all the easier given the novelty of his unabashed patriotism. The troubadour made this more than clear in 1972: 'My ambition? I guess you could say it's to sing Canada to the world.'[21] Connors even launched Boot Records in 1971 as a means of supporting non-mainstream acts often overlooked by the industry. 'I'd like to help keep some young singers and musicians from having as tough a time getting started as I did, and I'd like to promote Canadian talent.'[22] Among those he aided was east coast singer-songwriter Stephen 'Stevedore Steve' Foote, a performer cut from a similar cloth. As Foote told *Canadian Composer* about his engagement with Canada, 'it's not a matter of fitting Canadianism into my tunes so much as it is … well, you can only write what's in your heart, for lack of a better word. If you are a patriot at heart then everything that comes out will be flavoured that way.'[23]

While up-and-coming performers were wary about their success seeming to be due to the regulation, and the few nationalistic acts ended up

frustrated that there was no qualitative measure to include their domestically situated works, those with an established career not only distanced
themselves from nationalism but commonly decried the entire situation.
Part of their animosity towards the regulation was due to radio stations
'burning out' their singles. One week into the regulation, Ritchie Yorke
predicted that 'you'll hear "American Woman" once a day. You'll even
hear old Canadian singles that the stations turned down when they were
first released. You'll hear Joni Mitchell album tracks till you hate them
(if you don't already) and Paul Anka may stage a revival. Anything to
avoid playing Canadian singles by new Canadian artists, which obviously
was the whole point of the legislation.'[24] To little surprise, soon after, Jim
Kidd of Montreal's CFCF remarked that 'the percipient listener might
well have gotten the impression that AM radio stands for Anne Murray.'[25]
Along with Murray, Gordon Lightfoot became such a staple that, as Cam
Perry, station manager of Edmonton's CJCA only half joked, 'if the two
were to take out American citizenship tomorrow, Canadian radio will be
finished.'[26] Overplay led Ian Tyson to describe the regulation as 'a lot of
nonsense' because it did not 'make up for any lack of imagination on a
dumb jockey's part. In a lot of Canada, these … disk jockeys are so unim-
aginative and spend so little time researching what is happening in the
Canadian recording industry that 30 per cent seems to come out as Gord
Lightfoot and Anne Murray.'[27]

Almost needless to say, many performers were not impressed with the
outcome of the regulation.[28] They had no need for the regulation; nor,
it seemed, did they care all that much about the national imperative.
Career interests could only be harmed by nationalism and the regulation. 'I resent the hell out of guys like Juneau who take nationalism too
far,' Tyson scathingly told *Maclean's*.[29] Such talk was common from the
outspoken songwriter, whose sense of self and place was more regional
than national. 'I don't feel any kinship to Quebec or Ontario,' he later
remarked, again targeting Trudeau's intervention, complaining that
'this bicultural policy that we've got here in Canada is just plain dumb …
why do we allow people in Lethbridge to demand a trial in French? It
wastes money. It's just a knee-jerk liberal thing.'[30] Burton Cummings,
a songwriter with a notorious bravado, similarly used an interview with
Maclean's to praise his band's pre-quota success and to label the regulation a 'joke.'[31] So too did Terry Jacks of the Poppy Family, who had a hit
with 'Seasons in the Sun': 'The legislation was lobbied for by a bunch of
crybabies who couldn't get their records sold.'[32]

But no one was more vocal than Gordon Lightfoot. The regulation and any related semblance of patriotism were nothing but a hindrance to his career, the highly established and acclaimed singer-songwriter told Robert Markle in a *Maclean's* interview: 'The CRTC did absolutely nothing for me. I didn't need it, ab-so-lute-ly *nothing* ... Canadian content is fine if you're not doin' well. But I'm in the music business and I have a huge American audience. I'm going to do Carnegie Hall for the second time. I really like to record down there, but I like to live up here. I really dig this country, but I'm not going to bring out any flags. I'm an entertainer. *I'm in the music business.*'[33] It is worth noting that in that same year Lightfoot admitted to Yorke that he commonly played up his popularity in the United States while talking to Canadians, but, when it came down to it, he saw himself as simply singing about what was around him: 'In Canada, I'd tell people about my success in the U.S. I'd say I was doing really well down there, but that I didn't intend to live there. I was trying to play everyone for a while, but didn't deliberately try to make my songs more Canadian with obvious lyrics. I simply write the songs about where I am and where I'm from. I take situations and write poems about them. That's about all there is.'[34]

All the while, *RPM* continued to keep an eye on the airwaves, identifying which singles did and did not meet the MAPL criteria. Sometimes the comments were tongue-in-cheek. 'No, music directors – the Beatles do not classify as Canadian content because John Lennon spent 16 days here in 1970,' Yorke remarked in the 12 February 1971 issue of *RPM*.[35] More often, though, *RPM* helped stations navigate the MAPL system or called them out on their false tabulations:

Alice Cooper: the entire group is American, they perform their own compositions. Jack Richardson and Bob Ezrin produced the 'Love it to Death' album IN CHICAGO. They do not qualify in any way as Canadian content.

Teegarden and Van Winkle: both Americans, they did intend to record in Toronto, but due to an accident, did not. Intent to record in Canada does not constitute Canadian content.

Steppenwolf: the only Canadian-born member of the group is Jerry Edmonton who is not a featured performer and does not compose any of the group's material. They have been resident in California for over four years. Nothing by the group qualifies as Canadian in any way.

Three Dog Night: one member of the group is from Canada. Nothing by them qualifies unless it is written by him (Floyd Sneed).

Mountain: only one member, Corky Laing, is Canadian. Nothing by Mountain qualifies unless it is written by him or another Canadian Composer.[36]

Further, songs by Crosby, Stills, Nash, and Young only counted if Neil Young was the principal author of the track; merely being a member of the band was not sufficient. 'Lucretia MacEvil' and 'Hi De Ho' by Blood, Sweat and Tears could be counted towards the quota because they were composed by David Clayton-Thomas. 'Me and Bobby McGee' by Janis Joplin did not count because the two Canadian band members were only backup musicians.[37]

While *RPM* was vigilant about informing radio stations about Canadian content releases for the sake of ensuring opportunities, record labels had much to gain by doing the same. MCA Records mailed what it called 'Care Packages' of more than 4000 records (LPs and singles) to radio stations, including releases by Tom Northcott ('I Think It's Going to Rain Today'), Christopher Kearney ('Rocking Chair Ride'), and the Irish Rovers ('The Marvelous Toy').[38] Likewise, Capitol Records compiled and issued the *Capitol Records Guide to Canadian Content Programming*, a double-record set of thirty songs, some of which, in a rather strategic decision, were written by Canadians but sung by established American artists.[39]

Yet why should a radio station bother to air tracks recorded by record companies when it was possible to acquire interests in the recording and publishing industry and keep the royalties? After all, the regulation did not stipulate that the music had to be acquired from an external source. CHUM had begun to make this move in early 1970, during the time of the Maple Leaf System and, soon after the CRTC proposed the regulation, acquired Summerlea and Winterlea Music Publishing from Bob Hahn. CHUM Vice-President Larry Solway, faced by criticism for the station's vertical integration, retorted that the decision was 'a natural expansion of CHUM Radio's interest in the development of Canadian talent.'[40] MUCH Records – an anagram of CHUM – went on to record singles for such acts as Michel Pagliaro ('Give Us One More Chance') and George Olliver ('I May Never Get to See You Again' and 'Shine'). Six months after CHUM formed MUCH, the Canadian Association of Broadcasters followed suit by raising enough capital from its members to form Astra Records and purchase Laurentian Music and Rideau Music from Bob Hahn.[41]

Ritchie Yorke was aghast at what he saw as a blatant attempt to undermine and cash in on the regulation: 'We are absolutely against any domination of Canada's infant music industry by licensed users of the publicly-owned airwaves,' he told readers of *RPM*. 'We believe it is vital that we must all fight tooth and nail against this potential invasion.'[42] For radio stations to move into the recording and publishing rights industries certainly seemed to be a conflict of interest. Yorke went on to compile examples of the transgression, reporting that over a two-day period CHUM gave as much if not more airplay to 'Ordinary Man' by Freedom North, a single on its label, than any other single. The situation was compounded by the absence of singles described by Yorke as 'outstanding' and meriting airtime.[43] Not surprisingly, defenders of this vertical integration showed little remorse. For Kevin Frillman, chief announcer at CFOS-Owen Sound, the move was justified in terms of recording quality. 'My guess is that CHUM thinks it can just plain make a better phonograph record.'[44] However, even with (arguably) favourable amounts of airplay, the singles failed to establish MUCH and Astra Records as major players in the industry. The controversy did, on the other hand, make more than clear that although the MAPL system ensured opportunities, the selection of music came down to radio programmers. The overplaying of established acts, a reliance on singles of short length, the avoidance of songs tailored to Canadian audiences, and the airtime given to tracks from which stations stood to reap royalties were all barriers to the airwaves.

RPM certainly contained a nationalist streak, but even this paled compared with some of the writing that appeared in consumer periodicals, notably pieces by Jack Batten, William Westfall, Jon Ruddy, and Myrna Kostash.[45] Where *RPM* had been primarily concerned with industry, others were more interested in identity. *Maclean's*, *Saturday Night*, and *Chatelaine* were powerful platforms for nationalistic journalism, with popular music interwoven into stories of news, politics, culture, and entertainment. To these periodicals, music started to take on a cultural value not simply for its own sake but because, given the anemic industry and abundance of American imports, it embodied all that was deemed wrong in other sectors of Canadian society. Given exposure in these periodicals, the struggle for a 'Canadian music' was as much about the struggle for an independent Canada.

In early 1971 *Maclean's* took a step forward by launching a music column and, in the following year, published cover stories on Anne Murray and Leonard Cohen along with a multi-page interview with

Stompin' Tom Connors.[46] For the likes of *Maclean's* writer Jon Ruddy, the problem was not just that acts were being overlooked, but that too many of them, citing singles by Motherlode and the Guess Who on the chart at that time, 'were indistinguishable in style and content from the others [and thus] is another indication of U.S. pop-culture power.'[47] Ruddy envisioned the creation of a 'Canadian' sound, something severed from the international ebb and flow, that could be used as a means of separating Canadians from Americans and delivering a blow to American 'hegemony.' It was to be not music for music's sake but music for nation's sake.[48]

Others were keen to assert the Canadianness of popular music by using metaphor in the place of evidence, even vesting national value within acts that had left Canada and were now entrenched members of other scenes. Jack Batten, for example, informed the readers of *Chatelaine* that 'the Band is carrying its peaceful sound, the passive message of Canadian country rock, to the whole pop world.'[49] Just what in the music made it exclusively Canadian went unexplained. In a similar vein, Batten related how 'a fresh sound has been floating through the wild, rich, international world of pop music in the last year, and to the surprise of exactly no one who follows the shifting trends in rock, soul, jazz, rhythm 'n' blues and pop, it's a sound that is as characteristically Canadian as the rolling western prairies or the gentle hills of the Ontario countryside.'[50]

Folk and folk rock acts of international acclaim fit well with these metaphors and were particularly attractive because they offered external validation and a non-threatening musical style that was easily integrated into the pre-existing belief that Canada was a nation of open spaces. Gillian Mitchell has already noted that 'the image of Canada as a natural and pure land was persistent in the views of the nationalists and the press in the late 1960s and early 1970s, when the desire to "Canadianise" native-born musicians was strongest.'[51] Less nationalist attention, particularly among those who were inclined to romanticize, was given to the likes of Mainline, who, although actively nationalistic, were less respectable because of their rock and roll antics.[52] Although the band released the brazenly titled *Canada Our Home and Native Land* and often incorporated beavers and the Canadian flag on concert posters, their nationalism was matched by a tendency towards debauchery, the beavers and the flag blending with pornographic caricatures of women and concerts featuring strippers and elements of burlesque. 'We were never shy about being Canadians, but I think Canada was shy about us,' Mike McKenna has recalled.[53]

Although *Maclean's* offered a pulpit for columnists to treat popular music as ideologically national, John Macfarlane, associate editor and author of the new column on popular music, showed signs of restraint.[54] Macfarlane noted how the nationalist imperative skewed the ability to assess music on its own terms, often reminding readers that one should not be quick to praise music simply because it was created by Canadians. As he brazenly argued in December 1971,

Is all this made-in-Canada music we're listening to distinguishable in any way from the imported product? Has the Poppy Family really enriched our musical experience? Don't misunderstand me: I'm really happy that Doctor Music and the Stampeders and Anne Murray have been given a chance to compete fairly with Americans. But don't ask me to get weepy about the fact that had it not been so I might have been denied songs like 'One More Mountain To Climb,' 'Sweet City Woman,' and 'Talk It Over In The Morning.' The point being that most of the music we're making in Canada these days is no better than what spills over the border from the United States – and I refuse to be persuaded that I am showing something less than true patriot love if I say so.[55]

Opportunities for domestic talent, according to Macfarlane, were important; but to praise songs simply because they were made by Canadians was unacceptable. Nonetheless, the nationalist imperative was starting to gain ground.

Theorist Simon Frith has noted that 'music seems to be a key to identity because it offers, so intensely, a sense of both self and others, of the subjective in the collective.'[56] As explored in the introduction to this book, the positions taken by Batten, Ruddy, and others reflected how this 'sense' of seeing oneself in a national community of music was taking place with significant intensity at the turn of the 1970s. The baby boom generation had come of age as citizens of a country and members of a nation, mediating not only gender, class, generational, and other socio-economic identities through music but a national one as well. The attempt to reclaim 'their' expatriated artists was among the more powerful of this mediation. In this mindset, Gordon Lightfoot and the like were familial descendants of the Group of Seven and national brethren to Canadians as a whole. For performers to decry the regulation, or even distance themselves from nationalist ideology, mattered not. The transformation of performers into 'artists,' a description seeped in cultural capital and one that came along at the same time as the shift from 'rock and roll' as juvenile entertainment to 'rock' as serious expression, validated the idea that popular music was inherently national.

While English-speaking performers routinely distanced themselves from nationalism, many of their French-speaking counterparts eagerly embraced the Quebec nationalism that had emerged in the early 1960s and thrived into the 1970s. For them the Canadian content regulation had not been necessary because songwriters, audiences, and radio stations were already celebrating their community, and dream of nationhood, through song. This was particularly true for chansonniers, singers of a traditional folk genre who had captured the imaginations of audiences with tunes that were often nostalgic in character and that drew a line between the rural past, political present, and sovereign future. In the words of Jon Ruddy of *Maclean's*, 'the chansonniers of the new Quebec, most though not all of them separatists, are folk heroes in a way that is hard for an English-speaking Canadian to grasp.'[57] Chansonniers combined the roles that theorist of nationalism Anthony D. Smith has attributed to 'historians, linguists and writers [who] attempt to rediscover the community's past and to elaborate, codify, systematize and streamline into a single coherent ethno-history the various collective memories, myths and traditions that have been handed down piecemeal from generation to generation.'[58] In doing so they achieved significant positions within the Quebec 'ethnie,' a term Smith uses to describe an ethnic community shaped through a 'collective name,' 'a common myth of descent,' 'a shared history,' 'a distinctive shared culture,' 'an association with a specific territory,' and 'a sense of solidarity.'[59]

It was not only accepted but expected that celebrated chansonnier Gilles Vigneault would talk about ethnic survival in an interview with *Canadian Composer*. Vigneault told the interviewer that Canada is

an extraordinary country; all the same, it's not a bad idea to start to hose down the house when you see the forest burning ... Seen from Ontario, Quebec isn't sinking at all, not at all. But from inside Quebec, when you see English schools being built with tax money from French-speaking parents, schools where classes are given in English, when you see 40% of the students in a city of 100,000 people going to an English school, compared to 4% ten years ago, it's time you asked yourself a few questions about the harm, the neglect that the people in power are capable of visiting on a people and a culture and a language. Let's not kid ourselves. If young Quebeckers are becoming Anglicised – and they are, at a frightening and frightful rate around Montreal – well, that's it, it's the death knell.[60]

Songs were not alone in being mobilized for the task of nation-building, the interview made clear: so too were media opportunities to put forward the case for a sovereign Quebec. Performers were commonly as much promoters and propagandists as they were songwriters and entertainers.

Not all musicians in Quebec, though, were keen to back the nostalgic turn inwards being promoted by the chansonniers. A modern Quebec, the Quebec that was taking root in the wake of the Quiet Revolution, would best be served by empowering itself as a North American nation, argued famed performer Robert Charlebois, a charismatic musician who melded rock and roll, psychedelic sounds, 'joual' phrasing, and a distaste for an inward-looking separatism. As he asked Claude Gagnon in a 1969 interview with the *Canadian Composer*,

> How can you be a separatist when you are an inch and a half of the map above the U.S.? How can you be Quebecois when you ARE in the U.S. Look at the streets, the shops, the brands of food products, the stocks at the Exchange, the life insurance companies, automobiles, films on bill at the theatres, look at the Place Ville-Marie and then you come and tell me that we have a personal style. All that we have left is a couple of 'ceintures fléchées' and three Eskimo carvings. We live in a city that looks American, that has American values, on the American continent, handling money based on the American economy. Except that we have not got the same rights as the American. Our situation is worse than that of the Negroes or the Mexicans. We're the white-negroes of America.
>
> To seek refuge in separatism is a graceful way of blinding your eyes and plugging your ears, because when you repeat to yourself that you are 'Quebecois,' you deny that you are also the one who is making war in Vietnam. I'm no longer a separatist, not a confederationist; I'm not a republican not a democrat either. I think of myself as a leftist American, that is to say an anti-American American. I contest the way of life and the way of thinking that goes with that way of life. I am an American (since I live in North America) belonging to the Global Village that is the whole world. That is why, when I travel to California, I don't have the feeling of traveling, of going 'somewhere' else. Pretty soon, that 'somewhere else' will no longer exist geographically. You find 'Coca-Cola' and 'Esso' at the North Pole and in Africa; what more do you want.[61]

Indicative of his internationalism, Charlebois defied the turn inward by focusing on the European and the English-speaking Canadian markets. His success in the early 1970s with the single 'Lindberg' led to a high-profile performance at the Olympia in Paris, and, soon after, he broke into English-speaking Canada with the album *Superfrog*.[62] To Placide Gaboury of *Le Devoir*, Charlebois was an example of how 'one can be Québécois and at the same time avoid being closed in by an obsessed nationalism, that a Quebecker can be at ease anywhere in the world, and that one can be … creative in that world.'[63] Even the iconic chansonnier Félix Leclerc praised Charlebois's music, although not necessarily his politics. 'For me, the music is less important than the words, but for someone like Charlebois, music comes first. His music is aggressive; it upsets, mixes everything up, he takes it and produces an explosion of new sounds towards a new world. It is very beautiful. Charlebois is not a chansonnier; he is a musician … a chansonnier is … a man who makes songs.'[64]

Leclerc was willing, at least publicly, to accept the new sounds being offered by the likes of Charlebois. Not all chansonniers were so gracious, especially when it came to the psychedelic sounds that were tied to a lifestyle deemed detrimental to the quest for sovereignty. Tex Lecor, a chansonnier whose hits included 'Le frigidaire' and 'Noël au camp,' decried how

> the members of today's younger generation congregate in filthy pads where they stone themselves blind. I don't buy that. And that's why I sing 'Paurvre jeunesse' to them. 'Paurvre jeunesse, you've put yourselves to sleep with your sacraments of hash and pot; your brand of peace and love, I've had right up to here. You have to stand up straight to build a country – you don't build it with flowers and I-love-you's. Don't take the credit for what's going on today – the only people you help are the pushers and the mounties.'[65]

The nationalist dream came one step closer with the political victory of René Lévesque and the Parti Québécois on 15 November 1976. Lévesque had outlined his goals for a Québécois nation almost a decade earlier in *An Option for Quebec*, a selection from which is worth quoting at length as it shares much with the works of chansonniers, particularly the anti-modernism and politicization of the ethnie:

> What is at stake? The right to live one's life, to live *our* life; the right of men to live, whether they are weak or powerful; the right of peoples and nations to live, whether they are large or small … We have a country to create, and very little time in which to do it … We are Québécois. What that means first and foremost – and if need be, all that it means – is that we are attached to this one corner of the earth where we can be completely ourselves: this

Quebec, the only place where we have the unmistakable feeling that 'here we can be really at home.'.. Until recently in this difficult process of survival we enjoyed the protection of a certain degree of isolation. We lived a relatively sheltered life in a rural society in which a great measure of unanimity reigned, and in which poverty set its limits on change and aspiration alike. We are children of that society, in which the *habitant*, our father or grandfather, was still the key citizen. We also are heirs to that fantastic adventure – that early America that was almost entirely French. We are, even more intimately, heirs to the group obstinacy which has kept alive that portion of French America we call *Québec*. All these things lie at the core of this personality of ours. Anyone who does not feel it, at least occasionally, is not – is no longer – one of us. But *we* know and feel that these are the things that make us what we are. They enable us to recognize each other wherever we may be. This is our own special wave-length on which, despite all interference, we can tune each other in loud and clear, with no one else listening ... For our own good, we must dare to seize for ourselves complete liberty in Quebec, the right to all the essential components of independence, i.e., the complete mastery of every last area of basic collective decision-making. This means that Quebec must become sovereign as soon as possible.[66]

Electoral success, then, was about much more than politics. To Lévesque and other thinkers they had come closer to nationhood. Lucien Francoeur, famed poet-rocker and founder of Aut'Chose, identified ethnic survival as his reason for voting for Lévesque. In a 1979 interview he explained that 'on November 15 I voted, like everyone else, for René Lévesque. I didn't vote for the P.Q. but rather above all for the preservation of our language, the preservation of a way of expressing oneself. I wanted us to end once and for all our submergence by the English ... There will be two nations in America, if the Quebecker has any sense: Quebec and the rest.'[67]

For those in the cultural sector who had been pushing for a more independent Quebec, electoral success meant that the burden of the task had become alleviated. It also meant a decrease in interest in their music; electoral success had made the chansonniers obsolete. Georges-Hérbert Germain, journalist and music critic, observed at the time that the chansonniers 'were precious before, like Communion; you listened with your hands clasped,' but the scene was now winding down, not unlike the change that had occurred a few years earlier in the United States in the wake of Vietnam and Watergate.[68]

Yet it was not just political victory that accounted for a decline in the role of the chansonniers. Many of the young, radical advocates of political change and a sovereign Québécois state, the ones who had taken to the streets and used music as an outlet for expressing nationalist ideology, were now adults and members of the 'establishment.' Over a decade and a half had passed since the Front de libération du Québec began its campaign of terror. The October crisis of 1970, with the FLQ kidnappings of British trade commissioner James Cross and Quebec minister of labour Pierre Laporte, culminating in the death of the latter, had passed. *Maclean's* summed up this change in a 1978 article:

> Pauline Julien made the occasional *anglais* visitor cower from her bristling, patriotic songs in the supercharged nationalistic atmosphere of clubs like Le Patriote back in the late '60s. Later, she was arrested under the War Measures Act of 1970; lately, she co-hosts an amiable afternoon chat show on TV for Radio-Canada. Yvon Deschamps' monologues on injustice ... and the history of Quebec, left crowds squirming in their seats, uncomfortable with their complacency. He's spent part of his summer holidays looking over scripts for proposed TV sitcoms offered him by the Norman Lear organization in Hollywood. And Patsy Gallant has already turned [Gilles Vigneault's sentimental Québécois classic] 'Mon Pays' into 'From New York to L.A.' [with new lyrics about becoming a star in these two cities].[69]

Political success and a decline in radicalism meant that simply singing an engaging tale about *la patrie* was no longer enough to make a performer popular. Musicianship was now essential. 'Ten years ago, people wanted to see chansonniers,' Yvon Deschamps noted to *Maclean's* in August 1978. 'If you sang about trawlers, the tide and fishing, you worked. Then there was the *engagé* period. Lots of *Québec libre*, and songs that, as [Gilles] Vigneault put it, had "a blizzard at the beginning, lots of open space in the middle and at the end, *la liberté*." Just because there's been a change in government doesn't change the fact that Vigneault is a great poet. But now the audience is coming to see the artist, not the style.'[70] Or, as put by Bob Beauchamp, program director of CKOI-FM Montreal, 'people don't feel the need to go out and prove they're Québécois by buying a certain album.'[71]

Whereas the Quiet Revolution had entailed a turn inward for songwriters who joined the Québécois struggle for nationhood, political victory brought with it an emancipating turn outwards and encouragement to succeed abroad. For many acts, France became a popular choice. Whereas performers like Leclerc had to go there in the early years to secure a career, now performers accepted in Quebec did so by choice, including Charlebois, Claude Léveillée, Jean-Pierre Ferland, Claude Gauthier, Diane Tell, Diane Dufresene, and Fabienne Thibeault, among others. A number of them even purchased homes in France to serve as a launching pad into the European market.[72] As Charlebois quipped, 'you cannot conquer the country without going and living there.'[73]

France shared a French-speaking market and was tied to the heritage of the ethnie, and as such was a non-threatening alternative to Quebec. Yet for some acts, particularly those who were coming of age at the tail end of the politicized period, musical interests meant a turn towards English-speaking markets. Michel Rivard, founder of rock band Beau Dommage, admitted that he felt little for the nationalism that had underwritten Quebec's music scene for almost two decades. His sense of self and place, he told *Canadian Composer* in 1977, was quite unlike that of the chansonniers and those who had looked to a romanticized past in blueprinting a Québécois future:

> Let's be serious! We're a long way from the problems the Blacks have. It was more a reaction to the culture here, to the songs of that time particularly. We were sick and tired of seagulls! We'd all lived in Montreal and we found it as alienating listening to the chansonniers and wanting to go and live at Percé or Natashquan, as the Beach Boy trip was, and the California scene ... So we tried to put over the poetry of our daily lives and of our own scene by using childhood, life on the streets, our pals, without the irony you lay on that sort of thing when you're 20.[74]

Likewise, Lucien Francoeur told *Canadian Composer* that he identified more with the modernity of North America than the anti-modernism offered by the chansonniers:

> I'm sorry to say it, but Gilles Vigneault and Félix Leclerc, however much I respect their abilities as poets, haven't been that important in my own formation. Francoeur's influences are American. I was marked by the counter-culture, by acid and the words of Timothy Leary and Jerry Rubin ... I continue to believe in a North-American Quebec with a coke machine in every kitchen, a bubble gum machine in every store and a Camaro in every garage ... We shouldn't have any illusions: the Quebecker cannot turn his Michelin tires in for snowshoes. The Quebecker must work alongside progress and technology.[75]

Although drawn to the offerings of modernity, particularly as epitomized by America, Francoeur was by no means a continentalist. Integration with the United States, to him, was a horrible fate, one that had already befallen English-speaking Canadians: 'It's only a question of time before English Canadians, who are nothing more and nothing less than hillbillies and by-products of the American machine, are completely assimilated.'[76] The Québécois could look to the United States for artistic inspiration, and even engage in an international music scene, without becoming American, argued a number of younger musicians. Nathalie Petrowski, entertainment columnist at *Le Devoir*, described this change as follows: 'The days when singers wrapped themselves in a Quebec flag and won an automatic following are gone. Kids now look to New York before anywhere else.'[77]

To draw upon external influences and focus on markets abroad was increasingly acceptable if not encouraged, at least in terms of instrumentation. Using the English language, however, was a different matter. Language was a core component of the ethnie. Not only had nationalists made clear the importance of language, but so too did the provincial government. In 1974 Premier Robert Bourassa passed Bill 22, the Official Language Act, making French the sole language of the province, and three years later his successor René Lévesque expanded its reach with Bill 101. This, however, did not stop some performers from placing the linguistic needs of their music before alliance to the politics of the Québécois national project. For the members of Leyden Zar it was possible to identify as francophone and use French almost exclusively in daily life but, when it came time to record or perform, they chose to use English. 'It's not a political choice for us, it's something else,' explained a band member in a 1981 interview. 'English is an instrument for us, like a guitar or a synthesizer. It's a question of rhythm, of flexibility ... We've been listening to American rock exclusively for 15 years. Our influences don't come from here, but from somewhere else, and we're much closer to the Beatles than to Félix Leclerc.'[78] Even child star René Simard, the first Quebec singer to headline in Las Vegas, reportedly experienced criticism from his fellow Quebeckers for using English.[79]

Celine Dion would face a similar rebuking. In 1990 the Association du disque, de l'industrie du spectacle québécois et de la vidéo, the annual French-speaking music awards, selected Dion as the anglophone artist of the year, a 'comeuppance,' Larry LeBlanc of *Billboard* called it, for releasing her record *Unison* in English.[80] In refusing the award, Dion controversially exclaimed: 'I am not an Anglophone; I am a Québécoise,' implying that one could not be both Québécois and anglophone.[81] As a result of the controversy, the award was renamed 'Artiste québécois s'étant le plus illustré hors Québec' (Quebec artist most illustrious out-side of Quebec). Yet this would not be the end of the language issue at the awards show. Two years later Dion and Roch Voisine were both told that they could not sing in English at the show. Dion wished to perform a single from her latest English-language album *The Colour of Love* and reacted to the decision by refusing to sing; Voisine relented and sang a song in French. 'I still think most of the time in English, and I write most of my songs first in English, then translate them into French,' Voisine had told *Maclean's* a year earlier.[82] For now, though, the last word on the issue of language in the French music industry fittingly goes to a predic-tion offered by Robert Charlebois in 1982: 'I think that the thing that could most destroy Quebec and its artists is narrow-mindedness. Quebec culture is the same in any language, just as American culture is the same. Authors from here who know how to use English as well as French will have a fantastic advantage in a short while.'[83] Dion certainly benefited from that linguistic edge but in doing so found her authenticity as a Québécois called into question. The nationalism that had underwritten the age of the chansonniers had declined but it was certainly not gone.

'If you listened to pop radio in the early seventies, it was easy to believe that Burton Cummings was the voice of Canada,' wrote Geoff Pevere and Grieg Dymond on the early days of Canadian content in *Mondo Canuck: A Canadian Pop Culture Odyssey*.[84] Radio stations relied heavily on over-play, selective play, and non-MAPL songs, frustrating up-and-coming and established acts alike. While aspiring performers were concerned that their success seemed to be owing to nationalism and the regulation, for those who already had a career the over exposure soured their position even more. Station owners within the Canadian Association of Broad-casters went so far as to venture into vertical integration in hopes of turn-ing a regulation into a profit. No wonder, then, that Walt Grealis told the readers of *RPM*: 'While the industry was gearing itself to go into pro-duction and was working toward getting production budgets extended, the broadcast-producers were at their usual best (having lost the battle to quash the legislation) contriving to either take advantage of ... [the regulation] or at least make the ruling look ridiculous. They have suc-cessfully accomplished both.'[85]

Although musicians commonly kept a safe distance from the national-ism of the times, looking on the regulation as a means of providing oppor-tunities to access the airwaves, many other Canadians were beginning to engage in music in ideologically national terms and what it meant to be members of a nation. In turn, whether they wanted it or not, performers, particularly of the folk rock singer-songwriter vein, were being elevated to the status of artist and national representative. Much had changed since the days of immoral dancing to racy lyrics and frantic screaming at the concerts of lanky boys with 'mop top' hair. Music in Canada was becoming Canadian music, a nationalization spearheaded by columnists and periodicals interested in rallying nationalist sentiments, industry figures seeking to ensure their economic interests, and the fans themselves, as they, individually and collectively, used music as a means of envisioning themselves as members of a national community.

Although the Canadian content regulation, and its relationship to nationalism, was pronounced in English-speaking Canada, it did not even appear on the radar of the Québécois. The regulation was not needed in a radio market where station programmers gave plentiful airtime to domestic acts, not only continental rock and rollers but the folksy chansonniers who acted as pipelines for nationalist sentiments. Identifying along national lines, let alone crafting songs tied to the Québécois myth-symbol complex, was encouraged in a way that would make the likes of Bob Bossin and Stompin' Tom Connors envious. For the Québécois the milestone was not the start of the Canadian content regulation but the election of the Parti Québécois in 1976, an achievement that ironically diminished the role of the chansonniers as cultural vanguards. Although what followed was an opening of the French-speaking musical community, this did not extend so far as to singing in English, as linguistic fears were still strong. After all, even with the Parti Québécois in power, the survival of the Québécois was still at stake.

8

'The Nation's Music Station': Television and the Idea of Canadian Music

Ms. [Joni] Mitchell, born in Canada, has lived for many years in the United States – as have other [Juno Award] Hall of Fame winners, Hank Snow, Paul Anka, and the late Guy Lombardo. Only Oscar Peterson, chosen two years ago, still lives in this country.

– *Canadian Composer*, 1981[1]

'Gentlemen,' began the letter Stompin' Tom Connors passionately read aloud at a press conference held at his Boot Records office on 31 March 1978,

> I am returning herewith the six Juno Awards that I once felt honoured to receive but which I am no longer proud to have in my possession. As far as I'm concerned you can give them to the border jumpers who didn't receive an award this year and maybe you can have them presented by some American.
>
> I feel that the Junos should be for people who are living in Canada, whose main base of business operations is in Canada, who are working toward the recognition of Canadian talent in this country, and are trying to further the export of such talent from this country to the world, with a view to proudly showing off what we can contribute to the world market.
>
> Until the academy appears to comply more closely with aspirations of this kind, I will no longer stand for any nominations nor will I accept any award given.
>
> Yours very truly, Stompin' Tom Connors[2]

Connors then hailed a taxi and had the driver take the letter and all six of his Junos back to the awards committee. The Junos, he tried to make clear in his protest, had gone from celebrating domestic musicians and industry enthusiasts to becoming a televised platform for a select few performers, often non-residents, who were on the rosters of the powerful multinational record labels. For him, 'Canadian' meant actually living in Canada and contributing to the music scene and industry in the country. For the Canadian Academy of Recording Arts and Sciences (CARAS), though, television offered the ultimate advertising tool, a means of vesting international artists with national credibility.

The Juno Awards were not the first television showcase for musicians; the lineage includes such programs as the country-folk *Don Messer's Jubilee*, folk-pop *Singalong Jubilee*, and the numerous country and western shows like *Cross-Canada Barn Dance* and the personality-driven variety shows *Stompin' Tom's Canada*, *The Tommy Hunter Show*, and *Nashville North* (later *The Ian Tyson Show*). In terms of rock and roll, television broadcasters were much more cautious, particularly in the early years. The CBC, the only television network before the launch of CTV in 1961, was primarily interested in adult audiences, and the social undesirability of rock and roll raised concerns that advertisers would withdraw their sponsorship rather than be associated with the music. Many programmers simply disliked the racket that was being passed off as music.[3] In this regard, the CBC was less open than broadcasters in Britain, where television in the 1950s offered a range of programming, from 'bandstand' shows like *Hit Parade*, *6–5 Special*, and *Dig This!* to the music entertainment of *Off the Record* and *Juke Box Jury*. With the broadening of rock and roll to 'pop' came a new generation of programs, none more notable than *Ready, Steady, Go* and *Top of the Pops*.[4] The importance of *Top of the Pops* can be seen in how it routinely attracted approximately 17 million viewers a week during the mid- to late 1960s.[5]

Still, the CBC could not completely overlook a style of music that was of tremendous public discussion, if only to give audiences a taste of what it was all about. Even the CBC's otherwise 'respectable' *Cross-Canada Hit Parade* featured a performance by Bill Haley and His Comets in February 1956, a broadcast that, according to Paul Rutherford, attracted 'rave reviews from the teen audience – but at the cost of turning off adults.'[6] What one finds, then, is a very apprehensive, at most concessionary, approach to rock and roll. 'Television might offer a cleaned-up version of teen hits,' Rutherford noted, 'but it would neglect the hardcore rock … The rebellious world of youth was one realm of fantasy primetime television wasn't going to highlight.'[7]

Teenagers were instead offered programs that used a house band to perform the top radio hits – usually American and British – of the day. These shows were not platforms for celebrating national musical acts or even for giving opportunities to singer-songwriter 'artists,' as neither of these paradigms yet existed. Rather, local groups acted as jukeboxes that offered renditions of the big hits, as was common for 'hit parade' shows the world over. The shows were regionally produced as a means of entertaining kids after school (revealing how little of national value the network saw in 'pop' music). As Jeffrey Ridley of the United Empire Loyalists has recalled, 'just as radio stations were regional so too was CBC TV which produced national shows broadcast nationally, and local shows broadcast locally; and the pop music shows aimed at our generation were always local.'[8] Teenagers in Ontario, for example, could turn to *Music Hop*, a Toronto-based program launched in October 1963 that aired from 5:30 to 6:00 p.m. on Thursdays and was hosted by Alex Trebek.

The popularity of *Music Hop* and the mainstreaming of rock and roll finally caught the attention of CBC's national network in 1964, and five local programs were stitched together into a cross-Canada broadcast: Vancouver (*Let's Go*, hosted by famed disc jockey Red Robinson, with the Classics as house band), Montreal (*Jeunesse Oblige*), Winnipeg (*Hootenanny*), Toronto (*Music Hop*, with Trebek now replaced by disc jockey Davie Mickie), and Halifax (*Frank's Bandstand*). For the 1967 season all of the cities adopted the name *Let's Go*, and the series was renewed in 1968 for a final season under the name *Where It's At*.

By bringing together broadcasts from across Canada in a time when there was little coast-to-coast radio airplay, the series provided isolated regional groups with an opportunity to attract audiences elsewhere. Burton Cummings, who with the Guess Who formed the house band on the Winnipeg segment for the 1967-9 seasons, has described the broadcast as being invaluable in terms of exposure:

> So every week, like clockwork at 5:30 p.m., on Thursday, there we were in everybody's living rooms. Not only the salaries were great, but it gave us that national vibe. It was the first time we were known, from Newfoundland right to Victoria. When the first season ended we went out to Vancouver to play a gig one time, and I'll never forget it. Randy and I were walking downtown to get some new shirts and vests for onstage, and we started getting chased by girls and stuff, purely from the profile we had from the weekly TV show. It was absolutely fascinating – it was kind of like being the Monkees, you know.[9]

The opportunity was also not lost on Eddie Sossin, musical director for the Montreal segment and an advocate for the English-speaking bands struggling in Quebec, who explained to *RPM* in the summer of 1968 that the Montreal segment tried to 'use all the English talent we can find because there's not really much outlet for them, especially if they're a single act, not a group. Then we try and show the rest of Canada what Quebec is doing entertainment wise.'[10]

Still, although it aired from coast to coast, *Let's Go*, by its very nature, was an assembly of 'local' shows. Despite this, music historian John Einarson has stated that the national exposure outweighed any regional implications: 'Although the very nature of the series underscored the fragmented regional state of Canadian music, it ultimately helped break down those barriers by creating national audiences for artists from all parts of Canada.'[11] Further, although *Let's Go* used house bands to perform radio hits that were for the most part non-Canadian, it did provide opportunities for the occasional original piece. Burton Cummings has credited *Let's Go* producer Larry Brown for making this possible: 'He said, you know, I'm not gonna let you do a whole show of stuff, but you know, one or two a week maybe, or a couple every second week, and we'll see how it wears on the public. If we get any mail, well, that'll encourage you guys – well Randy and I were just like, you could have knocked us over with a feather. I mean, this was the chance to do original stuff on a national show, on TV.'[12] The result was that songs like 'Undun,' 'No Time,' and 'These Eyes' were slipped in among renditions of 'White Room,' 'Hey Jude,' and 'Time of the Season.'[13]

The CBC series competed against CTV's *After Four*, which launched in 1965, aired on Saturdays at 4:00 p.m, and was hosted by Carole Taylor and Johnny F. Bassett (son of CFTO station owner John F. Bassett). The next year audiences were offered *A Go-Go '66*, teaming local disc jockeys with house band Robbie Lane and the Disciples, a group that had made its name by opening for Ronnie Hawkins and the Hawks and eventually took over as his backing band. Although the show offered teenagers access to rock and roll, Paul Rutherford has emphasized how the music was made more palatable by having the bands dress in 'jackets and ties, with neat hair. Lane supposedly had a style "which bridges [the] rock 'n' roll and crooner eras."'[14] By the next season the show incorporated go-go dancers and changed its name to *It's Happening*. For its 1968–9 (and final) season the Disciples were replaced as house band by the more psychedelic Carnival (retaining Robbie Lane).[15]

Not everyone was happy to see television promote rock and roll, particularly on the taxpayer-funded CBC. *Maclean's* television columnist 'Strabo' certainly spoke for many Canadians in the simply titled 'Let's

Quit Subsidizing Music Shows,' published in May 1965: 'No nation's identity is going to stand or fall on the ability of its television stars to sing "Mrs. Brown You've Got a Lovely Daughter," as it just might stand on the ability of some newscasters to focus attention on common problems, crises and triumphs.'[16] The problem was not that CBC programs offered renditions of popular non-Canadian hits as opposed to Canadian hits, which of course were rather rare, but that rock and roll was being aired at all. Still, the music industry trade paper *Billboard* was impressed with the activities of the CBC, reporting, in the same year as Strabo's complaint, that the radio network's weekly teen program *Action Set* was helping to bridge the national divide. To *Billboard,* maybe music programming was what Canadian unity needed:

> While a Royal Commission on Bilingualism and Biculturalism goes into its second year of the weighty problem of two cultures in one country, CBC Radio's teen-oriented 'Action Set' show is experimenting with playing a disk from the French-Canadian hit parade each week in its otherwise English-language program. French-Canadians hear American English-language disks on their French radio stations, but seldom, if ever, does the average Canadian hear French-language hit parade material. Pop music may prove to be a force in bringing about national unity.[17]

Less than a decade later the emergence of 'Canadian rock and roll' as an ideological assertion empowered by baby boomers coming of age as members of a national project, and given legislative tangibility and airplay by the Canadian content regulation, reshaped the television broadcasting experience. Still, a recording industry was necessary to provide original singles and the transition from hit parade jukeboxes to featured artists. Recording industry entrepreneurs and the Canadian content regulation had combined to make this a reality. In February 1976, Martin Melhuish of *Maclean's* offered a succinct summary of the change:

> The number of Canadian-owned record companies has risen to more than 40 from fewer than 10 before the [Canadian content] rulings were introduced in January, 1971. Multinational record companies have all established Canadian talent development divisions. Royalty payments made by the major Canadian Performing Rights Association [the Composers, Authors and Publishers Association of Canada] – CAPAC – to Canadian songwriters quadrupled from $364,000 in 1968 to $1,333,000 in 1974. First-rank recording studios have blossomed all over the country. (Toronto now has

10 16-track studios compared to two before 1970 and Edmonton has had a busy 16-track studio since 1973).[18]

Although the number of studios quickly mushroomed, they tended to be centred in Toronto. Terry Brown of Toronto Sound, whose clients included Crowbar, Edward Bear, the Stampeders, Downchild Blues Band, and Tom Cochrane, estimated that as of 1974 approximately 80 per cent of English-language recording was done in Toronto, primarily at the half-dozen major studios.[19] Nonetheless, by decade's end there were over a hundred recording studios in Canada, and in March 1979 *Canadian Musician* magazine was launched as a source of industry information and advice.[20]

Television offered a chance to sell the recordings that came in the wake of the Canadian content regulation to an audience that increasingly thought of music in national terms. These were not simply people buying goods but citizens consuming a national identity. Philip Auslander has noted that 'the music industry specifically sets out to endow its products with the necessary signs of authenticity'; this can be extended to include not only the correct clothing and mannerisms but also national affiliation.[21]

The appropriation of the Juno Awards into a television spectacle reveals the degree to which the recording industry managed to benefit from the nationalist imperative. Initially launched in 1964 by *RPM* as the Gold Leaf Awards, it was an annual readers-based poll that did not have an actual ceremony until 23 February 1970, one week after the Canadian Radio and Television Commission proposed the Canadian content regulation. What was supposed to be a low-key affair of 125 invited guests at St Lawrence Hall in Toronto ended up attracting approximately 250 attendees.[22] The performers who won an award – a trophy in the shape of a metronome – were for the most part the same ones who had won in previous polls. The Guess Who took the top vocal-instrumental group for the third year in a row; Gordon Lightfoot was the folk artist of choice for the fifth year; Dianne Leigh won the female country singer award for the fifth time, and the male version went to Tommy Hunter for the third year running; Andy Kim and Ginette Reno took home the top male and female vocalist awards.[23] By the next year the event, now renamed the Juno Awards in tribute to Pierre Juneau of the CRTC, drew approximately 600 attendees yet was still a relatively low-key affair: dinner consisted of sandwiches assembled by the wife of Stan Klees.[24]

The tone of the event quickly changed once the Canadian content regulation was in place. 'Walt Grealis, *RPM*'s publisher, used to cart in the booze and homemade sandwiches himself,' *Time* (Canada) noted in its coverage of the 1972 awards. 'This year, nearly 1,000 record company executives, broadcasters and performers turned out for a do at Toronto's Inn on the Park that was resplendent with gold-coated waiters and caviar.'[25] The laid-back celebratory nature had likewise transformed into arguments between various industry camps over their interests; record producers complained about the lack of access to radio airtime, while broadcasters complained about the lack of quality albums to fill the quota. Tensions certainly were not helped when J. Robert Wood of CHUM, responding to the issue of airing new Canadian singles, told his radio programming peers to 'follow the golden rule of radio – when in doubt, don't.'[26]

Still, animosity did not prevent the participants from enjoying the weekend-long lead-up to the Monday night gala. The predictable daytime boozing in the hospitality suites of record labels – the big ones being MCA, Columbia, GRT, Capitol, and Quality – was followed by a concert at Toronto's Victory Theatre featuring Mainline. True to the band's reputation for nationalism and risqué performances, the show not only included topless go-go girls and strippers but also 'an unannounced girl,' who, as Flohil described in *Canadian Composer*, 'is naked in seconds, and the audience cheers as she starts to – how does one describe this in a family magazine? – as she starts to do interesting things with a stuffed beaver. Indicative, one supposes, of Canadian culture.'[27] After this evening of debauchery, the next day's awards gala was somewhat anti-climactic. The winners had already been announced (no sealed envelope) and the list was rather predictable: Anne Murray won for female vocalist of the year; Gordon Lightfoot won male vocalist; Bruce Cockburn took home the folksinger award; Tom Connors picked up the award for country singer; and the Stampeders, riding the hit 'Sweet City Woman,' won the award for instrumental group of the year.

Although the event was now a gala affair, it continued to be run by *RPM* with winners selected through a poll of the trade magazine's readers. Yet the poll did not make the major record companies all that happy as it reflected general popularity as opposed to sales. The Canadian Recording Industry Association (CRIA), a representative body strongly influenced by the foreign-owned multinational record companies that made up much of the industry, wanted to replace the celebration of industry with a televised awards show that promoted commercial acts whose sales could be furthered.[28] To this end, in early 1974, the CRIA warned *RPM* that an alternative event, a televised Maple Music Awards, would be launched unless their demands for control over the Junos were met. Faced by a power struggle, Grealis agreed to have the Junos administrated by a new body, the Canadian Music Awards Association (as of the following year the Canadian Academy of Recording Arts and Sciences). With this change of hands came a replacement of the *RPM* reader poll with a voting system limited to members of the label-dominated CARAS. This meant a significant narrowing of who got to vote on a reduced, and multinational-record-industry-friendly, list of possible recipients. 'The music industry tried to ensure its promotional interests by taking control of the Juno Awards away from Grealis,' sociologist David Young has noted. 'The industry-oriented categories that Grealis had created, such as Canadian Content Record Company, were dropped at the 1975 Juno Awards in favour of categories that had a promotional role for recordings or artists and would help to encourage sales.'[29]

Grealis and Klees were increasingly pushed to the side until, in 1977, CARAS took full control. A decade later, Richard Flohil of *Canadian Composer* summarized this changing of hands as follows: 'The Junos became a nationally televised annual event designed to be a promotion for the entire Canadian recording industry. This aspect of the Junos is central to understanding the event. It is *promotion* ... sales, spotlighting established names rather than artists with limited appeal, packed far as possible with Canadian stars, and hosted by an internationally-known (Canadian) celebrity.'[30] Put more critically, under CARAS the televising of the Junos as a celebration of 'national' music allowed the multinational record labels to extend the event to the internationally famous expatriates on their foreign, primarily American, divisions, while increasing audience size for the broadcast by drawing upon foreign-residing star power. It was thus fitting that the first host of the televised Junos in 1975 was Paul Anka, a long-absent songwriter who was experiencing a revival thanks to the hit '(You're) Having My Baby.'

Yet, not everyone bought into such a liberal identification of what constituted Canadian music. The presence of 'border jumpers' such as Anka at the event infuriated Stompin' Tom Connors, a performer and label entrepreneur who had contributed much to the domestic industry and to the struggle of non-commercial acts for airplay. And that was only one of Connors's problems with the show. Not only were expatriates being featured but there were few opportunities for aspiring performers less likely to draw viewing audiences. Connors was, ironically, part of the problem, a Junos veteran who had swept the Best Country Male Artist (renamed Country Male Vocalist of the Year in 1975) from 1971 to 1975, won the Country Album of the Year in 1974 for *To It and At It*, and was nominated for both Country Male Vocalist of the Year and Folksinger of the Year in 1976 and 1977. The lack of fresh blood and several questionable award nominees and winners at the 1977 event must have brought him close to giving up on it all. Not only did Gordon Lightfoot (Folk Singer of the Year and Composer of the Year) and Murray McLauchlan (Country Male Vocalist) win awards as they had done for many years, but industry veteran Burton Cummings won for Best Male Vocalist and Most Promising Male Vocalist; Colleen Peterson won Most Promising Female Vocalist despite having won a similar Gold Leaf Award a decade earlier; Patsy Gallant followed her Best Female Vocalist award with a performance of 'From New York to L.A.' (an American-centric reworking of the treasured Québécois chanson 'Mon Pays'); Paul Anka was again nominated (chalking up ten nominations in the previous three years despite having left Canada two decades earlier); and an award was given to Peter Frampton for Best Selling International Album. Even Heart, a band that had only recently moved from Seattle to Vancouver, won for Group of the Year.[31]

When the nominee list for the 1978 Junos showed little change, Connors made his stand. First, he withdrew his nomination for Best Male Country Vocalist in hopes that a less-established artist would have a chance at winning. In making this gesture Connors wanted other established nominees to follow suit, but to no avail. Two days after the Junos were aired and awards were given to the usual suspects, Connors called a press conference at his Boot Records office and returned all six of his Junos to CARAS. To show that this was not a publicity stunt, he also announced that he was going to refrain from performing for one year, an absence which, in the face of the industry's unwillingness to change, turned into a hiatus of almost two decades.

Connors was not alone in his frustration with the direction of the Junos. Many in the French-speaking industry felt ostracized as well. According to David Young, 'very few Francophones received Junos during that decade [of the 1970s]; CRTC chair Pierre Juneau was presented with a special award in 1971 while singer Ginette Reno and pianist André Gagnon each won two Junos in subsequent years. To the limited extent that Francophones performed on the awards ceremony after it was first televised in 1975, the French language was not heard. Gagnon played an instrumental piece in 1977, and Reno performed a medley of the year's top English-language hits two years later.'[32] Because of this, representatives of the French-speaking industry withdrew from the Junos in 1978 and launched the annual Association du disque et de l'industrie de spectacle Québécois, nicknamed the Félix awards after celebrated chansonnier Félix Leclerc, first held on 23 September 1979.[33] The Félix awards not only celebrated francophone music but revealed the degree to which the English- and French-speaking industries operated separately and how a 'Canadian' music did not exist in pan-national terms.

Nonetheless, the televised award show succeeded in celebrating what was by now a multigenerational approach to music as ideologically national. Baby boomers and their offspring found their musical icons to be celebrated as part of their nation. Award nominees and winners during the 1970s and early 1980s included country-folk leaders Gordon Lightfoot, Bruce Cockburn, and Murray McLauchlan; Celtic-roots performers Figgy Duff and Ryan's Fancy; rock and rollers April Wine, Beau Dommage, Harmonium, Max Webster, Triumph, Trooper, Chilliwack (previously the Collectors), Bachman-Turner Overdrive; progressive rockers Saga, Zon, and, most famously, Rush; 'hair bands' Platinum Blonde, Honeymoon Suite, Glass Tiger, and Loverboy (formed out of Streetheart); and the two competitors for the crown as the 'boy next door,' Bryan Adams and Corey Hart.

This multigenerational musical fraternalism was all the more solidified by the televising of Northern Lights, the Canadian contribution to a series of nation-based fundraisers to combat starvation in Ethiopia that culminated in Live Aid in 1985.[34] The event brought revered Canadian musical icons, young and old, from around the globe back to the country to collaborate in a song, music video, and CBC television special. Attention to the Ethiopian crisis originated, at least in music industry terms, when Bob Geldof, singer of the Irish band the Boomtown Rats and a social activist, brought British and Irish performers together under the moniker Band Aid for a charity-based single 'Do They Know It's Christmas.' After Band Aid's top-charting success, a collection of American musicians assembled as USA For Africa and had a hit with the Michael Jackson and Lionel Ritchie song 'We Are the World.' At about the same time, famed Canadian expatriate record producer David Foster and songwriters Bryan Adams and Jim Vallance created 'Tears Are Not Enough,' while Bruce Allen, Adams's manager, assembled famed performers for the recording session. Gordon Lightfoot, Burton Cummings, Anne Murray, Joni Mitchell, Dan Hill, Neil Young, Corey Hart, Bruce Cockburn, Geddy Lee of Rush, and Mike Reno of Loverboy were given solo lines; duets and triplets included some solo singers (Adams and Mike Reno) along with Carroll Baker, Ronnie Hawkins, Murray McLauchlan, Paul Hyde of the Payola$, Carole Pope of Rough Trade, and a French-Canadian trio comprised of Veronique Beliveau, Robert Charlebois, and Claude Dubois. Additional performers contributing to the chorus included Liona Boyd, Tom Cochrane, Kim Mitchell, Oscar Peterson, and Sylvia Tyson.

Northern Lights was loaded with celebrity capital and embodied the idea that even expatriates who had been absent for decades were, when it came down to it, first and foremost Canadian. It was no less than a multigenerational 'family reunion.' Robert Wright has noted:

> This was more than a charitable gathering; it was, as the CBC's commercial-
> ly-released film production of the session evinced, a celebration of the Ca-
> nadian pop music tradition, and a triumph of nationalism ... Like the music
> media that had criticized the Canadian performers who left the country in
> the late 1960s and deified those who remained, Canadians rallied momen-
> tarily around a mythic nationalism, a sentiment of such power that it could,
> even in the cynical, selfish 1980s, suspend disbelief. The significance of the
> closing sequence in the CBC film was not that beleaguered Ethiopia was
> receiving lifesaving wheat but that the wheat was Canadian. Perhaps this is
> why Bruce Cockburn, still as sensitive to political opportunism in Canada
> as he was during the 'golden age' of Canadian pop music, chose to stay in
> Europe over the winter of 1986.[35]

The release of singles based on national and geographic groupings as opposed to generation, genre, record label, or other such affiliation is a testament to rock's nationalization and how the issue of residency does not matter when it comes to a familial 'bond' that transcends borders.

The climax of the fundraising campaign for Ethiopian relief was Live Aid, a concert that took place on 13 July 1985, with shows in London and Philadelphia broadcast live on television via satellite to a billion and a half viewers in over a hundred countries. The star-studded lineup included Michael Jackson, Elton John, Madonna, Lionel Ritchie, U2, Phil Collins, and, notably, Bryan Adams, among dozens of other heralded international acts. Out of the event came approximately 50 million towards the famine in Ethiopia – a total that had increased to 120 million a year after Geldof undertook a fundraising tour and meetings with governments in the United States, Europe, and Australia.[36] Of course, the money came not from the millionaire performers but from the audiences, while those who performed at the high-profile event benefited from the exposure.

According to Geldof, 'jockeying for position' on the televised slots was endemic.[37] Donating their time to the event also raised the image of rock and rollers from decadent rebels to politically conscious, self-sacrificing role models. Live Aid, simply put, made good economic and public relations sense. A couple of weeks after the event, Bryan Adams made clear that his personal interests lay elsewhere: 'Why do things have to be polluted with social issues all of the time? I write about loneliness, which affects more people than nuclear war, more than starvation.'[38]

The international telecast of Live Aid, and the video recordings made for Band Aid, USA For Africa, and Northern Lights, worked well with what was increasingly becoming an age of 'music television' and, now at its forefront, the music video. 'Video' did not, as the Buggles professed, 'kill the radio star' but quite the opposite: it helped to revive a struggling recording industry by engaging youths in the celebrity lifestyles that went with rock and roll. The turn of the 1980s had been tough for the recording industry. At the time, Richard Flohil of *Canadian Composer* had noted that 'record companies, more and more, are sticking with what's safe, predictable, "commercial," and inexpensive – this is not the time to spend money on music that may not sell. Radio stations, as ever alert to what is already working in the United States, don't exactly encourage a diversity of taste ... The eighties are not going to be comfortable.'[39] Indeed, the Canadian subsidiaries of the major multinational record labels shared this attitude, reducing their production of Canadian content by almost half over the course of the 1980s.[40] Labels tightened their belts further by encouraging performers to record in label-owned studios, placing in jeopardy many of the studios created in the wake of the Canadian content regulation. Those that managed to stay in business often did so by relying on established clients, creating advertising jingles, and by reducing rates.[41]

A stimulus to the industry came in 1982 with the creation of the Foundation to Assist Canadian Talent on Records (FACTOR), a non-profit organization designed to loan money to aspiring artists and struggling labels, and the outcome of the CRTC requirement that radio broadcasters provide economic encouragement to emerging talent (Musicaction was formed in 1985 as an extension of FACTOR into the French-speaking market).[42] Applicants were to submit a demo tape, and, if successful, the funds would go towards studio time, or, if the applicant was a record label, money could be used to cover operating costs. Loans were to be paid back from sales and royalties plus 1 per cent interest to be put towards future FACTOR projects. Participating members contributed

$355,255 during the first year of FACTOR, of which $295,000 was allocated to 37 projects (amounts ranged from $2,000 to $25,000, with the
average being $7,767).[43] By 1986 over $800,000 had been lent through
FACTOR.[44] The federal government, having put its support behind the
Canadian content regulation a decade and a half earlier, now extended
its support to include financial aid through the Sound Recording Development Program (SRDP) under the aegis of the Department of Communications in 1986.[45] Given the commercial imperative of the SRDP, it
made sense that FACTOR and Musicaction were selected to co-adminis-
trate its funds.

Whereas the Juno Awards had aided the industry in a time of growth, a
new generation of music television programs and channels helped reinvigorate consumer desire. Although audiences could tune into the likes
of *The NewMusic*, launched in 1979 by City-TV, and *The CHUM Top 30* as
of 1983, the major force in developing music within a national discourse
was MuchMusic, a specialty music video cable channel and self-proclaimed 'nation's music station' that began airing in 1984.[46] MuchMusic established itself as a Canadian, and much lower-budget, variation of
Music Television, or MTV, a twenty-four-hour music cable channel that
began in the United States in August 1981.[47] As Jack Banks has noted, the
'music video revitalised a troubled record industry suffering a prolonged
recession by prompting renewed consumer interest in pop music and
successfully developing several new recording acts like Madonna, Cyndi
Lauper and Boy George with provocative visual images.'[48] Not surprisingly, the Canadian industry wanted to follow suit. Communications scholar
Ira Wagman has already told of how 'with the tremendous success of
American broadcaster MTV in promoting new musical talent, the English Canadian sound recording industry saw a music video channel as a
lifeline, one not dissimilar to the Canadian content regulations enacted
in 1970.'[49]

Even though MuchMusic was a cable station, as opposed to using the
limited airwaves, the CRTC decided that fair competition with traditional
broadcasters meant that the station had to dedicate some of its resources
to Canadian content. To this end, MuchMusic agreed to set aside 2.4 per
cent of its annual gross revenue (or $100,000, whichever was higher)
towards a fund for the production of music videos and would air 10 per
cent Canadian content in 1984–5, 20 per cent in 1985–6, and 30 per cent
as of the 1986–7 season.[50] By the early 1990s the amount of videos quan-
tifying as Canadian in content, using a modified version of the MAPL
criteria established by the CRTC, had levelled off at approximately 35

per cent.[51] Acquiring a sufficient number of music videos, particularly Canadian ones, would take time, so MuchMusic initially only screened six hours of programming that was then repeated over the course of the day. Filling even this limited number of hours meant having to rely upon the low-budget videos of groups that otherwise might have been rejected, thereby helping to seed the boom of the grassroots, independent acts of the national scene during the mid-1980s to mid-1990s. It also meant a reliance on non-video content like interviews with artists and cheaply made game shows. Michael Barclay, Ian A.D. Jack, and Jason Schneider convincingly argue that 'in the infancy of the music video medium, pretty much any Canadian artist with a half-decent visual idea suddenly had a national audience.'[52]

Two years after the start of MuchMusic, City-TV founder and head of MuchMusic Moses Znaimer expanded into the French-speaking market with MusiquePlus. 'There is a motherlode of talent for us to keep building on,' Znaimer explained to *Maclean's* about the new venture.[53] Yet, although there was much in the way of talent, there were even fewer videos than in English-speaking Canada. MusiquePlus started with only about 100 videos in its library and was limited to four hours of programming a day (repeated once).[54]

MuchMusic was a wise investment. Unlike traditional television broadcasters, there was no worry about the high cost of producing or acquiring programs. Videos, after all, acted as commercials, and exposure was exactly what the industry needed.[55] Communications theorist Will Straw has noted that MuchMusic not only offered exposure but did so by placing it within a national paradigm:

> When MuchMusic began operating in 1984, its effect on the marketing and consumption of music was immediately evident. MuchMusic offered a national outlet for new and current music in a country whose radio broadcasting has, for the most part, been local in scale … At the same time, MuchMusic has contributed to the embedding of music within complex layers of discourse *about* music, surrounding it with performer gossip, concert news and other information. These have played a clear role in the current success of Canadian performers. If the traditional weakness of English-Canadian music has much to do with its failure to develop the apparatus of celebrity (apparatus so evident in Francophone Quebec), music video networks have worked to remedy this.[56]

Though MuchMusic audiences and musicians were being linked as members of a national community, this was not simply a musical but an ideologically national phenomenon. Barclay, Jack, and Schneider have noted that 'MuchMusic allowed Canadian youth to see reflections of themselves in their compatriot musicians, which did a lot to increase the importance of the Canadian celebrity.'[57]

Much of this national connection took place external to the music itself. Terry David Mulligan shared moments on the streets of Vancouver with west coast bands on *MuchWest* while Mike Campbell did the same with east coast groups on *MuchEast*; *City Limits* (and later *The Wedge*) turned the microphone over to the artists themselves; *The NewMusic* used a newsmagazine show format to discuss the latest musical happenings across the country; and *Intimate and Interactive* brought musicians into MuchMusic for a 'special events' performance and question-and-answer period. *Intimate and Interactive* was even exclusively Canadian for the first eighteen months of production.[58] The national communalism made possible by *Intimate and Interactive* manifested itself in moments such as the September 2002 appearance of the Tragically Hip. Asked 'what is the craziest stereotype you've ever heard about Canada or Canadians?' the band's singer-songwriter Gord Downie responded 'that we're not patriotic.' Audience reaction was tremendous. 'At that point,' John Wright, Millard Gregory, and Sarah Riegel tell about the incident, 'the crowd [that had] gathered both in the studio and outside on the street broke into a spontaneous rendition of "O Canada."'[59] Author Kip Pegley has even argued that the multicultural makeup of the MuchMusic VJs and the street-level engagements of the studio played into the national self-image as a multicultural mosaic.[60]

MuchMusic built upon the nationalistic loyalty of its viewers by launching an annual televised awards ceremony in 1990. The first Canadian Music Video Awards consisted of a three-week-long train trip across Canada with awards handed out to high-profile acts along the way. 'We put a studio in a baggage car,' David Kines of MuchMusic recalled in a 2002 interview. 'When the train stopped, we'd open the doors and bands would play. People came off and on – like the Northern Pikes and Bruce Cockburn.'[61]

While MuchMusic started off by filling its programming hours with low-budget domestic video releases and interviews that spotlighted the musical experience in national terms, with growth came a focus on exporting a polished American-style channel to foreign markets. MuchMusic left behind its 'nation's music station' motto, took on a network logo that placed its name within a globe, and changed the name of the Canadian

Music Video Awards to the less geographically specific MuchMusic Video Awards; the network's national identity was swapped for a corporate one. Needless to say, then, the MuchMusic that had once travelled across Canada handing out awards from a train had long passed; as of the early 2000s its awards show had become, in the words of Shanda Deziel, 'all about the glitz – in recent years stars like Denzel Washington and Anne Heche have shown up unexpectedly.'[62] Matthew Good, who owed much of his rise on the national level to MuchMusic during the heydays of the 1990s, was not impressed with MuchMusic's change in direction. 'You have a national music television station where new artists aren't going to get broken unless there's clout behind them. Sometimes maybe a few people get played on "The Wedge" [on MuchMusic], but I mean it's not the same thing, where they're going to spin some relatively unknown artist's VideoFACT video in heavy rotation.'[63] Equally unimpressed was Colin MacKenzie of Sloan's Murderecords label in an interview with *Billboard* in 1998: 'MuchMusic has now, basically, slammed the door on independent music, as far as I'm concerned ... I appreciate what MuchMusic does with new music. [But] there is no space or opportunity for an up-and-coming band to make an appearance on MuchMusic now.'[64]

MuchMusic had little need for grassroots videos now that its vault was filled with polished videos by acts on the rosters of multinational record labels; just as important, the station was starting to change towards a predominantly non-video format much as MTV had done. The music in the music videos had only been one part of what drew audiences; musical lifestyles, and that of celebrities across the board, captivated audiences and offered a variety of identities that youths could appropriate for themselves. In their study of youths and popular music, Peter Christenson and Donald Roberts have already pointed out that 'the visual images and narratives of MTV clearly have more potential to form attitudes, values, or perceptions of social reality than does the music alone.'[65] In some ways this was nothing new. Teen magazines had done well cashing in on the teenager desire to know more about, and to emulate, the musicians they revered. What advice did Paul Anka have about dating? What did each of the Beatles like to eat for breakfast? The video age, however, took celebrity stardom and lifestyle to a new level, all the more so with in-studio interviews and entertainment magazine shows that dished gossip and offered behind-the-scenes exposés. The ability of lifestyle segments to hold onto viewers more efficiently than did music videos certainly encouraged a shift in programming. Kip Pegley has told of how 'music video shows, which are categorized as "short" programming, usually achieve less than 1 percent ratings, whereas longer-format shows, which air for thirty minutes or more, receive higher ratings for longer periods. This increased viewing time, of course, is critical for advertising revenue because rating systems often did not register viewing practices under a half an hour in length.'[66]

The music video age, then, gave way to celebrity lifestyles, and Much-Music became less of a music video channel and more of a pop-cult or lifestyle broadcaster, offering such foreign imports as the teenage drama *The O.C.*, the weight-loss competition *Celebrity Fit Club II*, and Flavor Flav of Public Enemy's quest for bootylicious love in *Flavor of Love*, alongside so-called MuchOriginals like *Stars Gone Wild* about 'our favourite Hollywood stars and infamous rich kids ... musicians and celebrities like 50 Cent, Lindsay Lohan, Paris Hilton, and many more' and *Popaganda*, 'a big-themed hour that pulls back the veil on the most controversial and compelling stories in music and entertainment.'[67] These programs allowed MuchMusic to focus on selling itself in foreign markets through such affiliates as MuchMusic Argentina and MuchMusic Malaysia.[68] The Canadian content that the affiliates brought along for the ride did little to contribute to the national imperative, though. Pegley, in researching MuchMusic's move into the Finnish market, found that there was little means of distinguishing Canadian and American content.[69]

MuchMusic's desire to break through internationally even led to a challenge to MTV in 1994 with the launch of MuchUSA (initially mixing MuchMusic content with American material), which folded in 2003 only to be challenged in turn by MTV Canada.[70] After years of trying to get around regulatory issues that sheltered MuchMusic in the Canadian market, MTV finally managed to do so by joining with CTV and reworking the latter's talktv into MTV Canada. Doing so, though, meant maintaining the talktv's 'lifestyle-talk' format and a significant amount of Canadian content: 68 per cent minimum overall and 71 per cent during prime time.[71] MTV Canada's inability to focus on music was not as much a barrier as one might think because the network had years earlier took the lead in changing from music to general pop-cult programming. With its licensing agreement having clamped the distribution of music videos, the summer of 2008 witnessed the CTVglobemedia group launch of MTV2 in Canada as a digital specialty channel capable of offering up to 10 per cent music videos alongside 'edgier' programming that targeted a 12- to 24-year-old demographic interested in 'wild stunts and pranks, extreme sports, live concerts, comedy, music videos, animation, and much, much more.'[72]

Further, the teaming of MTV Canada and CTV meant that MTV Canada could focus on airing MTV's non-music programming and adding Canadian content equivalents, such as a domestic version of *MTV Cribs* (featuring the homes of Canadian celebrities, particularly those of internationally known expatriates whose episodes would be sellable to affiliates), while CTV could air MTV's music and non-music programs alike, including MTV Canada's launch party featuring Kanye West and Sam Roberts.[73] There was a slight irony that CTV operated more like the original MTV than did MTV Canada, yet fitting given that CTV had brought Canadians the likes of the American-produced *The Monkees* in the 1960s (let alone decades of American programming).[74]

Whereas MuchMusic was initially poised against the duo of MTV Canada and CTV, in mid-2007 CTVglobemedia acquired CHUM's specialty channels, including MuchMusic and MuchMoreMusic, bringing them all under the same corporate umbrella; from this point on they were not so much competitors as corporate compatriots. Although MuchMusic had long aired MTV programming, there was now an almost perverse appropriateness to broadcasting the likes of the *MTV Europe Music Awards* and the *MTV New Year's Eve Masquerade*.[75] And, on the other side, MTV was bringing Canadian acts to the rest of the world, although audiences did not know them as such. Possessing '50 MTV-branded services worldwide serving 171 territories' meant that, as Graciela Martinez-Zalce has noted, Alanis Morissette 'arrived in Mexico through an American filter. She has even won several Grammy Awards … a large Mexican audience has grown up listening to rock music in English, so Canadian groups such as Crash Test Dummies, Barenaked Ladies, Sarah McLachlan, and k.d. lang have achieved a target market here, though perhaps only a few of the buyers know the origins of what they are taking home.'[76]

MuchMusic and MTV Canada still offer viewers musical content, but these days it is less in the form of music videos than it is live performances and interviews limited to a few programs like *Much on Demand* and *MTV Live*. Yet music videos are still in demand, even if relegated to the digital cable specialty channel PunchMuch or, as is more accessible to audiences, online resources. According to a report by Marise Strauss, music videos comprised 80 and 87 per cent of a combined 120 million streaming 'hits' on (respectively) mtv.ca and muchmusic.com during 2007.[77] Streaming provided access to videos of Canadians and non-Canadians alike. Tellingly, although Canadian rock sensation Hedley took awards for best video, best director, best cinematography, and best rock video at the 2008 MuchMusic Video Awards, Barbadian singer Rihanna won the award for the most-watched video on muchmusic.com.[78]

Grassroots acts could no longer depend on music videos as a means of reaching television audiences and began looking to alternatives, even commercials that years earlier would have been regarded as 'selling out.' Bryan Borzykowski, in *Marketing*, noted that 'with MuchMusic rarely playing music videos, and radio devoting its airtime to major artists, lesser-known acts are finally realizing the benefits of ad exposure,' a move that benefited such acts as Joel Plaskett, Bedouin Soundclash, the Be Good Tanyas, and the Golden Dogs, all of whom sold their songs for use by Zellers.[79] 'For proof,' Borzykowski pointed out, 'look at the Toronto-based reggae pop trio Bedouin Soundclash. Until the band landed a song in one of Leo Burnett's Zellers ads, the group was playing tiny dives across the country. In August, the band's sophomore album debuted at #2 on the Canadian charts.'[80]

In 2006, the Juno Awards entered a new era as a televised promotional device for the multinational record labels. Pamela Anderson, a starlet unconnected to the music industry outside of her famous sexual episodes with rock and rollers, was flown in from Los Angeles as host, and fellow expatriate Bryan Adams was scheduled to be inducted into the Canadian Music Hall of Fame. For him to be inducted by Chris Martin of Coldplay, a fellow citizen of England (Adams having moved there and taken up citizenship), was an irony that likely escaped most viewers. Just as telling was the other reason why Martin attended the award show: Coldplay shared the International Album of the Year award with the Black Eyed Peas, the two bands having somehow tied and both consequently getting to perform during the televised segment.[81] Only a few acts were given airtime, with non-commercial ones relegated to ceremonies held before the televised event. No doubt Coldplay and Black Eyed Peas helped to draw the 1.7 million viewers in Canada, a reported 26 per cent more than the Grammy Awards, and an awards show viewership only eclipsed by the Academy Awards and the Golden Globes.[82]

Canadians were not the only audience of interest to the producers of the Junos, however. As of that year, in what was a massive coup, CARAS and CTV teamed with MTV and VH1 to air the program to potentially a quarter of a billion households in Australia, China, India, Italy, Latin America, Malaysia, Portugal, Singapore, Taiwan, the United Kingdom, and, of course, the United States.[83] Much had changed since 1970, when a couple of hundred people came together at St Lawrence Hall for such awards as 'Best Company for Canadian Content' and ate homemade sandwiches. Still, there were moments of Canadiana, although with a choreographed feel, as when Pamela Anderson arrived arm in arm with a pair of strapping Mounties.[84]

From *Let's Go* and *After Four* to the Juno Awards and MuchMusic, television has offered an opportunity for Canadians to construct a national discourse around popular music. Whereas the early years made use of television performers as jukeboxes for Top 40 hits, the coming of coast-to-coast programs and opportunities to perform original singles helped to break down regionalism and develop audiences for a few select acts. At the turn of the 1970s television came to serve not only industrial but national interests by infusing music with a celebratory national discourse. Television played an important role in the transition from music in Canada to Canadian music. Just as revealing, and examined in the next chapter, is how a handful of global multimedia conglomerates encouraged the paradigm shift while reaping the economic benefits of the Canadian content regulation.

9

'Takin' Care of Business':
How Multinationals Underwrote
the Canadian Music Industry

The Canadian music business is not yet as rotten as the U.S. scene. But it's showing signs of catching up.

                                  – Bruce Cockburn, 1971[1]

It is unfortunate but true that as long as our major record companies are controlled by their American head offices, Canadian acts will not receive the priority
that they deserve. The Canadian market just isn't as lucrative as our southern
neighbor's.

                              – Editorial Board, *Rock Express*, 1986[2]

I'm a musical explorer and not just a pop songwriter. Alanis Morissette writes
words, someone else helps set it to music, and then she's kind of stylized into
the part.

                                       – Joni Mitchell, 1999[3]

'When you sign with True North you sign with True North and the individual attention that goes with it but you also sign with Columbia Records,
which is the best company in the world.'[4] True North Records owner
Bernie Finkelstein, spinning his sales pitch in a 1971 interview with *RPM*,
took great pride in the distribution agreement between his label and a
major American-based multinational. The declaration stands out if only
for its timing. After all, this was a period of intense anti-Americanism and
nationalistic grassroots mobilizations against American ownership and
cultural imperialism. Finkelstein was certainly a member of this nationalistic generation: his passion for aiding local music despite the economic
risks saw him managing the Paupers and Kensington Market in the late
1960s and launching True North Records in 1970 as a platform for such
artists as Bruce Cockburn, Murray McLauchlan, Luke Gibson, and Keith

McKie.[5] Such initiatives led *RPM* to praise him as 'a patron of the arts' and, in the words of John Macfarlane of *Maclean's*, 'the Jack McClelland of the Canadian music business.'[6] Yet for Finkelstein to extol Columbia Records in a time of activism against American branch plants was not all that inflammatory, at least not among those who understood how the music industry operated. Good business sense meant that Finkelstein and other label owners had to put aside nationalistic grievances and participate in a relationship for which there was no viable alternative. True North followed in the footsteps of such labels as Roman Records and its distribution agreement with Capitol for singles by the Paupers and David Clayton-Thomas and Yorktown's deal with Capitol to distribute the Ugly Ducklings. Nor was Finkelstein the only one flying in the face of nationalistic angst. Frank Davies of Love Productions and Daffodil Records, formed in 1970, credited its domestic distribution agreement with Capitol with setting the stage for signing Crowbar and King Biscuit Boy with Paramount Records in the United States and getting A Foot in Coldwater on Island in the UK and Elektra in the U.S.[7] The reality was that True North and other labels had little choice but to deal with the major multinationals that had developed the most extensive means of distributing products.

Being a record label owner in Canada was far from a cakewalk. Rock and roll offered much to radio stations and record stores but not so much to those who started up a label, at least not before the advent of the Canadian content regulation. Prospects had looked good in the mid-1960s as early rock and roll, British Invasion, and folk offered audiences for such entrepreneurial adventurers as Tamarac Records, Bigland, Roman Records, Chateau, Canatal, ACT, Can Cut, and Quality Records. Yet the optimism did not pan out as radio stations, and the record stores that based their offerings on the CHUM Chart, had little need for domestic recordings. It took a few more years before the Canadian content regulation promised to make the recording industry into a viable business sector. It was not a coincidence that on 20 January 1971, less than a week after the regulation had come into play, that the Canadian Independent Record Production Association (CIRPA) was formed as a non-profit body to represent the interests of label owners. Its imperatives were laid out in a press release:

1. To act as a forum for the gathering, discussion and dissemination of information relating to the business of independent record production.

2. To corporately strive for a higher standard of production quality in Canada resulting in greater rewards for the entire Canadian music industry.
3. To collectively support the growth of the talent community in Canada.
4. To make available to Canadian independent record producers an organization within which they can combine their talents, reputations, present and potential financial and political forces and direct them towards the solution of problems faced by independent record producers as a group.[8]

Membership in CIRPA required that over 50 per cent of a label's shares be owned by Canadian citizens.[9] Among the initial board members were Bernie Finkelstein (True North Records), Jack Richardson (Nimbus 9 Productions), and Terry Brown (Toronto Sound recording studio). Over the next few years the association would go on to include Daffodil, Boot Records, Tuesday Music, Revolver, Aquarius, Nick Records, Treble Clef Records, Axe Records, MWC Records, Mushroom Records, and Woodshed Records, among others.

Label entrepreneurs were not going it alone. Ritchie Yorke, the Australian-born music journalist who had made a mission out of aiding the industry, saw great promise for domestic and foreign-owned labels to come together and expand international sales. Having spent time abroad, Yorke brought with him a particular interest in tapping into the European market. 'Stay Awhile' by the Bells, according to statistics compiled by Yorke, sold over a million copies in North America but not even 1,000 in England. Of the Guess Who's twelve singles and six albums that were a hit on their home continent, only 'American Woman' charted on the Top 30 in England. And, although sixteen Canadian records made it into the *Billboard* charts in 1970, only 'Snowbird' and 'American Woman' made a dent in Europe.[10] Yorke concluded that the recording industry needed a junket, a gathering of foreign reporters and industry folk commonly used in Europe to introduce the youth-oriented press of other markets to a country's talent.

The Maple Music Junket was an idea put forth by Yorke in the 14 August 1971 issue of *RPM*. What was needed was funding to bring at least a hundred journalists, columnists, radio industry representatives, and other industry professionals to Canada for three days of concerts and networking. The major multinational subsidiaries had shown enthusiasm for expanding their share of the industry in the wake of the Canadian content regulation and, Yorke thought, could be brought onside to join with the domestically owned labels interested in getting their goods abroad. Yet, given that the multinationals were primarily in Canada to distribute foreign recordings, one could not expect them to handle the expenses alone. The federal government needed to ante up a substantial share. Yorke therefore spun the proposal to the government as a chance for it to affirm its support for the recording industry. 'The Maple Music Junket, we firmly believe, represents a unique opportunity for the Canadian Government to further demonstrate its belief in the growth and widening acceptance of Canadian music throughout the world ... The time has now come to capitalize on the very real and very large potential of Canadian music on a global basis.'[11]

Federal interest in the music scene was certainly not without precedent. Not only had the CRTC expanded the Canadian content regulation to include radio broadcasting but, a year before Yorke proposed the junket, the government had sent a contingent of musicians and bands to Expo '70 in Japan to show off the sorts of music available in Canada. English-language acts that made the trip included the Travellers, John Allan Cameron, the Poppy Family, Ian and Sylvia, the Guess Who, the Irish Rovers, the Collectors, and the Marshmallow Soup Group, while the French-speaking acts were les Bel Canto, les Bel Air, Jean-Pierre Ferland, Claude Léveillée, Gilles Vigneault, Renée Claude, André Gagnon, and les Contretemps.[12] The petition worked. Pierre Juneau and the CRTC brought the federal government onboard, although given Pierre Trudeau's enthusiasm for youth culture the decision should not have been a surprise. In fact, the rhetoric used by the prime minister in a letter to junket participants was nationalistic in its celebration of an essentialized Canadian music. 'Our contemporary music expresses in a unique, enjoyable and often powerful way our ideas and emotions as a people. Knowing and appreciating our music enables us and music lovers from other countries to know Canadians better.'[13] It was no less than a declaration that musicians could serve as cultural representatives of the nation. The CRTC provided a $30,000 grant, and the Canadian Record Manufacturers Association joined with various labels, publishers, and other industry participants to pool together $50,000. Maple Music Inc. was formed to administer the junket with a board of directors composed of Yorke and representatives from the Canadian Record Manufacturers Association, Capitol, Columbia, Polydor, Trans-Canada, and Quality. Given their support of the initiative and role in the music scene, honourary directorships were bestowed upon representatives from CAPAC, BMI, CIRPA, and the Ontario Council for the Arts.[14]

Over one hundred reporters and industry representatives from fifteen

European countries were flown to Canada to check out the French- and English-speaking markets. Showcases were established for such top-sellers as Richard and Marie-Claire Séguin, Vos Voisine, the Poppy Family, George Hamilton IV, Murray McLauchlan, Christopher Kearney, Bruce Cockburn, the Stampeders, the Perth County Conspiracy, Edward Bear, Mashmakhan, April Wine, Pepper Tree, Lighthouse, Fludd, Anne Murray, and Crowbar, the latter's massive stage show not surprisingly involving a naked go-go dancer jumping out of a cake. Out of the event came exposure for Canadian acts in the European market and an opportunity for labels, recording studios, and other industry participants to mingle and network with their foreign counterparts.[15] 'This music had always been American – transatlantic – as far as we were concerned,' Andy Gray of the *New Musical Express* in Britain reported, 'now we know who's a Canadian musician and what's Canadian music.'[16] The impression seemed to be shared by Wilder Penfield of *Canadian Composer*. 'Canadian music, with one stroke, has been severed from the North American mix. Just who is Canadian may not be remembered for long, but the distinction itself is not a conscious thing in the European media.'[17]

Penfield was not off the mark in pondering the brevity of the distinction. When the junket failed to become a regular occurrence, Canadian groups soon blended back into the North American whole. The federal government was apparently happy with the initial event and offered to participate in a repeat, even going so far as to raise the possibility of establishing a Maple Music office in London as a gateway into the European market, but the major multinational subsidiaries backed away from the possibility. Yorke not surprisingly took the outcome rather hard. 'I gathered later,' he told Richard Flohil of *Canadian Composer* in October 1976, 'that they had had the word from their various head offices: Stop crowing about Canadian talent, and get back to the day-to-day business of meeting the quotas on the established lines of product. Me? I got disgusted and quit … And now when I talk to Europeans about Canadian music, they say: "You guys made all that noise. What happened? Where's the follow-up?" And they forgot about it, and we let a golden opportunity slip by.'[18]

Yorke's comments, though bitter, contained an element of truth. The subsidiaries of multinational record labels existed first and foremost to sell foreign-produced recordings in the Canadian market, and this relationship had changed only to a minor degree with the new demand for Canadian content recordings. Bobby Curtola, former teenage heartthrob, opined in a 1971 interview that multinationals had gone from disregarding the domestic scene to now supporting talent because 'it's a damn good investment,' but he did not note the difference between investing in acts benefiting from Canadian content airtime and trying to break acts into foreign markets.[19] Even domestic investment was questionable at times, what Yorke frustratingly called 'the token efforts, and the tokenism is even worse than not signing an artist in the first place – they'll sign someone, throw a little press party, and sit around hoping that the records'll sell, but not really giving much of a damn one way or the other.'[20] Yorke shared this point of view with Larry Evoy, lead singer of Edward Bear, a group that had signed with Capitol. The label, Evoy told Mike Quigley of the *Georgia Straight* in the summer of 1970, was proving to be 'cautious' and 'hesitant' about signing domestic bands, while RCA was taking the opposite approach and 'just scooping up all kinds of bands and not doing anything with them … just scooping up people, but that's not gonna do any good, because if you get grabbed with a mess of others, you just get lost in the rush.'[21]

Capitol not only did much to market Edward Bear but it did so by tapping into nationalism through blending emotionally charged metaphors with a subtle assertion of international success. As one advertising poster declared, 'Like a fresh breeze from the North, Canadian talent is crossing borders and boundaries to gain greater international recognition. And Capitol's got the best.'[22] Capitol's use of national iconography was taken to its highest point in the 'Sounds Canadian' advertising campaign with its red and white record store displays covered in maple leaves and the placing of stickers on the albums of such artists as Edward Bear, Gene MacLellan, Mother Tucker's Yellow Duck, and Anne Murray. It even released a *Sounds Canadian* album featuring a variety of acts and a cover image of a record painted to resemble the flag and donned with the tag line 'Capitol captures the sounds of outstanding Canadian artists.'[23] Evoy was not all that comfortable with the campaign, however. His uneasiness came in part from the aesthetics. 'That "Sounds Canadian" sticker … makes it look like a 99 cent album,' Evoy complained to Quigley. 'You know, here's an album cover that Paul [Weldon, the band's organist] took a lot of time to figure out, because it's subtle, and then you get this big red and white thing – SOUNDS CANADIAN – Ugh!'[24] But, more revealingly, Evoy was also uncomfortable with the record company pointing out that the album was Canadian. Selling an act along national lines had yet to become common let alone a point of pride. 'Proclaiming that it's Canadian,' he noted, 'there's still that feeling that Canadian talent is second rate, and making a point of saying it [is Canadian] isn't such a hot idea.'[25]

Despite the questionable campaign, Edward Bear benefited from signing with Capitol. To be with a major multinational label, whether directly
or through a distribution agreement secured by a domestic label, was
essential to getting your albums into the hands of radio stations and
record stores from coast to coast. A comprehensive list of domestic labels
and artists holding distribution deals with multinational labels is beyond
the scope of this chapter, particularly given the frequency with which
affiliations were altered (Trooper, for example, was distributed by MCA,
RCA, and Warner at different times over the course of a decade), but
a sampling tells much about the role of the majors in the success of
domestic acts. RCA's roster included the Guess Who, April Wine, Lighthouse, Stonebolt, Ryan's Fancy, and Triumph. EMI-Capitol had Anne
Murray, Crowbar, Edward Bear, Beau Dommage, Pierre Lalonde, Streetheart, Prism, Helix, the Powder Blues Band, A Foot in Coldwater, Glass
Tiger, and Corey Hart. A&M signed Chilliwack, Leyden Zar, Cano, and
the Payola$. Columbia's roster included Mashmakhan and Loverboy.
Polygram/Polydor had agreements with Saga, Goddo, and Martha and
the Muffins. Mercury signed Rush, Max Webster, and Bachman-Turner
Overdrive. CBS had Zon, Offenbach, Rough Trade, Gowan, Platinum
Blonde, and the Diodes (the first Canadian punk band to get a major
label contract).

Not only was a deal with a multinational necessary, let alone common,
but it not hinder a tremendous national credibility; the music scene was
comfortably evolving as ideologically national yet industrially multinational. One has only to look at Rush, a band whose success was due to
resources and opportunities outside of Canada – and multinational ones
within Canada – but nonetheless thrived as what Nicholas Jennings of
Maclean's called 'perhaps the quintessential Canadian musical heroes.'[26]
Dating back to 1968 but taking its final configuration in 1974 with the
coming of drummer and songwriter Neil Peart, Rush cracked the American (and, in turn, Canadian) market thanks in part to the support of
Donna Halper at WMMS in Cleveland. With the backing of American
booking agency ATI, the band signed to Mercury Records in Chicago
before launching its own label.[27] Over the decades that followed, Rush
established itself as an international act. According to academic Durrell
Bowman, an expert on Rush, three-quarters of the band's hardcore fans
reside in the United States, and one-eighth in Canada, and there are
album sale 'guesstimates' of '40 million worldwide, 30 million in the U.S.,
5 million in Canada, and much of the remaining 5 million split almost
evenly between the U.K., Japan, and Brazil. Thus, Rush's success cannot

be explained as a mainly Canadian phenomenon, and the band's music almost never references Canadian topics in any case.'[28] Rush owed much to its breakthrough south of the border, the support of Mercury, and a national capital that even extended to the Canadian Consular General W.J. Collett, who bestowed an award on the group in 1979 as 'Canadian ambassadors of music.'[29] There was little to no incompatibility between being underwritten by a multinational label and thriving in ideologically national terms; if anything, multinational support affirmed the quality of the act as something in which to take pride (more will be said about this in the next chapter).

Relationships with multinationals were not always so rosy, though. After all, popular music operated first and foremost within the world of commerce. The relationship between CBS and the Diodes testifies as to how unstable these relationships could be. CBS backed the Diodes on their first release but, when the sales were not as high as expected, the label did not release the band's sophomore album. 'CBS signed us hoping to make a quick, effortless bundle from the punk thing,' the band complained in a 1979 interview with *Canadian Composer*. 'When that didn't materialize, they stopped trying.' CBS, on the other hand, defended its action as simple business sense: 'We don't feel the band has lived up to its potential in terms of the market we had envisaged for it in Canada.'[30] Yet, when the band continued to draw attention, CBS got back on board and released the second album.

The reaction of CBS to the tentative success of the Diodes was also indicative of the economic downswing that occurred at the turn of 1980s. Sales were suffering across the board and expenses were rising as the age of the singles came to be replaced by that of LPs and massive advertising campaigns. Labels were taking on fewer acts for the sake of support-ing a smaller number on a larger scale. Whereas in the mid-1970s one often finds a budget of $40,000 for recording and $10,000 for promo-tion, by the end of the decade the amount was upwards of $125,000.[31] Costs became all the more exorbitant with the advent of music videos. As early as 1983, Walt Grealis argued that videos were essential to break-ing a new act and had added 20 per cent to the production cost of an album.[32] This percentage quickly rose as the use of videos increased and labels attempted to outdo their competition by creating works that often approached cinematic quality. As Robert Roper, A&R manager at WEA Music, admitted to *Maclean's* in late 1986, 'videos have doubled the cost of making records. The other end of the equation is that we sign fewer acts.'[33] Typical of the times was when Capitol signed Tokyo, changed their name to Glass Tiger, and sank $200,000 into music videos alone, out of which came 'Don't Forget Me' (hitting No. 2 on *Billboard*).[34]

Spending big money was not as risky as one might think. The major multinationals struck a deal with MTV that allowed labels to place videos of its choice on 10 per cent of MTV's playlist in exchange for giving the music station exclusive access to 20 per cent of a label's video output.[35] The results were striking. A *Billboard* survey determined that only two of the 131 clips on MTV over the course of a twenty-four-hour period were by artists signed to an independent label, and even then the videos involved an established act: James Brown collaborating with Afrika Bambaataa (Tommy Boy Records) and blues guitarist Johnny Winter (Alligator Records).[36] The strategy in effect allowed labels to push specific videos on MTV until they cracked the market and were in turn picked up by radio stations.[37] The agreement reeked of the payola controversy of decades earlier, but, given that no money was exchanged, it was a legal exclusive distribution agreement.

Signing with the Canadian subsidiary of a multinational meant that one had limited access to such powerful tools. Little wonder, then, that some performers opted to go directly to the American office, although this was not all that easy to do. Gerry Young, former Polygram representative and owner of Current Records, explained to *Canadian Musician* in the summer of 1986 that 'today ... the world takes Canada seriously enough to look harder at what we have. Walk an unsigned Canadian project into a U.S. company and they'll ask why you can't get anything going in your hometown. It's a valid point.'[38] Yet in that same year, the Vancouver-based 54-40 attracted attention for bucking the norm and signing directly to the American office of Warner. Having regularly travelled down the coast from Vancouver to California before ever crossing over the mountains into Alberta, the band was more established in Seattle, Portland, and San Francisco than it was across Canada. Only after signing with Warner did 54-40 make its first trip inland.[39]

Geoffrey Kelly, singer-songwriter and multi-instrumentalist in Spirit of the West, understood why many bands bypassed the domestic subsidiary. He found himself increasingly frustrated by the inability of his label, Warner Canada, to crack the band's *Go Figure* in the American market. Kelly and his bandmates had to instead push the album as an import through the distribution company Cargo. 'Our Canadian label has tried to make it happen down in the States but it just hasn't happened and I don't think they have the power to make it happen,' he complained in a 1992 interview with *Canadian Musician*. 'That's why so many Canadian bands just bypass being signed at home and go directly to an American or British label. That's where things are happening, and if you get signed in the States or England things are going to happen for you at home anyways.'[40]

Signing directly with the American office did not make the executives at the Canadian subsidiaries all that happy, yet there was an understanding of why bands did so. Although the subsidiaries were part of the same multinational label, they operated relatively autonomously, often struggling to get the American offices to pick up a single or an album. Michael Roth, head of Sony Canada A&R, explained to Larry LeBlanc of *Billboard* that the American counterparts tended to overlook Canadian acts until offered evidence of high sales or, as was occasionally the case, impressed by a concert or showcase. 'We've had the U.S. company say no initially and change their mind after they saw the act or saw [sales] happen here. Our Lady Peace was a good example. We got no answers from our U.S. label initially, and we finally got it out on Relativity a year after we released it here.'[41] Roth experienced a similar lack of attention when trying to pitch the Philosopher Kings: 'We couldn't get [U.S. representatives] to come up and give them a good look after the album was released. Then last year Jason Jordan [A&R at Columbia in New York] heard them play at the Montreal Jazz Festival and was blown away by their performance, so the album was released in the U.S.'[42] Similarly, the Tragically Hip scored its deal with MCA Records after label president Bruce Dickinson saw them perform at the Horseshoe Tavern in Toronto in 1987.

Not only were acts going south but some American A&R representatives were even starting to travel north, bypassing their Canadian colleagues and treating the Canadian market on continental terms. Jane Siberry, Jeff Healey, the Tragically Hip, Maestro Fresh-Wes, k.d. lang, Alannah Myles, Barenaked Ladies, Colin James, the Pursuit of Happiness, and Sloan were but a few acts who attracted this sort of attention.[43] Such poaching did not go over well, of course, and maintaining good relations and maximizing the ability to sell in both markets often led to co-signing agreements. Nine American A&R representatives showed up to an I Mother Earth showcase in 1992, for example, leading to a joint project between the Canadian and American branches of EMI-Capitol.[44] Likewise, Moist signed a deal with the Canadian affiliate of EMI-Capitol but with guaranteed support from the American office. In opting not to sign directly to the American office, Keith Maryanovich, manager of Moist, told *Canadian Musician* that 'we didn't want to sign a U.S. deal.

As a Canadian band, we want to build up our home market, and Canadian labels are supportive of Canadian products. So we ended up with a worldwide record deal with certain promotional commitments from the U.S. company.'[45]

Maryanovich took pride in signing with what he called a 'Canadian label,' but EMI Canada (previously Capitol Canada) was, in actuality, a foreign-owned subsidiary of British-based EMI-Capitol, a multinational label whose Canadian subsidiary (and those elsewhere) was primarily designed to distribute and promote foreign recordings. These subsidiaries did substantially less to support domestic acts than did Canadian-owned labels. According to a survey conducted for the Federal Cultural Policy Review Committee in the early 1980s, the top four multinational labels accounted for almost 80 per cent of album sales in Canada, but it was the domestically owned labels, holding onto a small margin of the market, that produced more than 50 per cent of Canadian content albums.[46]

EMI Canada, as with the other multinational subsidies, was a domestic face on the Janus head of a multinational corporation that, along with a handful of peers, had spent the past several decades securing a hold over the global recording industry. Although the rise of independent labels and the anti-commercialism of rock and roll in the late 1960s had challenged the multinationals, during the 1970s the multinationals regained the sort of control that had existed in the days of Tin Pan Alley. Evidence of this reclaiming of power, Jon Savage argues, can be seen in the control gained over the 1960s psychedelic bands, counter culture groups, and 'even the most recalcitrant hippies.'[47] This taming of the youthquake was cemented by what author Robert Burnett identifies as a 'reconstruction period' that occurred between 1970 and 1973: 'First, they increased central control over the creative process through deliberate creation and extensive promotion of new artists, long-term contracts and reduced autonomy for producers. The majors also consolidated their leading position in the manufacturing and distribution of recordings. During the period the majors also made extensive use of illegal promotion such as payola (the playing of records on the radio for cash) and legal promotion which the independents could not match.'[48]

Consolidation of the music industry took place on a stunning level during the 1970s and especially in the early 1990s following the absorption of the multinational labels into vertically integrated multimedia conglomerates that spanned the gamut of production and distribution. Burnett provides a fascinating overview of the mergers:

Japanese electronic giant Sony purchased CBS records for $2.2 billion [U.S.] and then purchased Columbia Pictures for $3.4 billion [U.S.]. Time/Life's 1990 merger with Warner Communications created Time Warner, the world's largest communications company and significantly, the only American enterprise of that magnitude in a world dominated by Bertelsmann (Germany), Hachette (France) and Murdoch's News Corporation. Polygram Records, itself a subsidiary of the Netherlands multinational electronics giant Philips, acquired both Island Records and A&M Records. British EMI, a division of multinational Thorn, acquired independent music publishers SBK as well as Chrysalis Records and Virgin Records. The German BMG, a division of media giant Bertelsmann, purchased both RCA Records and Arista Records. And last but not least, in 1990 Matsushita Electric Industrial, which is twice the size of Sony, purchased MCA, parents of Universal Pictures and MCA Records.[49]

The result was a consolidation of the music industry under the umbrellas of six major corporations, each operating globally and capable of taking a single act through all stages of A&R, recording, production, album pressing, publicity, and the securing of air and video time. As of the mid-1990s, Burnett noted, consolidation meant that there were

> six firms in the international music industry that can be defined as transnational phonogram companies. One is American owned (Warner), two are Japanese (Sony, MCA), one is German (BMG), one is British (EMI) and one is Dutch owned (Polygram [although, in fact, it is also partially German-owned]). Each of these major firms is itself a division of an even larger electronics or communications conglomerate. BMG Music, formerly RCA, was until 1986 a division of the American electronics giant, Radio Corporation of American/General Electric. It is now owned by the German, Bertelsmann Music Group (BMG) which in turn is a division of the world's largest publisher, the Bertelsmann Publishing Group. EMI Records is a division of the Thorn-EMI electronics corporation [which also has Virgin Music Group and Capitol], while the majority of Polygram is owned by the Philips electronic corporation [and includes Poyldor, Mercury, MGM, Decca, A&M, Island Records, and Motown]. Warner Music is a division of the communications giant, Time Warner [and includes Atlantic, Elektra, Maverick, Reprise, and Sire, among others]. Sony Music was previously CBS Records, a division of the broadcasting conglomerate Columbia Broadcasting Systems until late 1987 when it was sold to the Japanese Sony electron-

ics corporation. MCA was bought by the Japanese Matsushita company in 1990. All six of the phonogram majors have branch subsidiaries throughout Europe and the Americas.[50]

These labels together had a hold on at least 80 per cent of the market in the United States, Japan, France, Germany, Austria, Ireland, Sweden, Italy, Portugal, Switzerland, and the United Kingdom in the early 1990s, and accounted for over 90 per cent of the sales of recorded music in Canada as of 1994.[51]

A further consolidation of power over the music industry took place at the turn of the century. The Canadian-owned beverage company Seagram, looking to broaden its holdings, pared the number of firms from six to five by purchasing MCA from Matsushita in 1995 for $5.5 billion (U.S.) and Polygram for $10 billion (U.S.) in 1998, creating Universal Music Group. This venture was short-lived, though, as Seagram's entertainment holdings were bought by France-based Vivendi in 2000 for $34 billion (U.S.). Three years later, Vivendi merged its entertainment wing with General Electric to form NBC Universal. In 2004 Sony and BMG brought together the bulk of their music holdings to form Sony BMG Music Entertainment, thereby taking the list of major players down to four: EMI Music Group, Universal Music Group, Sony BMG Music Entertainment, and Warner Music Group. As of 2006 these four multinationals had maintained approximately the same market share as previously held by the six companies, taking in about 90 per cent of Canadian recording industry revenue (with sales revenue hovering around $800 million).[52]

Statistics aside, the multinationals and their domestic subsidiaries made possible a decade-long upsurge of musical nationalism. Michael Barclay, Ian A.D. Jack, and Jason Schneider, in a nationalistic statement, have explained that 'there was never a single defining moment, but in 1985, Canadian rock-'n'-roll was not only at the vanguard of the nation's cultural identity, it also proudly carried that identity around the world. The heady decade that followed saw the arrival of countless homegrown stars and an accompanying stream of classic recordings ... what bound all of them together was the fact that they made music on their own terms, writing about their own experience and those of other Canadians.'[53] The rhetoric and tropes offered by these authors were by now rather common: musicians as channellers of an undefined national essence; musical acts as 'homegrown' within the native soil; a myth, presented as fact, of collective solidarity (and even a national communalism); a perpetuation of the image of rock and rollers as defying the status quo while now doing so as compatriots against foreign musical hegemony. And all of this now took place not only in Canada but, in an unadulterated form, on the world stage.

This phenomenon was given its grassroots, nationally situated tone through such avenues as MuchMusic, the popularity of live music, retail outlets that sold releases on consignment, and radio stations (particularly 'alternative' FM and college radio) that gave airplay to aspiring acts. CFNY-FM in Toronto was one of these radio stations. Nigel Best, at that time manager of Barenaked Ladies, credited CFNY with doing much for the band. 'Thank goodness a CFNY exists. We've probably received a half-million dollars of airtime on that station in the course of the year.'[54] Similarly, Dave Bidini of the Rheostatics has recalled 'driving to Brampton, Ont., to give the [CFNY] station's programmer, David Marsden, a recording of our first studio session … and driving home hoping he'd play it on the radio. He almost always did.'[55]

For the Rheostatics, topic choices added to their sense of Canadianness, as they drew upon established and emotionally loaded national iconography. 'For "The Ballad of Wendel Clark,"' Bidini has explained, 'me and Dave [Clark, the band's drummer] thought we'd write about our favourite hockey player 'cause it's something we know about. We wrote about going across Canada in "Canadian Dream" because it's something we wanted to do.'[56] Their interest in Canadian iconography even drew the attention of the National Gallery of Canada and led to a commission to create a soundtrack for an exhibition of Group of Seven works. Likewise, the Tragically Hip drew on such figures as explorer Jacques Cartier, painter Tom Thomson, and hockey player Bill Barilko. As with Bidini, singer-songwriter Gord Downie of the Hip explained to *Maclean's*: 'I really can't help myself. That's the Canada I discovered from travelling it. As a writer, you're always on the search for something new to say, or at least some new way to shed light on an old word. I'm pretty sure there haven't been many rock songs written about these people, these events, these landscapes, these images. Yet there's so much raw material to be mined.'[57] The Hip are, interestingly, rather passive and even slightly cynical in their nationalism, employing identifiers within lyrics but refraining from the sort of explicit anti-Americanism that worked so well for the Guess Who. Downie even braved disapproval by wearing a Boston Bruins hockey jersey in the music video for 'Courage' (his godfather is Harry Sinden, the team's former general manager and coach).

The Hip's popularity along national lines has been furthered by their lack of profile outside of Canada, a phenomenon interpreted by some of their fans as a sign of how Canadians are indeed different from Americans. Apparently, only Canadians can understand and appreciate the band, and the Hip thus act as a catalyst for national inclusiveness. As noted by John Wright, Millard Gregory, and Sarah Riegel, 'being a fan of the Hip becomes a marker of Canadian-ness, something shared by a generation of Canadians from which Americans are by-and-large excluded.'[58]

The phenomenon was nothing new. Bands such as the Guess Who and Lighthouse, Nicholas Jennings has reminisced, 'were homegrown heroes, local acts that had gone on to become stars.'[59] Or, as Tom Harrison of *Canadian Musician* remarked about the Guess Who, 'I remember how my classmates of John Henderson Junior High School in East Kildonan [Winnipeg] were thrilled that one of our bands had a hit on the radio. It had never happened before. For those of us who never got closer to the Beatles than watching their DC8 fly overhead, the idea of a local group actually side by side on the charts with "I Want To Hold Your Hand" was inconceivable.'[60] Yet such statements attest to the fact that acts existed on a local or, at most, regional level. The 'Canadian' homegrown hero had yet to exist on a significant level because a national scene, both geographically and ideologically, for the most part did not exist until it was made possible by the airplay, media coverage, recording industry, and coast-to-coast touring circuit that emerged following the Canadian content regulation.

As of the 1990s, musicians were metaphorical conquistadors who not only fought foreign musical hegemony but went abroad and dominated such events as the Grammy Awards. National jubilance erupted in 1996 when Canadians won eleven awards: Alanis Morissette, riding the success of *Jagged Little Pill*, won Best Rock Song for 'You Oughta Know,' Best Female Performance, Album of the Year, and Best Rock Performance; country singer Shania Twain scored Best Country Album for *The Woman in Me*; and Joni Mitchell took awards for Pop Album of the Year and Best Recording Package for *Turbulent Indigo*.[61] The next year Celine Dion joined the pack by taking Album of the Year for *Falling into You*. The greatest triumph, however, came in 1999, when Twain, Morissette, and Celine Dion, along with other Canadian-born talent, were nominated for twenty-six awards and won seventeen.[62]

Yet, in critical terms, their success represented not a Canadian defiance of American musical hegemony but simply their existence as part of the ebb and flow centred in the United States, with many of the

major acts even living in the United States. Morissette, who had won a
Juno in 1992 for the most promising female vocalist for the self-titled
Alanis, headed to Los Angeles in 1994, worked with producer Glen Bal-
lard (with whom she co-wrote *Jagged Little Pill*), and signed with Madonna's Maverick Records. Twain hailed originally from Timmins, Ontario,
but signed with Mercury Nashville Records and recorded *The Woman in
Me* with famed British producer Robert 'Mutt' Lange, with whom she
lived in upstate New York (before moving to Switzerland).[63] Joni Mitchell had long been a part of the American industry, maintaining homes
in the United States and Canada. And Dion, signed to Columbia and
Epic, recorded abroad and lived in Florida before following in the footsteps of crooners Paul Anka and fellow Quebecker René Simard by relocating to Las Vegas. Backstage at the 1996 Grammy Awards, Twain told
reporters: 'I never really was aware of the border. I like to keep it that
way actually, even now.'[64] But this self-identification and the fact that her
career was underwritten by resources outside of Canada did not stop
Brian D. Johnson of *Maclean's,* in the nationalist parlance by now so
common, from calling her 'Canadian music's no-nonsense sex symbol'[65]
and informing readers that 'she leads a country [music] invasion from
the north.'[66]

Such nationalist narratives are not all that accurate and certainly
not honest in the face of the multinational reality. The nationally conscious and celebratory music scene was made possible by, and in line
with the interests of, multinational record labels. In early 1992 music
journalist Nicholas Jennings counted eighty-four commercially popular musicians and bands on the rosters of the multinationals.[67] It is
worth offering a small sample of the signings: Warner/WEA had 54-40,
Spirit of the West, Great Big Sea, Colin James, the Killjoys, Loreena
McKennitt, Moxy Frïvous, the Odds, Jane Siberry, the Skydiggers, the
Waltons, Weeping Tile, Blue Rodeo, Natalie MacMaster, Wide Mouth
Mason, Alanis Morissette, and the Rheostatics. On the Sony label were
Our Lady Peace, Celine Dion, Chantal Kreviazuk, and the Bourbon
Tabernacle Choir. The MCA/Universal/Geffen supported the Tragi-
cally Hip, Sloan, Barenaked Ladies, and the Watchmen. BMG/RCA
had the Cowboy Junkies, Sarah McLachlan, Crash Test Dummies, and
Treble Charger. The EMI/Capitol/Virgin Music Group included I
Mother Earth, King Cobb Steelie, Rita MacNeil, John McDermott,
Tea Party, Moist, the Rankin Family, Tom Cochrane, Grapes of Wrath,
Leahy, Moist, Change of Heart, Rita MacNeil, the Northern Pikes, 13
Engines, Leslie Spit Treeo, and even Stompin' Tom Connors following

his return to the scene in 1990.[68] Finally, and still merely the tip of the iceberg, Polygram handled the Doughboys, Ashley McIsaac, and Jann Arden.[69]

Many of these acts chose to sign to the multinationals following their success as an independent. Spirit of the West, for example, released three independent albums before signing with WEA Music of Canada, an affiliate of Time-Warner.[70] Harpist Loreena McKennitt went from selling albums from the trunk of her car to joining first with Warner's Canadian and then American offices. The Rankin Family released two Juno-winning independent albums before signing with EMI Canada. Both Sloan and Barenaked Ladies turned their independently recorded cassette tapes into contracts with one of the hottest alternative rock labels, Sire, a division of Geffen/Warner. In other cases the multinationals stuck to the tried-and-true task of picking up acts already discovered by domestically owned labels. Alternative folk-rocker Hayden owed much of the success of *Everything I Long For* to the support of the domestically owned Sonic Unyon but then jumped ship in favour of Outpost (Geffen/Warner).[71]

Not all acts were eager to sign with a multinational label, though. The lure of money and promotion seemed to come at the cost of the personal attention and ongoing support offered by the Bernie Finkelsteins of the industry. There was a lot of risk in being valued as a commodity in a quickly changing industry, as singer-songwriter Andrew Cash opined to *Canadian Composer*. 'A record deal often isn't all it's cracked up to be. Most Canadian record companies are U.S.-owned subsidiaries ... What's the point of pinning your hopes on a big contract and allowing yourself to be moulded and processed if you end up getting dropped after one or two records, just because the U.S. parent company wasn't interested or didn't allow time for you to develop an audience and style? Who wants to be a has-been?'[72]

Cash seemed justified in his concern when the bubble began to burst in the mid-1990s. 'A lot of money is being pissed away because of the feeding frenzy,' Al Mair of Attic Records observed in an interview with Larry LeBlanc in early 1995. 'A lot of the acts being signed don't ... cut it.'[73] Labels soon realized that they had taken on too many acts too quickly and as a result began to purge their rosters. The end of the boom was furthered by changes in the retail and broadcasting sectors. Many retailers, including the influential HMV, stopped taking independent releases on consignment, thereby gutting an important means of accessing consumers.[74] MuchMusic was increasingly turning away from its grassroots origins and using a lot of non-video content, as explored in chapter eight. And even CFNY seemed to change its format so that independent acts had less chance at airplay. The heyday was over.

Many contracts were not renewed as labels attempted to re-centre themselves following the feeding frenzy. The situation was not unlike that of the early 1970s when the major labels were quick to sign acts in hopes of cashing in on the Canadian content regulation only to acquire a glut of bands that ended up languishing. For some acts the freedom was welcome after what they viewed as corporate neglect. The Cowboy Junkies had turned the success of their second independent release, *The Trinity Sessions*, into a contract with RCA, only to be unhappy with the results and switch to Geffen before giving up on multinationals and reviving their own Latent Records label.[75] Similarly, the Bourbon Tabernacle Choir were pleased when their Sony distribution deal came to an end because, keyboardist and vocalist Chris Brown has explained, they felt that sales were due more to years of touring and a personal rapport with audiences than anything done by Sony.[76] Even Sloan seemed eager to leave behind a record contract that had helped make them the pre-eminent east coast rock band. 'It was such a dream come true to be signed to a major label in the United States and we were doing well in Canada,' vocalist Patrick Pentland described in an interview with *Canadian Musician*, 'and as soon as we put out [sophomore release] *Twice Removed* in Canada there was a lot of positive response – but we woke up when Geffen said "What the hell is this? You can't put this out. This doesn't sound like *Smeared*."'[77]

Although Sloan went on to found its own label, Murderecords, the band was still not free from reliance upon the multinationals. Being an independent meant more control over what they could release, but they still needed distribution, in this case a contract with MCA Canada. No domestically owned label had yet to successfully compete with the multinationals in terms of distribution in the English-speaking market. This situation looked like it was about to change in 1999, however, when Allen Gregg, manager of the Tragically Hip, founded the Song Company by absorbing Attic Records and establishing connections to handle recording, publishing rights, and distribution. At the time, academic Will Straw took this to be a sign of change in the long-standing relationship in which domestically owned labels hunted out talent and the multinationals distributed the bands that were discovered. 'This development stood as the clearest proof yet that the two-tiered system of the previous 25 years had broken down,' Straw argued in the autumn of 2000.[78] Yet this alternative had a short lifespan. As Straw noted a mere three years later, the Song Company had filed for bankruptcy, unable to handle slumping sales, problems with distribution rights, and plagued by questionable internal activities.[79]

If the Song Company had managed to survive it would have continued to be the only vertically integrated, domestically owned label in English-speaking Canada and, as such, a counterpart to Les Disques Audiogram in Quebec. Les Disques Audiogram, founded in 1984, integrated recording (Le Studio in Montreal), promotion (Spectra-scène; Montréal Festival du Jazz; and Association du disque, de l'industrie du spectacle québécois et de la vidéo), distribution (Select; MusicCor), and sales (Archambault Musique record and music instrument chain).[80] Les Disques Audiogram thrived in the gap left by the withdrawal of the multinational labels from the French-speaking market during the economic restructuring of the 1980s. Just as important was the eagerness of consumers for domestic recordings. In fact, as sociologist Line Grenier has discussed, many of the record labels that became a part of this association had actually been founded by distributors who already had access to audiences and simply needed products to fill the demand.[81]

The closest that English-speaking Canada had to a vertically integrated, nationally empowered label as of the end of the decade was MapleCore, but it was a far cry from the dream of nationalists. MapleCore, formed in 2000, became one of the most important players in the Canadian music scene by owning two labels (MapleMusic Recordings for alternative and rock music and Open Road Recordings for country music), promotional sites (Maplemusic.com and Umbrellamusic.com), and a distribution outlet (MapleNationWide). True to its moniker, MapleCore portrayed itself as passionately patriotic: 'We are trying to corner the market on being Canadian,' MapleCore president and CEO Grant Dexter unabashedly told Larry LeBlanc in the summer of 2004. 'If you want to know about independent Canadian bands or buy their CDs or merchandise, we're the place. If you are not signed to a major label, we're the place to come.'[82] MapleCore's national capital was ensured when it brought onboard over 300 domestic acts, including such 'CanRock Renaissance' staples as the Lowest of the Low, the Cowboy Junkies, and the Skydiggers, along with hot up-and-comers Kathleen Edwards, Sam Roberts, Peter Elkas, and the Dears.[83] Yet, tellingly, since 2002 MapleCore has been financed in part, and has its distribution handled, by Universal Music Canada.

Neither the failed Song Corporation nor the thriving MapleCore offered a viable alternative to a system in which domestically owned labels depended on foreign-owned multinationals. EMI handled distribution for Nettwerk Productions, Marquis, Aquarius, and Popular; Warner handled Sonic Records and Stony Plain; and Universal, according to *Time*, 'distributes 25 indie labels and holds stock in two,' among its roster Albert Music, MapleMusic Recordings, Somerset Entertainment, 604, and, notably, True North Records.[84] Bernie Finkelstein and his True North Records had led the way decades earlier in bringing together domestic and multinational labels, but there was a significant change on the horizon: in 2008 the long-standing beacon of nationalist inspiration was sold by Finkelstein to Linus Entertainment.[85] Nonetheless, even the wave of 'hip' alternative labels over the course of the decade had to rely upon the multinationals. Arts & Crafts, which included Broken Social Scene, Feist, and the Constantines, signed with EMI Music Canada, while Last Gang, with Metric, Death From Above 1979, and Tricky Woo, signed with Warner. To be 'independent' was fully compatible with the idea of having a deal with a multinational.

Garry Newman, CEO and president of Warner Music Canada, was certainly not impressed by the antics of his American counterparts: 'American A&R people are constantly in this country, and they don't tell us they are here,' he complained in 2003.[86] Since the mid-1980s it had become rather commonplace for the American offices to extend their sphere to Canada and sign the most promising acts. More recently this has included such stars as Nickelback, Sum 41, Diana Krall, Nelly Furtado, Deborah Cox, Finger 11, Avril Lavigne, Simple Plan, the New Deal, Andy Stochansky, Hot Hot Heat, Three Days Grace, the Constantines, the Weakerthans, Michael Bublé, K-oS, the Trews, Billy Talent, Hedley, and Hawksley Workman.[87] Ritchie Yorke used to complain that the Canadian subsidiaries were doing little to contribute to the domestic industry, particularly when it came to showcasing them on the world stage. Decades later the subsidiaries were not only underwriting the success of many domestic acts but having to fight off their foreign counterparts when it came to signing talent.

What had not changed was the symbiotic relationship between domestically owned labels and the multinationals. Larry LeBlanc, in a 2006 report for the Canadian Association of Broadcasters, found that cutbacks by the multinationals in the mid-1990s had led to an even greater relationship with domestic labels 'via pressing and distribution (P&D) agreements, co-ventures, and licensing deals.'[88] The outcome would be no surprise to Robert Burnett, who a decade earlier had observed that multinationals needed to 'to create numerous and varied satellite or auxiliary labels that will develop new talent and feed the enormous worldwide distribution networks they have established.'[89]

Simply put, the Canadian recording industry is a domestic component of a global system of production and distribution lorded over by multinationals whose primary purpose is to spread foreign-produced recordings to consumers. Will Straw is correct in noting that 'international record companies operating in Canada devised the distribution systems on which a generation of Canadian-owned record companies came to depend for national distribution.'[90] The relationship, however, has been highly symbiotic. Although major-label subsidiaries would sometimes sign an act directly, the status quo was for multinationals to rely upon domestic labels to discover talent and to then enter distribution agreements. Perhaps no description could better capture the crux of the relationship than one made by Mark Jowett of Nettwerk Records in a 1988 interview with *Maclean's*: 'We offer Capitol some new artistic blood, and they in turn provide us with the all-important distribution.'[91]

The legacy of this is seen, at least in part, in acts being able to make a living in Canada without first making it in the United States. Bruce Cockburn and Crowbar were among the first beneficiaries of a relationship that has come to include the likes of the Tragically Hip. The relationship also fostered a sense of the Canadian music scene as operating on its own terms, an entity separate from American hegemony, yet all the while being underwritten by multinationals reaping the fruits of the Canadian content regulation. To Canadians caught up in celebrating their national music scene, the details were easily lost amid patriotism.

10

'(Everything I Do) I Do It for You': Bryan Adams and the *Waking Up the Neighbours* Controversy

Bryan Adams did not mince words at a press conference held in January 1992 during a tour stop in Sydney, Nova Scotia. On the road to support his latest album, *Waking Up the Neighbours,* he displayed much savvy in spinning a media frenzy:

> For the Canadian government to consider me un-Canadian is ridiculous. If you go to America or England, or almost any other country in the world, they don't have those kinds of stipulations on their artists. They're rewarded on the basis of their music, not government regulation. You would never hear Elton John declared un-British. You just wouldn't. It's a disgrace. The Canadian government should get out of the music business entirely. There are a lot of artists who have been successful in Canada who can't get arrested anywhere in the world and I think it's breeding mediocrity.[1]

Over the previous few months Adams and his manager Bruce Allen had been rallying public attention to how the singer-songwriter had supposedly been declared 'un-Canadian' by the federal government. Or, as Allen brazenly put it on the CBC *Evening News,* 'to say Bryan Adams is not a Canadian is absurd. Bryan Adams is a Canadian!'[2] Technically, the situation was somewhat different. *Waking Up the Neighbours* did not quantify for inclusion in the minimum amount of airtime set aside for recordings using domestic talent and resources because the criteria required at least two of four components – performer, lyricist, composer, and/or recording studio. Adams received only one point for being the performer. The lyrics and music were co-written with British producer Robert 'Mutt' Lange, and much of the album was recorded, mixed, and mastered in London and New York City. The album, in sum, was primarily created by non-Canadians using resources outside of Canada, and thus radio stations could not claim it towards the small amount of airtime ensured for domestic recordings.

Months of interviews fuelled the fire as Adams continued to equate the Canadian content regulation with government interference in the music industry and called upon his fellow performers to abandon the Canadian industry:

> If anyone came up to me and asked me for advice, I'd tell them to stay away from the Canadian music business. It's full of politics and bureaucracy. It's trouble. Don't sign to a Canadian company. Don't sign to a Canadian publisher. Go south of the border. You'll get a better deal … I think it's a disgrace and I think it's a shame that we have to deal with this kind of stupidity all the time … Fuck you! That's all I've got to say to those guys. Fuck you man! … I think it's garbage. Canadian music will prevail regardless of government regulation. The hypocrisy of what happened to me is indicative of how stupid CanCon really is … We don't need the Canadian government to tell people what to play.[3]

This was not the first time that Allen, who had handled Bachman-Turner Overdrive, Prism (featuring songwriter Jim Vallance), Loverboy, the Payola$, and Adams, among others, had tried to generate controversy for the sake of publicity. In April 1983 he made a spectacle out of Anne Murray's decision not to pick up her own Juno award; not coincidentally, Loverboy and Adams were up for awards. Allen later admitted to *Maclean's* that he 'used the shtick to get some attention for the awards, and it worked.'[4] He knew that success was as much if not even more about image and publicity than it was the music itself. As Thomas Hopkins of *Maclean's* had previously pointed out about Allen's ability to create acts, 'Loverboy was no accident.… The band was planned right down to the hot reds and yellows the group wears onstage … Allen, drawing on his BTO experience, told Loverboy how to dress, the order in which to play its songs and even what to say as between-song patter.'[5] Loverboy was big, but Adams was even bigger, with an image that needed to be crafted and protected. In 1984 Allen even interrupted an interview between, and demanded the tape recording of, Adams and a Much-Music video jockey when the singer began to stumble and contradict himself.[6] That was the year when Adams, co-writing with Jim Vallance, picked up steam and national attention with the massive-selling *Reckless*, featuring the singles 'Summer of '69,' 'Run to You,' 'Somebody,' 'Heaven,' 'One Night Love Affair,' and even a duet with Tina Turner called 'It's Only Love.'

Waking Up the Neighbours, coming after the relative downturn of 1987's *Into the Fire* (selling only 1.5 million copies compared with the 10 million of *Reckless*), deserved no less promotion than that stirred up by a controversy.[7] After all, despite declarations that imply otherwise, Adams and Allen were not surprised that *Waking Up the Neighbours* did not meet the MAPL criteria; they knew this to be the case at the time of recording. Allen even admitted to Larry LeBlanc of *Billboard* that 'we could have fudged the credits and that would have been the end of it. It happens all the time and it's B.S. That's not what happened. It was a definitive collaboration between Mutt and Bryan.'[8] Nor did Adams need inclusion in quota. Even without being counted towards the minimum amount of airtime, '(Everything I Do) I Do It For You' and each of the other singles from the album could still be aired nineteen times a week per station – in other words, almost three times a day, every day, on each station. Any gain in airtime would likely be marginal as pushing the track too much beyond that level might risk burnout, a by-product of the regulation that had raised concerns for decades. What was to be gained was publicity for the new single and the assertion of Adams's Canadianness in the face of an increasing amount of time spent abroad and, only a few years later, the decision to make his home in London as a British citizen. At the very least, the spectacle was instructive about how Adams viewed the Canadian content regulation: not as a means of ensuring opportunities for a breadth of domestic talent but, much like the multinational labels that ruled over the domestic industry, an obsolete tool that had little value in increasing the popularity of acts of most interest to foreign markets. Exporting a select few performers, not supporting the domestic industry, was what mattered. The event also further underlined that there was no incompatibility between being internationally situated within the multinational music industry and thriving in ideologically national terms; one could go so far as to call for the abandonment of the industry and still be lauded as a national hero.

Adams and Allen were not alone in stirring up controversy over the course of 1992. The highly charged publicity campaign, which pandered to the media's obsession with the question of Canadian identity, offered tremendous fodder for proponents in the press (or simply those who valued a sensationalistic story) and radio station programmers with an axe to grind against CRTC. Because the Canadian content regulation was poorly understood by the general public and even by many of those who reported on the music industry, the difference between a means of ensuring domestic access to the airwaves and a qualitative declaration of Canadianness became easily confused. Two decades of nationalization had created powerful rhetoric, tropes, and hyperbole. What followed was not an attempt to clarify the role of the regulation but to distort it within undefined and grandiose essentializations of Adams as the quintessential Canadian outrageously denationalized by cold government bureaucracy. Commonplace were such declarations as the one by Paul Myers that Adams 'is the international Ambassador of Canadian Rock, symbolic of all things Canadian in countries as disparate as England and Vietnam,' and Don Shafer's assertion that Adams had 'become the underdog who's not welcome in his own country because he's not Canadian anymore, according to the government. Every kid on the street is saying, "Wait a minute, Bryan's the all-Canadian kid." I don't care how you rationalize it, it's dumb.'[9] Such statements were as powerful as they were unqualified, brazenly sensationalistic, and simply inaccurate.[10]

Such provocative and misleading rhetoric did not go unanswered. Adams had, after all, not only decried being declared 'un-Canadian' but also called for an end to the Canadian content regulation. Brian Chater, president of the Canadian Independent Record Production Association, certainly spoke for many people when he told Adams to 'piss off ... obviously [the Canadian content regulation] has helped you.'[11] Similarly, argued Jan Matejcek of the Society of Composers, Authors and Music Publishers of Canada in an open letter to Adams, 'do you think your songs, such as "Let Me Take You Dancing" (1979), "Cuts Like a Knife" (1983), "Straight through the Heart" (1983), "Heaven" (1984), up to "Summer of '69" (1985), could have become the most performed Canadian songs by Canadian radio stations without the backing of the CRTC regulations?'[12] And there was certainly much truth to the opinion of Bernie Finkelstein, whose True North Records dated back to the start of the regulation, that 'CanCon is the cornerstone of the industry. We'd simply be lost without it.'[13]

One of the most interesting suggestions came from Larry LeBlanc, who shared with others the desire to clarify the actualities of the regulation as a measure designed to ensure greater musical diversity and opportunities for emerging acts. LeBlanc first noted that counting *Waking Up the Neighbours* towards the airtime would have meant less opportunity for other talent and that Adams was begrudging the assistance that had aided him in the early years.[14] But, even more revealing, LeBlanc recommended that Adams and other international stars should relinquish their inclusion in the regulation in order to prevent radio stations from filling the quota with international hits that would otherwise be aired.[15] The suggestion was reminiscent of the stand taken by Stompin' Tom Connors a decade and a half earlier when he returned his Juno awards to protest a recording industry that celebrated established 'border jumpers' to the exclusion of up-and-coming acts. Connors had hoped that others would follow his lead but no one else stepped forward. Nor did Adams.

The controversy was exacerbated when Adams complained that the Canadian content regulation made it possible for acts to be popular in Canada but not abroad. Although the ability of the domestic industry to operate self-sufficiently had been one of the underwriting forces of the regulation, for Adams music was interwoven with commercial aspirations and an international Weltanschauung. Here was someone who, as he told Maclean's in 1987, 'never believed there was a border,' and although born in Kingston, Ontario, to British parents stationed at a military base, had lived in five countries – Canada, Britain, Israel, Portugal, and Austria – by his teens, eventually spending time in England before making it his permanent home in 1995.[16] Adams thus not surprisingly rankled many people when he declared that 'there are a lot of artists who have been successful in Canada who can't get arrested anywhere in the world and I think it's breeding mediocrity.'[17] As one music fan wrote to the editors of Maclean's, 'as for Canadian content regulations promoting mediocrity, I think that you just have to listen to any recent album by Canadians such as Tom Cochrane, the Infidels, Kim Mitchell, the Holly Cole Trio or the Tragically Hip to realize that both artistically and lyrically, Bryan Adams's Waking Up the Neighbours is definitely one of the most mediocre albums of 1991. Viva CanCon.'[18] Or, as music journalist Nicholas Jennings opined, 'Blue Rodeo and 54-40 make a mockery of Adams's CanCon criticisms … Canadian pop is proving itself to be a vibrant, adventurous – and anything but mediocre.'[19] In fact, for academic David J. Jackson, Blue Rodeo stands out as not only an example of a highly talented band virtually ignored in the United States but one whose ability to thrive in Canada has resulted in an important ideological contribution:

> The collection of songs Blue Rodeo have produced tell Canadian stories, utilize Canadian images and places, and critique the U.S. as well as Canada. They enhance the vocabulary available for use by English-speaking Canadians when they think about what it means to be Canadians. In this sense they may contribute to the discovery, creation, and re-creation of the cultural

identity of English-speaking Canadians ... With over 50 million album sales
in Canada per year, this is an important contribution.[20]

Many acts rejected Adams's 'mediocrity' comment, but perhaps none
more so than Tom Cochrane, a performer who enjoyed tremendous
success in Canada yet little attention outside of the country and who
triumphed over Adams at the Junos in 1992: 'There's some incredible
music being made in this country,' Cochrane trumpeted the night of
his Juno victory. 'Anyone who says Canadian music is mediocre can go
to hell.'[21] Cochrane, whose 'Life Is a Highway' on the album *Mad Mad
World* was a top seller in Canada, won for Songwriter of the Year, Male
Vocalist of the Year, Single of the Year, and Album of the Year, whereas Adams, who had also been nominated in those categories, won for
Producer of the Year, Canadian Entertainer of the Year, and, fittingly,
the International Achievement Award. (*Waking Up the Neighbours* had
been included in the Junos because the Canadian Academy of Recording Arts and Sciences did not operate along the criteria used by the
CRTC). Cochrane's success at the Junos was all the richer given the
animosity between Cochrane and Bruce Allen, his manager during the
formative years of his career. Only a few years earlier, Allen had bitingly
told *Canadian Musician* that he had 'begged Tom Cochrane to come
to the West Coast, but he put his lifestyle ahead of his career. So he's
still living in Toronto and he's still hitting only 152 on *Billboard*.'[22] The
relationship had been further strained when Allen, having used management funds to help re-stock the band after instruments were stolen
during a 1982 tour, repossessed much of Cochrane's gear.[23] Cochrane,
not willing to let Allen get away with this, hit back with a song fittingly
titled 'Citizen Cane.'

Cochrane, not unlike Stompin' Tom, the Tragically Hip, the Rheostatics, and other acts that situated themselves within national iconography
and identifiers, drew fans who felt a national connection. Cochrane's
song 'Big League,' for example, about a hockey player who won a scholarship only to be killed in a car crash soon after, was based on a true
story and described by Cochrane as 'a comment on that whole process
of growing up with the sport of hockey, something that most Canadian
boys relate to.'[24] The ability to make a career in Canada singing about
topics not necessarily of interest to audiences outside of the country was
deemed a strength. 'Because I grew up here,' he explained in a 1992
interview with *Canadian Musician*, 'Canada is a large part of what I'm

made of as a writer. I've built up a tremendous camaraderie with my fans over the years; the support I have received is unbelievable. So to pick up and move, or brush them off, would feel like I'm deserting my fans. There's no way I would let that happen.'[25]

Cochrane won the battle at the Junos, but in the end Adams won the war, or at least something close to it. The CRTC, faced by a national controversy, formed a task force of representatives from the Canadian Recording Industry Association, the Society of Composers, Authors and Music Publishers of Canada, the Canadian Country Music Association, the Canadian Independent Record Production Association, the Canadian Music Publishers Association, and the Songwriters' Association of Canada to assess the effectiveness of the regulation and to recommend changes. Although Adams called for an end to the regulation, Bruce Allen wanted it to be changed so that any recording involving a performer of Canadian citizenship could be counted no matter the composer, lyricist, or recording studio.[26] Facilitating the promotion and exportation of 'stars,' rather than ensuring opportunities for the industry as a whole, was what best suited their interests. Allen's position was shared by the multinational record labels, which had more to gain from a celebrity system that privileged performers, particularly those who could be exported internationally, than from the domestic recording industry.[27] After all, the multinationals had grown from being a means of pressing and distributing foreign-recorded singles in Canada to a method of exporting select Canadian talent abroad; support for acts primarily of interest in Canada was less economically lucrative.

To little surprise, advocates of a strong recording industry dismissed any attempt to gut the Canadian content regulation. 'MAPL recognizes the input of the entire industry,' Al Mair, president of the Canadian Independent Record Producers Association and of Attic Records, pointed out to Larry LeBlanc. 'The big single expense in making a record is the studio bill. Canadian artists are leaving here to take money outside the country to make records.'[28] Similarly, Paul Spurgeon, legal counsel for the Society of Composers, Authors and Music Publishers of Canada, remarked, 'if they took M [music composer] and L [lyricist] out, the government would be penalizing a very important part of the creative community, composers and lyricists … If it weren't for performing rights, there probably wouldn't be much of a business here because so many of the acts are reliant on performing rights to survive.'[29] There was certainly some truth to these assertions. Songwriting was often a first step towards stardom for aspiring performers, as success in this regard offered the economic freedom to embark on their own performing careers. Gordon Lightfoot, Joni Mitchell, and Leonard Cohen, three of the most highly praised of artists, were among those whose first major opportunities came as songwriters. At the time of the *Waking Up the Neighbours* controversy this tradition was being carried on by the likes of Marc Jordan, whose 'Rhythm of My Heart' was charted by Rod Stewart, and famed songwriter Shirley Eikhard, author of Bonnie Raitt's hit 'Something to Talk About.'[30]

On 14 January 1992, the CRTC announced that the task force had made its recommendations. The result was a degree of support for the status quo but not without amendments favouring those who collaborated with non-Canadians:

> 1. The existing flexibility and simplicity of the MAPL system should be retained. It has delivered specific, clear benefits to all participants in the Canadian music and broadcast industries.
> 2. In order to recognize the increased amount of collaboration between songwriters in the creation of songs, the existing regulation should be modified so that where a song is co-written by a Canadian and a non-Canadian, where the Canadian songwriter is credited with at least fifty percent of the composer's share respecting the music and at least fifty percent of the writer's share respecting the lyrics, that song should qualify for one of the two required 'points.'[31]

The CRTC followed the task force by opening the recommendations, and the question itself, to public comment. Responses included increasing the value of the artist component to two points, having it mean automatic inclusion or even require it to be mandatory; establishing a point for record studio producer (not just location of studio); giving consideration for copyright ownership; and possibly eliminating expatriates who had been absent from the domestic scene for an excessive period.[32] At the very least, the submissions were far from unanimous. 'After having been in effect for 21 years,' the commission noted, some people thought that 'the regulation should be amended to require Canadian content to qualify on four rather than on two counts, while still others have argued that the regulation is no longer necessary or desirable.'[33]

In the end, none of the public submissions was incorporated, and the CRTC went forward with the proposal that one point would be awarded when a Canadian contributed at least 50 per cent to both the music and lyrical composition, and that the decision would be retroactive to September 1991 (thereby including *Waking Up the Neighbours*).[34] Although the commission was willing to shift the MAPL system in favour of collaborations with non-Canadians, there was no support for decreasing the point value of the other elements. As Bill Allen, director of public affairs at the CRTC, remarked to Larry LeBlanc soon after the decision, the regulation served not just to promote performers but 'also to encourage production in Canada and also Canadian lyricists and composers to work as well.'[35]

Over the next few years it became clear that in allowing the regulation to include collaborations with non-Canadians, particularly by Canadians who were internationally famous and likely to receive airplay anyway, the CRTC made it all the easier for radio stations to rely upon established acts. There was now an even greater number of recordings, many of which were already being played but not tabulated towards the minimum amount of airtime that could be counted. As Peter Diemer, vice president of national promotion at EMI Music Canada, complained to Larry LeBlanc at the time, 'there's always a lot of domestic traffic, and we hear, "Our Canadian content quota is full this week," regularly. Or we hear "We didn't add any Canadian content this week."'[36] The lack of airtime for new acts was brought to the forefront during the CRTC's 1998 Review of the Commercial Radio Policy, but, despite talk of a bonus system to encourage airplay for so-called 'emerging artists,' the regulator opted to pass on the idea out of concerns that it might lead to a reduction of the overall level of MAPL criteria music.[37]

The problem did not go away, though; it emerged again during the 2006 Review of the Commercial Radio Policy. According to a survey conducted by the Canadian Recording Industry Association in preparation for the CRTC review, radio stations were only picking up 1 per cent of newly released Canadian content recordings, and of 5142 artists of all national origins spun over the course of a six-week period, almost 80 per cent of spins went to only the top 10 per cent of acts.[38] Not surprisingly, at the top of the list was Bryan Adams. Whereas the average across the board was 215 spins, Adams clocked in at 10,397, or over 48 times more than the average.[39] This narrowcasting owed in large part to a growing interest in serving audiences in their thirties and forties, a demographic with established musical interests that were all the easier to serve thanks to the proliferation of back catalogues reissued on compact disc.[40]

The Canadian Association of Broadcasters (CAB), despite admitting that emerging artists were neglected, was unwilling to have its member stations change their programming priorities without an incentive from the regulator. Glenn O'Farrell, president of the CAB, made this clear in the association's submission to the Review of the Commercial Radio Policy. 'Because [a song or artist] is new, because it's untested, it's a commercial risk you are taking to put that into play lists with the possibility of turning off an audience member.'[41] Or, as the CAB put it another way, 'the majority of the commercial radio industry agrees that bringing emerging artists to air is an inherently risky venture in the radio business.'[42] In an act of bravado, the association explained that its members were unwilling to change if the regulator did not offer an incentive designed to reduce the overall amount of Canadian content:

> Our proposal for a new bonus system is based on the application of a credit for the airplay of music from 'emerging Canadian artists': while songs would still qualify as Canadian when meeting two out of four MAPL (Music, Artist, Production, Lyrics) categories, an additional 25 percent credit would be applied to the airplay of an 'Emerging Canadian Artist.' A Canadian artist would be considered an Emerging Canadian Artist up until 12 months from the date they reach the Top 40 in spins on BDS [Broadcast Data Systems] or Mediabase all format charts or become gold certified for the first time. The CAB strongly believes that this incentive system will encourage music programmers to take risks by playing more emerging artists and to move off track sooner, thereby reducing burn on Canadian artists.[43]

Yet, tellingly, the CAB hinged the proposed bonus system upon a change to the regulation in which 'the maximum floor for Canadian content [was to] be 30 percent, so that any station playing more Emerging Artists would not move beyond this point.'[44] This would be a significant reduction given that the CRTC had increased the Canadian content level to 35 per cent in 1998 and, as of the turn of the decade, began requiring that many new licensees provide at least 40 per cent.

The Canadian Independent Record Production Association (CIRPA), founded in 1971 to represent the interests of domestically owned labels, argued against the proposed bonus system on the grounds that it might lead to an overall reduction in the use of domestic recordings.[45] If the CAB was willing to have the quota increased to 45 per cent, and agree that 'Canadian-owned and controlled independent recorded masters should be allocated 50 percent of the Canadian content airplay,' then a bonus system might be workable.[46] This idea was certainly in line with the Broadcasting Act's requirement that 'each broadcasting undertaking shall make maximum use, and in no case less than predominant use, of

Canadian creative and other resources in the creation and presentation of programming' and that the airwaves were to 'include a significant contribution from the Canadian independent production sector.'[47]

The fight with the Canadian Association of Broadcasters was only one conflict that CIRPA had to endure. Nettwerk Records, True North Records, Aquarius Records, Children's Group, Anthem Records, and Linus Entertainment – all domestically owned labels – severed their tie with the Canadian Recording Industry Association (CRIA) upon reading a draft of the brief to the CRTC that called for increasing the artist component of the MAPL system to 1.5 while reducing the recording component to 0.5. The recommendation favoured the interests of the four major foreign-owned labels (EMI Music Canada, Sony BMG Music Canada, Universal Music Canada, and Warner Music Canada) in the association by prioritizing performers over the recording industry. Further, as LeBlanc reported about the revolt, the CRIA

> suggests easing current quota restrictions on Canadian artists recording or co-writing outside the country ... The CRIA [also] wants to reallocate funding from the Foundation to Assist Canadian Talent on Records, diverting it away from independents. Toronto-based FACTOR distributes funds from the federal government and Canadian broadcasters to companies in Canada's independent sector. The CRIA is suggesting that a portion of FACTOR monies could be allocated instead to Radio Star Maker Fund, a broadcaster initiative that supports the marketing of recordings by more mainstream Canadian artists, whether on major or independent labels.[48]

Donald Tarlton of the Donald K. Donald Group and Aquarius Records made his frustration clear: 'What are foreign-owned, multinational companies doing commenting on Canada's cultural policies and funding programs?'[49] There was likely much bristling when the CRIA's submission not only went forward with the recommendations but also argued that 'the ultimate objective is to focus on creating Canadian stars and developing talent that can be exported.'[50] The event brings to mind Will Straw's observation as to how 'cultural nationalists who, for decades, called on large record companies to take an interest in Canadian music now find them actively doing so, with possibly devastating effects on the domestic recording industry.'[51]

In December 2006, seven months after launching the review, the CRTC again decided against the idea of a bonus system. The 125 per cent credit proposed by the CAB was deemed likely to reduce the overall amount of Canadian recordings. Instead, a 'case by case' system was to be instituted, possibly involving a 'commitment' to be made at the time of licensing (new, renewed, and transferred).[52] The CRTC's decision, it is worth noting, was not unanimous. Two commissioners objected to what they viewed as kowtowing to the interests of broadcasters and the CRTC's unwillingness to take action on a major problem. Commissioner Stuart Langford made his dissent clear in an attachment to the decision:

> Lack of imagination ... appears to be the hallmark of the majority [of CRTC commissioners] reaction to the plight of Canada's new and emerging artists. Rather than solving the problem by requiring FM licensees to provide airplay opportunities for as many Canadian artists as possible, the majority has decided to duck the problem today and leave it to be solved on a case-by-case basis during future licence renewal processes. This is simply unacceptable. To say to emerging artists that some day down the road things will improve is the regulatory equivalent of promising pie in the sky when you die. The Commission's case-by-case approach ... leaves most Canadian musical talent out of the new radio policy as they were left out of the old. The case-by-case approach will result, not in the establishment of a clear regulatory directive supporting these artists but in the equivalent of a crazy quilt policy made up of dozens, perhaps hundreds, of rulings, each more or less different than the last. If flexibility is necessary, the better way is to set a standard and put the onus on licensees either to meet it or to apply to the Commission for a variation in light of their particular circumstances. Supporting new and emerging Canadian artists by playing their music should be the rule, not doing so, the exception. The majority has got it backwards. As to the sort of bonus or credit systems the CAB and other industry representatives suggested, I say no. With the right to exclusive use of valuable and scarce public property, a radio frequency, comes a duty to Canadians. Broadcasters should not have to be bribed to do their duty.[53]

Langford cut to the core of something commonly overlooked among the sales figures and the celebration of performers: the Broadcasting Act made clear that the airwaves are a publicly owned resource to be used to encourage communication among the citizenry and that radio stations have been granted a privilege in getting to use those airwaves to make money. A decade earlier the CRTC had even affirmed that 'the MAPL system and the minimum requirements for Canadian content have two essential objectives: To ensure that Canadian artists and their works have access to Canadian airwaves and to support a Canadian-based music and ·

recording industry.'[54] To Langford, the unwillingness of the CRTC to pass legislation that would ensure these objectives was a sign that the regulator was offering little more than empty words.

The *Waking Up the Neighbours* controversy and the issues that arose in its wake revealed significant changes in the industry over the past few decades. Bart Testa and Jim Shedden have argued that 'the episode revealed both that the protective scaffolding of Cancon had done its job and had become irrelevant. The musicians it had enabled were now stronger than the rules themselves.'[55] Some musicians had indeed grown to a level in which the regulation was not necessary and, in the case of Adams, carried enough national and public clout to garner support in a rally for change. This did not mean that the regulation was irrelevant, however. As I have argued elsewhere, the episode revealed the degree to which aspiring musicians struggled not only against the established foreign acts favoured by radio stations but also those holding Canadian citizenship who would likely be played regardless of the regulation yet nonetheless had their singles count towards Canadian content airtime.[56] Whereas the regulation had initially helped to establish access to the airwaves, all the more so because of the lack of Canadian content to fill the quota, there was now an abundance of recordings, from back catalogues to new releases, of established acts and multinational-backed up-and-coming stars. Without a significant change to the Canadian content regulation that would take this into account, the system no longer served the fundamentals that the CRTC continued to claim as being the backbone of the system.

If anything made the regulation irrelevant, which is certainly an overstatement, it was the advent of other delivery systems better able to bring audiences together with new acts. Radio had been the unrivalled cornerstone of music in Canada until the advent of 'music television' in the 1980s, but during the 2000s other delivery systems took hold in the gap left behind by changes in radio station and music video network formats that relied on back catalogues and catered to older audiences. Even a radio station like CFNY, having brought bands like Rheostatics, Hayden, and Barenaked Ladies to air, has been criticized for supposedly shifting its priorities. 'When CFNY was "on the edge,"' Yvonne Matsell, a talent booker and music event organizer, has remarked, 'it was interesting because they'd play stuff nobody else would play, and you'd always have a diverse sense of what was out there. Now it's so formatted, and I think it's just awful. You're not able to hear people like Ron Sexsmith on the radio – it's all word of mouth, and sometimes that takes a lot longer to get places. And by that time, the artist's label has dropped them.'[57] Yet Alan Cross, a CFNY cornerstone and well known for 'The Ongoing History of New Music,' disagrees. In his view, the station continues to do much to bring new music to the air, evidenced by the support given to such acts as City and Colour, Stars, Tokyo Police Club, the Constantines, and Mother Mother.[58]

At the very least, aspiring bands and eager listeners alike began turning to the Internet for its ease of access and a greater variety than was offered by radio. The Internet offers a level of interaction that radio cannot match and has become the top means by which people discover new music, reducing, but not eliminating, the role of radio in this regard. Not only does the Internet make possible official and fan-based websites that offer photos, tour dates, and sound bites, but interactive 'community' sites such as YouTube, Facebook, and MySpace allow users to pipeline streaming video and music and to host discussions.[59] There are also podcasts and streaming radio programs that provide exposure and access to music that otherwise might not be heard, for example, IndieCan, a podcast of Canadian 'indie' talent that made its way onto XM Satellite Radio and, as of late 2008, was getting 100,000 or so downloads each month.[60]

Major multimedia players have joined in on the new delivery systems, as with CBC Radio 3's combination of Internet streaming, podcasting, and availability on SIRIUS Satellite Radio. For example, SIRIUS and CBC Radio 3 broadcast North by Northeast (NXNE) concerts, an important showcase of up-and-coming talent. Among the many other Internet options are Bell Canada's 'All Access Music' and 'All Access Music to Go' music subscription and download services, and AOL Music Canada's videos, downloads, and such special events as the streaming of a live in-house concert and question and answer period with Feist.[61]

MP3 downloads have become a staple of the Internet music experience, ranging from illegal peer-to-peer sites, the pay-per-tune option of iTunes, and direct sales from band and label websites that make available music that had traditionally been the reserve of retail stores and merchandise tables at concerts. The number of online digital album downloads, according to Nielsen SoundScan Canada, jumped 93 per cent between 2006 and 2007.[62] Even Stompin' Tom Connors, now signed with EMI in a distribution deal, had songs available on iTunes as of 1 July 2008 (appropriately, Canada Day), although the use of an alternative delivery system did not squelch his fervour that had been brewing for decades.[63] 'I've never had a hit song on any hit parade,' he reflected a few months after his start on iTunes. 'Out of 50 albums, it's amazing. They tell me I don't fit the format or I'm too Canadian or I'm too country or I'm too this or I'm too that ... I'm too something. Whatever it is, I don't fit the format.'[64] Although Connors never enjoyed mainstream radio success, even he benefited from the Internet.

Alternatives to radio, then, have revolutionized the ways in which musical acts make their way into the recording industry and establish a fan base. Larry LeBlanc has recently noted that it is now common to see 'bands build an audience from touring and from Internet-driven marketing, particularly in the absence of mainstream retail and radio support.'[65] Entertainment lawyer Chris Taylor of Last Gang Records, a label that includes Metric and Death from Above 1979, explained to LeBlanc that 'online marketing is exploding and [international] borders are coming down with the Internet. That's created a snowball effect ... American and foreign labels have opened up their doors to Canadian music.'[66] Arcade Fire, for example, made a mark in the United Kingdom and drew the praise of Coldplay, U2, and David Bowie, among others, before Canadian radio caught on.

The Internet has proven to be a bastion for a new generation of acts, offering international prospects while maintaining a grassroots, do-it-yourself base. Broken Social Scene, Metric, Jill Barber, Joel Plaskett, the Stars, the Trews, Arcade Fire, Wolf Parade, and Feist, to name but a few, have all benefited from non-traditional delivery systems. For Feist, the use of her single '1234' from *The Reminder* in a commercial for Apple's iPod contributed to a rash of downloads, streaming hits, and what ended up being the top-selling digital album of 2007 in Canada, beating out the likes of Amy Winehouse and Kanye West. Arcade Fire, almost as impressively, came in fourth.[67] The Internet was doing for new music what many radio stations were not; the Canadian Recording Industry Association has noted that 'the number of spins devoted to more "gold" artists such as Bryan Adams in a sample of ... broadcast weeks exceeded the number of spins to Arcade Fire by a factor of over 10.'[68] Perhaps this conservatism and reliance upon established acts is why, despite competition from the Internet, commercial private radio stations in Canada have held their own, with total profits rising 5.5 per cent in 2007.[69] Video did not kill the radio star; nor, it seems, did the Internet kill the radio station.

Speaking with *Goldmine* in 1993, Bruce Cockburn recalled how the dream of a domestic industry that operated on its own terms, with no need for artists to head to the United States in order to get airplay at home, was shared by many of his generation:

> It was traditional at the time I started out for Canadian artists to come down to the United States, get a reputation and then be accepted back into Canada as something significant. It really had been almost impossible, or had been up to that point for somebody to start off in Canada and acquire an audience in Canada. There was a lot of nationalist feeling that grew through the '60s and early '70s, and a lot of us felt that this was kind of an ass backwards way of doing things and we should try and do what we could in Canada and then worry about other countries and see if we couldn't make that go. That's what governed my thinking for a long time.[70]

Paul Anka, the Crew Cuts, Ian and Sylvia, Joni Mitchell, Neil Young, Leonard Cohen, and those who would go on to form the Band, among many others, had left during the 1950s and 1960s because radio stations aired little other than singles listed in American trade papers and charts. This exodus and public support for the idea that performing and industry talent alike should have opportunities on the publicly owned airwaves had prompted the CRTC into instituting the MAPL system. Decades after the regulation came into place, however, much has changed, as radio stations now possess a tremendous number of recordings, back catalogues, and new releases to fill the airtime quota. Whereas aspiring acts had once been given little chance by radio stations that relied on imports, it was now internationally established, if not foreign-residing, Canadian artists who were the barrier to accessing airwaves, their abundant catalogues used to fill the quota. Although radio stations had relied upon a few internationally proven acts at the start of the regulation, at least opportunities trickled down; now there was an abundance of acts and a change to the regulation that made it all the more possible for stations to rely upon established acts.

When the regulation was first instituted, rock and roll was only in the initial stages of nationalization, and its advocates thought primarily in industrial terms and the maturing baby boom generation slowly incorporated the music as a way of seeing themselves in a world of nations. Now 'Canadian' rock and roll was full blown and the difference between quantitatively assessing an album's use of domestic resources and qualitatively assessing a performer's 'Canadianness' was not always so clear. This was all the more so when misleading and sensationalistic voices, tugging at a deep-seated fraternalism, were given ample media coverage.

For Gordon Lightfoot, the Guess Who, and other established acts, the legislation was frustrating on an industrial level; for Adams it was made out to be problematic on an ideological one.

A couple of decades of growth and nationalization had set the scene for a crisis that erupted in 1992, a national controversy that was not so much about the quota as it was about identity politics, the desire for publicity, conflicting opinions on the role of government intervention, and antagonism between, on one side, radio stations and multinational labels, and, on the other, the domestic recording industry and those who felt that opportunities for domestic talent should not have to hinge upon interests situated outside of the country. And, when the CRTC undertook a move that was antithetical to the regulation, it said much about how musicians vested with national value have the ability, especially when backed by radio broadcasters with a grudge and media eager for sensationalized stories, to destabilize the very system that aided their initial success and to deprive those who came after them. Songs that predominantly involved non-citizens and non-domestic resources were now not only imported to Canada, as had long been the case, but were now easier to count towards the small amount of airtime ensured for Canadian content; the irony is not that Adams was *excluded* but that 'Mutt' Lange and foreign recording studios were now *included*.

Over the next few years a lot of the uproar, jilted passions, and mudslinging that characterized the *Waking Up the Neighbours* controversy and the conflict over access to the airwaves started to seem almost moot, as new technologies came about that made the old ways less important. Stations and labels could continue to fight over the specifics of the MAPL system and quota percentages, proposing incentives to prompt stations into risking airtime on 'emerging' acts – adding an 'E' to make the MAPL into the MAPLE system, as Alan Cross has described it – but bands and fans were nonetheless accessing new music thanks to streaming music, podcasts, MP3 providers, and a lot of old-fashioned concerts and merchandise tables. After all, despite revolutionary changes, there was something to be said for the basics. As Kevin Young of *Canadian Musician* quipped in a discussion of illScarlett's success, 'the best way to get people to buy your music is still to play it for them, slap a record down in front of them, and hope they pull out their wallets and buy it.'[71]

Conclusion

I've never thought about a record being American or Canadian or English.
— Sandra Thompson, age 16, 1969[1]

The effort to define Canadian music falters and then fails precisely because there is no such thing as 'the Canadian sound' any more than one can define the 'great American novel.'
— Gene Lees, music critic and columnist, 1972[2]

Canadians aren't spoken about in songs. I feel that's what we lack and that's what's wrong with our country right now.
— Stompin' Tom Connors, 1992[3]

The last thing in the world we would want to be is poster people for some sort of Canadian scene.
— Texas-born Win Butler, Arcade Fire, 2005[4]

On her induction into the 2007 Canadian Songwriters Hall of Fame, Sylvia Tyson was said to be 'one of those rare artists whose work is at the very foundation of a nation's music. Sylvia and her pure, poignant songs are right there at that point of contact where pieces of hers identify a culture and speaks for its people.'[5] Audience applause offered all the evidence necessary to prove this to be true; they were emotionally engaged in 'their' music and national identity. To those who were citizens of a country who wanted to feel a sense of belonging to a nation, Sylvia was able to tap into the essence of Canadianness, even if that essence was less than clear. Being able to say that she could do so, that a Canadian music as an expression of 'us' existed, was in some ways all that the audience needed. They felt it to be true.

'Music in Canada' has become 'Canadian music.' This included not only folksingers like Tyson but even the rock and rollers who had earlier been the recipients of public ridicule, outrage, and bans. Society had earlier shown much disapproval for song lyrics about 'hot pistols' and 'long and tall' women, immorally gyrating hips, and girls screaming and fainting at the concerts of mop-topped boys. The *Vancouver Sun* warned parents that Elvis Presley was a pedophilic predator and that daughters should be prevented from attending his concerts even if it meant having to 'kick them in the teeth'; Allan Fotheringham of *Maclean's* forewarned Torontonians about the chaos to come with the arrival of the Beatles; and Vancouver's city council went so far as to discuss the possibility of rounding up hippies, along with their psychedelic music and lifestyle, into ghettos.

Parents, teachers, city councillors, religious leaders, and other social authorities had criticized the music, but to the baby boom generation the experiences had been a means of mediating socio-economic identities, particularly those of gender and class, defining their individual, collective, and generational sense of selves. They screamed and cavorted at concerts and danced at sock hops to the Top 40 tunes (almost exclusively imports) heard on CHUM; mimicked the likes of the Arkansas-born Ronnie Hawkins and the revolving doorway of musicians who backed him as the Hawks; co-opted British identifiers by taking such monikers as the British Modbeats; escaped into anti-modern Anglo-Celtic ballads and empowered the folk songs of Woody Guthrie and Pete Seeger; and, for those who wanted to make a career in music, got by with whatever resources could be scrounged together. For the 1950s rock and roll band the Asteroids this meant driving across the Maritimes to the closest recording studio; for Little Caesar and the Consuls a shot at stardom entailed heading to New York City; and for Chad Allan and the Expressions the opportunity to record the single 'Shakin' All Over' came about by lucking into a one-track Ampex in a Winnipeg television studio. Many other musicians would instead simply choose to move to the industrial hubs located in the United States since getting big in Canada usually required first becoming a hit south of the border. Labels and recording facilities were almost as rare as were radio stations willing to spin a domestic single when there were already plenty of proven hits from the United States that could be aired. If there was a strong grassroots following or a local rock and roll contest then a band had a shot at getting heard on the airwaves, but if that dream happened, as it did for the Ugly Ducklings in Toronto and the Haunted in Montreal, there was little expectation that the single would get picked up anywhere else. Only on a rare occasion would a hit be heard from coast to coast, and even then any awareness of its origins was limited at best. For teenagers tuning into the radio, there was nothing to discern Bobby Curtola's 'Hand in Hand with You' from the songs of Frankie Avalon or Ricky Nelson.

To grow up in Canada in the 1950s and 1960s was to engage in music within highly localized scenes that were fed international hits from domestic and American over-the-border stations. Music scenes stretched up and down the continent, shaped by mountains and prairies and rust belts and even language, as in the case of French speakers who shared little ground with those elsewhere on the continent. The Detroit R&B circuit looped up through southern Ontario and back down again, bringing visiting musicians and, in the case of Ronnie Hawkins, establishing an American cornerstone for the Toronto scene. Likewise, the California-based psychedelic scene had outposts along the west coast, bringing the Grateful Dead and Jefferson Airplane to Vancouver and taking the likes of the Collectors to San Francisco. Consequently, Vancouver-based acts shared more with their American peers than they did with the Guess Who in Winnipeg or the Paupers and Kensington Market in Toronto. If the acts in Canada shared anything it was their interest in foreign recordings, their inability to develop a domestic recording career, and their lack of knowledge about what was happening in Canadian cities outside of their own.

Popular music initially existed as something that was more *in* Canada than *of* Canada in the minds of its youthful consumers, industrial entrepreneurs, and social critics, but as of the mid-1960s, when the baby boom generation was becoming young adults, music became a means for them to mediate their political and national identities. Sock hops and decrees of puppy love gave way to an evolution in songwriting that saw the rise of the singer-songwriter, particularly in folk and folk rock, that transformed performers into poets and artists and offered songs of social commentary that rallied the like-minded into utopian communities. That Leonard Cohen had already established himself in the world of literature before making his way into 'pop' music certainly helped to affirm this process, as did the lyrical complexity and social relevance found in songs by Neil Young, Joni Mitchell, Gordon Lightfoot, and the Band, among others.

That so many of the increasingly acclaimed Canadian-born singer-songwriters lived in, and were becoming to be identified as citizens of, the United States irked many nationally sensitive Canadians. The period of the mid-1960s to the early 1970s was the time of a new nationalism characterized by anti-Americanism, socialist politics, a desire to 'buy back' the Canadian economy, and a mobilization of the arts and mass media for the sake of the nation. Filmmakers, journalists, painters, television show producers, authors, magazine publishers, and the like joined together in critiquing Americanization and asserting Canadian identity in a time of national jubilance buoyed by the Centennial and Expo '67 celebrations. Yet, interestingly, singer-songwriters absented themselves from this nationalist cause, many of them already having packed up and moved to the United States. When it came to using songwriting as a tool of national expression, there were no English-speaking Canadian equivalents to Félix Leclerc, Gilles Vigneault, and other chansonniers who used music to mediate a national sense of self at the advent of the Quiet Revolution in the early 1960s. In respect to linking popular music and nationhood the Québécois were years ahead of the rest of Canada.

With the interweaving of music and nationalism came a push to make opportunities available for domestic talent, particularly in the face of the continued talent drain and radio station reliance on American singles. The Canadian content regulation of 1970 was designed to ensure opportunities for music and recording industry talent alike and set the foundation for a viable industry, although over time it became misunderstood by the public, particularly due to the spin doctoring of those who have been eager to misconstrue the quantitative legislation with a qualitative assessment of Canadianness. Following the start of the regulation, radio stations maintained their ability to select the singles that would receive allotted airtime and continued to rely upon proven performers, much to the frustration of aspiring and established acts, but opportunities nonetheless trickled down. What followed was no less than an industrial revolution with a bevy of new artists, labels, studios, managers, venues, and even coast-to-coast touring routes that made it possible for a pan-Canadian music scene to develop. The need to fill airtime prompted radio stations to share singles that previously would only have been heard regionally, leading to a levelling of playlists across the country and furthering the idea of a Canadian music.

With the Canadian content regulation came a boom in production and in turn the need to market and sell the bevy of goods. The Canadian Recording Industry Association, which represented both the domestically owned labels and multinational subsidiaries, needed marketing opportunities in a country where exposure had long been a weak point. What followed was a successful takeover of the Juno Awards and its reinvention as a televised promotional tool for domestic and expatriate acts alike, all the while affirming the public attachment to 'their' music. Whereas shows such as *Let's Go* and *After Four* had brought audiences international Top 40 tunes performed by house bands, groups were now being featured as national artists with their own singles, not only on the Junos but, in time, on such programs as *The New Music, Ear to the Ground,* and the music videos shown on MuchMusic, the self proclaimed 'nation's music station.'

The heyday of the music video network, spanning from the mid-1980s to the mid-1990s, celebrated both 'grassroots' and internationally famous 'homegrown heroes,' from the Rheostatics and the Tragically Hip to Bryan Adams to Shania Twain. Flag waving became endemic at concerts. All the while, and unnoticed by the public, the music scene was increasingly underwritten by multinational media conglomerates, which reaped the benefits of the Canadian content regulation. The irony of the Canadian content regulation was that an industry had been built that did not so much compete with the multinationals as it became integrated into a symbiotic relationship; domestic labels provided multinationals with talent in exchange for access to distribution networks. That the subsidiaries of the multinationals managed to establish themselves as 'national' labels on a par with their domestically owned competition was a testament to the extensiveness of their involvement in the scene and the lack of public knowledge as to the workings of the industry.

Radio and music television did much to boost the national profile of Canadian acts during the 1980s and 1990s, but by the 2000s the influence of these delivery systems, particularly in regards to breaking new acts, waned as radio station formats turned towards an older demographic and music videos gave way to celebrity lifestyle programming. The decrease in opportunities for up-and-coming and independent acts on MuchMusic and its recently introduced compatriot MTV Canada resulted in a turn to Internet streaming video and music sites, podcasts, and pay-per-track downloads. Corporate giants have seen fit to join in, as with Yahoo! Canada's 'Up Your Music' competition in 2007 in which over 300 independent acts uploaded videos that went on to be viewed over two hundred thousand times and were ranked by over thirty thousand votes.[6] According to Kerry Munro of Yahoo! Canada, 'this contest is probably the country's biggest online battle of the bands ... Music and video have had a huge impact online and we are happy to provide users with the tools to connect them with up-and-coming Canadian artists and include them in the process of choosing the winner.'[7]

Exactly what constitutes Canadian music continues to be open to debate, with various factions indulging in inherently subjective, highly nationalistic, and reductively selective judgments in declaring what is and is not Canadian, winning public affirmation thanks to the emotional sway of nationalism and ease with which people can opt in to the national sense of self. 'We' share the Tragically Hip not only because they make occasional lyrical references to Canadian locations and historical figures but because, as their lack of popularity abroad attests, they can only be understood by 'us.' On the other side of the spectrum, Shania Twain, who lives and records abroad, has achieved international popularity thanks to a multinational label, yet she is nonetheless 'ours' because she was born in Canada. Even those who have been gone for decades and whose careers were built abroad, such as Paul Anka and Neil Young, can still be claimed as Canadian because of their place of birth. This nationalist imperative requires little evidence other than the emotional pang it evokes when Ian Menzies of *Canadian Musician* declares that 'now, like no other time in our history, the music we're making is truly international, but its strength is truly Canadian,' or Thomas Hopkins of *Maclean's* informs readers that when Triumph jokes that '"our music is for beer drinkers" ... the "eh?" though silent, is understood,' or Brian D. Johnson states that 'there's something unmistakably Canadian about [Alanis Morissette's] earnest style, her goodwill – and her resistance to industry types trying to package her.'[8]

What constitutes 'Canadian music' cannot be exclusively or singularly defined. There can be no clear winner in such a skewed debate, no clear answer to such an ambiguous question. Rather, what we can do is explore why and how music and national identity have come to be conflated. At the heart of it was a shift that occurred in the late 1960s and into the early 1970s in which popular music became reconfigured as a means of mediating not only socio-economic identities, particularly those of gender, class, and generation, but a national one as well. The change from 'music in Canada' to 'Canadian music' has been characterized not by the emergence of a 'Canadian sound' but in an emotional, patriotic, and fraternal connection to music as a means of mediating a national sense of self.[9] This ideological Canadianization has taken place alongside an industrialization in which domestic and multinational record labels have symbiotically thrived among opportunities made possible by the Canadian content regulation. All the while, nationalization has taken place largely outside of the activities of singer-songwriters, musicians, and performing talent themselves, with many of them hesitant to have their craft subsumed into reductive national categories or appropriated for nation-building. Few have been as sensitive to this phenomenon as Bruce Cockburn. To identify, categorize, and juxtapose a 'Canadian' versus 'American' music was overly simplistic, he explained in an interview for a 1972 *Saturday Night* cover story. 'While it is true that the music I was hearing and playing was a product of what went down in America, it was also just music. Sometimes music does exist as an artifact, as a thing with an existence separate from its original context so that it is *from* it but not *of* it.'[10] Cockburn understood the nationalist imperative, but for many other Canadians the difference between *from* and *of* was immaterial. For them, 'music in Canada' had become 'Canadian music.'

Notes

Introduction

1 Ritchie Yorke, *Axes, Chops and Hot Licks: The Canadian Rock Music Scene* (Edmonton: Hurtig, 1971), 25.
2 Richard Flohil, 'Interview! Gilles Vigneault,' *Canadian Composer*, June 1974, 10.
3 Richard Flohil, 'Interview! Murray McLauchlan,' *Canadian Composer*, May 1974, 18.
4 Tom Harrison, '54-40 without a Fight,' *Canadian Musician*, August 1986, 43.
5 Courtney Tower, 'Musicians Play a Canada Rock,' *Maclean's*, 4 February 1970, 4.
6 As Tyson reportedly told an audience in Greenwich Village in 1965 before performing 'Four Rode By,' 'there were hardly any bad guys in Canadian history like you had down here, and I always felt deprived as a kid. So I searched through our history and finally found some real bad guys in my own home town, Kamloops, British Columbia.' Jack Batten, 'Sweet Song of Success,' *Maclean's*, 21 August 1965, 15.
7 Tower, 'Musicians Play a Canada Rock.'
8 Many songwriters and musicians, Robert Wright has already noted, were deeply suspicious of nationalism, while, at the same time, a number of journalists, particularly those writing for *Maclean's* and other domestically focused periodicals, were attempting to juxtapose a Canadian against an American music scene and assert a musical sovereignty in a time of rabid anti-Americanism. Wright singles out William Westfall of the *Canadian Forum* and Jack Batten and Jon Ruddy of *Maclean's* (among other periodicals). Robert Wright, '"Dream, Comfort, Memory, Despair": Canadian Popular Musicians and the Dilemma of Nationalism, 1968–1972,' *Journal of Canadian Studies* 22, no. 4 (Winter 1987–8): 30.

9 Courtney Tower, 'Canada Report,' *Maclean's*, 4 February 1970, 1; italics in
   original.
10 Ibid., 1–5.
11 Interestingly, in 1965 the U.S. Armed Forces launched a campaign to
   improve the image of country and western music among troops serving
   abroad, including prohibiting the nicknames 'hick,' 'hillbilly,' and 'music
   from the sticks' in favour of 'country,' 'western,' 'CandW,' 'American folk
   music,' and 'music of America.' The U.S. Armed Forces found a lot of patriotic value in what it called 'an integral part of the American cultural heritage and of the American way of life.' As *Billboard* columnist Omer Anderson
   noted, 'aside from giving the soldier what he wants in the way of music,
   the military has discovered that country music is an important adjunct to
   instilling loyalty and a sense of duty to country into members of the Armed
   Forces'; thus, 'military personnel, military publications and the military
   radio network are under orders to stress the American folk character of the
   idiom.' Omer Anderson, 'U.S. Launches European Drive to Aid Country
   Music Image,' *Billboard*, 25 December 1965, 24, 33.
12 Among the best scholarly examinations of the relationship between youth
   and popular music is Peter G. Christenson and Donald F. Roberts, *It's Not
   Only Rock and Roll: Popular Music in the Lives of Adolescents* (Cresskill, NJ:
   Hampton Press, 1998).
13 Peter Gzowski, 'Dylan: An Explosion of Poetry,' *Maclean's*, 22 January 1966,
   20; italics in original.
14 In 1976 the Canadian Radio and Television Commission became the Canadian Radio-television and Telecommunications Commission. This intervention was a component of a much larger process of Canadianization that
   entailed the federal government using its powers and moneys to encourage
   the production and consumption of domestically produced arts and mass
   media for the sake of pan-national unity.
15 Pierre Juneau, quoted in Yorke, *Axes, Chops and Hot Licks*, x.
16 I am indebted to Benedict Anderson for this metaphor, 'stretching the
   short, tight skin of the nation over the gigantic body of the empire.' Benedict Anderson, *Imagined Communities: Reflections on the Origin and Spread of
   Nationalism* (London: Verso, 1991), 86.
17 Gillian Mitchell, *The North American Folk Music Revival: Nation and Identity in
   the United States and Canada, 1945–1980* (Burlington, VT: Ashgate, 2007),
   146.
18 Ritchie Yorke, *Axes, Chops and Hot Licks*, 49.
19 Bob Johnston, 'Bob's Radio Review,' unidentified newspaper, Library and
   Archives Canada, MG30, D304, vol. 22, file 22-27, circa 1970–1.

20 Nicholas Jennings, *Before the Gold Rush: Flashbacks to the Dawn of the Canadian Sound* (Toronto: Viking, 1997), 5. It is also worth noting that Jennings covered the domestically focused music boom of the 1990s for *Maclean's*.

21 Michael Barclay, Ian A.D. Jack, and Jason Schneider, 'Disclaimer,' *Have Not Been the Same: The CanRock Renaissance* (Toronto: ECW Press), no page.

22 As Peter Wade puts it about social identity, but in a statement just as true for national identity, 'there is a tendency to see social identity as a pre-formed thing which music simply expresses.' 'Music, Blackness and National Identity: Three Moments in Columbia History,' *Popular Music*, 17, no. 1 (1998): 4.

23 Mary Harron, 'McRock: Pop as a Commodity,' in Simon Frith, ed., *Facing the Music: A Pantheon Guide to Popular Culture* (New York: Pantheon Books, 1988), 187–8.

24 Douglas Fetherling, *Some Day Soon: Essays on Canadian Songwriters* (Kingston, ON: Quarry Press, 1990), 10.

25 Ibid., 11.

26 Fetherling not only has written numerous books but was a literary reviewer and columnist for such periodicals as *Saturday Night*.

27 Marco Adria, *Music of Our Times: Eight Canadian Singer-Songwriters* (Toronto: Lorimer, 1990). I have previously critiqued these arguments in 'Of War Machines and Ghetto Scenes: English-Canadian Nationalism and The Guess Who's "American Woman,"' *American Review of Canadian Studies*, 33, no. 3 (Autumn 2003): 339–56.

28 Greg Potter, *Hand Me Down World: The Canadian Pop-Rock Paradox* (Toronto: Macmillan Canada, 1999) back cover, paperback version.

29 Ibid.

30 Rick Salutin, 'National Cultures in the Age of Globalization: The Case of Canada,' *Queen's Quarterly* 106, no. 2 (Summer 1999): 206.

31 See my discussion of this in 'Of War Machines and Ghetto Scenes.'

32 Barry K. Grant, '"Across the Great Divide": Imitation and Inflection in Canadian Rock Music,' *Journal of Canadian Studies* 21, no. 1 (Spring 1986): 122.

33 Bart Testa and Jim Shedden, 'In the Great Midwestern Hardware Store: The Seventies Triumph in English-Canadian Rock Music,' in Joan Nicks and Jeannette Sloniowski, eds, *Slippery Pastimes: Reading the Popular in Canadian Culture* (Waterloo, ON: Wilfrid Laurier University Press, 2002), 179.

34 Timothy Rice and Tammy Gutnik, 'What's Canadian about Canadian Popular Music? The Case of Bruce Cockburn,' in John Beckwith and Timothy J. McGee, eds, *Taking a Stand: Essays in Honour of John Beckwith* (Toronto: University of Toronto Press, 1995), 251, 252.

35 Ibid., 253.

36 Lehr presents an understanding of the regulation based upon two relatively random statements, one each from Pierre Juneau of the CRTC and
Alan Johnson of the CBC (despite the fact that CBC was not speaking for
the CRTC). The article fails to provide a sufficient background as to the
creation of the regulations, particularly the reasons why the CRTC avoided
qualitative measurements and the problems with restricting access to the
publicly owned airwaves to only those artists who limit their craft to national
identifiers. John Lehr, 'As Canadian as Possible ... Under the Circumstances: Regional Myths, Images of Place and National Identity in Canadian
Country Music,' in Beverley Diamond and Robert Winter, eds, *Canadian
Music: Issues of Hegemony and Identity* (Toronto: Canadian Scholars' Press,
1994), 271.
37 Ibid., 275, 279, 280.
38 Ibid., 280. A more balanced approach to country music in Canada is offered
by Bram Dov Abramson, who takes less of a dichotomized 'us' and 'them'
approach to a genre rooted within American iconography and realizes that
'the Canadian country music apparatus is itself a branch plant of transnational country music.' Bram Dov Abramson, 'Country Music and Cultural
Industry: Mediating Structures in Transnational Media Flow,' *Media, Culture
and Society* 24 (2002): 269.
39 Elaine Keillor, *Music in Canada: Capturing Landscape and Diversity* (Montreal and Kingston: McGill-Queen's University Press, 2006). Keillor is to be
applauded for compiling a survey that spans early aboriginal works and the
modern age of MP3 and electronica; perhaps partially due to the nature of
the task, the result is little more than encyclopedic.
40 Fetherling, *Some Day Soon*, 136; Keillor, *Music in Canada*, 243, 247.
41 Keillor, *Music in Canada*, 311.
42 Ibid., 312.
43 Ibid.
44 Cecily Devereux, '"Canadian Classic" and "Commodity Export": The Nationalism of "Our" Anne of Green Gables,' *Journal of Canadian Studies* 36, no. 1
(2001): 12.
45 Ibid., 25.
46 Robert Wright, '"Dream, Comfort, Memory, Despair": Canadian Musicians
and the Dilemma of Nationalism,' revised version, in *Virtual Sovereignty:
Nationalism, Culture and the Canadian Question* (Toronto: Canadian Scholars'
Press, 2004), 57.
47 See Ryan Edwardson, 'A Canadian Modernism: The Pre-Group of Seven
"Algonquin School," 1912–1917,' *British Journal of Canadian Studies* 17, no. 1

(2004): 81–92. Lightfoot not only learned much from non-Canadian musicians and recordings, particularly Bob Dylan and Bob Gibson, but even studied at the Westlake School of Modern Music in Los Angeles. Marjorie Harris, 'Gordon Lightfoot,' *Maclean's*, September 1968, 35.

48 Myrna Kostash, 'The Pure, Uncluttered Spaces of Bruce Cockburn,' *Saturday Night,* June 1972, 22.

49 Anthony D. Smith, *The Ethnic Origins of Nations* (New York: Blackwell, 1986), 15. Although Smith discusses this concept in reference to ethnic nationalism, it certainly extends to civic nationalism as well.

50 Anderson, *Imagined Communities*, 7. In this same vein, it is important to distinguish between 'country' and 'nation,' two terms often treated as interchangeable when, in fact, they are related but different; the geographic and material sites in which popular music has been developed cannot simply be retroactively or inherently thought of as national. A country is a political territory, usually but not always governed by a sovereign state, whereas a nation is an ideological construct given tentative shape and continuously reworked to fit changing socio-ethnic demographics and civic values.

51 As Anderson argues, the nation is imagined because 'the members of even the smallest nation will never know most of their fellow-members, meet them, or even hear of them, yet in the minds of each lives the image of their communion.' Ibid., 6.

52 Lawrence Grossberg, 'Another Boring Day in Paradise: Rock and Roll and the Empowerment of Everyday Life,' *Popular Music 4* (Cambridge: Cambridge University Press, 1984), 234.

53 For a discussion of the power of tropes and literary techniques within narratives, see Hayden White, *The Content of the Form: Narrative Discourse and Historical Representation* (Baltimore: Johns Hopkins University Press, 1987).

54 Lee Silversides, foreword to Martin Melhuish, *Oh What a Feeling: A Vital History of Canadian Music* (Kingston, ON: Quarry Press, 1996), a celebratory history of the Juno Awards. Melhuish was an obvious choice to author the book in conjunction with the Canadian Academy of Recording Arts and Sciences. One of his earlier works, *Heart of Gold: 30 Years of Canadian Pop Music* (Toronto: CBC Enterprises, 1983), offered a survey in what he called 'an anecdotal fashion but with an eye to historical perspective ... Those artists that appear here, I feel, best capture the essence of Canadian pop music in a national and international context.' The goal was made all the more revealing when he concluded the introduction with a wish that the book 'in a small way instill some pride in Canadians in the rich contemporary music that is part of their culture' (no page).

55 Larry LeBlanc, 'The Flip Side of Anne Murray,' *Maclean's*, November 1974, 90; italics in original.
56 John Macfarlane, 'What If Anne Murray Were an American?,' *Maclean's*, May 1971, 78.
57 Malka Marom, 'Face to Face,' *Maclean's*, June 1974, 66; Nicholas Jennings, 'Guess Who's Reborn,' *Maclean's*, 29 May 2000, 55.
58 Ian Tyson and Colin Escott, *I Never Sold My Saddle* (Toronto: Douglas and McIntyre, 1994), 43.
59 See discussions of this in chapters seven and eight.
60 Linda Kelley, 'Jane Siberry's Musical Dance In and Out of Time,' *Canadian Composer*, October 1985, 6.
61 For example, 'the Hip' have sung about Bobcaygeon, Jacques Cartier, Tom Thomson, and Bill Barilko of the Toronto Maple Leafs.
62 That being said, there is an eerie similarity between the aggressively masculine if not borderline misogynistic lyrics found in a lot of Gordon Lightfoot's early work ('That's What You Get (For Lovin' Me),' 'I'm Not Sayin,' 'Go Go Round,' etc.) and the lyrics of contemporary urban music.
63 Will Straw, 'In and Around Canadian Music,' *Journal of Canadian Studies* 35, no. 3 (Fall 2000): 175.
64 Douglas Ivison, 'Canadian Content: Cultural Specificity in English-Canadian Popular Music,' in Joy Cohnstaedt and Yves Frenette, eds, *Canadian Cultures and Globalization* (Montreal: Association for Canadian Studies, 1997), 52.
65 Ibid., 51.
66 Ibid., 52.
67 Testa and Shedden, 'In the Great Midwestern Hardware Store,' 185, 213. In the terms set forth by Testa and Shedden, region is 'first to mean region (the South, the Midwest, the East Coast, etc.); second, to indicate patterns of local development (e.g., 'rural,' 'urban,' 'ex-urban/industrial,' 'suburban,' etc.)' (197).
68 Ibid., 191.
69 Don DiNovo, Canadian Radio and Television Commission, *Public Hearing*, 21 April 1970, 1359.
70 Ibid., 186.
71 Larry Starr, Christopher Waterman, and Jay Hodgson, *Rock: A Canadian Perspective* (Don Mills, ON: Oxford University Press, 2009).
72 Simon Frith, 'Music and Identity,' in Simon Hall and Paul du Gay, eds, *Questions of Cultural Identity* (London: Sage, 1996), 109.
73 Simon Frith, 'Towards an Aesthetic of Popular Music,' in Richard Leppert and Susan McClary, eds, *Music and Society: The Politics of Composition, Performance and Reception* (Cambridge: Cambridge University Press, 1987), 137.

74 Peter Symon, 'Music and National Identity in Scotland: A Study of Jock Tamson's Bairns,' *Popular Music* 16, no. 2 (1997): 203–16.

75 Noel McLauchlin and Martin McLoone, 'Hybridity and National Musics: The Case of Irish Rock Music,' *Popular Music* 19, no. 2 (2000): 181–99.

76 Roy Shuker and Michael Pickering, 'Kiwi Rock: Popular Music and Cultural Identity in New Zealand,' *Popular Music* 13, no. 3 (1994): 261–78.

77 Christian Lahusen, 'The Aesthetic of Radicalism: The Relationship between Punk and the Patriotic Nationalist Movement of the Basque Country,' *Popular Music* 12, no. 3 (1993): 263–80; David Treece, 'Guns and Roses: Bossa Nova and Brazil's Music of Popular Protest, 1958–68,' *Popular Music* 16, no. 1 (1997): 1–29; Peter Manuel, 'Marxism, Nationalism and Popular Music in Revolutionary Cuba,' *Popular Music* 6, no. 2 (May 1987): 161–78.

78 Edward Larkey, 'Just for Fun? Language Choice in German Popular Music,' *Popular Music and Society* 24, no. 3 (Fall 2000): 5–6.

1 Lonely Boys and Wild Girls

1 Mac Reynolds, 'Daughter Wants to See Elvis? "Kick Her in the Teeth!"' *Vancouver Sun*, 31 August 1957, 1.

2 Quoted in Bob Blackburn, 'Elvis Every Bit a Pro – Honest He Is!' *Ottawa Citizen*, 4 April 1957, 1.

3 Correspondence with Norm Sherratt, February 2008.

4 John Kirkwood, 'Rock 'n' Roll Seen "Emotion, Not Sin": Pastor Joins Sun Staffer in Viewing First Outburst in City,' *Vancouver Sun*, 28 June 1956, 3.

5 Doug Owram, *Born at the Right Time: A History of the Baby Boom Generation* (Toronto: University of Toronto Press, 1997), 137.

6 John Clare, 'The Scramble for the Teen-age Dollar,' *Maclean's*, 14 September 1957, 19.

7 Ibid., 112.

8 Robert Thomas Allen, 'How to Live with a Teen-age Daughter,' *Maclean's*, 31 August 1957, 12. For an account of his own childhood, see *My Childhood and Yours: Happy Memories of Growing Up* (Toronto: Macmillan, 1977).

9 Jane and Mary Allen, 'How to Endure a Father,' *Maclean's*, 31 January 1959, 19.

10 Owram, *Born at the Right Time*, 153.

11 Paul Friedlander, *Rock and Roll: A Social History* (Boulder, CO: Westview, 1996), 22.

12 Nicholas Jennings, *Fifty Years of Music: The Story of EMI Music Canada* (Toronto: Macmillan, 2000), 16.

13 Ibid.

14 Steve Chapple and Reebee Garofalo, *Rock 'n' Roll Is Here to Pay: The History and Politics of the Music Industry* (Chicago: Nelson-Hall, 1977), 232–3.

15 Marc Eliot, *Rockonomics: The Money behind the Music* (New York: Carol, 1993), 49.

16 Wes Smith, *The Pied Pipers of Rock 'n' Roll: Radio Deejays of the 50s and 60s* (Marietta, GA: Longstreet Press, 1989), 7.

17 Before he emigrated to Israel in 1982, Dov Ivry's name was Jon Everett.

18 Correspondence with Dov Ivry, January 2008.

19 Robinson and Greg Potter have amassed anecdotes and photos from his years as a disc jockey and spanning entertainment and shows throughout the twentieth century in *Backstage Vancouver: A Century of Entertainment Legends* (Vancouver: Harbour, 2004).

20 Quoted in Brandon Yip, 'Rockin' back the Clock,' *Vancouver Courier*, 7 July 2004, 1.

21 Ibid.

22 Simon Frith, *Performing Rites: On the Value of Popular Music* (Cambridge: Harvard University Press, 1996), 131; italics in original. This is also discussed in Peter Wicke, 'Rock Music: A Musical-Aesthetic Study,' *Popular Music 2* (Cambridge: Cambridge University Press, 1982): 219–43.

23 Correspondence with Dov Ivry, January 2008.

24 'New Pop Records,' *Time*, 4 April 1955, 68–9. *Time* (Canada) is a split-run version of *Time* magazine that is printed in Canada primarily with content from the original publication and some domestic material added.

25 'Yeh-Heh-Heh-Hehs, Baby,' *Time*, 18 June 1956, 86.

26 Ibid.

27 'Rock 'n' Rollers Deny Music Immoral,' *Vancouver Sun*, 27 June 1956, 2.

28 Quoted in ibid.

29 Photo caption, *Vancouver Sun*, 28 June 1956, 3.

30 Stanley Bligh, 'He's Nauseated: Sun Music Critic on Rock 'n' Roll: "Ultimate in Musical Depravity,"' *Vancouver Sun*, 28 June 1956, 3.

31 Barbara Moon, 'What You Don't Need to Know about Rock 'n' Roll,' *Maclean's*, 7 July 1956, 51.

32 Ibid., 51.

33 Ibid., 52.

34 Ibid., 53.

35 William T. Bielby, 'Rock in a Hard Place: Grassroots Cultural Production in the Post-Elvis Era,' *American Sociological Review* 69 (February 2004): 8.

36 Ibid.

37 Susan J. Douglas, *Where the Girls Are: Growing Up Female with the Mass Media* (Toronto: Random House, 1994), 94.

38 'Yeh-Heh-Heh-Hes, Baby,' *Time*, 18 June 1956, 86.
39 The history is well told in Peter Guarlnick's *Last Train to Memphis: The Rise of Elvis Presley* (Toronto: Little, Brown, 1994).
40 'Yeh-Heh-Heh-Hes, Baby,' *Time*, 18 June 1956, 52.
41 Randy Bachman and John Einarson, *Takin' Care of Business* (Toronto: McArthur, 2000), 33.
42 Joe Scanlon, '23,000 See Elvis – Late Show 15,000 His Largest Ever,' *Toronto Daily Star*, 3 April 1957, 2.
43 Ibid., 1.
44 'Flying Wedge Gets Elvis Safely Past Giddy Girls,' *Ottawa Citizen*, 3 April 1957, 1.
45 'Hoax Has Parliament Hopping for Presley,' *Ottawa Citizen*, 3 April 1957, 1.
46 Bob Blackburn, 'Elvis Every Bit a Pro   Honest He Is!' *Ottawa Citizen*, 4 April 1957, 1.
47 Interestingly, the Elvis concert shared the cover that day with a story on the apparent suicide of Herbert Norman, the Canadian ambassador to Egypt, who had been hounded by the Senate House Committee on Un-American Activities led by the junior senator from Wisconsin Joseph McCarthy.
48 Greg Connolley and Gerry Mulligan, 'The Police Kept It Peaceful,' *Ottawa Citizen*, 4 April 1957, 25.
49 Ibid.
50 Greg Connolley and Gerry Mulligan, 'The "Great Man" on Her Arm,' *Ottawa Citizen*, 4 April 1957, 25.
51 'Elvis Fans "Better Behave" – Police,' *Ottawa Citizen*, 1 April 1957, 3.
52 Reynolds, 'Daughter Wants to See Elvis?, 1.
53 Martha Robinson, 'Square Dancers Have Lots of Fun,' *Vancouver Sun*, 31 August 1957, 10.
54 John Kirkwood, 'Presley Fans Demented,' *Vancouver Sun*, 3 September 1957, 1.
55 Friedlander, *Rock and Roll: A Social History*, 54.
56 Ronnie Hawkins and Peter Goddard, *Ronnie Hawkins: Last of the Good Ol' Boys* (Toronto: Stoddart, 1989), 95.
57 Ritchie Yorke, 'Ronnie Hawkins,' *Rolling Stone*, 9 August 1969, 24.
58 Hawkins and Goddard, *Ronnie Hawkins*, 83.
59 Correspondence with Peter De Remigis, January 2008.
60 Yorke, 'Ronnie Hawkins,' 26.
61 'Ronnie Hawkins,' *Canadian Musician*, March/April 1981, 42.
62 Several of these are listed in Jennings, *Before the Gold Rush* (Toronto: Penguin, 1997), 11–13. See also Ira Nadel, *Various Positions: A Life of Leonard Cohen* (Toronto: Random House, 1996), 35.

63 Ian Tyson and Colin Escott, *I Never Sold My Saddle* (Toronto: Douglas and McIntyre, 1994), 17.
64 Jennings, *Before the Gold Rush*, 31.
65 John Mackie, '50s Vancouver Rock Reprised' *Vancouver Sun*, 31 January 2004, D3.
66 Ibid.
67 Correspondence with Dov Ivry, January 2008.
68 Ibid.
69 Ritchie Yorke, in *Axes, Chops and Hot Licks: The Canadian Rock Music Scene* (Edmonton: Hurtig, 1971), offers a rather bleak picture of radio station apathy and neglect. Gillian Mitchell, on the other hand, takes Yorke's position to task in noting the presence of radio broadcasters, including those at CHUM, in discussions of the local music scene in the 'After Four' section of the *Toronto Telegram*. Gillian Mitchell, *The North American Folk Music Revival: Nation and Identity in the United States and Canada, 1945–1980* (Burlington, VT: Ashgate, 2007), 151. Still, both would likely agree with the point that coverage was not only relatively limited but also characterized by a focus on local scenes as opposed to a national scene.
70 David Cobb, 'Pop Power,' *Toronto Telegram*, 29 July 1967, Showcase section, 6.
71 The Top 10 on the first CHUM Chart were: 'All Shook Up' (Elvis Presley), 'Love Letters in the Sand' (Pat Boone), 'I Like Your Kind of Love' (Andy Williams), 'Bye Bye Love' (the Everly Brothers), 'Start Movin' (In My Direction)' (Sal Mineo), 'Dark Moon' (Gale Storm), 'A White Sport Coat (And a Pink Carnation)' (Marty Robbins), 'Fabulous' (Charlie Gracie), 'Girl with the Golden Braids' (Perry Como), and 'Yes Tonight, Josephine' (Johnnie Ray).
72 CHUM Chart, 27 May 1957.
73 Jennings, *Before the Gold Rush*, 59.
74 Correspondence with Dov Ivry, January 2008.
75 Ibid.
76 Correspondence with Peter De Remigis, January 2008.
77 Ibid.
78 Correspondence with Norm Sherratt, February 2008.
79 Owram, *Born at the Right Time*, 156.
80 See, for example, Soren Schou, 'The Charisma of the Liberators: The Americanization of Postwar Denmark,' in Roger de la Garde, William Gilsdorf, and Ilja Wechselmann, eds, *Small Nations, Big Neighbour: Denmark and Quebec/Canada Compare Notes on American Popular Culture* (London: John Libbey, 1993), 65.

81 See Dick Bradley, *Understanding Rock 'n' Roll: Popular Music in Britain, 1955–1964* (Buckingham: Open University Press, 1992).

82 'Real Schräg,' *Time*, 8 December 1958, 38.

83 'Rittoru Dahring,' *Time*, 14 April 1958, 32.

84 Timo Toivonen and Antero Laiho, '"You Don't Like Crazy Music": The Reception of Elvis Presley in Finland,' *Popular Music and Society* 13, no. 2 (1999): 2.

85 Charles Hamm, 'Rock 'n' Roll in a Very Strange Society,' in Richard Middleton and David Horn, eds, *Popular Music 5: Continuity and Change* (London: Cambridge University Press, 1985), 159.

86 David Eggleton, *Ready to Fly: The Story of New Zealand Rock Music* (Nelson, NZ: Craig Potton, 2003), 8.

87 Michael Sturma, 'The Politics of Dancing: When Rock 'n' Roll Came to Australia,' *Journal of Popular Culture* 25, no. 4 (Spring 1992): 123, 124, 168. See also Lawrence Zion, 'Disposable Icons: Pop Music in Australia, 1955–63,' *Popular Music* 8, no. 2 (1989): 165–75.

88 Georg Maas and Hartmut Reszel, 'Whatever Happened to … : The Decline and Renaissance of Rock in the Former GDR,' *Popular Music* 17, no. 3 (1998): 269. Three months later the GDR banned 'beat music.'

89 Larkey, 'Just for Fun? Language Choice in German Popular Music,' *Popular Music and Society* 24, no. 3 (Fall 2000): 5–6.

90 Timothy W. Ryback, *Rock around the Bloc: A History of Rock Music in Eastern Europe and the Soviet Union* (New York: Oxford University Press, 1990), 33.

91 Ibid., 33.

92 Ibid., 114.

93 Ibid., 23.

94 Ibid., 24.

95 Ibid., 114.

96 'The Rock Is Solid,' *Time*, 4 November 1957, 56.

97 Ibid., 55.

98 Ibid., 56.

99 'American Abroad,' *Time*, 9 June 1958, 28.

100 Ibid.

101 'Rock 'n' Riot,' *Time*, 19 May 1958, 66.

102 Ibid.

103 Robert Burnet, *The Global Jukebox: The International Music Industry* (New York: Routledge, 1996), 29.

104 Statistic quoted in Simon Frith, *Sound Effects: Youth, Leisure, and the Politics of Rock 'n' Roll* (New York: Pantheon, 1981), 134.

105 Ibid.

106 Paul A. Gardner, 'What It Takes to Crash Tin Pan Alley at Fifteen,' *Maclean's*, 4 January 1958, 38.
107 Susan Mair, 'Paul Anka: The World's Reigning Juvenile,' *Maclean's*, 1 December 1962, 36.
108 Ibid.
109 For an overview of Curtola's career, see Yorke, *Axes, Chops and Hot Licks*, 158–63.
110 Richard Flohil, 'Burton Cummings,' *Canadian Musician*, March/April 1979, 17.
111 Rock and roll was connected to juvenile delinquency during the 1950s, but so too was other youthful consumerism, most notably comic books. See Bart Beaty, 'High Treason: Canadian Nationalism and the Regulation of American Crime Comic Books,' *Essays on Canadian Writing* 62 (Fall 1997): 85–107.

2 Guess Who?

1 Mike Cobb, 'Fans Successfully Held at Bay: It's Mad Day for Seattle as Beatles Come to Town,' *Vancouver Sun*, 22 August 1964, 1.
2 Guitarist Randy Bachman has told the story as if there had been only one shared microphone and amplifier, with everyone huddled around the former and plugged into the latter, but bassist Gary Petterson has stated that there were multiple microphones and amplifiers. See Tom Harrison, 'The Guess Who: Ballad of the Last 25 Years,' *Canadian Musician*, February 1988, 51.
3 Such a technical 'glitch' is questionable, but the explanation appears in multiple accounts offered by members of the band.
4 Petterson has identified George Struth of Quality Records as being the one to suggest the 'Guess Who?' promotional stunt. Mike Megaffin, 'Garry Peterson: Canadian Classic,' *Classic Drummer*, April/May/June 2006, 46.
5 Ibid.
6 John Einarson, *Shakin' All Over: The Winnipeg Sixties Rock Scene* (Winnipeg: Variety Club of Manitoba, 1987), 52.
7 Randy Bachman and John Einarson, *Takin' Care of Business* (Toronto: McArthur, 2000), 65.
8 Einarson, *Shakin' All Over*, 16.
9 Ibid., 54. Bachman and Einarson, *Takin' Care of Business*, 79.
10 Ibid., 80.
11 'The New Madness,' *Time*, 15 November 1963, 58.
12 Laurel Sercombe, '"Ladies and gentlemen ..." The Beatles: The Ed Sullivan

Show, CBS TV, February 9, 1964,' in Ian Inglis, ed., *Performance and Popular Music: History, Place and Time* (Hampshire: Ashgate, 2006), 10.

13 *Time*, for example, reported on the arrival in its 14 February 1964 issue.

14 Ian Inglis, 'Synergies and Reciprocities: The Dynamics of Musical and Professional Interaction between the Beatles and Bob Dylan,' *Popular Music and Society* 20, no. 4 (Winter 1996): 62.

15 Ian Inglis, "The Beatles Are Coming!' Conjecture and Conviction in the Myth of Kennedy, America, and the Beatles,' *Popular Music and Society* 24, no. 2 (Summer 2000): 93.

16 'Beatles Fan PNE Hoopla: Teenagers Swell Parade Crowds,' *Vancouver Sun*, 22 August 1964, 1.

17 William Littler, '20,000 Beatlemaniacs Pay So Much – for So Little,' *Vancouver Sun*, 24 August 1964, 1.

18 Stan Shillington, 'Beatle Mob Past Comparison: Only 100 Police between Youngsters and Disaster,' *Vancouver Sun*, 24 August 1964, 1.

19 Ibid.

20 Ibid.

21 *Vancouver Sun*, 24 August 1964, 9.

22 Allan Fotheringham, 'The Beatle Menace: How to Preserve Public Safety When Four Kids from Liverpool Visit Canada,' *Maclean's*, 19 September 1964, 1.

23 Ibid., 2.

24 Wendy Michener, 'How Elvis Survived the Faddish Years, and Why the Beatles May Go On Forever,' *Maclean's*, 19 September 1964, 68.

25 Ray Timson, '200 Girls Swoon in Battle of the Beatles,' *Toronto Daily Star*, 8 September 1964, 1.

26 'A Deafening Silence,' *Montreal Star*, 9 September 1964, 2.

27 Mary Harron, 'McRock: Pop as a Commodity,' 'The Enemy Within: Sex, Rock, and Identity,' in Simon Frith, ed., *Facing the Music: A Pantheon Guide to Popular Culture* (New York: Pantheon Books, 1988), 178.

28 Walter Pornovich, 'Stones Rolled So Secretly Admirers Gathered Moss,' *Montreal Star*, 23 April 1965, 4.

29 'A Deafening Silence,' *Montreal Star*.

30 Ralph Thomas and Morris Duff, 'Rolling Stones Show Violent and Vulgar,' *Toronto Daily Star*, 26 April 1965, 18.

31 Wilf Bell, '"Stones" Rock Ottawa,' *Ottawa Citizen*, 26 April 1965, 13.

32 Thomas and Duff, 'Rolling Stones Show Violent and Vulgar.'

33 Ibid.

34 Christy McCormick, '9,000 Teenagers Go Wild with Rock and Roll Hysteria,' *Montreal Star*, 30 October 1965, 3. That the newspaper printed the wrong

name is a sign of how far removed the staff members were from rock and roll.

35 Jes Odam, 'Rolling Stones Hit Town, Leave Agrodome Rocking,' *Vancouver Sun*, 2 December 1965, 3.

36 '36 Screaming Fans Carried from Wild "Rock" Jamboree,' *Vancouver Sun*, 20 July 1966, 1.

37 Quoted in ibid.

38 Georg Maas and Hartmut Reszel, 'Whatever Happened to … : The Decline and Renaissance of Rock in the Former GDR,' *Popular Music* 17, no. 3 (1998): 268.

39 Jack Batten, 'Hawks, Chicks and a Swinging Nest,' *Maclean's*, 20 March 1965, 25.

40 *Time*, 'Rock 'n' Roll: The Sound of the Sixties,' 21 May 1965, 71.

41 Ibid., 68.

42 Nicholas Jennings, *Fifty Years of Music: The Story of EMI Music Canada* (Toronto: Macmillan, 2000), 26.

43 Ibid., 33.

44 Burton Cummings, forward to Einarson, *Shakin' All Over*, viii.

45 Jennings offers not only band names but also images of the clothing styles in *Before the Gold Rush* (Toronto: Viking, 1997), chap. 4, 'Ticket to Ride.'

46 David Downing, *A Dreamer of Pictures: Neil Young, the Man and His Music* (New York: Da Capo Press, 1995), 9.

47 Einarson, *Shakin' All Over*, 18.

48 Ibid.

49 Jennings, *Before the Gold Rush*, 67.

50 Correspondence with David Bingham, January 2008.

51 Jennings, *Fifty Years of Music*, 28.

52 Ibid, 49.

53 Tim Perlich, 'Ugly Ducklings Float Back from Obscurity,' *NOW*, 4–10 February 1999. In Bell's defence, Bingham has explained 'that was just his thing. He really couldn't help it and he certainly enjoyed it and used it to his advantage!' Correspondence with David Bingham, January 2008.

54 Jennings, *Fifty Years of Music*, 35.

55 Keith Richards talks about the origins of their band name in Mick Jagger, Dora Loewenstein, Philip Dodd, and Charlie Watts, *According to the Rolling Stones* (San Francisco: Chronicle Books, 2003), 42. Paul McCartney talks about the influence of Buddy Holly's Crickets on their choice of name in McCartney, John Lennon, George Harrison, and Ringo Starr, *The Beatles Anthology* (San Francisco: Chronicle Books, 2000), 42.

56 Marden, interesting enough, had actually been born in London, and Dennis would later change his name to Mars Bonfire.
57 John Kay and John Einarson, *John Kay: Magic Carpet Ride* (Kingston, ON: Quarry Press, 1994), 127.
58 Jennings, *Before the Gold Rush*, 172.
59 Robert Giroux, *Le guide de la chanson québécoise* (Montreal: Triptyque, 1991), 50.
60 For a discussion of some of these as well as other groups offering covers of popular English-language songs, see André Loiselle, *À l'image d'une nation: le cinéma de Michel Brault et l'histoire du Québec contemporain* (Paris: L'Harmattan, 2005), 161.
61 Correspondence with Jurgen Peter, January 2008.
62 Correspondence with Jeffrey Ridley, January 2008.
63 Correspondence with Jurgen Peter, January 2008.
64 According to Bingham, 'both Roger [Mayne, the band's guitarist] and I would scour record shops and buy almost anything that we could find on the smaller U.S. R&B and blues labels. Garnett Mims was also a favourite of Roger's and of course we all loved anything by Jimmy Reed. The Coasters were another big influence on me while I was in high school. [Jerry] Leiber and [Mike] Stoller were just the best as far as songwriters and I paid attention to the way that they constructed songs.' Correspondence with David Bingham, January 2008.
65 Will Straw, 'Exhausted Commodities: The Material Culture of Music,' *Canadian Journal of Communication* 25, no. 1 (2000): 182.
66 On this topic, see C. Champion, 'A Very British Coup: Canadianism, Quebec, and Ethnicity in the Flag Debate, 1961–1965,' *Journal of Canadian Studies* 40, no. 3 (Fall 2006): 68.
67 The UEL band name change is discussed in the liner notes of UEL's *Notes from the Underground*, a collection of the band's music released in the late 1990s. The jackets were discussed in correspondence with Ridley.
68 Peter Shapiro, 'Paul Revere and the Raiders,' in Peter Buckley, ed., *The Rough Guide to Rock*, 3rd ed. (London: Penguin, 2003), 870. Although Paul Revere and the Raiders predated the British Invasion and owed their name in part to the real name of band member Paul Revere Dick, they nonetheless took to the sounds of the new genre, particularly that of the Rolling Stones, while ironically building on their image as a patriotic response to the bands from Britain.
69 David Eggleton, *Ready to Fly: The Story of New Zealand Rock Music* (Nelson, NZ: Craig Potton, 2003), 190.

70 Edward Larkey, 'Just for Fun? Language Choice in German Popular Music,' *Popular Music and Society* 24, no. 3 (Fall 2000): 5.
71 Correspondence with Jurgen Peter, January 2008.
72 Ibid.
73 Linda Martin and Kerry Segrave, *Anti-Rock: The Opposition to Rock 'n' Roll* (New York: Da Capo Press, 1993), 118.

3 From 'Tom Dooley' to 'Mon Pays'

1 Jack Batten, 'Sweet Song of Success,' *Maclean's*, 21 August 1965, 15.
2 'Folksinger's Biggest Wish: Hometown Date in Saskatoon,' *Saskatoon Star Phoenix*, 2 February 1968.
3 'Maclean's Reports,' 'A Black Sheep among the Separatists,' *Maclean's*, April 1969, 4.
4 'The Folk-Girls,' *Time*, 1 June 1962, 48.
5 'Sibyl with Guitar,' *Time*, 23 November 1962, 60.
6 Francis Child, *The English and Scottish Popular Ballads* (London: Henry Stevens, Son and Stiles, 1882), vii.
7 Ian McKay, *Quest of the Folk: Antimodernism and Cultural Selection in Twentieth-Century Nova Scotia* (Montreal and Kingston: McGill-Queen's University Press, 1994), 18; italics in original.
8 Lee Marshall, 'Bob Dylan: Newport Folk Festival, July 25, 1965,' in Ian Inglis, ed., *Performance and Popular Music: History, Place and Time* (Hampshire: Ashgate, 2006), 20. In making this statement Marshall is drawing upon David Whisnant, *All That Is Native and Fine: The Politics of Culture in an American Region* (Chapel Hill: University of North Carolina Press, 1983).
9 For an informative look at the selectivity of Sharp's work, particularly the act of self-censoring, see E.C. Cawte, 'Watching Cecil Sharp at Work: A Study of His Records of Sword Dances Using His Field Notebooks,' *Folk Music Journal* 8, no. 3 (2003): 282–313. John Murray Gibbon's role in promoting identity via folk festivals has been examined by Stuart Henderson in '"While There Is Still Time...": J. Murray Gibbon and the Spectacle of Difference in Three CPR Folk Festivals, 1928–1931,' *Journal of Canadian Studies* 39, no. 1 (Winter 2005): 139–75. For Marius Barbeau, see Lawrence Nowry, *Man of Mana: Marius Barbeau* (Toronto: NC Press, 1995), and Andrew Nurse, 'Tradition and Modernity: The Cultural Work of Marius Barbeau' (doctoral thesis, Queen's University, 1997), and '"But now things have changed": Marius Barbeau and the Politics of Amerindian Identity,' *Ethnohistory* 48, no. 3 (Summer 2001): 433–72. Helen Creighton's work has been meticulously examined in McKay, *Quest of the Folk*.

10 McKay, 21.

11 Vincent J. Roscigno, William F. Danaher, and Erika Summers-Effler, 'Music, Culture, and Social Movements: Song and Southern Textile Worker Mobilization, 1929–1934,' *International Journal of Sociology and Social Policy* 22, nos 1–3 (2002): 154–5.

12 Ibid., 153.

13 McKay, *Quest of the Folk*, 23–4.

14 Simon Frith, *Sound Effects: Youth, Leisure, and the Politics of Rock 'n' Roll* (New York: Pantheon, 1981), 28.

15 Martha Bayles, 'The Strange Career of Folk Music,' *Michigan Quarterly Review* 44, no. 2 (Spring 2005), 309–10. Bayles's biggest contribution to the field is *Hole in Our Soul: The Loss of Beauty and Meaning in American Popular Music* (New York: Free Press, 1994).

16 Although the Lomaxes acted as filters in cataloguing the music, separating the songs from those who were singing, one would be amiss not to acknowledge that, given the disinterest of the commercial music market in folk music, many of the traditional songs would likely have been lost without the passionate and genuine interest of enthusiasts. Simon Frith was certainly right in noting that musicians within the folk movement helped to preserve songs which would likely have disappeared under the weight of an enlarging commercial music industry, and, in fact, the performers even managed to posit a significant challenge to that industry during the 1930s and 1940s. Frith, *Sound Effects*, 28.

17 Gillian Mitchell, *The North American Folk Music Revival: Nation and Identity in the United States and Canada, 1945–1980* (Burlington, VT: Ashgate, 2007), 36.

18 Guthrie was a member of the Industrial Workers of the World and wrote a column for the *Daily Worker*. See Ed Cray, *Ramblin' Man: The Life and Times of Woody Guthrie* (New York: Norton, 2004).

19 Marc Eliot, *Rockonomics: The Money behind the Music* (New York: Carol Publishing, 1993), 103.

20 For a look at how such episodes contributed to Seeger's status, see Minna Bromberg and Gary Alan Fine, 'Resurrecting the Red: Pete Seeger and the Purification of Difficult Reputations,' *Social Forces* 80, no. 4 (2002): 1135–55.

21 Although Seeger did not make it to Canada, a few years later he accepted a rare opportunity to tour behind the Iron Curtain during the Cold War era, spending a month and a half in Czechoslovakia, Poland, and the Soviet Union starting in March 1964. During this time Seeger sang to and visited with workers, hosted symposiums on folk music, and so forth. Timothy W. Ryback, *Rock around the Bloc: A History of Rock Music in Eastern Europe and the Soviet Union* (New York: Oxford University Press, 1990), 36, 37. For Seeger's

involvement with *Singalong Jubilee*, see Ernest Dick, *Remembering Singalong Jubilee* (Halifax: Formac, 2004).

22 Nicholas Jennings, *Before the Gold Rush* (Toronto: Viking, 1997), 27.

23 For a concise academic overview of the folk scene, see Daniel J. Gonczy, 'The Folk Music Movement of the 1960s: Its Rise and Fall,' *Popular Music and Society* 10, no. 1 (1985): 15–32.

24 The sensation of 'Tom Dooley' also prompted the Grammy Awards, in a move signifying the arrival of folk music as a commercial genre, to create a folk music category after having to first bestow upon the Kingston Trio the award for Best Country and Western Performance. Nicholas Jennings, *Fifty Years of Music: The Story of EMI Music Canada* (Toronto: Macmillan, 2000), 18.

25 The sales level is listed in 'Tin Pan Alley,' *Time*, 11 July 1960, 70.

26 'Folk Frenzy,' *Time*, 11 July 1960, 54

27 Ibid.

28 See Bill Usher and Linda Page-Harpa, eds, *For What Time I Am in This World: Stories from Mariposa* (Toronto: Peter Martin, 1977).

29 Mitchell, *North American Folk Music Revival*, 81.

30 Ibid, 82.

31 Ibid, 75.

32 Ian Tyson and Colin Escott, *I Never Sold My Saddle* (Toronto: Douglas and McIntyre, 1994), 24.

33 Sylvia Fraser, 'Sylvia Tyson Gets It Together,' *Chatelaine*, January 1976, 58, 60.

34 Jennings, *Before the Gold Rush*, 32.

35 'Folk Frenzy,' *Time*, 11 July 1960, 54.

36 'Sibyl with Guitar,' *Time*, 23 November 1962, 60.

37 Ibid., 66.

38 'Let Us Now Praise Little Men,' *Time*, 31 May 1963, 61.

39 Jennings, *Before the Gold Rush*, 47, 48.

40 McKenzie Porter, 'An Evening Out with McKenzie Porter: The Naughty but Nice New Coffee Houses,' *Maclean's*, 23 March 1963, 29.

41 Jennings, *Before the Gold Rush*, 99.

42 Ibid., 100.

43 Ibid., 115. Sainte-Marie brought attention to the plight of North American natives in such songs as 'Now That the Buffalo's Gone,' 'My Country, 'tis of Thy People You're Dying,' and 'Bury My Heart at Wounded Knee.'

44 Jennings, *Before the Gold Rush*, 65–6.

45 For a look at Mitchell's early years, see Karen O'Brien, *Joni Mitchell: Shadows and Light* (London: Virgin Books, 2001).

46 Jennings, *Before the Gold Rush*, 79.

47 'Sylvia Tyson,' *Canadian Musician*, May/June/July 1984, 41.

48 Jack Batten, 'Sweet Song of Success,' *Maclean's*, 21 August 1965, 15, 38.

49 Jennings, *Before the Gold Rush*, 87-88.

50 Ibid., 111.

51 Ibid., 113. By 1970 the Mynah Bird had become an adults-only club in which one could 'body paint our beautiful, completely topless girls,' 'photograph our live nude beautiful models,' and also watch 'nude movies from Europe never before shown in a theatre or club in Canada. Only for those who will not be offended.' Advertisement for the Mynah Bird, *Globe and Mail*, 12 February 1970, 13.

52 'The Crying Voice,' *Time*, 15 February 1971, 10.

53 For an overview of his life see John Kay and John Einarson, *John Kay: Magic Carpet Ride* (Kingston, ON: Quarry Press, 1994).

54 'They Hear America Singing,' *Time*, 19 July 1963, 47.

55 Fraser, 'Sylvia Tyson Gets It Together,' 60.

56 Tyson and Escott, *I Never Sold My Saddle*, 27.

57 *Woman of Heart and Mind. Joni Mitchell: A Life Story* (DVD, Eagle Vision USA, 2003).

58 Richard Flohil, 'Burton Cummings,' *Canadian Musician*, March/April 1979, 17.

59 The critique certainly seemed all the more valid after the song was banned by many radio stations. Los Angeles disc jockey Bob Eubanks spoke for many radio station programmers when he told *Time*, 'How do you think the enemy will feel with a tune like that no.1 in America?' *Time*, 17 September 1965, 76.

60 Jerome L. Rodnitzky, 'The Sixties between the Microgrooves: Using Folk and Protest Music to Understand American History, 1963–1973,' *Popular Music and Society* 23, no. 4 (Winter 1999), 109.

61 Craig Morrison, 'Folk Revival Roots Still Evident in 1990s Recordings of San Francisco Psychedelic Veterans,' *Journal of American Folklore* 114, no. 454 (Fall 2001): 478–9.

62 Ryback, *Rock around the Bloc*, 34.

63 David Lewis Stein, 'The Peaceniks Go to La Macaza,' *Maclean's*, 8 August 1964, 11.

64 Myrna Kostash, *Long Way From Home: The Story of the Sixties Generation in Canada* (Toronto: Lorimer, 1980), xxiv–xxv.

65 *Time*, 'The Toronto Teach-In,' 15 October 1965, 17.

66 See Meg Luxton, 'Feminism as a Class Act: Working-Class Feminism and the Women's Movement in Canada,' *Labour/Le Travail* 48 (Fall 2001): 63–88.

67 Marie Welton and Evangelia Tastsoglou, 'Building a Culture of Peace: An Interview with Muriel Duckworth and Betty Peterson,' *Canadian Woman Studies* 22, no. 2 (Fall 2002/Winter 2003): 115–21.

68 Ritchie Yorke, 'Boosting Peace: John and Yoko in Canada,' *Rolling Stone*, 18 June 1969, 6.

69 *Time*, 'The War Babies from the U.S.,' 9 August 1968, 9.

70 Doug Owram, *Born at the Right Time: A History of the Baby Boom Generation* (Toronto: University of Toronto Press, 1997), 216.

71 See Ryan Edwardson, 'Kicking Uncle Sam out of the Peaceable Kingdom: English-Canadian "New Nationalism" and Americanization,' *Journal of Canadian Studies* 37, no. 4 (Winter 2002): 131–50.

72 See Ryan Edwardson, *Canadian Content: Culture and the Quest for Nationhood* (Toronto: University of Toronto Press, 2008).

73 Mitchell, *The North American Folk Music Revival*, 75.

74 Ibid., 167.

75 Yorke, *Axes, Chops and Hot Licks* (Edmonton: Hurtig, 1971), 5.

76 Jack Batten, 'Canada's Rock Scene: Going, Going ...,' *Maclean's*, February 1968, 34.

77 David Cobb, 'Pop Power,' *Toronto Telegram*, 29 July 1967, Showcase section, 5.

78 'Who's Provincial??' *RPM*, 19 August 1967, 7.

79 Bart Testa and Jim Shedden, 'In the Great Midwestern Hardware Store: The Seventies Triumph in English-Canadian Rock Music,' in Joan Nicks and Jeannette Sloniowski, eds, *Slippery Pastimes: Reading the Popular in Canadian Culture* (Waterloo, ON: Wilfred Laurier University Press, 2002), 184.

80 Ritchie Yorke, *Axes, Chops and Hot Licks*, 199.

81 Robert Markle, 'Early Morning Afterthoughts,' *Maclean's*, December 1971, 28; italics in original.

82 Yorke, *Axes, Chops and Hot Licks*, 123.

83 Neil Young, who did not have a green card, worked illegally until 1970. Originally published in Cameron Crowe, 'So Hard to Make Arrangements with Yourself,' *Rolling Stone*, 14 August 1975, reprinted in Dave Zimmer, *4 Way Street: The Crosby, Stills, Nash, and Young Reader* (Cambridge, MA: Da Capo Press, 2004).

84 Jimmy McDonough, *Shakey* (Toronto: Vintage Canada, 2003), 142.

85 'Lightfoot: The Lyrical Loner,' *Globe and Mail*, 18 June 1966, 15.

86 Ibid.

87 Gordon Lightfoot, liner notes to *Songbook* (Warner Archive/Rhino).

88 Ibid., 32.

89 'Cosmopolitan Hick,' *Time*, 8 November 1968, 53.

90 Tom Hopkins, 'Gordon's Song,' *Maclean's*, 1 May 1976, 39. Al Mair, at one time manager of Lightfoot's Early Morning Productions, stated: 'Lightfoot is one of your bigger male chauvinists and a leading exponent of the double standard' (ibid., 36).

91 Ibid, 42.

92 Jack Batten pointed out the 'male chauvinism' in Lightfoot's earlier works and reprinted part of a review from the *Village Voice* that noted that 'That's What You Get (For Lovin' Me)' and 'I'm Not Sayin'' 'makes even the [Rolling Stones' song] "Look at That Stupid Girl" seem a raving feminist by comparison.' Jack Batten, 'The Vulnerability of Gordon Lightfoot,' *Saturday Night*, July 1974, 24.

93 Daniel Francis, *National Dreams: Myth, Memory, and Canadian History* (Vancouver: Arsenal Pulp Press, 1997), 150.

94 Ibid., 152.

95 Kevin Young (writer and ex-member of Moist), 'Capturing the Essence of the Tragically Hip Live,' *Canadian Musician*, September/October 2004, 37.

96 Mitchell, *The North American Folk Music Revival*, 153.

97 Even 'Black Day in July' was a hit among commercial radio stations. Although the song was banned in Detroit, it was aired in Canada and was an over-the-border hit in Detroit via Windsor. Lightfoot, complaining about the ban, noted that 'it's number one in Detroit and it's the Canadian station. It's the only place in Canada to break a record in the U.S.' Lightfoot to Marjorie Harris, 'Gordon Lightfoot,' *Maclean's*, September 1968, 60.

98 Matthew Good, interviewed in the TV special *Shakin' All Over*, Soapbox Productions, 2006.

99 The first French-speaking one, if one is to use 'pop' to refer simply to 'popular,' was Félix Leclerc, predating Lightfoot by two years.

100 'Lightfoot,' *Canadian Composer*, September 1970, 4.

101 Robert Giroux, *Le guide de la chanson québécoise* (Montreal: Triptyque, 1991), 50.

102 Richard Flohil, 'Interview! Gilles Vigneault,' *Canadian Composer*, June 1974, 10.

103 Gerry Barker, 'The Lads Laze as the Girls Scream,' *Toronto Daily Star*, 8 September 1964, 9.

104 'Separatists Burn Flags,' *Toronto Telegram*, 8 September, 1964, 1.

105 Jane Champagne, 'Félix Leclerc: Returning Home to Canada,' *Canadian Composer*, December 1973, 46.

106 Pierre Nadeau, 'Gilles Vigneault lui-méme, par Pierre Nadeau,' *L'Actualité*, September 1979, 12.

107 Georges-Hébert Germain, 'Le Patriote: Ten Years of Quebec's Pioneering Nightclub,' *Canadian Composer*, March 1975, 10.
108 Jon Ruddy, 'Another Kind of Explosion in Quebec: Talent,' *Maclean's*, June 1969, 45.
109 Richard Flohil, 'Interview! Ritchie Yorke,' *Canadian Composer*, October 1976, 28.
110 Ibid., 11.
111 'A Black Sheep among the Separatists,' *Maclean's*, April 1969, 4.
112 Jon Ruddy, 'It Wasn't My Country Any More ...,' *Maclean's*, June 1969, 11.
113 Jack Batten, 'Sweet Song of Success,' *Maclean's*, 21 August 1965, 38.

4 'California Dreamin'

1 Richard Flohil, 'Interview! Gilles Vigneault,' *Canadian Composer*, June 1974, 10.
2 Malka Marom, 'Face to Face,' *Maclean's*, June 1974, 66.
3 Susan Lumsden, 'Leonard Cohen Wants the Unconditional Leadership of the World,' *Weekend Magazine*, reprinted in Michael Gnarowski, *Leonard Cohen: The Artist and His Critics* (Toronto: McGraw-Hill Ryerson, 1976), 70.
4 Ralph J. Gleason, *Rolling Stone*, 17 May 1969, 4.
5 Ibid., 6.
6 Greil Marcus, *Mystery Train: Images of America in Rock 'n' Roll Music* (New York: E.P. Dutton, 1975), 50–1.
7 Police harassment is discussed in Gillian Mitchell, *The North American Folk Music Revival: Nation and Identity in the United States and Canada, 1945–1980* (Burlington, VT: Ashgate, 2007), 127.
8 Ibid., 120–2.
9 Ibid., 113.
10 Sylvia Fraser, 'Sylvia Tyson Gets It Together,' *Chatelaine*, January 1976, 60.
11 Ian Tyson and Colin Escott, *I Never Sold My Saddle* (Toronto: Douglas and McIntyre, 1994), 27. Ian offered a similar explanation in a 1965 interview with *Maclean's*: 'We had a good look at American politics last fall when we campaigned with Lady Bird. We did it because we were like everybody else – afraid of Goldwater – and when the democrats asked us to do something, we had to say yes.' Jack Batten, 'Sweet Song of Success,' *Maclean's*, 21 August 1965, 38.
12 Ibid.
13 Tyson and Escott, *I Never Sold My Saddle*, 27.
14 Ibid.
15 Ibid., 48.

16 Ibid., 46.
17 Krise Granat May, *Golden State, Golden Youth: The California Image in Popular Culture, 1955–1966* (Chapel Hill: University of North Carolina Press, 2002), 167, 188.
18 For events at Berkeley, see Robert Cohen and Reginald Zelnik, eds, *The Free Speech Movement: Reflections on Berkeley in the 1960s* (Berkeley: University of California Press, 2002).
19 Peter Collier and David Horowitz, 'Slouching towards Berkeley: Socialism in One City,' *Public Interest* (Winter 1989), 54.
20 See Adam Rome, '"Give Earth a Chance": The Environmental Movement and the Sixties,' *Journal of American History* 90, no. 2 (September 2003): 525–54.
21 The song was written by John and Michelle back in their New Journeymen days and was based on Michelle's homesickness for California.
22 Nathan Rubin, *Rock and Roll: Art and Anti-Art* (Dubuque, IA: Kendall and Hunt, 1993), 94.
23 Peter Gzowski, 'Dylan: An Explosion of Poetry,' *Maclean's*, 22 January 1966, 40.
24 Zal Yanovsky would eventually end up far from his psychedelic roots owning and operating a high-end eatery and specialty cuisine shop in Kingston, Ontario.
25 William Echard, *Neil Young and the Poetics of Energy* (Bloomington: Indiana University Press, 2005), 15.
26 Although this story has been told in many places, one of the more lively accounts is offered by Nicholas Jennings, *Before the Gold Rush* (Toronto: Viking, 1997).
27 'The Crying Voice,' *Time* (Canada), 15 February 1971, 10.
28 For this period in Young's life, see John Einarson and Richie Furay, *For What It's Worth: The Story of Buffalo Springfield* (Lanham, MD: Cooper Square Press, 2004).
29 For an overview of the song's origins, see David Downing, *A Dreamer of Pictures: Neil Young, the Man and His Music* (New York: Da Capo Press, 1995), 71.
30 For an in-depth look at the times, see Michael Walker, *Laurel Canyon: The Inside Story of Rock-and-Roll's Legendary Neighborhood* (London: Faber and Faber, 2006).
31 'Joni Mitchell,' *Rolling Stone*, 17 May 1969, insert, 8.
32 The track would be recorded by CSNY before Mitchell got around to doing so on her 1970 album *Ladies of the Canyon*.
33 Review of 'Clouds,' *Melody Maker*, 27 September 1969, 22.
34 'Joni Mitchell Hangs It Up,' *Rolling Stone*, 13 December 1969, 12.

35 Ibid., 48.
36 Craig Morrison, 'Folk Revival Roots Still Evident in 1990s Recordings of San Francisco Psychedelic Veterans,' *Journal of American Folklore* 114, no. 454 (Fall 2001): 478.
37 Jerome L. Rodnitzky, 'The Sixties between the Microgrooves: Using Folk and Protest Music to Understand American History, 1963–1973,' *Popular Music and Society* 23, no. 4 (Winter 1999): 109.
38 'Born to Be Wild' was written by ex-Sparrow member Dennis McCrohan, who also used the names Dennis Edmonton and Mars Bonfire.
39 Kay and Steppenwolf are discussed, for example, in Martin Melhuish, *Heart of Gold* (Toronto: CBC Enterprises, 1983), and *Oh What a Feeling* (Kingston, ON: Quarry Press, 1996), as well as Jennings, *Before the Gold Rush.*
40 Melhuish, *Heart of Gold,* states that Kay became a citizen (82), but Kay has explained to biographer John Einarson that 'we had been in Canada long enough to apply for Canadian citizenship, but put it off while my parents considered a move to the states. For me, it was a dream come true.' John Kay and John Einarson, *John Kay: Magic Carpet Ride* (Kingston, ON: Quarry Press, 1994), 59, 84–5. Einarson has confirmed to me that 'John Kay did not become a Canadian citizen. We embrace him as our own, he was a landed immigrant in Canada and got his start here, but he has been an American citizen since the early 60s.' Correspondence with Einarson, May 2007.
41 Yorke, *Axes, Chops and Hot Licks* (Edmonton: Hurtig, 1971), 128.
42 Kay and Einarson, *John Kay,* 145.
43 'John Kay,' *Canadian Musician,* July/August 1983, 62.
44 Melhuish, *Heart of Gold,* 82.
45 'Is the World (or Anybody) Ready for Leonard Cohen?' *Maclean's,* 1 October 1966, 34.
46 For a history of the hotel see Joe Ambrose, *Chelsea Hotel Manhattan* (London: Headpress, 2007).
47 David Boucher, *Dylan and Cohen: Poets of Rock and Roll* (New York: Continuum, 2004), 105, 107.
48 Ibid., 139.
49 Half-page advertisement in *Rolling Stone,* 17 May 1969, insert, 13.
50 Boucher, *Dylan and Cohen,* 137.
51 Richard Goldstein, 'Beautiful Creep,' *Village Voice,* reprinted in Michael Gnarowski, ed., *Leonard Cohen: The Artist and His Critics* (Toronto: McGraw-Hill Ryerson, 1976), 44.
52 Review quoted in Ira Nadel, *Various Positions: A Life of Leonard Cohen* (Toronto: Random House, 1996), 159.
53 Jennings, *Before the Gold Rush,* 62.

54 Sue Palmer, 'The Saga of How Blood, Sweat and Tears Were Born,' *Melody Maker*, 19 July 1969, 17.

55 Yorke, *Axes, Chops, and Hot Licks*, 115.

56 Robert Wright, '"Dream, Comfort, Memory, Despair": Canadian Popular Musicians and the Dilemma of Nationalism, 1968–1972,' *Journal of Canadian Studies* 22, no. 4 (Winter 1987–8): 27–43.

57 Gillian Mitchell, *North American Folk Music Revival*, 155, 166.

58 Bill Flanagan, *Written in My Soul: Rock's Great Songwriters Talk about Creating Their Music* (Chicago: Contemporary Books, 1986), 121.

59 Marcus, *Mystery Train*, 44, 51.

60 Levon Helm, with Stephen Davis, *This Wheel's on Fire: Levon Helm and the Story of the Band* (London: Plexus, 1994), 129–30, 136.

61 Gzowski, 'Dylan,' 22.

62 For an interesting look at this period in his life, see Helm and Davis, *This Wheel's on Fire*.

63 Marcus, *Mystery Train*, 5, 6, 43.

64 Mitchell, *North American Folk Music Revival*, 165.

65 Bart Testa and Jim Shedden, 'In the Great Midwestern Hardware Store: The Seventies Triumph in English-Canadian Rock Music,' in Joan Nicks and Jeannette Sloniowski, eds, *Slippery Pastimes: Reading the Popular in Canadian Culture* (Waterloo, ON: Wilfred Laurier University Press, 2002), 189.

66 Helm and Davis, *This Wheel's on Fire*, 188.

67 Ralph J. Gleason, 'The Band,' *Rolling Stone*, 16 October 1969, 44.

68 'Down to Old Dixie and Back,' *Time* (Canada), 12 January 1970, 44.

69 Ibid., 41.

70 'The Band's in "The Pink,"' *RPM*, 30 September 1968, 2.

5 'Turn On, Tune In, Drop Out'

1 *Time*, 1 July 1966, 50.

2 *Time*, 'A Pallet, a Jug and "Grass,"' 11 August 1967, 13.

3 Greg Potter, *Hand Me Down World: The Canadian Pop-Rock Paradox* (Toronto: Macmillan Canada, 1999), 105.

4 Correspondence with Bill Henderson, March 2008.

5 Ron Verzuh, *Underground Times: Canada's Flower-Child Revolutionaries* (Toronto: Deneau, 1989), 5.

6 Yorke, *Axes, Chops and Hot Licks* (Edmonton: Hurtig, 1971), 55.

7 Verzuh, *Underground Times*, 64. The Vancouver club scene is also discussed in Hubert Harrison, 'The Pop Scene,' *Saturday Night*, July 1967, 41.

8 Verzuh, *Underground Times*, 59.

9 Jack Batten, 'How the Town's Fighting the Dread Hippie Menace,' *Maclean's*, August 1967, 52.

10 Ibid., 50.

11 Correspondence with Bill Henderson, March 2008.

12 Correspondence with Jeffrey Ridley, January 2008.

13 Ibid.

14 'The Ups and Downs of a Great Canadian Peace Festival,' *Maclean's*, July 1970, 48.

15 Although the Toronto Peace Festival did not come about, the name is now often used to refer to the Toronto Rock and Roll Revival.

16 Nicholas Jennings, *Before the Gold Rush* (Toronto: Viking, 1997), 163.

17 'O'Keefe Centre Presents – An Explosion,' *RPM*, 2 October 1967, 1.

18 Jennings, *Before the Gold Rush*, 2.

19 Nancy Elliott, 'There'll Be No More Passports to Bohemia,' *Maclean's*, 2 July 1966, 45; italics in original.

20 Jack Batten, 'Canada's Rock Scene: Going, Going ...,' *Maclean's*, February 1968, 32.

21 Jack Batten, 'How This Freaky Character Is Rocking Today's Pop Music,' *Saturday Night*, May 1968, 30.

22 Paul Williams, *The Crawdaddy Book: Writing (and Images) from the Magazine of Rock* (Milwaukee: Hal Leonard, 2002), 148.

23 Jack Batten, 'Canada's Rock Scene,' 42.

24 Ibid.

25 Jack Batten, 'How This Freaky Character,' 30.

26 Ibid.

27 *Time*, 'Holding Company,' 16 August 1968, 13.

28 David Butcher, 'Records,' *Rolling Stone*, 21 December 1968.

29 Jennings, *Before the Gold Rush*, 188.

30 Ritchie Yorke and Ben Fong-Torres, 'Hendrix Busted in Toronto,' *Rolling Stone*, 31 May 1969, 10.

31 Melinda McCracken, 'Street Singer,' *Maclean's*, March 1973, 84.

32 'Bikers Stomp at Canadian Festival,' *Rolling Stone*, 14 June 1969, 10.

33 'News from Music Capitals of the World,' *Billboard*, 25 December 1965, 33.

34 Cummings and Allan overlapped for about five months in early to mid-1966. John Einarson's books on Randy Bachman, the Guess Who, and the Winnipeg scene all offer accounts of these early years.

35 Young also reportedly played for them recordings by the Buffalo Springfield. Randy Bachman, quoted in 'Randy Bachman,' *Canadian Musician*, June 1979, 20.

36 Randy Bachman and John Einarson, *Takin' Care of Business* (Toronto: McArthur and Company, 2000), 123. The Guess Who was not alone in benefiting from early access to the sounds developing in England. According to David Eggleton in *Ready to Fly: The Story of New Zealand Rock Music,* Sounds Unlimited brought home the British take on psychedelia, particularly as offered by Hendrix and Cream, and had an edge over bands that had not yet heard the new sounds (38).

37 Bachman and Einarson, *Takin' Care of Business,* 131.

38 The show had its origins in a collection of other regional programs that will be talked about in chapter eight. The five cities, in order from Monday to Friday, were Halifax, Montreal, Toronto, Winnipeg, and Vancouver.

39 Bachman and Einarson, *Takin' Care of Business,* 132.

40 Kit Morgan, 'Canadian Coca-Cola Drive Centres on Pop Disk Groups,' *Billboard,* 7 August 1965, 1.

41 Ibid., 1, 22; 'A Wild Pair – Coca-Cola and Canadian Talent,' *RPM,* 27 January 1968, 8.

42 Michael O'Halloran, ed., *CBC Radio's Mountaintop Music: 25 Canadian Artists, Their Favourite Music and Books* (Calgary: Bayeux Arts, 2000), 121.

43 Ibid.

44 Ibid.

45 Ibid. Bachman and Einarson, *Takin' Care of Business,* 143.

46 Yorke, *Axes, Chops and Hot Licks,* 43.

47 Stan Lepka, 'Witness,' *Canadian Composer,* June 1969, 34.

48 Ibid., 32.

49 *Canadian Musician,* January/February 1981, 22–3.

50 Yorke, *Axes, Chops and Hot Licks,* 45.

51 Bachman and Einarson, *Takin' Care of Business,* 154.

52 Ibid., 152, 153. Further, in an interview with *Canadian Musician* in 1979, Randy Bachman told of how 'These Eyes' 'broke out in the States, Detroit to be exact. It came out in Canada earlier and had a very mild success. CHUM wouldn't go on it … We all chipped in our money and paid for an independent promotion man in Detroit … It caught on on various chains and became our first big hit. It was then that the song had a resurgence in Canada. It went top 5 and went gold 8 months later.' Bob Mackowycz, 'Randy Bachman,' *Canadian Musician,* May/June 1979, 20.

53 Yorke, *Axes, Chops and Hot Licks,* 28.

54 Nancy Edmons, 'Records,' *Rolling Stone,* 14 June 1969, 36.

55 Lester Bangs, 'Records,' *Rolling Stone,* 7 February 1970, 38.

56 John Einarson, *American Woman: The Story of The Guess Who* (Kingston, ON: Quarry Press, 1995), 45.

57 RCA advertisement, full page, with band sitting on doorway steps and small caption boxes for *Canned Wheat* and *Wheatfield Soul. Rolling Stone*, 13 December 1969, 19; italics in original.

58 Bachman and Einarson, *Takin' Care of Business*, 89-90.

59 See Ryan Edwardson, '"Of War Machines and Ghetto Scenes": English-Canadian Nationalism and The Guess Who's "American Woman,"' *American Review of Canadian Studies* 33, no. 3 (Autumn 2003): 339–56.

60 Einarson, *American Woman*, 95.

61 Robert Wright, '"Dream, Comfort, Memory, Despair": Canadian Popular Musicians and the Dilemma of Nationalism, 1968–1972,' *Journal of Canadian Studies* 22, no. 4 (Winter 1987–8): 34.

62 Juan Rodriguez, 'An Essay on Hype,' *Last Post*, April 1970, 43.

63 Simon Frith, 'Towards an Aesthetic of Popular Music,' in Richard Leppert and Susan McClary, eds, *Music and Society: The Politics of Composition, Performance and Reception* (Cambridge: Cambridge University Press, 1987), 140.

64 Ironically, it was Canadian-born Mike Myers who expressed the sentiment in his role as Austin Powers, and the film itself was produced by New Line Cinema, a division of Time Warner and one of the most powerful of American production companies.

65 Bachman and Einarson, *Takin' Care of Business*, 168.

66 Jack Batten, 'The Guess Who,' *Maclean's*, June 1971, 54, 55. It is worth noting that, two years after joining them on tour, Batten was set to publish a book on the Guess Who when the band threatened the publisher with so much litigation that the book was never published. Apparently, according to the affidavit, the Guess Who – and their lawyers – interpreted Batten's discussion of the 'bubble gum' characterizations of their music to be libellous. See Jack Batten, 'Confessions of a Retired Rock Critic,' *Saturday Night*, March 1973.

6 'Legislated Radio'

1 Ritchie Yorke, 'Can a Law Put Canada on the Hit Parade?' *RPM*, 9 September 1968, 6.

2 'Legislated Radio: Americanized Radio,' *RPM*, 22 June 1968, 3.

3 W.D. Whitaker, Canadian Radio and Television Commission, *Public Hearing*, 21 April 1970, 1316.

4 'Horizons Expanded for Our Musicians,' *RPM*, 9 January 1971, 14. The non-profit Canadian Talent Library, founded in 1952 by CFRB-Toronto and CJAD-Montreal, had 206 subscribing stations as of February 1971. 'McConnell Back into Studios for Third Set,' *RPM*, 13 February 1971, 2.

5 Jack Batten, 'One Man's Crusade to Canadianize Rock 'n' Roll' *Maclean's*, 8 August 1964, 46; italics in original.
6 Stan Klees, correspondence with author, July 2006.
7 Yorke, *Axes, Chops and Hot Licks* (Edmonton: Hurtig, 1971), 3.
8 Ibid., 4.
9 Born in Australia and with some experience in the British music industry, Yorke moved to Canada in July 1967. He soon picked up a job working as a junior promotion writer at CTV and, after lying to the *Toronto Telegram* about his relationship with Beatles manager Brian Epstein in order to secure a commission to write the latter's obituary, used the opportunity to establish himself as a music journalist and in turn become the *Global and Mail's* first full-time popular culture and music columnist. See Ritchie Yorke, 'After 19 Years, a Memoir,' *Canadian Composer*, July 1987, 18, 20.
10 See Kit Morgan, 'Canadian Indies Merge; BWO Own "Co-op" Label,' *Billboard*, 30 January 1965, 16, 19.
11 The first release was Dee and the Yeomen's 'Take the First Train Home' and 'Why, Why, Why,' produced by Stan Klees. See Kit Morgan, 'Canada,' *Billboard*, 25 September 1965, 32.
12 Kit Morgan, 'Canada Firms Look to Making Impact on National, Int'l Marts,' *Billboard*, 9 January 1965, 20.
13 Kit Morgan, 'Canada,' *Billboard*, 25 September 1965, 32. 'News from Music Capitals of the World,' *Billboard*, 25 December 1965, 33.
14 R.A. Chislett of the Compo Company, Ltd, quoted in Morgan, 'Canada Firms Look to Making Impact on National, Int'l Marts,' 20.
15 Ibid., 18.
16 Ibid.
17 Ibid., 20.
18 Stan Klees, 'Music Biz,' *RPM*, 7 October 1968, 3.
19 David Cobb, 'Pop Power,' *Toronto Telegram*, 29 July 1967, Showcase section, 5.
20 Stan Klees, 'Music Biz,' *RPM*, 6 April 1968, 2.
21 Stan Klees, correspondence with author, July 2006.
22 Ibid.
23 Stan Klees, 'Music Biz,' *RPM*, 22 June 1968, 10.
24 More specifically, in 1967 he sued reporter David Cobb, CHUM Limited, and CHUM's Robert McAdorey, over an article by Cobb in the Showcase section of the *Telegram* on 29 July 1967 in which McAdorey told Cobb that Klees was claiming to be blacklisted by CHUM. See 'Canadian Producer Launched Libel Action,' *RPM*, 2 December 1968, 7.
25 'Legislated Radio: A License to Make Money?' *RPM*, 20 April 1968, 3.
26 'Legislated Radio: Putting Broadcasters on the Same Competitive Basis,'

RPM, 27 April 1968, 3; 'Legislated Radio: Americanized Radio,' *RPM*, 22 June 1968, 3.

27 'Legislated Radio: A Study of Canadian Content,' *RPM*, 18 May 1968, 3. Ritchie Yorke has reported that the survey involved nine major cities. Yorke, 8.

28 'Legislated Radio: A Study of Canadian Content,' *RPM*, 18 May 1968, 3.

29 For an overview of the start of Canadian content regulations for television and other cultural sectors, see Ryan Edwardson, *Canadian Content: Culture and the Quest for Nationhood* (Toronto: University of Toronto Press, 2008).

30 'Legislated Radio: One Hundred Percent Canadian Content,' *RPM*, 11 May 1968, 3.

31 Klees, 'Music Biz,' *RPM*, 16 December 1968, 6.

32 'Legislated Radio: We Leave It to the Industry,' *RPM*, 6 July 1968, 3.

33 Yorke, 'Can a Law Put Canada on the Hit Parade?'

34 Maple Leaf System (statement of purpose), Kit Morgan, 'MLS,' *Canadian Composer*, March 1970, 29.

35 CHUM, 'The Maple Leaf System,' *Music Scene*, November-December 1969, 12.

36 Yorke, 9.

37 Morgan, 'MLS.'

38 Yorke, *Axes, Chops and Hot Licks*, 9.

39 See Edwardson, *Canadian Content: Culture and the Quest for Nationhood* (Toronto: University of Toronto Press, 2008), chap. 3, 'Institution to Industry: Mass Media and State Intervention, 1958–1966.'

40 Stan Klees, correspondence with author, July 2006.

41 'CCPAU Pressing CRTC,' *RPM*, 16 December 1968, 2.

42 CRTC, 'Proposed Amendments to the Radio (TV) Broadcasting Regulations,' 12 February 1970.

43 Ibid.

44 Don Hamilton, CAB Vice-President, Radio, Canadian Radio and Television Commission, *Public Hearing*, 16 April 1970, vol. 2, 551.

45 Ibid., 551–2. Six days after making representations in Ottawa at the CRTC hearings into Canadian content, the CAB reiterated this position in front of another federal body. See 'Brief to Be Presented to the House of Commons Committee on Broadcasting, Film and Assistance to the Arts on behalf of the Canadian Association of Broadcasters,' Standing Committee on Broadcasting, Film, and Assistance to the Arts, *Minutes of Proceedings and Evidence*, Appendix M, 22 April 1970.

46 Don Hamilton, Canadian Radio and Television Commission, *Public Hearing*, 16 April 1970, vol. 2, 553–5. The same position and recommendations were

repeated to the Standing Committee on Broadcasting, Film, and Assistance to the Arts, *Minutes of Proceedings and Evidence,* 22 April 1970.

47 John Funston, CKSL-London, Ontario, speaking on behalf of the CAB, Canadian Radio and Television Commission, *Public Hearing,* 16 April 1970, vol. 2, 604.

48 This was a minor change from the 1958 Broadcasting Act, which had phrased the obligation as 'predominantly Canadian in content and character.' Canada. Statutes of Canada. Broadcasting Act, 1958/1968.

49 Warren Davis, Canadian Radio and Television Commission, *Public Hearing,* 17 April 1970, 752.

50 Farley Mowat, ibid., 741.

51 Pierre Berton, ibid., 878.

52 Ritchie Yorke, ibid., 1162.

53 Ibid., 1157–8.

54 Ritchie Yorke, Canadian Radio and Television Commission, *Public Hearing,* 20 April 1970, 1159–60.

55 Ibid., 1159–60.

56 Ibid., 1165.

57 Ibid., 1160.

58 Commissioner (Mr Hylton), ibid., 21 April 1970, 1365.

59 Skip Prokop, ibid., 1346.

60 Ibid., 1349–50.

61 Ibid., 1363.

62 Allan Meyer, speaking on behalf of the Canadian Music Publishers Association, Canadian Radio and Television Commission, *Public Hearing,* 22 April 1970, 1539.

63 Ibid., 1535.

64 T. St Clair Low, Canadian Music Publishers Association, ibid., 1541.

65 Stan McDowell, '"I Too Like Beer-Drinkers' TV" Juneau Tells Jeering MPs,' *Toronto Daily Star,* 6 May 1970, 1.

66 MP Stafford, Canada, Standing Committee on Broadcasting, Film, and Assistance to the Arts, *Minutes,* 5 May 1970, 22: 26.

67 Pierre Juneau, ibid., 22: 25. The song had charted as no. 1 in Canada two weeks earlier, on 25 April 1970.

68 Ibid., 23: 45.

69 CRTC, 20 May 1970, Decision 70-99, instituted in SOR/70-256.

70 'Country 30 per cent; Easy Listening 10 per cent; Middle of the Road 15 per cent; and Contemporary 20 per cent.' CRTC, *FM Radio in Canada: A Policy to Ensure a Varied and Comprehensive Radio Service* (Ottawa: CRTC, 1975). In 1991, the FM band having become predominantly uniform, the level was

raised to the standard 30 per cent for mainstream stations. See Larry Leblanc, 'New Regs Redraw Canadian FM Map,' *Billboard*, 21 September 1991.

71 Roy Shuker and Michael Pickering, 'Kiwi Rock: Popular Music and Cultural Identity in New Zealand,' *Popular Music* 13, no. 3 (1994): 262.

72 Ibid., 270.

73 Ibid.

74 Ibid., 277.

75 Rocky Douché, 'The NZ Music Industry: A Scoping Review of the Contemporary Music Industry for Industry New Zealand' (R. Douché Consulting, 31 August 2001), 30. Shuker and Pickering, 'Kiwi Rock,' also report that the level was only about 5 per cent (269).

76 This moment of economic retaliation for cultural policy echoes that of the U.S. State Department's warning to the Canadian government that the Auto Pact would not be ratified if the Liberals passed the Canadian Paperback and Periodical Distributors Act in 1964. The federal government acquiesced to the American threat and exempted *Time* and *Reader's Digest* from the legislation which otherwise would have limited tax deductions for advertising in periodicals to those that were domestically owned. See Edwardson, *Canadian Content*, chap. 3: 'From Institution to Industry: Mass Media and State Intervention, 1958–1966.'

77 Skip Prokop, Canadian Radio and Television Commission, *Public Hearing*, 21 April 1970, 1351.

78 Chad Allan, 'The Pop Scene in Winnipeg,' *Music Scene*, July-August 1968, 6.

79 Jack Batten, 'Canada's Rock Scene: Going, Going ...,' *Maclean's*, February 1968, 34.

80 'Legislated Radio: Some Progressive Moves,' *RPM*, 29 June 1968, 3.

81 For example, the government created an Arts and Culture Policy (1968) in order to directly fund pro-unity arts activities; attempted to purge separatism from Radio-Canada and coerce the Canada Council for the Arts to withhold funding for artists who identified themselves as politically separatist; built upon the Canadian Film Development Corporation (which, as of 1968, began investing in feature film production) by establishing a voluntary quota agreement with Famous Players and Odeon Theatres and increased the capital cost allowance to encourage private sector investment in film production; provided block grants to book publishers and funded the translation of books between English and French; altered immigration laws to ensure opportunities for Canadian academics; and funded Canadian studies programs at home and abroad in order to draw attention to domestic issues and, in turn, reify a federal Canada. See Edwardson, *Canadian Content*, chap. 7, 'Saving Canada: Pierre Trudeau and the Mobilization of Culture.'

7 'Oh What a Feeling'

1 'The Canadian Sound,' *Time*, 1 February 1971, 9.
2 Bruno Dostie, 'Pop Music from a Quebec Perspective,' *Canadian Composer*, October 1977, 30.
3 Ritchie Yorke, *Axes, Chops and Hot Licks: The Canadian Rock Music Scene* (Edmonton: Hurtig, 1971), 153.
4 Nicholas Jennings, *Before the Gold Rush* (Toronto: Viking, 1997), 147.
5 Mike Quigley, 'Edward Bear Interview,' *Georgia Straight*, 5 August 1970.
6 Fergus Hambleton, 'The Bear,' *Canadian Composer*, May 1970, 7.
7 Murray McLauchlan, *Getting Out of Here Alive: The Ballad of Murray McLauchlan* (Toronto: Viking, 1998), 153.
8 Yorke, *Axes, Chops and Hot Licks*, 94.
9 Robert Wright, '"Dream, Comfort, Memory, Despair": Canadian Popular Musicians and the Dilemma of Nationalism, 1968–1972,' *Journal of Canadian Studies* 22, no. 4 (Winter 1987–8): 30.
10 Cockburn's earlier years are discussed in Jack Batten, 'From Bruce Cockburn to Youth – A Very Private Message,' *Maclean's*, January 1971. See also Jennings, *Before the Gold Rush*, 132.
11 Yorke, *Axes, Chops and Hot Licks*, 56.
12 Sue Carter Flinn, 'Life and Times,' *The Coast*, 12 October 2006, 25.
13 Ashley Collie, 'Bruce Cockburn,' *Canadian Musician*, September/October 1983, 43.
14 Yorke, *Axes, Chops and Hot Licks*, 102. Robert A. Wright has discussed parts of this in 'Dream, Comfort, Memory, Despair.'
15 Richard Flohil, 'From Crowbar to Sled Dog Races: Kelly Jay Moves On,' *Canadian Composer*, September 1988, 28.
16 'Daffodil's Crowbar Reaches for Top,' *RPM*, 14 August 1971, 3. Apparently a Crowbar necklace was also presented and a marijuana joint was slipped into the prime minister's pocket.
17 Terry David Mulligan, 'Canadian Productions Hotting Up in Van,' *RPM*, 13 March 1971, 3.
18 Roy MacGregor, 'Any More Messages Maestro?' *Maclean's*, February 1973, 86.
19 Rebecca Manson, 'Stringband's Decade of Canadian Folk Music,' *Canadian Composer*, January 1982, 34.
20 Alden Nowlan, 'What's More Canadian than Stompin' Tom?' *Maclean's*, August 1972, 44.
21 Ibid., 31.
22 Ibid., 44. Boot Records also involved business partners Jury Krytiuk and Mark Altman.

23 John Morris, 'Stevedore Steve: A Country Singer Talks about His Music,' *Canadian Composer*, February 1975, 30.

24 Ritchie Yorke, 'Monitor Your Favourite Station,' *RPM*, 23 January 1971, 17.

25 'The Canadian Sound,' *Time*, 1 February 1971, 9.

26 Ibid.

27 'Ian Tyson Raps CRTC,' unidentified newspaper, Library and Archives Canada, MG30, D304, vol. 2, file 'Canadian Content – correspondence, copies of newspaper clippings, 1952–1974.'

28 It is worth noting that Anne Murray did not worry about overexposure: 'I don't think it's possible to be over-played on radio … unless, of course, you're the only artist being played day and night.' Quoted in Yorke, *Axes, Chops and Hot Licks*, 102.

29 Quoted in Martin Melhuish, 'The 30% Solution: Still Music to a Lot of Ears,' *Maclean's*, 23 February 1976, 53.

30 'At Home on the Range: With Ian Tyson, the Cowboy and the Songwriter Are One and the Same,' *Western Report*, 4 April 1994, 26.

31 Melhuish, 'The 30% Solution,' 53.

32 Ibid.

33 Robert Markle, 'Early Morning Afterthoughts,' *Maclean's*, December 1971, 28; italics in original.

34 Yorke, *Axes, Chops and Hot Licks*, 82.

35 Yorke, 'There's No Truth to the Rumour …,' *RPM*, 13 February 1971, 12.

36 'Phoney Cancon Could Forfeit a License,' *RPM*, 17 April 1971, 14.

37 'More Cancon Guide,' *RPM*, 10 April 1971, 4. '*RPM* Bows Guide to Legit Cancon Discs,' *RPM*, 3 April 1971, 2.

38 'MCA "Care Package" to Needy Broadcasters,' *RPM*, 30 January 1971, 13.

39 'Capitol Sends Help to Canadian AM Stations,' *RPM*, 30 January 1971, 2.

40 Kit Morgan, 'MLS,' *Canadian Composer*, March 1970, 31.

41 Ritchie Yorke, 'Astra – A Prime Factor in the Record Industry?' *RPM*, 15 May 1971, 14.

42 Ibid., 22.

43 Yorke, *Axes, Chops and Hot Licks*, 215.

44 'Take Hiss Out of Cancon Discs,' letter to the editor, *RPM*, 24 April 1971, 19–20.

45 Wright, 'Dream, Comfort, Memory, Despair,' 40. Music is addressed in national terms in Myrna Kostash, 'The Pure, Uncluttered Spaces of Bruce Cockburn,' *Saturday Night*, June 1972.

46 The dates for Anne Murray, Leonard Cohen, and Stompin' Tom Connors were, respectively, May, June, and August of 1972.

47 Jon Ruddy, 'How to Become an American without Really Trying,' *Maclean's*, November 1969, 61.
48 Such a position is similar to Margaret Atwood's proclamation made only a few years later, in *Survival*, that what was important was 'Canadian literature, as *Canadian* literature – not just literature that happened to be written in Canada.' Margaret Atwood, *Survival* (Toronto: Anansi, 1972), 13; italics in original.
49 Jack Batten, 'Can. Pop,' *Chatelaine*, September 1969, 29.
50 Ibid., 27. Gillian Mitchell has previously quoted part of this line in discussing Batten's attempts to popularize the idea of a 'Canadian music.' *The North American Folk Music Revival* (Burlington, VT: Ashgate, 2007), 149.
51 Mitchell, *North American Folk Music Revival*, 155.
52 The group was originally named McKenna Mendelson Mainline.
53 McKenna, quoted in Jennings, *Before the Gold Rush*, 227.
54 In the words of Ritchie Yorke, '*Maclean's*, our national kaleidoscope of all things Canadian and long a prime offender, took a leap forward in 1971 with the appointment of a regular music columnist, John Macfarlane, who is at least partly sympathetic to what is happening in contemporary Canadian music.' *Axes, Chops and Hot Licks*, 203. John Macfarlane has in turn noted that Ritchie Yorke might not be the greatest of rock journalists out there, but that he was 'undeniably the most celebrated Canadian writer in the field.' Yorke's success was, in Macfarlane's opinion, due in part to never being 'one to worry about hyperbole.' John Macfarlane, 'Dear Ritchie, Oh How I Hate to Write,' *Maclean's*, December 1971, 94.
55 Ibid.
56 Simon Frith, 'Music and Identity,' in Simon Hall and Paul du Gay, eds, *Questions of Cultural Identity* (London: Sage, 1996), 110.
57 Jon Ruddy, 'Another Kind of Explosion in Quebec: Talent,' *Maclean's*, June 1969, 41.
58 Anthony D. Smith, *Nations and Nationalism in a Global Era* (Cambridge: Polity Press, 1995), 65.
59 Anthony D. Smith, *The Ethnic Origins of Nations* (New York: B. Blackwell, 1986), 15, 22–9.
60 Richard Flohil, 'Interview! Gilles Vigneault,' *Canadian Composer*, June 1974, 10, 14.
61 Claude Gagnon, 'Who Is Robert Charlebois?' *Canadian Composer*, May 1969, 34–6.
62 'People are beginning to recognize me for what I am, an internationalist,' Charlebois told Louis-Bernard Robitaille, 'Charlebois Is Synonymous with Quebec,' *Canadian Composer*, December 1973, 24.

63 Reprinted in 'Super Frog,' *Time*, 18 December 1972, 6d.
64 Jane Champagne, 'Félix Leclerc: Returning Home to Canada,' *Canadian Composer*, December 1973, 22.
65 Pierre Vincent, 'Tex Lecor – "Last of the Real Quebeckers" – Finds Success at Last,' *Canadian Composer*, April 1972, 8.
66 René Lévesque, *An Option for Quebec* (Toronto: McClelland and Stewart, 1968), 8, 14, 27; italics in original.
67 Nathalie Petrowski, 'Interview: Lucien Francoeur,' *Canadian Composer*, March 1979, 18.
68 Wayne Grimsby, 'The Morning After the Night Before,' *Maclean's*, 7 August 1978, 56.
69 Ibid.
70 Ibid., 56.
71 Wayne Grimsby, 'Hewers of Funk, Drawers of Glamor,' *Maclean's*, 19 April 1982, 63–4.
72 Robitaille, 'Charlebois Is Synonymous with Quebec,' 26. Anthony Wilson-Smith, 'Upbeat Sounds for Francophone Blues,' *Maclean's*, 15 September 1986, 61.
73 Wilson-Smith, 'Upbeat Sounds,' 61.
74 Bruno Dostie, 'Pop Music from a Quebec Perspective,' 32.
75 Petrowski, 'Interview: Lucien Francoeur,' 18.
76 Ibid., 14.
77 Nathalie Petrowski, *Le Devoir*, quoted in Anthony Wilson-Smith, 'Upbeat Sounds,' 61. As noted by Wayne Grimsby ('Hewers of Funk') in 1982, 'the chansonnier tradition that nourished Quebec's musical heroes of the '60s … has given way to the funky vitality of American-style pop music' (63).
78 Nathalie Petrowski, '"American" Rock from Quebec,' *Canadian Composer*, June 1981, 12.
79 James Quig, 'Mommas' Boy,' *Maclean's*, 19 September 1977, 48.
80 Larry LeBlanc, 'Carmen Reigns at 15th Félix Awards,' *Billboard*, 30 October 1993, 54.
81 See David Young, 'Céline Dion, the ADISQ Controversy, and the Anglophone Press in Canada,' *Canadian Journal of Communication* 24 (1999): 515–37.
82 Barry Came, 'Roch 'n' Roll,' *Maclean's*, 1 June 1992, 49.
83 Robert Charlebois, quoted in Marc Desjardins, 'Interview! Robert Charlebois,' *Canadian Composer*, April 1982, 5.
84 Geoff Pevere and Grieg Dymond, *Mondo Canuck: A Canadian Pop Culture Odyssey* (Scarborough, ON: Prentice-Hall, 1996), 71.
85 Walt Grealis, 'Production Suspended,' *RPM*, 20 February 1971, 4.

8 'The Nation's Music Nation'

1 'Pop Music's New Wave Finally Washes over the Juno Awards,' *Canadian Composer*, March 1981, 25.

2 Tom Connors, *Stompin' Tom and the Connors Tone* (Toronto: Viking, 2000), 367–8.

3 Paul Rutherford, *When Television Was Young: Primetime Canada 1952–1967* (Toronto: University of Toronto Press, 1990), 215.

4 Paul Fryer, '"Everybody's on Top of the Pops": Popular Music on British Television, 1960–1985, *Popular Music and Society* 21, no. 3 (Fall 1997): 158.

5 Ibid, 156.

6 Rutherford, *When Television Was Young*, 215.

7 Ibid.

8 Correspondence with Jeffrey Ridley, January 2008.

9 Michael O'Halloran, ed., *CBC Radios Mountaintop Music: 25 Canadian Artists, Their Favourite Music and Books* (Calgary: Bayeux Arts, 2000), 121.

10 '"Let's Go" – C.B.C. Montreal,' *RPM*, 15 June 1968, 13.

11 Randy Bachman and John Einarson, *Takin' Care of Business* (Toronto: McArthur and Company, 2000), 131.

12 O'Halloran, ed., *CBC Radios Mountaintop Music*, 121.

13 Ibid., 121. Several of these songs are available on the CD compilation of the Guess Who, *Let's Go*, released by Maximum Canada, 2005.

14 Rutherford, *When Television Was Young*, 216.

15 *RPM*, 13 July 1968, 2.

16 'Strabo on Television: Let's Quit Subsidizing Music Shows,' *Maclean's*, 15 May 1965, 64.

17 *Billboard*, 'CBS [sic] Has Something for Everyone in Its Fare,' 13 November 1965, 20.

18 Martin Melhuish, 'The 30% Solution: Still Music to a Lot of Ears,' *Maclean's*, 23 February 1976, 53. The CAPAC merged in 1990 with the Performing Rights Organization of Canada to form the Society of Composers, Authors and Music Publishers of Canada.

19 Taking into consideration French-language recording, most of which was done in Quebec, Toronto's hold on the national market was around 60 per cent (and included some French-language recording). Richard Flohil, 'Interview! Terry Brown,' *Canadian Composer*, February 1974, 12.

20 *Canadian Musician*, March/April 1979, 7. Its first issue included interviews with Burton Cummings and Murray McLauchlan, articles on shopping for a synthesizer and recording studio design, and columns dedicated to playing and recording techniques.

21 Philip Auslander, 'Seeing Is Believing: Live Performance and the Discourse of Authenticity in Rock Culture,' *Literature and Psychology* 44, no. 4 (1998): 6.

22 Sean Larose, *Walter Grealis: The Man behind the Music* (Whitby, ON: Master Print, 2004), 22.

23 'Kim, Reno, Lightfoot among Award Winners,' *Globe and Mail*, 23 February 1970, 13.

24 This apparently entailed over sixty loaves of bread. Larose, *Walter Grealis*, 24.

25 'The Canadian Sound,' *Time* (Canada), 27 March 1972, 10.

26 Richard Flohil, 'RPM's Big Weekend: Top 40 Radio Meets the Bigtime Record Business,' *Canadian Composer*, April 1972, 26.

27 Ibid.

28 David Young explains that the acts receiving awards and those performing on the telecast both experience a boost in sales. 'For instance, in the week after Chantal Kreviazuk performed on the 2000 Juno Awards and won in two major categories, the sales of her nominated album went up by 106 per cent. There were also significant sales jumps for others who performed that year, including Amanda Marshall and Diana Krall. A sales boost can emerge from winning Junos or even being nominated for awards, but performances on the ceremony have the biggest impact on album purchases.' David Young, 'Ethno-Racial Minorities and the Juno Awards,' *Canadian Journal of Sociology* 31, no. 2 (Spring 2006): 194.

29 David Young, 'The CBC and the Juno Awards,' *Canadian Journal of Communication* 30, no. 3 (2005): 347. Further, Young has identified the combination of the Canadian content regulation, CBC, and federal funding as evidence that the Juno Awards facilitate the 'promotional state.' See Young, 'The Promotional State and Canada's Juno Awards,' *Popular Music* 23, no. 3 (2004): 271–89. The struggle over the Junos is also discussed in Larose, *Walter Grealis*.

30 Richard Flohil, 'Junos Promote Canadian Music,' *Canadian Composer*, November 1987, 24–6.

31 See 'The 1977 Juno Awards,' *Canadian Composer*, April 1977, 20.

32 Young, 'Ethno-Racial Minorities and the Juno Awards,' 195.

33 Ibid., 191.

34 Interestingly, little attention has been paid to national identity in discussions about Live Aid. According to Neal Ullestad discussions of the event have largely become polarized over whether it was one of rebellion or co-optation. 'One view holds that Live Aid was a renewal of the spirit of rock 'n' roll, a revitalisation of the audience, musicians and industry in a socially relevant way. The other preponderant view has it that Live Aid was just another example of pop rock's cooptation, a rip-off of the hard work that put together such other musical/political expressions as the British Coal

Miners Benefits, and at best well-intentioned charity and philanthropy without political significance other than that individual concern and sharing
was kept within corporate and government channels.' Ullestad, 'Rock and
Rebellion: Subversive Effects of Live Aid and "Sin City,"' *Popular Music* 6, no.
1 (January 1987): 68.

35 Robert Wright, '"Dream, Comfort, Memory, Despair": Canadian Popular
Musicians and the Dilemma of Nationalism, 1968–1972,' *Journal of Canadian
Studies* 22, no. 4 (Winter 1987–8): 40.

36 Mark J. Prendergast, *Irish Rock: Roots, Personalities, Directions* (Dublin: The
O'Brien Press, 1987), 273.

37 As David Rowe has pointed out, 'if it could raise 50 million for Ethiopian
famine through the agency of pop stars and their record companies, how
much is routinely and daily accumulated by them when it is business as
usual?' Rowe, *Popular Cultures: Rock Music, Sport and the Politics of Pleasure*
(London: Sage, 1995), 55. Bob Geldof, *Is That It?* (Markham, ON: Penguin,
1986), 288.

38 Jane O'Hara, 'The Master of Rock 'n' Roll Romance,' *Maclean's*, 5 August
1985, 55.

39 Richard Flohil, editorial, *Canadian Composer*, February 1981, 2.

40 Statistics listed in Line Grenier, 'The Aftermath of a Crisis: Quebec Music
Industries in the 1980s,' *Popular Music* 12, no. 3 (1993): 210.

41 See Marc Desjardins, 'The Studio Scene in Quebec,' *Canadian Composer*,
December 1982.

42 Initial members of FACTOR included CHUM Ltd, Moffat Communications
Ltd, Rogers Radio Broadcasting Ltd, the Canadian Independent Record
Production Association, and the Canadian Music Publishers Association.

43 'FACTOR Releases Its First Financial Statement on Record Production Aid,'
Canadian Composer, March 1983, 30, 32.

44 Canada, *Report of the Task Force on Broadcasting Policy* (Ottawa: Minister of
Supply and Services, 1986), 409.

45 The program now operates under the Department of Canadian Heritage.

46 On basic cable as of September 1989.

47 For discussions of the early years of MTV, see Alan Cross, *Over the Edge: The
Revolution and Evolution of New Rock* (Toronto: Prentice-Hall, 1997); Lawrence Grossberg, '"You [Still] Have to Fight for Your Right to Party": Music
Television as Billboards of Post-Modern Difference,' *Popular Music* 7, no. 3
(1988): 315–32; and Will Straw, 'Music Video in Its Contexts: Popular Music
and Post-Modernism in the 1980s,' *Popular Music* 7, no. 3 (1988): 247–66.

48 Jack Banks, 'Video in the Machine: The Incorporation of Music Video into
the Recording Industry,' *Popular Music* 16, no. 3 (1998): 293.

49 Ira Wagman, 'Rock the Nation: MuchMusic, Cultural Policy, and English Canadian Music Video Programming, 1979–1984,' *Canadian Journal of Communication* 26, no. 4 (2001): 49.

50 This fund was given shape as the Video Foundation to Assist Canadian Talent (or Videofact). Jeff Bateman, 'A Progress Report,' *Music Scene*, March-April 1985, 9. In 1998 the CRTC noted that MuchMusic 'is in a profitable situation and considers that it is realistic to expect the licensee to contribute a greater proportion of its gross revenues to the production of Canadian music videos,' with the amount increasing to the larger amount of 5 per cent or $300,000. CRTC, quoted in Kirk LaPoint, 'MuchMusic Swallows CRTC Rules,' *Billboard*, 12 November 1988, 68.

51 Nick Krewen and Larry LeBlanc, 'Budgets Challenge Canada's Directors,' *Billboard*, 21 March 1992, 52.

52 Michael Barclay, Ian A.D. Jack, and Jason Schneider, *Have Not Been the Same: The CanRock Renaissance, 1985–95* (Toronto: ECW Press, 2001), 29–30.

53 Anthony Wilson-Smith, 'Upbeat Sounds for Francophone Blues,' *Maclean's*, 15 September 1986, 61.

54 Ibid., 62. This amount was increased to 5 per cent in 1988. LaPoint, 'MuchMusic Swallows CRTC Rules,' 68.

55 The Matthew Good Band, for example, with hits including 'Everything Is Automatic,' 'Hello Time Bomb,' and 'Strange Days,' stood out in the mind of Shawn Marino, international marketing manager at Universal Music Canada, as an example of the video network's promotional power. 'MuchMusic absolutely had a lot to do with the success of the Matthew Good Band. MuchMusic put all of the band's videos in heavy rotation and supported the act right out of the box when a lot of people didn't know who they were.' Quoted in Carla Hay, 'Music Television: A Global Status Report: MuchMusic and Its Sisters Dominate Canada,' *Billboard*, 17 February 2001, 1.

56 Will Straw, 'Sound Recording,' in Michael Dorland, ed., *The Cultural Industries in Canada* (Toronto: Lorimer, 1996), 109. Similarly, Bart Testa and Jim Shedden have argued that MuchMusic provided 'Canadian rock with something it always lacked, an equivalent to a rock press. Featuring interviews with musicians, rock-related news, regularly centred on local scenes across Canada, and "lifestyle" segments, MuchMusic resembles a rock-magazine format, just what Canadian rock fans never had before, though these were familiar apparatuses in Great Britain and the U.S. thirty years ago. It is the rock press (and not radio) that is the main vehicle of celebrity … MuchMusic spreads this powerful promotional apparatus over the entire country, which radio, always local, never did.' Bart Testa and Jim Shedden, 'In the Great Midwestern Hardware Store: The Seventies Triumph in English-

Canadian Rock Music,' in Joan Nicks and Jeannette Sloniowski, eds, *Slippery Pastimes: Reading the Popular in Canadian Culture* (Waterloo, ON: Wilfred Laurier University Press, 2002), 211.

57 Barclay, Jack, and Schneider, *Have Not Been the Same*, 56.

58 Larry LeBlanc, '"Intimate & Interactive" boosts acts,' *Billboard*, 5 July 1997, 42.

59 John Wright, Millard Gregory, and Sarah Riegel, 'Here's Where We Get Canadian: English-Canadian Nationalism and Popular Culture,' *American Review of Canadian Studies* 32, no. 1 (Spring 2002): 23.

60 Kip Pegley, *Coming to You Wherever You Are: MuchMusic, MTV, and Youth Identities* (Middletown, CT: Wesleyan University Press, 2008), 35.

61 Shanda Deziel, 'Rock 'n' Roll,' *Maclean's*, 17 June 2002, 10.

62 Ibid.

63 Kevin Young, 'The World According to Good,' *Canadian Musician*, November/December 2005, 34.

64 Paul Cantin, 'It's All Too "Much,"' *Billboard*, 10 January 1998, 40.

65 Peter G. Christenson and Donald F. Roberts, *It's Not Only Rock and Roll: Popular Music in the Lives of Adolescents* (Cresskill, NJ: Hampton Press, 1998), 64.

66 Pegley, *Coming to You*, 17.

67 Canada NewsWire, 'The Celebrity Obsessed Get Their Fill with MuchMusic's Fall Line-Up,' 9 August 2007, 1. Canada NewsWire, 'MuchMoreMusic's Fall Programming Puts Pop Culture Lovers to the Test,' 10 August 2007, 1.

68 There was even a Much arabyeah in the Middle East, although it collapsed within a few months. Habib Battah, 'Crowded House,' *Variety*, 1 October 2007, B1.

69 Pegley, *Coming to You*, 108.

70 The failure of MuchUSA, and its replacement, Fuse, is discussed by Jack Banks, 'Keeping "Abreast" of MTV and Viacom: The Growing Power of a Media Conglomerate,' in Janet Wasko, ed., *A Companion to Television* (Malden, MA: Blackwell, 2005), 256–69.

71 Larry LeBlanc, 'CTV Wants, and Gets, Its MTV,' *Billboard*, 22 October 2005, 20.

72 Anonymous, 'MTV2 to Launch in Canada on Aug. 1 with New Original Music Video Show,' *Canadian Press*, 16 July 2008.

73 Angela Pacienza, 'MTV Canada Blasts Off with VIP Bash Featuring Kanye West, Sam Roberts,' Canadian Press NewsWire, 19 April 2006.

74 Michael Nolan, *CTV: The Network That Means Business* (Edmonton: University of Alberta Press, 2001), 129.

75 Canada NewsWire, 'MuchMusic and MTV Bring the "MTV Europe Music

Awards 2007" to Canadians Thursday, Nov. 1,' 18 October 2007, 1. Canada
NewsWire, 'MuchMusic Airs MTV New Year's Eve Masquerade on December
31,' 19 December 2007, 1.

76 Graciela Martinez-Zalce, 'Popular Music: Exchanges between Mexico and
Canada,' in Joy Cohnstaedt and Yves Frenette, eds, *Canadian Issues: Canadian Cultures and Globalization, Association for Canadian Studies* 19 (1997):
65–6. MTV's movement into non-American markets has also been discussed
in Gregory Lee, 'The "East Is Red" Goes Pop: Commodification, Hybridity
and Nationalism in Chinese Popular Song and Its Televisual Performance,'
Popular Music 14, no. 1 (1995): 98; and Keith Roe and Gust de Meyer, 'One
Planet – One Music? MTV and Globalization,' in Andreas Gebesmair and
Alfred Smudits, eds, *Global Repertoires: Popular Music within and beyond the
Transnational Music Industry* (Aldershot, UK: Ashgate, 2001), 33–44.

77 Marise Strauss, 'MTV, MuchMusic Online Streaming Explosion,' *Playback:
Canada's Broadcast and Production Journal*, 21 January 2008, 6.

78 Lee-Anne Goodman, 'B.C. Rockers Hedley the Big Winner at MMVAs as
Event Marred by Major Downpours,' *Canadian Press*, 16 June 2008.

79 Bryan Borzykowski, 'Classic Hits Have Been Replaced by an Indie Vibe as
the Soundtrack of Choice for TV Ads,' *Marketing*, 15 October 2007, 26.

80 Ibid.

81 Notably, the International Album of the Year award was introduced in 1975,
at that time called the Best Selling International Album, the first year the
event was televised; Pamela Anderson did not catch onto the fact that the
Junos honoured non-Canadians and came under fire during a press conference for the event when she identified Coldplay and Black Eyed Peas as
examples of the outstanding groups to recently come out of Canada.

82 Canada NewsWire, '1.7 Million Watch 2006 Juno Awards on CTV,' 3 April
2006.

83 Canada NewsWire, 'The 2006 Juno Awards to Reach Quarter Billion Audience on Five Continents,' 30 March 2006.

84 Karen Bliss, 'Coldplay, Peas Storm Canada,' *Rolling Stone*, 3 April 2006.

9 'Takin' Care of Business'

1 Ritchie Yorke, *Axes, Chops and Hot Licks: The Canadian Rock Music Scene*
(Edmonton: Hurtig, 1971), 56.

2 Editorial board, 'Express Delivery,' *Rock Express* 102 (May 1986): 7.

3 Brian D. Johnson, 'Reinventing Alanis Morissette,' *Maclean's*, 8 March 1999,
51. Johnson also reports that Morissette claims to have never listened to
Mitchell until after *Jagged Little Pill* had drawn comparisons.

4 Jim Smith, 'Finkelstein … A Patron of the Arts,' *RPM*, 3 April 1971, 23.
5 Ibid., 6.
6 Ibid.; John Macfarlane, 'Dear Ritchie, Oh How I Hate to Write,' *Maclean's*, December 1971, 94.
7 Nicholas Jennings, *Fifty Years of Music: The Story of EMI Music Canada* (Toronto: Macmillan Canada, 2000), 81. See also 'Love Productions's First Birthday,' *RPM*, 1 May 1971, 16.
8 Release as reprinted in 'CIRPA Announces Aims and Objectives,' *RPM*, 6 February 1971, 2. CIRPA was not actually incorporated as a non-profit organization until July 1975. That the association had to be formed in the first place, Walt Grealis argued, 'was a signal that something was drastically wrong in the industry.' Walt Grealis, 'Production Suspended,' *RPM*, 20 February 1971, 4.
9 Roger Wallin and Krister Malm, *Big Sounds from Small Peoples: The Music Industry in Small Countries* (New York: Pendragon Press, 1984), 110.
10 Maple Music Junket proposal, reprinted in Ritchie Yorke, 'Everyone Has a Stake in the Maple Music Junket,' *RPM*, 7 August 1971, 12.
11 Ibid.
12 Barbara Beckett, 'At Osaka,' *Canadian Composer*, May 1970, 11.
13 Pierre Trudeau in a letter to Maple Music Junket participants, quoted in Canadian Radio and Television Commission, *Annual Report*, 1972, 18.
14 The full list of board members, including honourary members: Arnold Gosewich (Capitol), Fred Wilmot (Columbia), Evert Garretsen (Polydor), Jean-Paul Rickner (Trans-Canada), Lee Farley (Quality), Bert Betts (CRMA), Ritchie Yorke, Jan Matejcek (CAPAC), Harold Moon (BMI), Jack Richardson (CIRPA), and Louis Applebaum (OCA). Wilder Penfield, 'Maple Music Junket,' *Canadian Composer*, September 1972, 18.
15 Ibid., 22.
16 Doug Fischer, 'The Little Music Magazine That Could,' *Ottawa Citizen*, 14 June 2003, J1.
17 Penfield, 'Maple Music Junket,' 22.
18 Richard Flohil, 'Interview! Ritchie Yorke,' *Canadian Composer*, October 1976, 28.
19 Yorke, *Axes, Chops and Hot Licks*, 162–3.
20 Flohil, 'Interview! Ritchie Yorke,' 28.
21 Mike Quigley, 'Edward Bear Interview,' *Georgia Straight*, 5 August 1970.
22 Jennings, *Fifty Years of Music*, 54.
23 *Sounds Canadian* includes tracks by Pierre Lalonde, Anne Murray, Brian Browne, Donna Ramsay, Gary Buck, Edward Bear, Bobby Curtola, Claude Valade, and Gene MacLellan.

24 Quigley, 'Edward Bear Interview.'
25 Ibid.
26 Nicholas Jennings, 'Rock 'n' Roll Royalty,' *Maclean's*, 30 September 1991, 67.
27 Richard Flohil, 'Living the Rock and Roll Lifestyle,' *Canadian Composer*, January 1975, 8.
28 Durrell Bowman, 'Permanent Change: Rush, Musicians' Rock, and the Progressive Post-Counterculture' (doctoral thesis, University of California,Los Angeles, 2003), 7.
29 David Farrell, 'From the Music Capitals of the World,' *Billboard*, 6 January 1979, 67.
30 'Diodes Break with Their Record Company in Fight about Expectations, Music Quality,' *Canadian Composer*, March 1979, 44.
31 David Farrell, 'Music Report from Canada: Sunny Skies and a Rosy Forecast,' *Billboard*, 27 January 1979, C-3. Or, as Earl Rosen, executive director of the Canadian Independent Record Production Association, summarized a few years later, the days in which one could take a chance on an artist by putting an album together for $50,000 had come to an end. Kirk LaPointe 'A Billboard Spotlight on Canada,' *Billboard*, 31 January 1987, C-12.
32 David Hayes, 'Videos Now a Fact of Life,' *Music Scene*, November-December 1983, 8.
33 Pamela Young, 'Rock's Road to Success,' *Maclean's*, 24 November 1986, 60.
34 Ibid.
35 Jack Banks, 'Video in the Machine: The Incorporation of Music Video into the Recording Industry,' *Popular Music* 16, no. 3 (1998), 297.
36 Ibid., 306.
37 Ibid., 297.
38 Johnathan Gross, 'You Too Can Conquer the U.S.A,' *Canadian Musician*, June 1986, 38.
39 '54-40: On the Road,' *Canadian Musician*, August 1993, 36. The band released three albums with Warner Bros. before switching to Sony Music in 1990 and making a major mark with *Dear Dear*. Nicholas Jennings, 'Plucking for Glory,' *Maclean's*, 10 August 1992, 46.
40 Chris Gudgeon, 'New Haunts for Spirit of the West,' *Canadian Musician*, June 1992, 41.
41 Larry LeBlanc, 'Sony Music Takes on the World,' *Billboard*, 22 June 1996, 62.
42 Ibid.
43 Will Straw, 'Sound Recording,' in Michael Dorland, ed., *The Cultural Industries in Canada* (Toronto: Lorimer, 1996), 97. Larry LeBlanc, 'Label Affiliates Mull Border-Crossing,' *Billboard*, 5 December 1992, 52.

44 LeBlanc, 'Label Affiliates Mull Border-Crossing,' 52.

45 Karen Bliss, 'Attention! You Can Make and Sell Your Own Record,' *Canadian Musician*, April 1995, 54.

46 Canada. *Report of the Federal Cultural Policy Review Committee* (Ottawa: Minister of Supply and Services, 1982), 240.

47 Jon Savage, 'The Enemy Within: Sex, Rock, and Identity,' in Simon Frith, ed., *Facing theMusic: A Pantheon Guide to Popular Culture* (New York: Pantheon, 1988), 162–3.

48 Robert Burnett, *The Global Jukebox: The International Music Industry* (New York: Routledge, 1996), 107. The result was more than clear by the late 1970s. As Richard Flohil pointed out to readers of *Canadian Composer*, 'the major record companies achieved an unheard of integration through every channel of the business – from recording, manufacturing, and packaging, all the way through wholesaling and retailing,' Richard Flohil, editorial, *Canadian Composer*, February 1981, 2.

49 Burnett, *Global Jukebox*, 18.

50 Ibid., 50–1.

51 Robert Burnett, 'Dressed for Success: Sweden from Abba to Roxette, *Popular Music* 11, no. 2 (1992): 143. Burnett, *Global Jukebox*, 2.

52 Larry LeBlanc, *The Music Industry in Canada*, report produced for the Canadian Association of Broadcasters, February 2006, 4.

53 Michael Barclay, Ian A.D. Jack, and Jason Schneider, *Have Not Been the Same: The CanRock Renaissance, 1985–95* (Toronto: ECW Press, 2001), book cover.

54 Larry LeBlanc, 'With Bare Necessities, 'Naked Ladies Turn Heads,' *Billboard*, 11 January 1992, 32.

55 Dave Bidini, 'The Ballad of the Rheos,' *Globe and Mail*, 29 March 2007, R3. Bidini has gone on to become a prolific author, most notably writing an autobiographical sketch of life on the road in *On a Cold Road* (Toronto: McClelland and Stewart, 1998).

56 Howard Druckman, 'Indie Bands Make Their Mark,' *Canadian Composer*, October 1988, 22.

57 Kevin Young, 'From the Hip,' *Maclean's*, 11 December 2000, 48.

58 John Wright, Millard Gregory, Sarah Riegel, 'Here's Where We Get Canadian: English-Canadian Nationalism and Popular Culture,' *American Review of Canadian Studies* 32, no. 1 (Spring 2002): 23.

59 Nicholas Jennings, *Before the Gold Rush: Flashbacks to the Dawn of the Canadian Sound* (Toronto: Viking, 1997), 2.

60 Tom Harrison, 'The Guess Who: Ballad of the Last 25 Years,' *Canadian Musician*, February 1988, 49.

61 Peter Howell, 'Canadians Grab 11 Grammys,' *Toronto Star*, 19 February 1996, C7.

62 Judith Timson, 'The Season of the Diva,' *Maclean's*, 8 March 1999.

63 Robert Wright has already noted that 'in 1991, Shania Twain was "discovered" at a Huntsville, Ontario, resort but signed her first record deal with Mercury Nashville. In a slight variation on the same theme, Alanis Morissette abandoned the Canadian music scene altogether in 1993 after two albums with MCA Canada, obliterating her dance-pop past and signing with Madonna's Maverick Records label.' 'Gimmie Shelter: Cultural Protectionism and the Canadian Recording Industry,' in Wright, *Virtual Sovereignty: Nationalism, Culture and the Canadian Question* (Toronto: Canadian Scholars' Press, 2004), 89.

64 Barbara Wickens, 'Grammy Night in Canada,' *Maclean's*, 11 March 1996, 50.

65 Brian D. Johnson, 'Shania Revealed,' *Maclean's*, 23 March 1998, 50.

66 Ibid., 52.

67 Nicholas Jennings, 'Domestic Bands Win Acclaim,' *Maclean's*, 27 January 1992, 52.

68 Nicholas Jennings, 'A Rebel's Return,' *Maclean's*, 14 May 1990, 63.

69 This list has been accumulated through various industry advertisements published by the record labels and includes acts signed directly and through distribution agreements with domestics and/or subsidiaries.

70 Nicholas Jennings, 'Melancholy Mavericks,' *Maclean's*, 19 March 1990, 52.

71 Nicholas Jennings, 'Plucking for Glory,' *Maclean's*, 10 August 1992, 46.

72 Greg Quill, 'The "Indies" Fight On,' *Canadian Composer*, April 1986, 18.

73 Larry LeBlanc, 'Alternative Surge Creates Canada A&R Frenzy,' *Billboard*, 4 February 1995, 72. Mair certainly knew the scene. Having cut his teeth as business manager of Gordon Lightfoot's Early Morning Productions in the late 1960s, he and Tom Williams, a former promotion head at WEA Records of Canada, launched Attic in 1973 with a sizeable $300,000 investment and built it into one of the biggest of the domestically owned labels. Larry LeBlanc, 'Attic Chief Reveals Indie's Secrets,' *Billboard*, 15 August 1992, 36. Over the course of the next decade and a half Attic, in the assessment of Richard Flohil, 'had sold $40 million worth of records at retail, paid $9 million in production costs and artists' royalties, paid out $5 million in songwriting and publishing royalties, and earned more than $6 million in foreign income. Attic had paid out more than $1.75 million in federal sales taxes, and spent $7 million in manufacturing costs. And, along the way, Attic had released more than 160 albums, which included more than 1,500 compositions.' 'Canada's Leading Independent Record Company Celebrates 15th Anniversary,' *Canadian Composer*, November 1998, 24.

74 LeBlanc, *The Music Industry in Canada*, 5.
75 See Nicholas Jennings, 'Junkies Inc.,' *Maclean's*, 7 May 2001. In fairness, it is worth noting that RCA seemed to show its support by re-releasing the album and going so far as to fly in press from Italy, France, and Britain to attract attention for their follow-up release *The Caution Horses*. Jennings, 'Melancholy Mavericks.'
76 Ian Menzies, 'The Bourbon Tabernacle Choir,' *Canadian Musician*, August 1995, 38–9.
77 Karen Bliss, 'Sloan Can't Stop Pop,' *Canadian Musician*, October 1996, 40.
78 Straw, 'In and Around Canadian Music,' *Journal of Canadian Studies* 35, no. 3 (Fall 2000): 180.
79 Will Straw, 'No Future? The Canadian Music Industries,' in David Taras, Frits Pannekoek, and Maria Bakardjieva, eds, *How Canadians Communicate* (Calgary: University of Calgary Press, 2003), 212, 213.
80 Ibid., 213.
81 Line Grenier, 'The Aftermath of a Crisis: Quebec Music Industries in the 1980s,' *Popular Music* 12, no. 3 (1993): 212, 213.
82 Larry LeBlanc, 'MapleCore's Indie Arena,' *Billboard*, 28 August 2004, 55.
83 Ibid.
84 Laura Blue, 'What It Means To Go "Indie,"' *Time* (Canada), 4 April 2005, 47. Larry LeBlanc, 'The Great White North Heats Up,' *Billboard*, 12 April 2003, 48.
85 Anonymous. 'Linus Entertainment Takes Over True North Records,' *Canadian Musician*, March/April 2008, 18.
86 LeBlanc, 'The Great White North Heats Up.'
87 Ibid.
88 LeBlanc, *The Music Industry in Canada*, 7. LeBlanc further explains that 'since the multinationals control their own distribution, and distribute their own records as well as foreign-owned independent labels, and those of Canadian-controlled record labels, they dominate the Canadian music market. Their strategies and trade practices are the defacto industry practices – particularly in distribution and at retail. Also a sizable portion of Canada's music talent pool is, in fact, signed to multinational sources outside the country … Their enormous impact is further enhanced by their control or access to a range of media. They can cross-market or negotiate product across multiple media including through recordings, films, television and advertising. Multinationals are all involved in coordinating record and video production, signing and promoting artists, distributing product to retailers and wholesalers. These companies may also be involved in music publishing. While most multinationals have made significant investments in Cana-

dian music, their core activity is maximizing the sale of recordings made by the parent and fellow subsidiaries' (5–6).

89 Burnett, *The Global Jukebox*, 61.

90 Will Straw, 'In and Around Canadian Music,' *Journal of Canadian Studies* 35, no. 3 (Fall 2000): 179.

91 Mark Jowett, Nettwerk Records, quoted in Nicholas Jennings, 'Vancouver's Rock 'n' Roll Explosion,' *Maclean's*, 21 March 1988, 63.

10 '(Everything I Do) I Do It for You'

1 Larry LeBlanc, 'Bryan Adams to Government: "Get Out of the Music Biz,"' *Billboard*, 25 January 1992, 44.

2 Canadian Broadcasting Corporation, *Evening News*, 12 September 1991.

3 Statements assembled from Geoff Pevere and Grieg Dymond, *Mondo Canuck: A Canadian Pop Culture Odyssey* (Scarborough, ON: Prentice-Hall, 1996), 2; Brian D. Johnson and Pamela Young, 'Rock on a Roll,' *Maclean's*, 27 January 1992, 49; and Larry LeBlanc, 'Cochrane Cleans Up at Juno Awards,' *Billboard*, 11 April 1992, 41.

4 Malcolm Gray, 'The Manager with the Midas Touch,' *Maclean's*, 6 June 1983, 48.

5 Thomas Hopkins, 'Canadian Rock Rolls South,' *Maclean's*, 14 June 1982, 46, 47.

6 Rachelle Chapman, 'Much, Much Less,' *Ryerson Review of Journalism* (Spring 2003). http://www.rrj.ca/issue/2003/spring/387/ (accessed 16 April 2009).

7 Johnson and Young, 'Rock on a Roll,' 48.

8 Larry LeBlanc, 'Oh Canada: New Adams Set Fails MAPL Grading System,' *Billboard*, 28 September 1991, 74.

9 Paul Myers, 'Bryan Adams Gets Upwardly Mobile Down South,' *Canadian Musician*, August 1996, 40. Don Shafer, quoted in Larry LeBlanc, 'Oh Canada.'

10 Even the most straightforward of semiotic readings easily identifies how his chosen identifiers – white T-shirt, leather jacket, and rebelliousness – were more in line with popular representations of the 'all-American boy next door' cemented in such icons as James Dean. For seminal explorations of semiology see Roland Barthes, *Mythologies* (Paris: Éditions du Seuil, 1957) and *Elements of Semiology* (London: Jonathan Cape, 1967).

11 Larry LeBlanc, 'Cancon Debate Heats Up Toronto Meet,' *Billboard*, 11 April 1992, 66.

12 Jan Matejcek, open letter to Adams, reprinted in Larry LeBlanc, 'Bryan Adams to Government: "Get Out of the Music Biz."'

13 Nicholas Jennings, 'Domestic Bands Win Acclaim,' *Maclean's*, 27 January 1992, 52.

14 Larry LeBlanc, '"Canadian-Content" Discontent,' *Billboard*, 29 February 1992, 40.

15 LeBlanc, 'Cancon Debate Heats Up Toronto Meet.'

16 Nicholas Jennings, 'The Superstar,' *Maclean's*, 6 July 1987, 34.

17 LeBlanc, 'Bryan Adams to Government: "Get Out of the Music Biz."'

18 Letters, *Maclean's*, 10 February 1992, 6.

19 Nicholas Jennings, 'Rocking Sounds,' *Maclean's*, 13 July 1992, 46.

20 David J. Jackson, 'Peace, Order, and Good Songs: Popular Music and English-Canadian Culture,' *American Review of Canadian Studies* 35 (Spring 2005): 39.

21 LeBlanc, 'Cochrane Cleans Up at Juno Awards.'

22 Perry Stern, 'Bruce Allen Is Hot,' *Canadian Musician*, December 1986, 38.

23 Bill Reynolds, 'Red Rider: Victory Day for Tom Cochrane,' *Canadian Musician*, October 1988, 41.

24 Ibid.

25 Richard Chycki, 'His Victory Day in a Mad, Mad World,' *Canadian Musician*, April 1992, 34.

26 LeBlanc, 'Cancon Debate Heats Up Toronto Meet.'

27 See discussion of this in LeBlanc, 'Oh Canada.' Further, the CRTC discussed this possibility in 1998: 'The Commission recognizes that allowing a recording to automatically qualify as Canadian if the principal artist is Canadian may ensure some additional access for Canadian artists to radio play lists. The Commission notes, however, that, under such a regime, a recording made outside of Canada of a non-Canadian song would qualify as Canadian, provided the performing artist is Canadian. The Commission is not convinced that such a change would assist in achieving the second objective, namely the support of a Canadian-based recording industry. The Commission also notes that many of the artists who would benefit from such a change have already received considerable international success.' CRTC Public Notice 1998-41.

28 LeBlanc, 'Oh Canada.'

29 Ibid.

30 Eikhard had achieved an impressive status as a songwriter over the previous two decades. In 1971 *RPM* reported that Anne Murray's hit single 'It Takes Time' 'was written by fifteen year old Shirley Eikhard, an Oshawa schoolgirl, now being wooed by record companies – as a performer.' 'Anne Murray Success Pattern Grows and Grows,' *RPM*, 17 April 1971, 3.

31 CRTC Public Notice 1992-32, 30 April 1992.

32 Ibid., and CRTC Public Notice 1993-5, 29 January 1993.
33 CRTC Public Notice 1992-32, 30 April 1992. Or, as noted in CRTC Public
    Notice 1993-5, 29 January 1993, 'some preferred retention of the status quo,
    while others advocated the abolition of the Canadian content regulation
    altogether.'
34 CRTC Public Notice 1993-5.
35 Larry LeBlanc, 'Foreign Co-Writers Score in Revised CanCon Rules,' *Bill-
    board*, 13 February 1993, 51.
36 Peter Diemer, quoted in Larry LeBlanc, 'Industry Seeks CanCon Review,'
    Billboard, 30 March 1996, 53.
37 CRTC Public Notice 1998-41.
38 Canadian Independent Record Production Association, 'Submission
    Regarding Broadcasting Notice 2006-1,' 15 May 2006, 2.
39 Canadian Recording Industry Association, 'Re: Broadcasting Notice of
    Public Hearing CRTC 2006-1: Review of the Commercial Radio Policy,' 15
    March 2006, 200.
40 The reissuing of back catalogues and the targeting of this demographic are
    discussed in Jody Berland and Will Straw, 'Getting Down to Business: Cultural
    Politics and Policies in Canada,' in Benjamin Singer, ed., *Communications in
    Canadian Society*, 4th ed. (Scarborough, ON: Nelson Canada, 1995), 332–60.
41 'Less Dinosaur Rock, More New Music on the Radio?' *Globe and Mail*, 15
    May 2006.
42 Canadian Association of Broadcasters, '"Then ... Now: Private Radio's
    Changing Realities," A Submission to the Canadian Radio-television Tel-
    ecommunications Commission with Respect to Public Notice 2006-1,' 15
    March 2006, 7.
43 Ibid., 92–3.
44 Ibid., 93.
45 Canadian Independent Record Production Association, Canadian Radio-
    television and Telecommunications Commission, *Hearing Transcript*, 15 May
    2006, 4–5; Canadian Independent Record Production Association, 'Submis-
    sion Regarding Broadcasting Notice 2006-1,' 15 May 2006, 9.
46 Ibid., 38.
47 Broadcasting Act, 1991, sections 3(1)(f), and 3(1)(i)(v).
48 Larry LeBlanc, 'Indie Revolt up North,' *Billboard*, 29 April 2006, 18.
49 Ibid.
50 Canadian Recording Industry Association, 'Re: Broadcasting Notice,' 29.
51 Will Straw, 'Sound Recording,' in Michael Dorland, ed., *The Cultural Indus-
    tries in Canada* (Toronto: Lorimer, 1996), 97.
52 CRTC Public Notice 2006-158.
53 Stuart Langford, CRTC Public Notice 2006-158. Langford dissented from

the CRTC's recommendations because he felt that the majority of commissioners favoured broadcasters over the need to ensure Canadian content and opportunities for new acts.

54 CRTC Public Notice 1998-41.

55 Bart Testa and Jim Shedden, 'In the Great Midwestern Hardware Store,' in Joan Nicks and Jeannette Sloniowski, eds, *Slippery Pastimes: Reading the Popular in Canadian Culture* (Waterloo, ON: Wilfrid Laurier University Press, 2002), 207.

56 See Edwardson, *Canadian Content: Culture and the Quest for Nationhood* (Toronto: University of Toronto Press, 2008).

57 Michael Barclay, Ian A.D. Jack, and Jason Schneider, *Have Not Been the Same: The CanRock Renaissance* (Toronto: ECW Press, 2001), 656.

58 Alan Cross, conversation with author, January 2009.

59 The author himself founded a 'list-serve' for the band Big Sugar in the early 1990s so that fans could inform each other as to tour dates, the success of which led to the band's management taking it over.

60 Anonymous, 'IndieCan Celebrates 100th Broadcast,' *Canadian Musician*, November/December 2008, 18.

61 Telecomworldwire, 'Bell Introduces All Access Music Services in Canada,' 5 July 2007, 1; Canada NewsWire, 'AOL Canada Launches New Music Channel,' 9 May 2007, 1.

62 Martha Worboy, 'Canadians Getting in Tune with Digital Music,' CanWest News, 5 January 2008, 1.

63 Anonymous, 'Stompin' Tom's 'Bud the Spud' to Be Made Available Digitally on Canada Day,' Canadian Press, 30 June 2008.

64 Cassandra Szklarski, 'Canadian Legend Stompin' Tom Laments Lack of Radio Play, Patriotism,' Canadian Press, 24 October 2008.

65 Larry LeBlanc, 'Canada Gets Hot,' *Billboard*, 1 April 2006, 27; Larry LeBlanc, 'Snowball Effect,' *Billboard*, 23 June 2007, 12.

66 LeBlanc, 'Snowball Effect.'

67 Worboy, 'Canadians Getting in Tune with Digital Music.'

68 Canadian Recording Industry Association, 'Re: Broadcasting Notice,' 21.

69 Statistic according to the CRTC. 'Canadian Radio Continues to Thrive,' *Canadian Musician*, September/October 2008, 15.

70 Bruce Cockburn, interview with *Goldmine* reprinted in Ian Menzies, 'Bruce Cockburn,' *Canadian Musician*, December 1993, 37.

71 Kevin Young, 'illScarlett,' *Canadian Musician*, July/August 2008, 36.

Conclusion

1 Jon Ruddy, 'How to Become an American without Really Trying. Your First

Move? Get with the "Canadian" Music Scene: It's as Yankee as Dylan and Drive-ins,' *Maclean's*, November 1969, 61.

2 Gene Lees, 'Producing Great Sounds in Spite of Ourselves,' *Maclean's*, August 1972, 70.

3 Stompin' Tom Connors, quoted in Nancy Lanthier, 'Stompin' Tom Shares a Few Bon Mots,' *Canadian Composer*, Summer 1992, 6–7.

4 Brendan Canning, 'The Insider's Guide to Indie Rock,' *Time*, 4 April 2005, 55.

5 Andrew Craig, *Canadian Songwriters Hall of Fame 2007*, Cansong Productions, 2007.

6 Canada NewsWire, 'Online Battle of the Bands Begins – Canadians Pick the Winner,' 24 April 2007, 1.

7 Ibid.

8 Ian Menzies, 'Musical Milestones,' *Canadian Musician*, April 1994, 51. Thomas Hopkins, 'Canadian Rock Rolls South,' *Maclean's*, 14 June 1982, 46. Brian D. Johnson, 'Alanis in Wonderland,' *Maclean's*, 25 February 2002, 56.

9 Robert Wright has already noted that 'the path to success in New York and Stockholm and Tokyo lay in developing the generic sounds of the increasingly globalized corporate 'playlist,' which actually meant reducing the 'Canadianness' of Canadian recorded product.' Robert Wright, 'Gimmie Shelter: Cultural Protectionism and the Canadian Recording Industry,' in Wright, *Virtual Sovereignty: Nationalism, Culture and the Canadian Question* (Toronto: Canadian Scholar's Press, 2004), 88. Along these same lines, Bart Testa and Jim Shedden have argued that 'the national-culturalist objective was never more than a hopelessly vague critical ideal. Canadian musicians had pragmatically figured out how to occupy the higher tiers of the international industry both musically and commercially and did without it ... Canada's enduring capability in rock chronology becomes, by the 1990s, the regular capacity to generate rock records that slot smoothly into all radio and wide-reaching concert venues ... The Cancon regulations of 1971 cleared the ground and made it possible, finally by the mid-1980s, for Canadian music acts to prosper and thrive. None of this, however, ensured that a uniquely Canadian style or approach to music would develop.' 'In the Great Midwestern Hardware Store: The Seventies Triumph in English-Canadian Rock Music,' in Joan Nicks and Jeannette Sloniowski, eds, *Slippery Pastimes: Reading the Popular in Canadian Culture* (Waterloo, ON: Wilfried Laurier University Press, 2002), 210.

10 Myrna Kostash, 'The Pure, Uncluttered Spaces of Bruce Cockburn,' *Saturday Night*, June 1972, 22; italics in original.

Bibliography

Abramson, Bram Dov. 'Country Music and Cultural Industry: Mediating Structures in Transnational Media Flow.' *Media, Culture and Society* 24 (2002): 255–74.

Adria, Marco. *Music of Our Times: Eight Canadian Singer-Songwriters*. Toronto: Lorimer, 1990.

Allan, Chad. 'The Pop Scene in Winnipeg.' *Music Scene*, July-August 1968.

Allen, Jane and Mary. 'How to Endure a Father.' *Maclean's*, 31 January 1959.

Allen, Robert Thomas. 'How to Live with a Teen-Age Daughter.' *Maclean's*, 31 August 1957.

– *My Childhood and Yours: Happy Memories of Growing Up*. Toronto: Macmillan, 1977.

Ambrose, Joe. *Chelsea Hotel Manhattan*. London: Headpress, 2007.

Anderson, Benedict. *Imagined Communities: Reflections on the Origin and Spread of Nationalism*. London: Verso, 1991.

Anderson, Omer. 'U.S. Launches European Drive to Aid Country Music Image.' *Billboard*, 25 December 1965.

Arsenault, Tim. 'Sloan: Canada's Grunge Rockers Get Smeared.' *Canadian Musician*, December 1992.

Atwood, Margaret. *Survival*. Toronto: Anansi, 1972.

Auslander, Philip. 'Seeing Is Believing: Live Performance and the Discourse of Authenticity in Rock Culture.' *Literature and Psychology* 44, no. 4 (1998): 1–25.

Bachman, Randy, and John Einarson. *Takin' Care of Business*. Toronto: McArthur, 2000.

Bangs, Lester. 'Records.' *Rolling Stone*, 7 February 1970.

Banks, Jack. 'Video in the Machine: The Incorporation of Music Video into the Recording Industry. *Popular Music* 16, no. 3 (1998): 293–309.

– 'Keeping "Abreast" of MTV and Viacom: The Growing Power of a Media Conglomerate.' In Janet Wasko, ed., *A Companion to Television*, 256–69.Malden, MA: Blackwell, 2005.

Barclay, Michael, Ian A.D. Jack, and Jason Schneider, *Have Not Been the Same: The Canrock Renaissance.* Toronto: ECW Press, 2001.

Barker, Gerry. 'The Lads Laze as the Girls Scream.' *Toronto Daily Star*, 8 September 1964.

Barthes, Roland. *Mythologies.* Paris: Éditions du Seuil, 1957.

– *Elements of Semiology.* London: Jonathan Cape, 1967.

Bateman, Jeff. 'A Progress Report.' *Music Scene*, March-April 1985.

Battah, Habib. 'Crowded House.' *Variety*, 1 October 2007.

Batten, Jack. 'One Man's Crusade to Canadianize Rock 'n' Roll.' *Maclean's*, 8 August 1964, 46.

– 'Hawks, Chicks and a Swinging Nest.' *Maclean's*, 20 March 1965.

– 'Sweet Song of Success.' *Maclean's*, 21 August 1965.

– 'How the Town's Fighting the Dread Hippie Menace.' *Maclean's*, August 1967.

– 'Canada's Rock Scene: Going, Going ...' *Maclean's*, February 1968, 34.

– 'How This Freaky Character Is Rocking Today's Pop Music.' *Saturday Night*, May 1968.

– 'Can.Pop.' *Chatelaine*, September 1969.

– 'From Bruce Cockburn to Youth – A Very Private Message.' *Maclean's*, January 1971.

– 'The Guess Who.' *Maclean's*, June 1971.

– 'Confessions of a Retired Rock Critic.' *Saturday Night*, March 1973.

– 'The Vulnerability of Gordon Lightfoot.' *Saturday Night*, July 1974, 24.

Bayles, Martha. *Hole in Our Soul: The Loss of Beauty and Meaning in American Popular Music.* New York: Free Press, 1994.

– 'The Strange Career of Folk Music.' *Michigan Quarterly Review* 44, no. 2 (Spring 2005): 304–17.

Beaty, Bart. 'High Treason: Canadian Nationalism and the Regulation of American Crime Comic Books.' *Essays on Canadian Writing* 62 (Fall 1997): 85–107.

Beckett, Barbara. 'At Osaka.' *Canadian Composer*, May 1970.

Bell, Wilf. '"Stones" Rock Ottawa.' *Ottawa Citizen*, 26 April 1965.

Berland, Jody, and Will Straw. 'Getting Down to Business: Cultural Politics and Policies in Canada.' In Benjamin Singer, ed., *Communications in Canadian Society*, 4th ed., 332–60. Toronto: Nelson, 1995.

Bidini, Dave. *On a Cold Road.* Toronto: McClelland and Stewart, 1998.

– 'The Ballad of the Rheos.' *Globe and Mail*, 29 March 2007.

Bielby, William T. 'Rock in a Hard Place: Grassroots Cultural Production in the Post-Elvis Era.' *American Sociological Review* 69 (February 2004): 1–13.

Bingham, Dave. Correspondence with author, January 2008.

Blackburn, Bob. 'Elvis Every Bit a Pro – Honest He Is!' *Ottawa Citizen*, 4 April 1957.

Blair, Ian. 'Frontline Rocker.' *Maclean's*, 27 February 1989.

Bligh, Stanley. 'He's Nauseated: Sun Music Critic on Rock 'n' Roll: 'Ultimate in Musical Depravity.' *Vancouver Sun*, 28 June 1956.

Bliss, Karen. 'Attention! You Can Make and Sell Your Own Record.' *Canadian Musician*, April 1995.

– 'Sloan Can't Stop Pop.' *Canadian Musician*, October 1996.

– 'Coldplay, Peas Storm Canada.' *Rolling Stone*, 3 April 2006.

Blue, Laura. 'What It Means to Go "Indie."' *Time* (Canada), 4 April 2005.

Borzykowski, Bryan. 'Classic Hits Have Been Replaced by an Indie Vibe as the Soundtrack of Choice for TV Ads.' *Marketing*, 15 October 2007.

Boucher, David. *Dylan and Cohen: Poets of Rock and Roll.* New York: Continuum, 2004.

Bowman, Durrell. *Permanent Change: Rush, Musicians' Rock, and the Progressive Post-Counterculture.* Doctoral thesis, University of California (Los Angeles), 2003.

Bradley, Dick. *Understanding Rock 'n' Roll: Popular Music in Britain, 1955–1964.* Buckingham: Open University Press, 1992.

Bromberg, Minna, and Gary Alan Fine. 'Resurrecting the Red: Pete Seeger and the Purification of Difficult Reputations.' *Social Forces* 80, no. 4 (2002): 1135–55.

Burnett, Robert. 'Dressed for Success: Sweden from Abba to Roxette, *Popular Music* 11, no. 2 (1992): 141–50.

– *The Global Jukebox: The International Music Industry.* New York: Routledge, 1996.

Butcher, David. 'Records.' *Rolling Stone*, 21 December 1968.

Came, Barry. 'Rock 'n' Roll.' *Maclean's*, 1 June 1992.

Canada. Statutes of Canada. Broadcasting Act, 1958/1968/1991.

– Standing Committee on Broadcasting, Film, and Assistance to the Arts, *Minutes of Proceedings and Evidence*, April/May 1970.

– *Report of the Federal Cultural Policy Review Committee.* Ottawa: Minister of Supply and Services, 1982.

– *Report of the Task Force on Broadcasting Policy.* Ottawa: Minister of Supply and Services, 1986.

Canada Newswire. 'The 2006 Juno Awards to Reach Quarter Billion Audience on Five Continents.' 30 March 2006.

– '1.7 Million Watch 2006 Juno Awards on CTV.' 3 April 2006.

– 'Online Battle of the Bands Begins – Canadians Pick the Winner.' 24 April 2007.

– 'AOL Canada Launches New Music Channel.' 9 May 2007.

– 'The Celebrity Obsessed Get Their Fill with MuchMusic's Fall Line-up.' 9 August 2007.
– 'MuchMoreMusic's Fall Programming Puts Pop Culture Lovers to the Test' 10 August 2007.
– 'MuchMusic and MTV Bring the "MTV Europe Music Awards 2007" to Canadians Thursday, Nov. 1.' 18 October 2007.
– 'MuchMusic Airs MTV New Year's Eve Masquerade on December 31.' 19 December 2007.
– 'Canadian Independent Music Takes International Stage as SIRIUS Satellite Radio Broadcasts Exclusive Live Concerts from North by Northeast (NXNE).' 2 June 2008.
Canadian Association of Broadcasters, 'Brief to Be Presented to the House of Commons Committee on Broadcasting, Film and Assistance to the Arts on Behalf of the Canadian Association of Broadcasters.' Standing Committee on Broadcasting, Film, and Assistance to the Arts, *Minutes of Proceedings and Evidence*, Appendix M, 22 April 1970.
– '"Then ... Now: Private Radio's Changing Realities." A Submission to the Canadian Radio-television Telecommunications Commission with Respect to Public Notice 2006-1.' 15 March 2006.
Canadian Composer. Various issues.
Canadian Independent Record Production Association. Press release. Reprinted in 'CIRPA Announces Aims and Objectives.' *RPM*, 6 February 1971.
– 'Submission Regarding Broadcasting Notice 2006-1.' 15 May 2006.
– Hearing transcript. 15 May 2006.
Canadian Musician. Various issues.
Canadian Radio and Television Commission / Canadian Radio-television and Telecommunications Commission. 'Proposed Amendments to the Radio (TV) Broadcasting Regulations.' 12 February 1970.
– *Public Hearing*, April 1970.
– Decision 70-99. 20 May 1970.
– *Annual Report*. 1972.
– *FM Radio in Canada: A Policy to Ensure a Varied and Comprehensive Radio Service.* Ottawa: CRTC, 1975.
– Public Notice 1992-32.
– Public Notice 1993-5.
– Public Notice 1998-41.
– Public Notice 2006-158.
– *Hearing Transcript*. 15 May 2006.
Canadian Recording Industry Association. 'Re: Broadcasting Notice of Public Hearing CRTC 2006-1: Review of the Commercial Radio Policy.' 15 March 2006.

Canning, Brendan. 'The Insider's Guide to Indie Rock.' *Time* (Canada), 4 April 2005.

Cantin, Paul. 'It's All Too "Much."' *Billboard*, 10 January 1998.

Cawte, E.C. 'Watching Cecil Sharp at Work: A Study of His Records of Sword Dances Using His Field Notebooks.' *Folk Music Journal* 8, no. 3 (2003): 282–313.

Champagne, Jane. 'Félix Leclerc: Returning Home to Canada.' *Canadian Composer*, December 1973.

Champion, C.P. 'A Very British Coup: Canadianism, Quebec, and Ethnicity in the Flag Debate, 1964–1965.' *Journal of Canadian Studies* 40, no. 3 (Fall 2006): 68–99.

Chapman, Rachelle. 'Much, Much Less.' *Ryerson Review of Journalism* (Spring 2003). http://www.rrj.ca/issue/2003/spring/387/ (accessed 16 April 2009).

Chapple, Steve, and Reebee Garofalo. *Rock 'n' Roll Is Here to Pay: The History and Politics of the Music Industry*. Chicago: Nelson-Hall, 1977.

Child, Francis. *The English and Scottish Popular Ballads*. London: Henry Stevens Sons and Stiles, 1882.

Christenson, Peter G., and Donald F. Roberts. *It's Not Only Rock and Roll: Popular Music in the Lives of Adolescents*. Cresskill, NJ: Hampton Press, 1998.

CHUM. 'The Maple Leaf System.' *Music Scene*, November-December 1969.

Chycki, Richard. 'His Victory Day in a Mad, Mad World.' *Canadian Musician*, April 1992.

Clare, John. 'The Scramble for the Teen-Age Dollar.' *Maclean's*, 14 September 1957.

Cloonan, Martin. 'State of the Nation: "Englishness," Pop, and Politics in the mid-1990s.' *Popular Music and Society* 21, no. 2 (Summer 1997): 47–70.

Cobb, David. 'Pop Power.' *Toronto Telegram*, Showcase Section, 29 July 1967.

Cobb, Mike. 'Fans Successfully Held at Bay: It's Mad Day for Seattle as Beatles Come to Town.' *Vancouver Sun*, 22 August 1964.

Cohen, Robert, and Reginald Zelnik, eds. *The Free Speech Movement: Reflections on Berkeley in the 1960s*. Berkeley: University of California Press, 2002.

Cohen, Ronald D. *Rainbow Quest: The Folk Music Revival and American Society, 1940–1970*. Amherst: University of Massachusetts Press, 2002.

Collie, Ashley. 'Bruce Cockburn.' *Canadian Musician*, September/October 1983.

Collier, Peter and David Horowitz. 'Slouching towards Berkeley: Socialism in One City.' *Public Interest* (Winter 1989): 47–68.

Connolley, Greg, and Gerry Mulligan, 'The Police Kept It Peaceful.' *Ottawa Citizen*, 4 April 1957.

– 'The "Great Man" on Her Arm.' *Ottawa Citizen*, 4 April 1957.

Connors, Tom. *Stompin' Tom and the Connors Tone*. Toronto: Viking, 2000.

Cray, Ed. *Ramblin' Man: The Life and Times of Woody Guthrie.* New York: Norton, 2004.

Cross, Alan. *Over the Edge: The Revolution and Evolution of New Rock.* Scarborough, ON: Prentice Hall, 1997.

– Conversation with author, January 2009.

CTVglobemedia 'MTV's Blowin' Up with Jamie Kennedy Premieres May 27 on "MTV on CTV."' Press release. 16 May 2006. http://media.ctv.ca/mtv/releases/release.asp?id=8674andnum=2andyyyy=2006 (accessed 27 February 2008).

De Remigis, Peter. Correspondence with author, January 2008.

Desjardins, Marc. 'Interview! Robert Charlebois.' *Canadian Composer,* April 1982.

– 'The Studio Scene in Quebec.' *Canadian Composer,* December 1982.

Devereux, Cecily. '"Canadian Classic" and "Commodity Export": The Nationalism of "Our" Anne of Green Gables.' *Journal of Canadian Studies* 36, no. 1 (2001): 11–28.

Deziel, Shanda. 'Rock 'n' Roll.' *Maclean's,* 17 June 2002.

Dick, Ernest. *Remembering Singalong Jubilee.* Halifax: Formac, 2004.

Dostie, Bruno. 'Pop Music from a Quebec Perspective.' *Canadian Composer,* October 1977.

Douché, Rocky. 'The NZ Music Industry: A Scoping Review of the Contemporary Music Industry for Industry New Zealand.' R.P. Douché Consulting, 31 August 2001.

Douglas, Susan J. *Where the Girls Are: Growing Up Female with the Mass Media.* Toronto: Random House, 1994.

Downing, David. A *Dreamer of Pictures: Neil Young, the Man and His Music.* New York: Da Capo Press, 1995.

Druckman, Howard. 'Indie Bands Make Their Mark.' *Canadian Composer,* October 1988.

Echard, William. *Neil Young and the Poetics of Energy.* Bloomington: Indiana University Press, 2005.

Edmons, Nancy. 'Records.' *Rolling Stone,* 14 June 1969.

Edwardson, Ryan. 'Kicking Uncle Sam Out of the Peaceable Kingdom: English-Canadian "New Nationalism" and Americanization.' *Journal of Canadian Studies* 37, no. 4 (Winter 2002): 131–50.

– "Of War Machines and Ghetto Scenes": English-Canadian Nationalism and the Guess Who's "American Woman."' *American Review of Canadian Studies* 33, no. 3 (Autumn 2003): 339–56.

– 'A Canadian Modernism: The Pre–Group of Seven "Algonquin School." 1912–1917.' *British Journal of Canadian Studies* 17, no. 1 (2004): 81–92.

– *Canadian Content: Culture and the Quest for Nationhood.* Toronto: University of Toronto Press, 2008.

Eggleton, David. *Ready to Fly: The Story of New Zealand Rock Music.* Nelson, NZ: Craig Potton, 2003.

Einarson, John. *Shakin' All Over: The Winnipeg Sixties Rock Scene.* Winnipeg: Variety Club of Manitoba, 1987.

– *American Woman: The Story of the Guess Who.* Kingston: Quarry Press, 1995.

– Correspondence with author, May 2007.

Einarson, John, and Richie Furay. *For What It's Worth: The Story of Buffalo Springfield.* Lanham, MD: Cooper Square, 2004.

Eliot, Marc. *Rockonomics: The Money behind the Music.* New York: Carol, 1993.

Elliott, Nancy. 'There'll Be No More Passports to Bohemia.' *Maclean's,* 2 July 1966.

Farrell, David. 'From the Music Capitals of the World.' *Billboard,* 6 January 1979.

– 'Music Report from Canada: Sunny Skies and a Rosy Forecast.' *Billboard,* 27 January 1979.

Fetherling, Douglas. *Some Day Soon: Essays on Canadian Songwriters.* Kingston: Quarry Press, 1990.

Fischer, Doug. 'The Little Music Magazine That Could.' *Ottawa Citizen,* 14 June 2003.

Flanagan, Bill. *Written in My Soul: Rock's Great Songwriters Talk about Creating Their Music.* Chicago: Contemporary Books, 1986.

Flinn, Sue Carter. 'Life and Times.' *The Coast,* 12 October 2006.

Flohil, Richard. 'Lightfoot.' *Canadian Composer,* September 1970.

– '*RPM*'s Big Weekend: Top 40 Radio Meets the Bigtime Record Business.' *Canadian Composer,* April 1972.

– 'Interview! Terry Brown.' *Canadian Composer,* February 1974.

– 'Interview! Murray Mclauchlan.' *Canadian Composer,* May 1974.

– 'Interview! Gilles Vigneault.' *Canadian Composer,* June 1974.

– 'Living the Rock and Roll Lifestyle.' *Canadian Composer,* January 1975.

– 'Interview! Ritchie Yorke.' *Canadian Composer,* October 1976.

– 'Burton Cummings.' *Canadian Musician,* March/April 1979.

– Editorial, *Canadian Composer,* February 1981.

– 'Junos Promote Canadian Music.' *Canadian Composer,* November 1987.

– 'From Crowbar to Sled Dog Races: Kelly Jay Moves On.' *Canadian Composer,* September 1988.

– 'Canada's Leading Independent Record Company Celebrates 15th Anniversary.' *Canadian Composer,* November 1998.

Fotheringham, Allan. 'The Beatle Menace: How to Preserve Public Safety When Four Kids from Liverpool Visit Canada.' *Maclean's,* 19 September 1964.

Francis, Daniel. *National Dreams: Myth, Memory, and Canadian History.* Vancouver: Arsenal Pulp Press, 1997.

Fraser, Sylvia. 'Sylvia Tyson Gets It Together.' *Chatelaine*, January 1976.

Friedlander, Paul. *Rock and Roll: A Social History*. Boulder, CO: Westview, 1996.

Frith, Simon. *Sound Effects: Youth, Leisure, and the Politics of Rock 'n' Roll*. New York: Pantheon, 1981.

– 'Towards an Aesthetic of Popular Music.' In Richard Leppert and Susan McClary, eds, *Music and Society: The Politics of Composition, Performance and Reception*, 133–49. Cambridge: Cambridge University Press, 1987.

– *Performing Rites: on the Value of Popular Music*. Cambridge: Harvard University Press, 1996.

– 'Music and Identity.' In Simon Hall and Paul du Gay, eds, *Questions of Cultural Identity*, 108–27. London: Sage, 1996.

Fryer, Paul. '"Everybody's on Top of the Pops": Popular Music on British Television, 1960–1985. *Popular Music and Society* 21, no. 3 (Fall 1997): 153–71.

Gagnon, Claude. 'Who Is Robert Charlebois?' *Canadian Composer*, May 1969.

Gancher, David. 'Records.' *Rolling Stone*, 11 June 1970.

Gardner, Paul A. 'What It Takes to Crash Tin Pan Alley at Fifteen.' *Maclean's*, 4 January 1958.

Gatehouse, Jonathon. 'Anka's Back, Baby!' *Maclean's*, 1 July 2005.

Geldof, Bob. *Is That It?* Markham, ON: Penguin, 1986.

Germain, Georges-Hébert. 'Le Patriote: Ten Years of Quebec's Pioneering Nightclub.' *Canadian Composer*, March 1975.

Giroux, Robert. *Le guide de la chanson québécoise*. Montreal: Triptyque, 1991.

Gleason, Ralph J. 'The Band.' *Rolling Stone*, 17 May 1969.

– 'The Band.' *Rolling Stone*, 16 October 1969.

Globe and Mail. Various issues.

Gnarowski, Michael. *Leonard Cohen: The Artist and His Critics*. Toronto: McGraw-Hill Ryerson, 1976.

Gonczy, Daniel J. 'The Folk Music Movement of the 1960s: Its Rise and Fall.' *Popular Music and Society* 10, no. 1 (1985): 15–32.

Goodall, Peter. *High Culture, Popular Culture: The Long Debate*. St Leonards, NSW: Allen and Unwin Pry, 1995.

Goodman, Lee-Anne. 'B.C. Rockers Hedley the Big Winner at MMVAs as Event Marred By Major Downpours.' *Canadian Press*, 16 June 2008.

Gorman, Paul R. *Left Intellectuals and Popular Culture in Twentieth-Century America*. Chapel Hill: University of North Carolina Press, 1996.

Grant, Barry K. '"Across the Great Divide": Imitation and Inflection in Canadian Rock Music.' *Journal of Canadian Studies* 21, no. 1 (Spring 1986): 116–27.

Grealis, Walt. 'January 18th, a Day Like Any Other ...' *RPM*, 30 January 1971.

– 'Production Suspended.' *RPM*, 20 February 1971.

Grenier, Line. 'The Aftermath of a Crisis: Quebec Music Industries in the 1980s.' *Popular Music* 12, no. 3 (1993): 209–27.

Grimsby, Wayne. 'The Morning after the Night before.' *Maclean's*, 7 August 1978.
– 'Hewers of Funk, Drawers of Glamor.' *Maclean's*, 19 April 1982.
Gross, Johnathan. 'You Too Can Conquer the U.S.A.' *Canadian Musician*, June 1986.
Grossberg, Lawrence. 'Another Boring Day in Paradise: Rock and Roll and the Empowerment of Everyday Life.' *Popular Music 4*, 225–58. Cambridge: Cambridge University Press, 1984.
– '"You [Still] Have to Fight for Your Right to Party": Music Television as Billboards of Post-modern Difference.' *Popular Music* 7, no. 3 (1988): 315–32.
Guarlnick, Peter. *Last Train to Memphis: The Rise of Elvis Presley.* Toronto: Little, Brown, 1994.
Gudgeon, Chris. 'New Haunts for Spirit of the West.' *Canadian Musician*, June 1992.
Gzowski, Peter. 'Dylan: An Explosion of Poetry.' *Maclean's*, 22 January 1966.
Hambleton, Fergus. 'The Bear.' *Canadian Composer*, May 1970.
Hamm, Charles. 'Rock 'n' Roll in a Very Strange Society.' In Richard Middleton and David Horn, eds, *Popular Music 5: Continuity and Change*, 159–74. London: Cambridge University Press, 1985.
Harris, Marjorie. 'Gordon Lightfoot.' *Maclean's*, September 1968.
Harrison, Hubert. 'The Pop Scene.' *Saturday Night*, July 1967.
Harrison, Tom. '54-40 without a Fight.' *Canadian Musician*, August 1986.
– 'The Guess Who: Ballad of the Last 25 Years.' *Canadian Musician*, February 1988.
Harron, Mary. 'McRock: Pop as a Commodity.' In Simon Frith, ed., *Facing the Music: A Pantheon Guide to Popular Culture*, 173–220. New York: Pantheon Books, 1988.
Hawkins, Ronnie, and Peter Goddard. *Ronnie Hawkins: Last of the Good Ol' Boys.* Toronto: Stoddart, 1989.
Hay, Carla. 'Music Television: A Global Status Report: MuchMusic and Its Sisters Dominate Canada.' *Billboard*, 17 February 2001.
Hayes, David. 'Videos Now a Fact of Life.' *Music Scene*, November-December 1983.
Helm, Levon, with Stephen Davis. *This Wheel's on Fire: Levon Helm and the Story of the Band.* London: Plexus, 1994.
Henderson, Bill. Correspondence with author. March 2008.
Henderson, Stuart. "While There Is Still Time ...': J. Murray Gibbon and the Spectacle of Difference in Three CPR Folk Festivals, 1928–1931.' *Journal of Canadian Studies* 39, no. 1 (Winter 2005): 139–75.
Hopkins, Thomas. 'Gordon's Song.' *Maclean's*, 1 May 1976.
– 'Canadian Rock Rolls South.' *Maclean's*, 14 June 1982.

Howell, Peter. 'Canadians Grab 11 Grammys.' *Toronto Star*, 19 February 1996.

Hutcheon, Linda. *Leonard Cohen and His Works*. Toronto: ECW Press, 1989.

Inglis, Ian. 'Synergies and Reciprocities: The Dynamics of Musical and Professional Interaction between the Beatles and Bob Dylan.' *Popular Music and Society* 20, no. 4 (Winter 1996): 53–79.

– '"The Beatles Are Coming!" Conjecture and Conviction in the Myth of Kennedy, America, and the Beatles.' *Popular Music and Society* 24, no. 2 (Summer 2000): 93–108.

Irving, Katrina. 'Rock Music and the State: Dissonance or Counterpoint?' *Cultural Critique* (Fall 1988): 151–70.

Ivison, Douglas. 'Canadian Content: Cultural Specificity in English-Canadian Popular Music.' In Joy Cohnstaedt and Yves Frenette, eds, *Canadian Cultures and Globalization*, 47–56. Montreal: Association for Canadian Studies, 1997.

Ivry, Dov. Correspondence with author, January 2008.

Jackson, David J. 'Peace, Order, and Good Songs: Popular Music and English-Canadian Culture.' *American Review of Canadian Studies* 35 (Spring 2005): 25–44.

Jagger, Mick, Dora Loewenstein, Philip Dodd, and Charlie Watts. *According to the Rolling Stones*. San Francisco: Chronicle Books, 2003.

Jennings, Nicholas. 'The Superstar.' *Maclean's*, 6 July 1987, 34.

– 'Vancouver's Rock 'n' Roll Explosion.' *Maclean's*, 21 March 1988.

– 'Melancholy Mavericks.' *Maclean's*, 19 March 1990.

– 'A Rebel's Return.' *Maclean's*, 14 May 1990.

– 'Rock 'n' Roll Royalty.' *Maclean's*, 30 September 1991.

– 'Domestic Bands Win Acclaim.' *Maclean's*, 27 January 1992.

– 'Rocking Sounds.' *Maclean's*, 13 July 1992.

– 'Plucking for Glory.' *Maclean's*, 10 August 1992.

– *Before the Gold Rush: Flashbacks to the Dawn of the Canadian Sound*. Toronto: Viking, 1997.

– 'Guess Who's Reborn.' *Maclean's*, 29 May 2000.

– *Fifty Years of Music: The Story of EMI Music Canada*. Toronto: Macmillan, 2000.

– 'Junkies Inc.' *Maclean's*, 7 May 2001.

Johnson, Brian D. 'Rock on a Roll.' *Maclean's*, 27 January 1992.

– 'Shania Revealed.' *Maclean's*, 23 March 1998.

– 'Reinventing Alanis Morissette.' *Maclean's*, 8 March 1999.

– 'Alanis in Wonderland.' *Maclean's*, 25 February 2002.

Johnson, Brian D., and Pamela Young, 'Rock on a Roll.' *Maclean's*, 27 January 1992.

Kay, John, and John Einarson. *John Kay: Magic Carpet Ride*. Kingston, ON: Quarry Press, 1994.

Keillor, Elaine. *Music in Canada: Capturing Landscape and Diversity* (Montreal and Kingston: McGill–Queen's University Press, 2006.

Kelley, Linda. 'Jane Siberry's Musical Dance in and out of Time.' *Canadian Composer*, October 1985.

Kirkwood, John. 'Rock 'n Roll Seen "Emotion, Not Sin": Pastor Joins Sun Staffer in Viewing First Outburst in City.' *Vancouver Sun*, 28 June 1956.

– 'Presley Fans Demented.' *Vancouver Sun*, 3 September 1957.

Klees, Stan. 'Music Biz.' *RPM*, 22 June 1968.

– 'Music Biz.' *RPM*, 7 October 1968.

– 'Music Biz.' *RPM*, 16 December 1968.

– 'MOT Snowball into MOR Programming.' *RPM*, 27 March 1971.

– Correspondence with author, July 2006.

Kostash, Myrna. 'The Pure, Uncluttered Spaces of Bruce Cockburn.' *Saturday Night*, June 1972.

– Long Way from Home: *The Story of the Sixties Generation in Canada*. Toronto: Lorimer, 1980.

Krewen, Nick, and Larry LeBlanc. 'Budgets Challenge Canada's Directors.' *Billboard*, 21 March 1992.

Kroes, Rob. *High Brow Meets Low Brow: American Culture as an Intellectual Concern*. Amsterdam: Free University Press, 1988.

Lahusen, Christian. 'The Aesthetic of Radicalism: The Relationship between Punk and the Patriotic Nationalist Movement of the Basque Country.' *Popular Music* 12, no. 3 (1993): 263–80.

Lanthier, Nancy. 'Stompin' Tom Shares a Few Bon Mots.' *Canadian Composer*, Summer 1992.

Lapointe, Kirk. 'A Billboard Spotlight on Canada.' *Billboard*, 31 January 1987.

– 'MuchMusic Swallows CRTC Rules.' *Billboard*, 12 November 1988.

Larkey, Edward. 'Just for Fun? Language Choice in German Popular Music.' *Popular Music and Society* 24, no. 3 (Fall 2000): 1–20.

Larose, Sean. *Walter Grealis: The Man behind the Music*. Whitby, ON: Master Print, 2004.

LeBlanc, Larry. 'The Flip Side of Anne Murray.' *Maclean's*, November 1974.

– 'New Regs Redraw Canadian FM Map.' *Billboard*, 21 September 1991.

– 'Oh Canada: New Adams Set Fails MAPL Grading System.' *Billboard*, 28 September 1991.

– 'With Bare Necessities, 'Naked Ladies Turn Heads.' *Billboard*, 11 January 1992.

– 'Bryan Adams to Government: "Get Out of the Music Biz."' *Billboard*, 25 January 1992.

– '"Canadian-Content" Discontent.' *Billboard*, 29 February 1992.

– 'Cancon Debate Heats Up Toronto Meet.' *Billboard*, 11 April 1992.

– 'Cochrane Cleans Up at Juno Awards.' *Billboard*, 11 April 1992.
– 'Attic Chief Reveals Indie's Secrets.' *Billboard*, 15 August 1992.
– 'Label Affiliates Mull Border-Crossing.' *Billboard*, 5 December 1992.
– 'Foreign Co-Writers Score in Revised Cancon Rules.' *Billboard*, 13 February 1993.
– 'Carmen Reigns at 15th Félix Awards.' *Billboard*, 30 October 1993.
– 'Alternative Surge Creates Canada AandR Frenzy.' *Billboard*, 4 February 1995.
– 'Industry Seeks CanCon Review.' *Billboard*, 30 March 1996.
– 'Sony Music Takes on the World.' *Billboard*, June 22 1996.
– '"Intimate and Interactive" Boosts Acts.' *Billboard*, 5 July 1997.
– 'The Great White North Heats Up.' *Billboard*, 12 April 2003.
– 'MapleCore's Indie Arena.' *Billboard*, 28 August 2004.
– 'CTV Wants, and Gets, Its MTV.' *Billboard*, 22 October 2005.
– *The Music Industry in Canada*. Report produced for the Canadian Association of Broadcasters, February 2006.
– 'Canada Gets Hot.' *Billboard*, 1 April 2006.
– 'Indie Revolt Up North.' *Billboard*, 29 April 2006.
– 'Snowball Effect.' *Billboard*, 23 June 2007.
Lee, Gregory. 'The "East Is Red" Goes Pop: Commodification, Hybridity and Nationalism in Chinese Popular Song and Its Televisual Performance.' *Popular Music* 14, no. 1 (1995): 95–110.
Lees, Gene. 'Producing Great Sounds in Spite of Ourselves.' *Maclean's*, August 1972.
Lehr, John. 'As Canadian as Possible ... Under the Circumstances: Regional Myths, Images of Place and National Identity in Canadian Country Music.' In Beverley Diamond and Robert Winter, eds, *Canadian Music: Issues of Hegemony and Identity*, 269–81. Toronto: Canadian Scholars' Press, 1994.
Lepka, Stan. 'Witness.' *Canadian Composer*, June 1969.
– 'Motherlode Recorded before Performing.' *Music Scene*, January-February 1970.
Lévesque, René. *An Option for Quebec*. Toronto: McClelland and Stewart, 1968.
Lightfoot, Gordon. Liner notes to *Songbook*. Warner Archive/Rhino, 1999.
Littler, William. '20,000 Beatlemaniacs Pay So Much – for So Little.' *Vancouver Sun*, 24 August 1964.
Loiselle, André. *À l'image d'une nation: le cinéma de Michel Brault et l'histoire du Québec contemporain*. Paris: L'Harmattan, 2005.
Luftig, Stacey. *The Joni Mitchell Companion*. New York: Schirmer Books, 2000.
Luxton, Meg. 'Feminism as a Class Act: Working-Class Feminism and the Women's Movement in Canada.' *Labour/Le Travail* 48 (Fall 2001): 63–88.
Maas, Georg, and Hartmut Reszel. 'Whatever Happened to ... The Decline and

Renaissance of Rock in the Former GDR.' *Popular Music* 17, no. 3 (1998):
267–77.

MacFarlane, John. 'Lightfoot: The Lyrical Loner.' *Globe and Mail*, 18 June 1966.

– 'What If Anne Murray Were an American?' *Maclean's*, May 1971.

– 'Dear Ritchie, Oh How I Hate to Write.' *Maclean's*, December 1971.

MacGregor, Roy. 'Any More Messages Maestro?' *Maclean's*, February 1973.

– 'To Hell with Bob Dylan: Meet Rush. They're in It for the Money.' *Maclean's*,
23 January 1978.

Mackie, John. '50s Vancouver Rock Reprised.' *Vancouver Sun*, 31 January 2004,
D3.

Mackowycz, Bob. 'Randy Bachman.' *Canadian Musician*, May/June 1979.

Maclean's. Various issues.

Mair, Susan. 'Paul Anka: The World's Reigning Juvenile.' *Maclean's*, 1 December
1962.

Manson, Rebecca 'Stringband's Decade of Canadian Folk Music.' *Canadian
Composer*, January 1982.

Manuel, Peter. 'Marxism, Nationalism and Popular Music in Revolutionary
Cuba.' *Popular Music* 6, no. 2 (May 1987): 161–78.

Marcus, Greil. *Mystery Train: Images of America in Rock 'n' Roll Music*. New York:
E.P. Dutton, 1975.

Markle, Robert. 'Early Morning Afterthoughts.' *Maclean's*, December 1971.

Marom, Malka. 'Face to Face.' *Maclean's*, June 1974.

Marshall, Lee. 'Bob Dylan: Newport Folk Festival, July 25, 1965.' In Ian Inglis,
ed., *Performance and Popular Music: History, Place and Time*, 16–27 Hampshire,
England: Ashgate, 2006.

Martin, Linda, and Kerry Segrave. *Anti-Rock: The Opposition to Rock 'n' Roll*. New
York: Da Capo, 1993.

Martinez-Zalce, Graciela. 'Popular Music: Exchanges between Mexico and
Canada.' In Joy Cohnstaedt and Yves Frenette, eds, *Canadian Cultures and Globalization*, 59–67. Canadian Issues 19. 23rd Annual Conference of the Association for Canadian Studies. Montreal: Association for Canadian Studies, 1997.

May, Krise Granat. *Golden State, Golden Youth: The California Image in Popular Culture, 1955–1966*. Chapel Hill: University of North Carolina Press, 2002.

McCartney, Paul, John Lennon, George Harrison, and Ringo Starr. *The Beatles
Anthology*. San Francisco: Chronicle Books, 2000.

McCormick, Christy. '9,000 Teenagers Go Wild with Rock and Roll Hysteria.'
Montreal Star, 30 October 1965.

McCracken, Melinda. 'Street Singer.' *Maclean's*, March 1973.

McDonald, Marci. 'Havin' My Son.' *Maclean's*, February 1975.

McDonough, James. *Shakey*. Toronto: Vintage, 2003.

McDowell, Stan. "'I Too Like Beer-Drinkers' TV" Juneau Tells Jeering MPs.'
  Toronto Daily Star, 6 May 1970.
McGrath, Paul. 'A Summer Celebration of Folk Music.' *Maclean's*, 12 July 1982.
McKay, Ian. *Quest of the Folk: Antimodernism and Cultural Selection in Twentieth-
  Century Nova Scotia* (Montreal and Kingston: McGill-Queen's University Press,
  1994.
McLauchlan, Murray. *Getting Out of Here Alive: The Ballad of Murray McLauchlan.*
  Toronto: Viking, 1998.
McLauchlin, Noel, and Martin Mcloone. 'Hybridity and National Musics: The
  Case of Irish Rock Music.' *Popular Music* 19, no. 2 (2000): 181–99.
Megaffin, Mike. 'Garry Peterson: Canadian Classic.' *Classic Drummer*, April/
  May/June 2006.
Melhuish, Martin. 'The 30% Solution: Still Music to a Lot of Ears.' *Maclean's*, 23
  February 1976.
– *Heart of Gold: 30 Years of Canadian Pop Music*. Toronto: CBC Enterprises, 1983.
– *Oh What a Feeling: A Vital History of Canadian Music*. Kingston, ON: Quarry
  Press, 1996.
Menzies, Ian. 'Bruce Cockburn.' *Canadian Musician*, December 1993.
– 'Musical Milestones.' *Canadian Musician*, April 1994.
– 'The Bourbon Tabernacle Choir.' *Canadian Musician*, August 1995.
Michener, Wendy. 'How Elvis Survived the Faddish Years, and Why the Beatles
  May Go on Forever.' *Maclean's*, 19 September 1964.
Mitchell, Gillian. The *North American Folk Music Revival: Nation and Identity in the
  United States and Canada, 1945–1980*. Burlington, VT: Ashgate, 2007.
Moon, Barbara. 'What You Don't Need to Know about Rock 'n' Roll.' *Maclean's*,
  7 July 1956.
Morgan, Kit. 'Canada Firms Look to Making Impact on National, Int'l Marts.'
  Billboard, 9 January 1965.
– 'Canadian Indies Merge; BWO Own "Co–Op" Label.' *Billboard*, 30 January 1965.
– 'Canadian Coca-Cola Drive Centres on Pop Disk Groups.' *Billboard*, 7 August
  1965.
– 'Canada.' *Billboard*, 25 September 1965.
– 'Canada.' *Billboard*, 25 December 1965.
– 'MLS.' *Canadian Composer*, March 1970.
– 'From the Music Capitals of the World.' *Billboard*, 6 January 1979.
Morris, John. 'Stevedore Steve: A Country Singer Talks about His Music.' *Cana-
  dian Composer*, February 1975.
Morrison, Craig. 'Folk Revival Roots Still Evident in 1990s Recordings of San
  Francisco Psychedelic Veterans.' *Journal of American Folklore* 114, no. 454 (Fall
  2001): 478–88.

Mulligan, Terry David. 'Canadian Productions Hotting Up in Van.' *RPM*, 13 March 1971.

Myers, Paul. 'Bryan Adams Gets Upwardly Mobile Down South.' *Canadian Musician*, August 1996.

Nadeau, Pierre. 'Gilles Vigneault lui-même, par Pierre Nadeau.' *L'Actualité*, September 1979.

Nadel, Ira. *Various Positions: A Life of Leonard Cohen*. Toronto: Random House, 1996.

Nash, Knowlton. 'Have Germs Already Made the H-Bomb Obsolete?' *Maclean's*, 26 March 1960.

Nolan, Michael. *CTV: The Network That Means Business*. Edmonton: University of Alberta Press, 2001.

Nowlan, Alden. 'What's More Canadian than Stompin' Tom?' *Maclean's*, August 1972.

Nowry, Lawrence. *Man of Mana: Marius Barbeau*. Toronto: NC Press, 1995.

Nurse, Andrew. 'Tradition and Modernity: The Cultural Work of Marius Barbeau.' Doctoral thesis, Queen's University, 1997.

– '"But Now Things Have Changed": Marius Barbeau and the Politics of Amerindian Identity.' *Ethnohistory* 48, no. 3 (Summer 2001): 433–72.

O'Brien, Karen. *Joni Mitchell: Shadows and Light*. London: Virgin Books, 2001.

Odam, Jes. 'Rolling Stones Hit Town, Leave Agrodome Rocking.' *Vancouver Sun*, 2 December 1965.

O'Halloran, Michael, ed. *CBC Radio's Mountaintop Music: 25 Canadian Artists, Their Favourite Music and Books*. Calgary: Bayeux Arts, 2000.

O'Hara, Jane. 'The Master of Rock 'n' Roll Romance.' *Maclean's*, 5 August 1985.

Ottawa Citizen. Various issues.

Owram, Doug. *Born at the Right Time: A History of the Baby Boom Generation*. Toronto: University of Toronto Press, 1997.

Pacienza, Angela. 'MTV Canada Blasts off with VIP Bash Featuring Kanye West, Sam Roberts.' Canadian Press Newswire, 19 April 2006.

Palmer, Sue. 'The Saga of How Blood, Sweat and Tears Were Born.' *Melody Maker*, 19 July 1969, 17.

Pegley, Kip. *Coming to You Wherever You Are: MuchMusic, MTV, and Youth Identities*. Middletown, CT: Wesleyan University Press, 2008.

Penfield, Wilder. 'Maple Music Junket.' *Canadian Composer*, September 1972.

Perlich, Tim. 'Ugly Ducklings Float Back from Obscurity.' *Now*, 4–10 February 1999.

Peter, Jurgen. Correspondence with author, January 2008.

Petrowski, Nathalie. 'Interview: Lucien Francoeur.' *Canadian Composer*, March 1979.

– '"American" Rock from Quebec.' *Canadian Composer*, June 1981.

Pevere, Geoff, and Grieg Dymond. *Mondo Canuck: A Canadian Pop Culture Odyssey*. Scarborough, ON: Prentice-Hall, 1996.

Poiger, Uta G. 'Rock 'n' Roll, Female Sexuality, and the Cold War Battle over German Identities.' *Journal of Modern History* 68, no. 3 (September 1996): 577–616.

Pond, Steve. 'Bruce Cockburn Launches a Hit: Fired by Christian Pacifism, the Canadian Singer Targets New, Worldwide Success.' *Rolling Stone*, 23 May 1985.

Pornovich, Walter. 'Stones Rolled So Secretly Admirers Gathered Moss.' *Montreal Star*, 23 April 1965.

Porter, McKenzie. 'An Evening Out with McKenzie Porter: The Naughty but Nice New Coffee Houses.' *Maclean's*, 23 March 1963.

Potter, Greg. *Hand Me Down World: The Canadian Pop-Rock Paradox*. Toronto: Macmillan, 1999.

Potts, Lynn. 'Horizons Expanded for Our Musicians.' *RPM*, 9 January 1971.

Prendergast, Mark J. *Irish Rock: Roots, Personalities, Directions*. Dublin: The O'Brien Press, 1987.

Quig, James. 'Mommas' Boy.' *Maclean's*, 19 September 1977.

Quigley, Mike. 'Edward Bear Interview.' *Georgia Straight*, 5 August 1970.

Quill, Greg. 'The "Indies" Fight On.' *Canadian Composer*, April 1986.

Reynolds, Bill. 'Red Rider: Victory Day for Tom Cochrane.' *Canadian Musician*, October 1988.

Reynolds, Mac. 'Daughter Wants to See Elvis?: "Kick Her in the Teeth!"' *Vancouver Sun*, 31 August, 1957.

Rice, Timothy, and Tammy Gutnik. 'What's Canadian about Canadian Popular Music? The Case of Bruce Cockburn.' In John Beckwith and Timothy J. McGee, eds, *Taking a Stand: Essays in Honour of John Beckwith*, 238–58. Toronto: University of Toronto Press, 1995.

Ridley, Jeffrey. Correspondence with author, January 2008.

Robinson, Martha. 'Square Dancers Have Lots of Fun.' *Vancouver Sun*, 31 August 1957.

Robinson, Red, and Greg Potter. *Backstage Vancouver: A Century of Entertainment Legends*. Vancouver: Harbour Publishing, 2004.

Robitaille, Louis-Bernard. 'Charlebois Is Synonymous with Quebec.' *Canadian Composer*, December 1973.

Rodnitzky, Jerome L. 'The Sixties between the Microgrooves: Using Folk and Protest Music to Understand American History, 1963–1973.' *Popular Music and Society* 23, no. 4 (Winter 1999): 105–22.

Rodriguez, Juan. 'An Essay on Hype.' *Last Post*, April 1970.

Roe, Keith, and Gust De Meyer, 'One Planet – One Music? MTV and Globalization.' In Andreas Gebesmair and Alfred Smudits, eds, *Global Repertoires: Popular Music within and beyond the Transnational Music Industry*, 33–44. Aldershot, UK: Ashgate, 2001.

Rolling Stone. Various issues.

Rome, Adam. '"Give Earth a Chance": The Environmental Movement and the Sixties.' *Journal of American History* 90, no. 2 (September 2003): 525–54.

Roscigno, Vincent J., William F. Danaher, and Erika Summers-Effler. 'Music, Culture, and Social Movements: Song and Southern Textile Worker Mobilization, 1929–1934.' *International Journal of Sociology and Social Policy* 22, no. 1–3 (2002): 141–74.

Rowe, David. *Popular Cultures: Rock Music, Sport and the Politics of Pleasure.* London: Sage, 1995.

RPM. Various issues.

Rubin, Joan Shelly. *The Making of Middlebrow Culture.* Chapel Hill: University of North Carolina Press, 1991.

Rubin, Nathan. *Rock and Roll: Art and Anti-Art.* Dubuque, IA: Kendall and Hunt, 1993.

Ruddy, Jon. 'Is the World (Or Anybody) Ready for Leonard Cohen?' *Maclean's*, 1 October 1966.

– 'Another Kind of Explosion in Quebec: Talent.' *Maclean's*, June 1969.

– 'It Wasn't My Country Any More ...' *Maclean's*, June 1969.

– 'How to Become an American without Really Trying. Your First Move? Get with the "Canadian" Music Scene: It's as Yankee as Dylan and Drive-Ins.' *Maclean's*, November 1969.

Rutherford, Paul. *When Television Was Young: Primetime Canada 1952–1967.* Toronto: University of Toronto Press, 1990.

Ryback, Timothy W. *Rock around the Bloc: A History of Rock Music in Eastern Europe and the Soviet Union.* New York: Oxford University Press, 1990.

Salutin, Rick. 'National Cultures in the Age of Globalization: The Case of Canada.' *Queen's Quarterly* 106, no. 2 (Summer 1999): 206–15.

Savage, Jon. 'The Enemy within: Sex, Rock, and Identity.' In Simon Frith, ed., *Facing the Music: A Pantheon Guide to Popular Culture*, 131–72. New York: Pantheon, 1988.

Scanlon, Joe. '23,000 See Elvis – Late Show 15,000 His Largest Ever.' *Toronto Daily Star*, 3 April 1957.

Schou, Soren. 'The Charisma of the Liberators: The Americanization of Postwar Denmark.' In Roger De La Garde, William Gilsdorf, and Ilja Wechselmann, eds, *Small Nations, Big Neighbour: Denmark and Quebec/Canada Compare Notes on American Popular Culture.* London: John Libbey, 1993.

Sercombe, Laurel. '"Ladies and Gentlemen ..." the Beatles: The Ed Sullivan

Show, CBS TV, February 9, 1964.' In Ian Inglis, ed., *Performance and Popular Music: History, Place and Time*, 1–15. Hampshire, England: Ashgate, 2006.

Shapiro, Peter. 'Paul Revere and the Raiders.' In Peter Buckley, ed., *The Rough Guide to Rock*, 3rd ed., 870. London: Penguin, 2003.

Sherratt, Norm. Correspondence with author, 2008.

Shillington, Stan. 'Beatle Mob Past Comparison: Only 100 Police between Youngsters and Disaster.' *Vancouver Sun*, 24 August 1964.

Shuker, Roy, and Michael Pickering. 'Kiwi Rock: Popular Music and Cultural Identity in New Zealand.' *Popular Music* 13, no. 3 (1994): 261–78.

Smith, Anthony D. *The Ethnic Origins of Nations*. New York: Blackwell, 1986.

– *Nations and Nationalism in a Global Era*. Cambridge: Polity Press, 1995.

Smith, Jim. 'Finkelstein ... A Patron of the Arts.' *RPM*, 3 April 1971.

Smith, Wes. The *Pied Pipers of Rock 'n' Roll: Radio Deejays of the 50s and 60s*. Marietta, GA: Longstreet Press, 1989.

Soapbox Productions. *Shakin All Over*, 2006.

Starr, Larry, Christopher Waterman, and Jay Hodgson. *Rock: A Canadian Perspective*. Don Mills, ON: Oxford University Press, 2009.

Stein, David Lewis. 'The Peaceniks Go to La Macaza.' *Maclean's*, 8 August 1964.

Stern, Perry. 'Bruce Allen Is Hot.' *Canadian Musician*, December 1986.

Storey, John. *An Introductory Guide to Cultural Theory and Popular Culture*. Athens: University of Georgia Press, 1993.

Strauss, Marise. 'MTV, MuchMusic Online Streaming Explosion.' *Playback: Canada's Broadcast and Production Journal*, 21 January 2008.

Straw, Will. 'Music Video in Its Contexts: Popular Music and Post-Modernism in the 1980s.' *Popular Music* 7, no. 3 (1988): 247–66.

– 'Sound Recording.' In Michael Dorland, ed., *The Cultural Industries in Canada*, 95–117. Toronto: Lorimer, 1996.

– 'Exhausted Commodities: The Material Culture of Music.' *Canadian Journal of Communication* 25, no. 1 (2000): 175–85.

– 'In and Around Canadian Music.' *Journal of Canadian Studies* 35, no. 3 (Fall 2000): 173–84.

– 'No Future? The Canadian Music Industries.' In David Taras, Frits Pannekoek, and Maria Bakardjieva, eds, *How Canadian Communicate*, 203–21. Calgary: University of Calgary Press, 2003.

Sturma, Michael. 'The Politics of Dancing: When Rock 'n' Roll Came to Australia.' *Journal of Popular Culture* 25, no. 4 (Spring 1992): 123–42.

Symon, Peter. 'Music and National Identity in Scotland: A Study of Jock Tamson's Bairns.' *Popular Music* 16, no. 2 (1997): 203–16.

Szklarski, Cassandra. 'Canadian Legend Stompin' Tom Laments Lack of Radio Play, Patriotism.' Canadian Press, 24 October 2008.

Telecomworldwire. 'Bell Introduces All Access Music Services in Canada.' 5 July 2007.

Testa, Bart, and Jim Shedden. 'In the Great Midwestern Hardware Store: The Seventies Triumph in English-Canadian Rock Music.' In Joan Nicks and Jeannette Sloniowski, eds, *Slippery Pastimes: Reading the Popular in Canadian Culture*, 177–216. Waterloo, ON: Wilfrid Laurier University Press, 2002.

Thomas, Ralph, and Morris Duff. 'Rolling Stones Show Violent and Vulgar.' *Toronto Daily Star*, 26 April 1965.

Time (Canada). Various issues.

Timson, Judith. 'The Season of the Diva.' *Maclean's*, 8 March 1999.

Timson, Ray. '200 Girls Swoon in Battle of the Beatles.' *Toronto Daily Star*, 8 September 1964.

Toivonen, Timo, and Antero Laiho. '"You Don't Like Crazy Music": The Reception of Elvis Presley in Finland.' *Popular Music and Society* 13, no. 2 (1999): 1–22.

Tower, Courtney. 'Canada Report.' *Maclean's*, 4 February 1970.

– 'Musicians Play a Canada Rock.' *Maclean's*, 4 February 1970.

Treece, David. 'Guns and Roses: Bossa Nova and Brazil's Music of Popular Protest, 1958–68.' *Popular Music* 16, no. 1 (1997): 1–29.

Tyson, Ian, and Colin Escott. *I Never Sold My Saddle*. Toronto: Douglas and Mcintyre, 1994.

Ullestad, Neal. 'Rock and Rebellion: Subversive Effects of Live Aid and "Sin City."' *Popular Music* 6, no. 1 (January 1987): 67–76.

United Empire Loyalists. *Notes from the Underground*. CD. Indiepool Canada, 1998.

Usher, Bill, and Linda Page-Harpa, eds. *For What Time I Am in This World: Stories from Mariposa*. Toronto: Peter Martin Associates, 1977.

Vancouver Sun. Various issues.

Verzuh, Ron. *Underground Times: Canada's Flower-Child Revolutionaries*. Toronto: Deneau, 1989.

Vincent, Pierre. 'Tex Lecor – "Last of the Real Quebeckers" – Finds Success at Last.' *Canadian Composer*, April 1972.

Wade, Peter. 'Music, Blackness and National Identity: Three Moments in Columbia History.' *Popular Music* 17, no. 1 (1998): 1–19.

Wagman, Ira. 'Rock the Nation: MuchMusic, Cultural Policy, and English Canadian Music Video Programming, 1979–1984.' *Canadian Journal of Communication* 26, no. 4 (2001): 47–62.

Walker, Michael. *Laurel Canyon: The Inside Story of Rock-and-Roll's Legendary Neighborhood*. London: Faber and Faber, 2006.

Wallis, Roger, and Krister Malm. *Big Sounds from Small Peoples: The Music Industry in Small Countries*. New York: Pendragon Press, 1984.

Welton, Marie, and Evangelia Tastsoglou. 'Building a Culture of Peace: An Interview with Muriel Duckworth and Betty Peterson.' *Canadian Woman Studies* 22, no. 2 (Fall 2002/Winter 2003): 115–21.

Whisnant, David. *All That Is Native and Fine: The Politics of Culture in an American Region.* Chapel Hill: University of North Carolina Press, 1983.

White, Hayden. The *Content of the Form: Narrative Discourse and Historical Representation.* Baltimore: Johns Hopkins University Press, 1987.

Wicke, Peter. 'Rock Music: A Musical-Aesthetic Study.' *Popular Music 2,* 219–43. Cambridge: Cambridge University Press, 1982.

Wickens, Barbara. 'Grammy Night in Canada.' *Maclean's,* 11 March 1996.

Williams, Paul. The *Crawdaddy Book: Writing (and Images) from the Magazine of Rock.* Milwaukee, WI: Hal Leonard, 2002.

Wilson-Smith, Anthony. 'Upbeat Sounds for Francophone Blues.' *Maclean's,* 15 September 1986.

Woman of Heart and Mind. Joni Mitchell: A Life Story. DVD. Eagle Vision USA, 2003.

Worboy, Martha. 'Canadians Getting in Tune with Digital Music.' CanWest News, 5 January 2008.

Wright, John, Millard Gregory, and Sarah Riegel. 'Here's Where We Get Canadian: English-Canadian Nationalism and Popular Culture.' *American Review of Canadian Studies* 32, no. 1 (Spring 2002): 11–34.

Wright, Robert. '"Dream, Comfort, Memory, Despair": Canadian Popular Musicians and the Dilemma of Nationalism, 1968–1972.' *Journal of Canadian Studies* 22, no. 4 (Winter 1987–8): 27–43.

– '"Dream, Comfort, Memory, Despair": Canadian Musicians and the Dilemma of Nationalism.' Revised version, in Wright, *Virtual Sovereignty: Nationalism, Culture and the Canadian Question,* 57–78. Toronto: Canadian Scholars' Press, 2004.

– 'Gimmie Shelter: Cultural Protectionism and the Canadian Recording Industry.' In Wright, *Virtual Sovereignty,* 79–98.

Yip, Brandon. 'Rockin' Back the Clock.' *Vancouver Courier,* 7 July 2004.

Yorke, Ritchie. 'Can a Law Put Canada on the Hit Parade?' *RPM,* 9 September 1968.

– 'Canadian Pop Groups.' *Music Scene,* July-August 1969.

– 'Ronnie Hawkins.' *Rolling Stone,* 9 August 1969.

– 'Boosting Peace: John and Yoko in Canada.' *Rolling Stone,* 18 June 1969.

– *Axes, Chops and Hot Licks: The Canadian Rock Music Scene.* Edmonton: Hurtig, 1971.

– 'Monitor Your Favourite Station.' *RPM,* 23 January 1971.

– 'There's No Truth to the Rumour ...' *RPM,* 13 February 1971.

– 'Astra – A Prime Factor in the Record Industry?' *RPM*, 15 May 1971.
– 'Everyone Has a Stake in the Maple Music Junket.' *RPM*, 7 August 1971.
– 'After 19 Years, a Memoir.' *Canadian Composer*, July 1987.
Yorke, Ritchie, and Ben Fong-Torres. 'Hendrix Busted in Toronto.' *Rolling Stone*, 31 May 1969.
Young, David. 'Céline Dion, the ADISQ Controversy, and the Anglophone Press in Canada.' *Canadian Journal of Communication* 24 (1999): 515–37.
– 'The Promotional State and Canada's Juno Awards.' *Popular Music* 23, no. 3 (2004): 271–89.
– 'The CBC and the Juno Awards.' *Canadian Journal of Communication* 30, no. 3 (2005): 343–65.
– 'Ethno-Racial Minorities and the Juno Awards.' *Canadian Journal of Sociology* 31, no. 2 (Spring 2006): 183–211.
Young, J.R. 'Records.' *Rolling Stone*, 7 March 1970.
Young, Kevin. 'From the Hip.' *Maclean's*, 11 December 2000.
– 'Capturing the Essence of the Tragically Hip Live.' *Canadian Musician*, September/October 2004.
– 'The World According to Good.' *Canadian Musician*, November/December 2005.
– 'Illscarlett.' *Canadian Musician*, July/August 2008.
Young, Pamela. 'Rock's Road to Success.' *Maclean's*, 24 November 1986.
Zimmer, Dave. *4 Way Street: The Crosby, Stills, Nash, and Young Reader* (Cambridge, MA: Da Capo, 2004).
Zion, Lawrence. 'Disposable Icons: Pop Music in Australia, 1955–63.' *Popular Music* 8, no. 2 (1989): 165–75.

Illustration Credits

Ian Blum: Joel Plaskett.
Gordon Campbell: Bryan Adams; Tom Cochrane.
Canadian Musician: Canadian Musician.
CBC Stills Archive: Paul Anka; *Let's Go* featuring the Guess Who; Northern
    Lights for Africa.
Trevor Connell: Gord Downie.
Tom Connors/Boot Records: Stompin Tom Connors.
Vern Craig: The Staccatos.
Wes Dakus: Wes Dakus & the Rebels.
Frank Davies: Kelly Jay of Crowbar; A Foot in Coldwater.
Michael Desjardins: Colin James and Sarah McLachlan; Honeymoon Suite;
    Corey Hart.
A. De Wilde: Stars.
Ryan Edwardson: Buffy Sainte-Marie; Jill Barber.
John Einarson: Neil Young with the Squires.
Bill Graham: Concert poster for the Buffalo Springfield.
Christie Greyerbiehl/Hardwood Records: Hayden.
Andrew Henwood: Ian Tyson.
Kirsten Harris Design: Ed Robertson of Barenaked Ladies.
Paul Leask: The Lords of London.
Library and Archives Canada: Gordon Lightfoot (Horst Ehricht , PA-189430);
    Félix Leclerc (National Film Board of Canada. Photothèque, PA-107872);
    Joni Mitchell (PA-211916).
Allan Nicholls: J.B. and the Playboys.
Scott Penner: Gordie Johnson.
Jurgen Peter: The Haunted.
Jeffrey Ridley: The United Empire Loyalists.

The Stampeders: The Stampeders.
Cameron Traviss: Trooper.
Les Vogt: Les Vogt and the Prowlers.
Craig Webb: The Rogues.
Norman Wong: Broken Social Scene.
York University Libraries, Clara Thomas Archives & Special Collections,
   Toronto Telegram fonds: Ronnie Hawkins and Robbie Robertson (F0433,
   image no. ASC05106); The Ugly Ducklings (F0433, image no. ASC05111);
   McKenna Mendelson Mainline (F0433, image no. ASC05110); Bruce
   Cockburn (F0433, image no. ASC05113).

Index